Introduction to
Biblical Literature

Introduction to
Biblical Literature
Second Edition

O. B. DAVIS

Chairman, English Department
Kent School

BOYNTON/COOK PUBLISHERS
HEINEMANN
PORTSMOUTH, NH

Boynton/Cook Publishers Inc.
A subsidiary of Reed Elsevier Inc.
361 Hanover Street
Portsmouth, NH 03801-3912
Offices and agents throughout the world

Library of Congress Cataloging-in-Publication Data

Davis, O. B.
      Introduction to Biblical literature / O.B. Davis. —2nd ed.
         p.   cm.
      ISBN 0-86709-227-0
      1. Bible. O.T.—Textbooks.   I. Title.
   BS 1194.D34 1988
   220.6' 1—dc 19   88-2801
                                                              CIP

Printed in the United States of America
03 02 01 00   EB   10 11 12 13

Preface to the Second Edition

Introduction to Biblical Literature is a textbook and an introduction. It is not an abridgement of the Bible, not a key to the mysteries of the Bible, and not a guide towards or away from personal religious commitment. This book's purpose is to inform and exercise its readers in some of the essentials of Biblical literature to the end that they may understand more about what goes on in the cultural currents they inhabit.

Serious students using this text should have easy access to the King James Version of the English Bible as well as to more contemporary translations. A good Biblical dictionary that includes basic maps will help, though the glossaries and appendices of some Bible editions may suffice.

The frame of reference intended and expected in this book is literary art as it is available, either directly or by translation, in the English language. Students who are alert to non-Biblical literature and language should find more to recognize than to be surprised by in *Introduction to Biblical Literature*.

The introductory notes and other essays in the book are one reader's reactions to the Biblical literature we are studying. At this distance, my feelings will not be hurt if you challenge such reactions, and you are invited to learn a great deal on your own from doing so. The "Considerations and Questions" that follow most of the selections are not tests or examinations unless teachers or students choose to make them so. They are meant to be suggestions for lines of inquiry, topics for discussion or written work, and devices by which you can make continuing appraisals of your progress.

The text here is that of *The Dartmouth Bible,* published by Houghton Mifflin Company, to whom I am indebted for their kind permission for its use. The type differences between the Bible text and my commentary have been emphasized in order to keep the two elements clearly separate for the reader.

Contents

I

An Introductory Note And An Investigation

"The English Bible, a book which,
if everything else in our language should
perish, would alone suffice to show
the whole extent of its beauty and power."

Thomas Babington Macaulay, "On John Dryden"

An Introductory Note

"The American habit of owning the Bible has survived into our times far better than the earlier American habit of reading it." So I wrote in the Introductory Note to the 1976 edition of this book, and I'm afraid I remember fancying the statement as mildly clever and pertinent. I am embarrassed by it now and think it more querulous than clever, more pompous than pertinent. However that may be, probably more Americans do read the Bible nowadays than did in 1976, but if so I think they read the Bible for good reasons not to our immediate purpose in this textbook. *Introduction to Biblical Literature* was designed to be and is designed to remain a text for the study of literature and the English language.

Of course a devotional application to Holy Writ may supply much of what is useful to the student of literature, and a literary application to the English Bible may lead some to religious devotion. Either result, though, is incidental; neither is to be counted on; neither is intended. Let me grant for the record that religious truth is much more important than are the benefits of a liberal education. Salvation, the Means of Grace, the Hope of Glory, Faith, and *Caritas* are, I allow and really believe, greater far than human art, knowledge, or wisdom. Yet human art, knowledge, and wisdom are our areas and our aims just now, and the job of pursuing them is quite important enough to deserve strenuous effort from such mortals as we be.

Less abstractly put, what we are immediately after is an understanding of the Bible not as religious property but as cultural property, or what William Blake called "the Great Code of Art."

Northrop Frye's *The Great Code: The Bible and Literature* (Harcourt Brace Jovanovich) appeared in 1982, so I did not have the benefits of that remarkable book when I prepared the first edition of *Introduction to Biblical Literature*. I knew, though, that Frye's was the book for me when I read very early on in his Introduction, "I soon realized that a student of English literature who does not know the Bible does not understand a good deal of what is going on in what he reads." My intention and hope for *Introduction to Biblical Literature* is that it will help start students towards understanding a good deal of what is going on in what they read.

Not many English teachers and not many of those who administer their curricular doings are apt to challenge the implications of Frye's observation. Not many will contest in theory what I hope and intend for this book. Yet it remains as I felt it was in 1976 that a great many potentially able and otherwise well-read American students and a startling number of their teachers are ignorant of or ridiculously wrong about what is actually in the Bible. That state of ignorance and error continues to be a gross impediment to understanding our literature and our language.

What accounts for this significant gap between principle and practice, between agreeing, at least by implication, on the importance of Biblical literature and failing to study it? Is it that administrators fear the following footfalls of Civil Liberties folks a-hunting for church/state separation violations? Can it be a parallel fear of offending religious groups within our scholastic clientele by presuming to read rather than worship? If teachers deal with the Old and New Testaments as "the Great Code of Art," such objections, however well intentioned in source and politically volatile in appearance, are frivolous in substance. We know where the roads paved with ignorant good intentions lead, and political timidity is surely unworthy of respectable prospectors after learning.

But I am optimistic enough to think that the main reason for too little Bible in our general curricula these days reflects neither on the character nor the capacity of those who teach and learn. In the closing decades of this American century, possibly more than ever in our history people responsible for the study of literature are the products of educations which omitted or scanted the Bible. Ironically, some intelligent teachers have actually learned what they know about the Bible from summary references in footnotes and other commentaries to secular texts. Such a back door route is better than no route at all, but is unlikely to provide much vision of the Great Code. What perhaps it can provide, indeed what I have seen it provide, is an intelligent consciousness of ignorance, one of the most valuable things for any teacher or student to have. Our ignorance, after all, if we recognize it, we can assail with knowledge.

Besides the English Bible itself, I have used and continue to use—for there is no end to this kind of assault—a number of supporting or auxiliary forces. Among those particularly helpful to me in preparing *Introduction to Biblical Literature* is Mary Ellen Chase's *The Bible and the Common Reader* (Macmillan 1971). As decidedly a common reader myself, I recommend this clear and witty commentary for its modest enlargements on most of the Biblical selections emphasized in this text. I am also indebted to Fleming James's *Personalities of the Old Testament* (Scribner's 1947) as an essential aid to understanding the nature of Biblical characterization. Although this book has been for years a standard curricular text in many theological seminaries, James's point of view sorts well with the literary student, and his vigorous style is uncluttered with clerical or theological specialties.

There are many excellent surveys of Old Testament history more recently in print than *History of the Hebrew Commonwealth*

(Scribner's 1935) by Albert Edward Bailey and Charles Foster Kent. I, however, have found nothing I liked better. The book is for the general studious reader, is fairly short, and is supplied with useful maps and chronological tables. For additional commentary on the Psalms, I suggest Mary Ellen Chase's *The Psalms for the Common Reader* (Norton 1962) and C.S. Lewis's *Reflections on the Psalms* (Harcourt 1958).

The urgency with which I recommend Northrop Frye's *The Great Code: The Bible and Literature* is just this side idolatry. *The Great Code* is not an easy book, but its rewards to any teacher of literature justify effort, effort which can rapidly become downright pleasurable. Perhaps what interested and affected me most in *The Great Code* is its compelling emphasis on the whole Bible's artistic unity, but I owe Frye much more besides. His earlier *Anatomy of Criticism* (Princeton 1957) helped me re-examine and clarify my notions of what literature consists of—a rather important thing to do before presuming to introduce *Biblical* literature. *Anatomy of Criticism's* abundance of Biblical reference has since 1982 tempted me to think of the book as, among other important things, a little like a voice in the wilderness announcing the coming of *The Great Code.* To recommend these two books to teachers of Biblical literature is to say too little: I positively would not and will not be without them. More temperately I will add, though, that in my experience the two Frye books are not for beginners. They go far beyond the matters and ideas of this text and to accompany them calls for at least having had the kind of "introduction" provided in *Introduction to Biblical Literature.*

In the 1976 edition of this book we let the New Testament off with two pages of general commentary. While the balance of the new *Introduction to Biblical Literature* is still heavily weighted on the Old Testament side, this time we have included the complete text of Mark's Gospel as well as what I intend to be pertinent references to other New Testament books. The decision to move in such a direction was chiefly urged by William Blake (via Northrop Frye). Blake, after all, did not annotate his engraving of the Laocoön group with the assertion that "the Old Testament" or even that "the Bible" is "the Great Code of Art"; he specified that "the Old and New Testaments are ...."

An Investigation

Perhaps I am mistaken. Perhaps more people know more about the Bible than I think they do. Here is an easy way to make a rough estimate of where at least *you* stand. These questions may encourage you to the belief that you start an introduction to the study of Biblical literature at an advantage. Or, they may dismay you with the conclusion that you know even less about the Bible than you thought. For the most accurate idea of your status check off only those questions to which you are sure your answers are correct and reasonably complete.

1. What does the title Genesis mean?
2. What are the two main divisions of the Bible?
3. To what event does the title Exodus refer?
4. How does the experience of Paul differ from that of the other "apostles" of Jesus?
5. Why did King James write the Bible?
6. What happens to Jonah after he is freed from the belly of the great fish?
7. On what circumstance is the famous "patience of Job" based?
8. What does it mean to call someone a "Judas"? Why?
9. What is the punishment or "curse" of Cain? Why does Cain receive it?
10. How does Genesis account for the coming of the children of Israel to live in Egypt?
11. Other than his defeat of Goliath, what is memorable about David?
12. Under what circumstances does Moses appear in the Bible? With what major events is he identified?
13. Can you name some official "Prophets" in the Bible? What do Prophets do?
14. What are the four "Gospels" of the New Testament? What do they have in common?
15. What is the characteristic way of life of John the Baptist?
16. What is the particular status of Abraham in the tradition of Israel?
17. Who is Pontius Pilate?
18. What is Samson's official position in Israel? What strengths and weaknesses does he bring to the office?
19. Who is Solomon?

20. "The Devil tempts Eve and she eats the apple." Is this in
    the Bible? Where? In what terms?

Here are my answers to the twenty questions. My responses
are not meant to be exhaustive, and with some research you may find
some of them debatable, but I think they will serve as check points for
your judgment of your own knowledge. If you find that you do pretty
well at this game, don't relax; these are easy questions and there are
many more where they came from. If you find that you don't do so well,
don't be discouraged; you know more than you did.

1. Genesis, which means "beginning," is the title of the
first book of the Bible. The book starts with an account of the creation of
the world: "In the beginning. . . ." It goes on to deal with the origins of
the nation of Israel.

2. The two main divisions of the Bible are commonly
called the Old Testament and the New Testament. The former deals
with the world of Israel before the birth of Jesus Christ; the latter with
the life of Jesus Christ and the years shortly afterwards. The Old
Testament is much longer, more diverse in form and authorship, and of
more literary importance than the New Testament.

3. "Exodus" means "going out" or departure. Exodus is the
second book of the Bible and is about the departure of the Israelites
from bondage in Egypt.

4. Paul, unlike the original twelve "apostles," was not an
associate of Jesus during his lifetime.

5. King James I of England did not write the Bible. He *did*,
in 1607, appoint fifty-four of the most learned men he could find to
make an authorized translation. They finished the job in the astonishing
span of three years, and the Authorized King James Version, published
in 1611, has been perhaps the most influential and certainly one of the
greatest pieces of English literature ever since.

6. After Jonah lands safely on the beach, he goes, as God
had commanded him to do in the first place, to the great and wicked city
of Nineveh. There he makes public announcements that the city will be
destroyed in forty days. The people of Nineveh, however, repent; God
decides not to destroy the place after all. At the end of the tale Jonah is
sitting on a hill near Nineveh, angry with God for His sentimental
suspension of justice.

7. In the everyday sense, Job's patience clearly has its
limits, as we can see by some of the things he says to his "comforters."
On the heroic and profounder level, the patience of Job is his resolute
loyalty to his God in spite of the terrible afflictions that God allows to
fall upon him. "Though he slay me, yet will I trust in him."

8. When we speak of someone as "Judas," we commonly are accusing that person of betraying a friend. The reference is to Judas Iscariot, an apostle who sells out Jesus to the high priests for thirty pieces of silver.

9. God punishes Cain for the murder of his brother Abel by sentencing him to wander, "a vagabond in the earth," bereft of the ordinary happiness and success which may come to other men. God, however, also sets a mark on Cain which warns other people against killing the murderer for his crime.

10. The account in Genesis tells of how Joseph, son of the patriarch, Jacob, is sold by his elder brothers into slavery in Egypt. There, Joseph rises to be business manager of that country. When a famine scourges the lands where his family live, they and their followers come to live with him in Egypt.

11. David is the greatest king of ancient Israel. Although subject to certain human failings, he represents the ideal of royal leadership in the Judaic tradition.

12. According to Exodus, Moses, born a Hebrew, is adopted by Pharaoh's daughter and is consequently brought up and educated in the Egyptian royal court. Somehow aware of his real identity as an Israelite, Moses takes action against the slavery and gradual genocide imposed on his people by the Egyptians. Moses is commonly identified with such events as: (a) his personal inspiration from God, whom he encounters in a burning bush in Midian; (b) the miracles by which Pharaoh is finally persuaded to allow the departure of the Israelites; (c) his receiving of the Decalogue, or Ten Commandments, on Mt. Sinai; (d) various other miracles (notably the parting of the Red Sea and the descent of "manna") by which the Israelites are sustained and disciplined in Exodus; (e) the introduction and maintenance of a rule by Law for the nation of Israel.

13. Elijah, Isaiah, Jeremiah, Ezekiel, Amos, among others, would do. The principal job of the Prophets appears to be telling authorities and other people what they are doing wrong and advising them of the consequences.

14. The four "Gospels" of the New Testament are about the life of Jesus Christ. Their names, in order of appearance in the Bible, are The Gospel According to Matthew, The Gospel According to Mark, The Gospel According to Luke, and The Gospel According to John. (There is a rhythm to "Matthew, Mark, Luke, and John" which makes the order fairly easy to remember.) The Gospels have various differences as to detail and emphasis, but each is clearly the work of a writer who absolutely believes that Jesus Christ is the son of God and Savior of the world.

15. John the Baptist, a New Testament evangelist who is a

few years older than Jesus, preaches repentance to the people around Jerusalem and baptizes those who repent. No respecter of authority, he lives outdoors in primitive clothes and on a diet of honey and locusts.

16. In the Judaic tradition as we encounter it in Genesis, Abraham is Father Abraham, the first identified member of the Chosen People, the first "patriarch" of Israel.

17. In the lifetime of Jesus, Palestine was part of the Roman Empire. It was the policy of the Empire to leave strictly local matters in the hands of local authorities, but to handle major economic and legal matters through a corps of military governors or "procurators." In the Gospel accounts, Pontius Pilate is, at the time of the trial and crucifixion of Jesus, Procurator of Judea, the area including and surrounding Jerusalem. Since capital punishment is a major legal matter, it was Pontius Pilate who authorized the execution of Jesus.

18. Samson is one of the "Judges" of Israel. He is physically extremely strong and possessed of a rude wit. Otherwise he appears to have no judicial strong points and a number of weak ones.

19. Solomon, the son of David, is the last king of the brief monarchy of united Israel. He has been reputed to be extremely wise. He built a great temple in Jerusalem and evidently enjoyed the company of a great many wives and concubines.

20. Genesis mentions neither "the Devil" nor an "apple" but reports only that a *serpent* persuaded Eve to eat of the *fruit* of the tree of the knowledge of good and evil.

II

Myth And Genesis

"The world is charged with the grandeur of God."

Gerard Manley Hopkins, "God's Grandeur"

1. A Note on Myth

Briefly, the language of concern is the language of myth.

NORTHROP FRYE, *The Stubborn Structure*

When I refer to certain episodes in Genesis as myths, I don't mean that I believe them to be untrue. A good many people do use the word "myth" to mean fantasy, falsehood, or distortion of history, but I do not. When I call, for example, the story of Adam and Eve a myth, I mean something about how that narrative makes its point, how its writer goes about his business. I mean that in this story the major importance of actual events is not that they literally occurred at some particular date and place, but that they reflect a partial glimpse of a reality beyond dates, places, and events themselves. I mean that this is one of those works of literature which deal with a vast ocean of experience that we can only swim in with the support of symbols (and, like the literal ocean, we can only see and enter tiny parts of it at a time). I don't necessarily mean that I disbelieve that there was a garden east of Eden where the first man and the first woman lived blissfully until a serpent got them in trouble. I do mean that for me the truth of this kind of literature, mythic literature, has nothing to do with whether I accept its historical accuracy or not.

Everyone knows that history is an important branch of knowledge and that historical writing is an important kind of literature. Indeed, we often use "historical" loosely as an adjective meaning "true." History's knowledge consists of conclusions drawn from events of the observable human past. The historical writer rests much of the case for his truth on evidence that the events he uses really happened in the space and time of this world. One way we can generally recognize the historical style, and thus the historical intent, in a piece of writing is by its emphasis on such matters as dates, statistics, rational cause-and-effect relationships, records, archeological remnants, and surviving proper names.

Myth is also an important branch of knowledge, and mythic writing is an important kind of literature. But mythic knowledge is not information logically concluded from literal events on the world calendar. Mythic knowledge is rather a matter of *recognition*. It is, in a sense, something we already know but do not realize without the help of the myth. In mythic literature, the case for truth rests on whether events embody, or make visible, part of what we somehow feel to be the way life is. How or why we feel this is a fascinating and mysterious matter over which depth-psychologists and philosophers continue to ponder and debate. That we human beings share a mass of "primordial" ideas about our existence few will deny. It is the business of myth and mythic literature to bring such ideas out of their abstract state, out of conscious and subconscious memory, and to let us see them. How shall we believe in what we have not seen? The test of mythic truth is in the response of recognition: "Yes, I know," we say in the presence of mythic truth, "that puts it right. That's how things are."

A good deal of myth's popular reputation for mendacity must depend on the strange and historically improbable quality of the characters and events which often inhabit mythic narrative. We might note in passing that history contains its own share of the strange and improbable. Forty years ago I did not consider the possibility of watching men literally walk on the moon. The main fallacy in this critical view of myth, however, is that it applies the criteria of historical truth to something quite different in process and purpose. Mythic truth does not depend on the probability of its events but on the strange familiarity of what they symbolize.

Yet history and myth are, along with other kinds of knowledge, complementary. We shall frequently see historical and mythic literature share a single page, perhaps a single sentence. The existence of a myth has often been a fact, an event of history, and myth often employs events certified by history for its own purposes. To call a story a myth is not to say that it may not also be historical. It is to contend that its apparent intent is mythic, the intent to expose a truth beyond history.

2. Creation and the Fall

Of Man's first disobedience, and the fruit
Of that forbidden tree . . .

JOHN MILTON, *Paradise Lost*

Subject to jest, parody, and relative neglect as they sometimes are, the first three chapters of the Bible are particularly important and rewarding. Along with much else, the myths of the Creation and the Fall that are recorded in these chapters appropriately present assumptions on which everything that follows in the Bible depends.

One of these is that the world and mankind have been specially created by a Supreme Will. The writers of the rest of the Bible conclude from this that what happens among people and to the earth is important beyond the interest that individual persons may feel as conscious organisms. Another assumption is that human life is a good deal less than ideal, but that this is the responsibility of mankind, not of the Supreme Will.

Perhaps you do not accept either or both of these assumptions. If that is the case, remember that everything you read and all the words you hear are predicated on assumptions, some set of given conditions. To talk with one another, we agree that certain words mean certain things. Such assumptions allow communication. As readers of literature we can make sense of what we read only if we grant, at least temporarily, the terms of writers.° The literature of the Bible assumes that what happens in the world is important to God, and that man is to a significant extent free to choose his own paths.

Here are some matters to consider as you study the first three chapters of Genesis.

1. Chapter 1 is the "happier" of the two accounts of the Creation. This story presents God's construction of the earth and mankind as wonderful fun. Again and again the Builder sees "that it was good," and He concludes that everything is "very good." In chapter 1 God says "Let there be" and "Let us make," and things happen accordingly. True, He does set, divide, create, call, and make, but in this context such active verbs do not signify the stress of toil.

In this first account God makes man and woman in His own image to hold unrestricted sovereignty over the rest of the earth. His only

---

° It is conceivable, for example, that one may not believe that romantic love is a real force in human affairs. Such a person will have to suspend that disbelief while attempting to understand *Romeo and Juliet.*

command to them is a genial "be fruitful and multiply." It is hard to find any hint in the first chapter of world problems to come.

2. Early in chapter 2, on the other hand, appears the idea that the construction of the heavens and the earth was "work," and that the divine constructor wants rest when He is finished. Chapter 2 picks up the Creation at the point where this work, the heavens and the earth, is concluded, but before God has made any living thing. When He makes man, He makes him of dust; fourteen verses later, when He makes woman, He makes her of a bone. Dust and bone: Is a faint stench of death already on the sweet air of Eden before the Fall?

Note how much more local and particular, in certain aspects, chapter 2 is than chapter 1. The male and female, unnumbered and unnamed, live on and replenish the earth in chapter 1. In chapter 2 Adam and Eve are put in a garden east of Eden. Furthermore, specific geographical boundaries, rivers, and countries are named, as well as precious minerals like gold and onyx stone. For the happy couple in God's garden these particulars do not imply economic competition or international politics, but we know and the writer of Genesis knows what has evolved from boundaries and wealth.

3. Not only are toil, death, politics, and economics manifested or implied in chapter 2 as they are not in chapter 1, but also the concept of crime and punishment and, by strong implication at least, that of sexual inequality.

4. We find furniture characteristic of pagan mythology, folklore, and fairy tale in chapters 2 and 3 as we do not in chapter 1. Consider the talking serpent and the magic tree with its magic fruit. In chapters 2 and 3 God gives reasons for what He does, and in the third chapter He walks in the garden "in the cool of the day" and cross-examines Adam and Eve face to face.

Genesis

1:1,2   In the beginning God created the heaven and the earth. And the earth was without form, and void; and darkness was upon the face of the deep. And the Spirit of God moved upon the face of the waters.

3,4   And God said, Let there be light: and there was light. And God saw the
5 light, that it was good: and God divided the light from the darkness. And God called the light Day, and the darkness he called Night. And the evening and the morning were the first day.

6   And God said, Let there be a firmament in the midst of the waters, and
7 let it divide the waters from the waters. And God made the firmament, and divided the waters which were under the firmament from the waters which
8 were above the firmament: and it was so. And God called the firmament Heaven. And the evening and the morning were the second day.

9   And God said, Let the waters under the heaven be gathered together unto
10 one place, and let the dry land appear: and it was so. And God called the dry land Earth; and the gathering together of the waters called he Seas: and God
11 saw that it was good. And God said, Let the earth bring forth grass, the herb yielding seed, and the fruit tree yielding fruit after his kind, whose seed is
12 in itself, upon the earth: and it was so. And the earth brought forth grass, and herb yielding seed after his kind, and the tree yielding fruit, whose seed
13 was in itself, after his kind: and God saw that it was good. And the evening and the morning were the third day.

14   And God said, Let there be lights in the firmament of the heaven to divide the day from the night; and let them be for signs, and for seasons, and for
15 days, and years: And let them be for lights in the firmament of the heaven
16 to give light upon the earth: and it was so. And God made two great lights; the greater light to rule the day, and the lesser light to rule the night: he
17 made the stars also. And God set them in the firmament of the heaven to
18 give light upon the earth, And to rule over the day and over the night, and
19 to divide the light from the darkness: and God saw that it was good. And the evening and the morning were the fourth day.

20   And God said, Let the waters bring forth abundantly the moving creature that hath life, and fowl that may fly above the earth in the open firmament
21 of heaven. And God created great whales, and every living creature that moveth, which the waters brought forth abundantly, after their kind, and
22 every winged fowl after his kind: and God saw that it was good. And God blessed them, saying, Be fruitful, and multiply, and fill the waters in the
23 seas, and let fowl multiply in the earth. And the evening and the morning were the fifth day.

24   And God said, Let the earth bring forth the living creature after his kind, cattle, and creeping thing, and beast of the earth after his kind: and it was so.
25 And God made the beast of the earth after his kind, and cattle after their kind, and every thing that creepeth upon the earth after his kind: and God saw that it was good.

26   And God said, Let us make man in our image, after our likeness: and let them have dominion over the fish of the sea, and over the fowl of the air, and

over the cattle, and over all the earth, and over every creeping thing that
27 creepeth upon the earth. So God created man in his own image, in the image
28 of God created he him; male and female created he them. And God blessed
them, and God said unto them, Be fruitful, and multiply, and replenish the
earth, and subdue it: and have dominion over the fish of the sea, and over
the fowl of the air, and over every living thing that moveth upon the earth.
29 And God said, Behold, I have given you every herb bearing seed, which is
upon the face of all the earth, and every tree, in the which is the fruit of a
30 tree yielding seed; to you it shall be for meat. And to every beast of the
earth, and to every fowl of the air, and to every thing that creepeth upon the
earth, wherein there is life, I have given every green herb for meat: and it
31 was so. And God saw every thing that he had made, and, behold, it was very
good. And the evening and the morning were the sixth day.
2 Thus the heavens and the earth were finished, and all the host of them.
2 And on the seventh day God ended his work which he had made; and he
3 rested on the seventh day from all his work which he had made. And God
blessed the seventh day, and sanctified it: because that in it he had rested
4 from all his work which God created and made. These are the generations
of the heavens and of the earth when they were created,
5 in the day that the Lord God made the earth and the heavens, And
every plant of the field before it was in the earth, and every herb of the
field before it grew: for the Lord God had not caused it to rain upon the
6 earth, and there was not a man to till the ground. But there went up a mist
7 from the earth, and watered the whole face of the ground. And the Lord God
formed man of the dust of the ground, and breathed into his nostrils the
breath of life; and man became a living soul.
8 And the Lord God planted a garden eastward in Eden; and there he put
9 the man whom he had formed. And out of the ground made the Lord God to
grow every tree that is pleasant to the sight, and good for food; the tree of
life also in the midst of the garden, and the tree of knowledge of good and
evil.
15 And the Lord God took the man, and put him into the garden of Eden to
16 dress it and to keep it. And the Lord God commanded the man, saying, Of
17 every tree of the garden thou mayest freely eat: But of the tree of the knowledge of good and evil, thou shalt not eat of it: for in the day that thou eatest
thereof thou shalt surely die.
18 And the Lord God said, It is not good that the man should be alone; I will
19 make him a help meet for him. And out of the ground the Lord God formed
every beast of the field, and every fowl of the air; and brought them unto
Adam to see what he would call them: and whatsoever Adam called every
20 living creature, that was the name thereof. And Adam gave names to all
cattle, and to the fowl of the air, and to every beast of the field; but for Adam
there was not found a help meet for him.
21 And the Lord God caused a deep sleep to fall upon Adam, and he slept;
22 and he took one of his ribs, and closed up the flesh instead thereof. And the
rib, which the Lord God had taken from man, made he a woman, and
brought her unto the man.
23 And Adam said, This is now bone of my bones, and flesh of my flesh:
24 she shall be called Woman, because she was taken out of man. Therefore
shall a man leave his father and his mother, and shall cleave unto his wife:

Myth and Genesis

25 and they shall be one flesh. And they were both naked, the man and his wife, and were not ashamed.

3   Now the serpent was more subtile than any beast of the field which the Lord God had made. And he said unto the woman, Yea, hath God said, Ye

2 shall not eat of every tree of the garden? And the woman said unto the ser-

3 pent, We may eat of the fruit of the trees of the garden: But of the fruit of the tree which is in the midst of the garden, God hath said, Ye shall not eat

4 of it, neither shall ye touch it, lest ye die. And the serpent said unto the

5 woman, Ye shall not surely die: For God doth know that in the day ye eat thereof, then your eyes shall be opened, and ye shall be as gods, knowing good and evil.

6   And when the woman saw that the tree was good for food, and that it was pleasant to the eyes, and a tree to be desired to make one wise, she took of the fruit thereof, and did eat, and gave also unto her husband with her; and

7 he did eat. And the eyes of them both were opened, and they knew that they were naked; and they sewed fig leaves together, and made themselves aprons.

8   And they heard the voice of the Lord God walking in the garden in the cool of the day: and Adam and his wife hid themselves from the presence of

9 the Lord God amongst the trees of the garden. And the Lord God called unto Adam, and said unto him, Where art thou?

10   And he said, I heard thy voice in the garden, and I was afraid, because I was naked; and I hid myself.

11   And he said, Who told thee that thou wast naked? Hast thou eaten of the tree, whereof I commanded thee that thou shouldest not eat?

12   And the man said, The woman whom thou gavest to be with me, she gave me of the tree, and I did eat.

13   And the Lord God said unto the woman, What is this that thou hast done? And the woman said, The serpent beguiled me, and I did eat.

14   And the Lord God said unto the serpent,

> Because thou hast done this, thou art cursed above all cattle,
>   and above every beast of the field;
> upon thy belly shalt thou go,
>   and dust shalt thou eat all the days of thy life:

15
> And I will put enmity between thee and the woman,
>   and between thy seed and her seed;
> it shall bruise thy head,
>   and thou shalt bruise his heel.

16   Unto the woman he said,

> I will greatly multiply thy sorrow and thy conception;
>   in sorrow thou shalt bring forth children;
> and thy desire shall be to thy husband,
>   and he shall rule over thee.

17   And unto Adam he said,

> Because thou hast hearkened unto the voice of thy wife,
>   and hast eaten of the tree, of which I commanded thee, saying,
>   Thou shalt not eat of it:
> cursed is the ground for thy sake;
>   in sorrow shalt thou eat of it all the days of thy life;

Introduction to Biblical Literature

18   Thorns also and thistles shall it bring forth to thee;
      and thou shalt eat the herb of the field:
19   In the sweat of thy face shalt thou eat bread,
      till thou return unto the ground;
    for out of it wast thou taken;
      for dust thou art,
      and unto dust shalt thou return.

20 And Adam called his wife's name Eve; because she was the mother of all
21 living. Unto Adam also and to his wife did the Lord God make coats of
skins, and clothed them.

22 And the Lord God said, Behold, the man is become as one of us, to know
good and evil: and now, lest he put forth his hand, and take also of the tree
23 of life, and eat, and live for ever: Therefore the Lord God sent him forth
24 from the garden of Eden, to till the ground from whence he was taken. So he
drove out the man: and he placed at the east of the garden of Eden cherubim,
and a flaming sword which turned every way, to keep the way of the tree
of life.

Considerations and Questions

1. The writers of the first three chapters assert that there was a time when the world and mankind were created, and that there was a time when human beings learned that it is possible to do wrong. In what sense are these historical statements rather than mythic ones?

2. Expressing, even imagining, what there was before there was anything is a problem that the writer who would describe the Creation must consider. Perhaps we should say that the writer must consider how to get around the problem, since the human mind must have something to start with. With what generalized condition of existence does the writer of chapter 1 start? To what extent is this Creation story a description of shaping, ordering, and furnishing?

3. One of the archetypal ideas embodied in chapter 1's Creation myth has to do with the place of Man in the order of created nature, as well as the function of Man as inhabitant of the place in the order. How does the writer of chapter 1 treat this matter? What hold do you think the feeling or attitude he presents has on the generations of humanity as you know them?

4. Another most persistent archetypal idea appears in widespread mythic representations of "the golden age." As students of history we may conclude that there never has been a time when humanity lived in uncompromised peace and plenty. As scientific observers we may conclude that human life is inevitably a costly, painful struggle. Yet there is an idea in mankind that it could be otherwise. It is an idea that has refused to die and an idea of such power that it has given fuel and motivation to innumerable attempts, great and small, to change the quality of human life. It is not difficult to see a connection between the universality, durability, and power of this idea and the numerous mythic assertions that there in fact *has* been such a time when everything was "very good," for a vision of a "golden age" in the past supports the possibility of a golden age in the present or future. Not only do all the mythologies include some sort of picture of a golden age, but the picture keeps cropping up in various forms throughout literature and life. Most of us, for example, have something in our consciousness known as "the good old days." Utopian literature, writing concerned with the achievement of, or blighted attempts to achieve, the perfect society, has been important and popular since the times of the earliest stories on record.

> The world's great age begins anew
> The golden years return.
> The earth doth like a snake renew
> Her winter weeds outworn. . . .

So Shelley begins his chorus from "Hellas" and so people strive with their imaginations, reason, arts, and sometimes violence to bring to birth new orders of society, new moralities, new technologies. A characteristic of the human species appears to be the thirst to restore something like that situation at the end of chapter 1 when God gave everything to humankind, "and, behold, it was very good."

5. Forbidden fruit, taboos, and "No trespassing" signs in one form or another are familiar facts of life. Not incidentally, the thing forbidden is an important piece of construction material for the work of building all kinds of narrative. Doing what one is not supposed to do, grasping what one is not supposed to have, establishes the plots of fairy tales, Elizabethan drama, Homeric epics, and last week's best-selling novel. In stories, we know that the mention of a taboo, a forbidden thing or action, is a sure signal that characters will soon attempt to violate it. Notice that such a signal appears in verse 17 of chapter 2. In fairy tales, mythology, and other kinds of symbolic narrative, what is forbidden is frequently magic. That is, it provides its possessor with powers beyond his natural human capacity. Generally, too, in such stories a clear statement of the consequences of violation accompanies the signal. Can you support, or refute, my proposition with plots you recall? What particular properties of the taboo-tree are signaled in chapter 2? In what sense are these properties "magic"? What are the consequences of trespass?

6. Granting that the forbidden tree of chapters 2 and 3 is an example of a common narrative pattern, what further symbolic or mythic meanings does it particularly evoke as "the tree of the knowledge of good and evil"? To what extent and in what sense may the trespass of Adam and Eve suggest a universal condition of human life—unto the present generation? (Consider that dogs and elephants die; only human beings contemplate death.)

7. There is another particular tree in the garden, in the story, and in the mythic significance of these chapters. God does not forbid this tree to Adam and Eve. Why not? But God does, in the end, put it out of their reach. Why?

8. That serpent is surely a "subtile" beast. (*The New English Bible* calls him "crafty.") Why do you suppose in the story he speaks only to Eve, not to Adam, and not, in the sentencing scene, to God? Do you find any reasons, implied or stated, for his undertaking the job of temptation?

When confronted by God, guilty Eve, in verse 13 of chapter 3, says that the serpent "beguiled" her ("tricked" in *The New English Bible*). God apparently agrees that this is so, for He gives the serpent a stiff sentence. In *Paradise Lost* John Milton accounts for some of Eve's susceptibility by the serpent's magnificent appearance and by the fact that he is the only "beast of the field" who can talk, but in the Genesis account the serpent influences the woman only through what he says and how he says it. What are the mechanics of this subtile success? How are his terms and his connections designed to reach simple Eve?

          Incidentally, I prefer, in the context of the story, "subtile" to "crafty" and "beguiled" to "tricked." Consider the effects which the alternate choices have on the extent of Eve's responsibility.

9. The dialogue between Eve and the serpent (3:1–5) and the woman's subsequent decision to take the forbidden fruit has had a peculiar fascination for generations of audiences. Part of this may be due to an ancient and widespread feeling that there is something mysterious and ambiguous about the feminine personality as contrasted with the male personality. The scornful masculine charge that women are less "reasonable" than men is often combined with the uneasy sense that "woman's intuition" and the "feminine mystique" may have powers beyond the scope of mere reason. Granting that Eve's seduction by the serpent marks her as irrational, vulnerable, and wrong; granting that the God of Genesis austerely sentences her and her daughters to subordination, is there still not something mysteriously vital and even admirable about this mythic Eve that is lacking in her husband? Can we completely condemn her pursuit of wisdom and beauty? It is Eve who takes the leap; plodding Adam only eats when she gives him the fruit.

10. For various reasons, the idea has gotten around over the centuries that the first *sin,* as accounted for in the book of Genesis, is sexual intercourse. It is hard to drag support for such a notion from chapter 1. There, God blesses His male and female and tells them to be fruitful and multiply. As regards human beings at least, there isn't any other explicitly sexual reference in that chapter. The writer of chapters 2 and 3, on the other hand, is concerned with the nakedness of the man and the woman and their significantly changing reaction to it. In chapter 2, "man shall leave his father and mother and cleave unto his wife . . . and they shall be one flesh." In chapter 3, God sentences woman to the pain of childbirth. Do you think, as some have, that "the forbidden fruit" should be taken as a symbol or metaphor for sexual activity? Do you think, for example, that the serpent is a sex symbol? Why or why not?

3. Cain and Abel

O my offense is rank, it smells to heaven;
It hath the primal eldest curse upon't,
A brother's murder.

WILLIAM SHAKESPEARE, *Hamlet*

Murder has been a problem and a mystery among human be-
ings in all places and in all ages excepting the mythical golden age, or, in
Biblical terms, before the Fall. Those occasional groups of humanity that
boast of having no recorded homicides have only dealt with the problem
for a flicker of time; they have not made the problem evaporate. There
remains an awareness in all mature human beings of the possibility that
they can murder or be murdered. The book which records virtually all
mankind's basic difficulties, the Bible, includes many murders, attempted
murders, and allusions to murder. The mythic "first murder" of Abel
by his brother Cain enacts the essential outlines of criminal homicide.

Here are some matters to take note of as you consider this short
and deceptively simple story.

1. This murder is fratricide. Throughout the tale it is emphasized that Cain and Abel are children of the same parents. This, of course,
may seem technically necessary for the action to be consistent with its
mythic setting; presumably there are no people alive who are not the offspring of Adam and Eve. Yet the writer does not appear to be much concerned with that kind of consistency, as certain events after the killing indicate. What the writer does appear to emphasize is a picture of murder whose
victim lives and works intimately with the murderer.

2. This murder is irrational. Cain does not assassinate for hire
nor can he apparently expect to inherit Abel's sheep. There is not even
the dubious logic of vengeance; Abel has not wronged Cain, nor does Cain
indicate a belief that he has.

3. This murder is punished. Although Cain commits a per-
fect crime so far as society's police and courts are concerned, nature ex-
poses him and God sentences him.

Genesis

4 And Adam knew Eve his wife; and she conceived, and bare Cain, and said,
2 I have gotten a man from the Lord. And she again bare his brother Abel.
And Abel was a keeper of sheep, but Cain was a tiller of the ground.

3 And in process of time it came to pass, that Cain brought of the fruit of the
4 ground an offering unto the Lord. And Abel, he also brought of the firstlings
of his flock and of the fat thereof. And the Lord had respect unto Abel and
5 to his offering: But unto Cain and to his offering he had not respect. And
Cain was very wroth, and his countenance fell.

6 And the Lord said unto Cain, Why art thou wroth? and why is thy
7 countenance fallen? If thou doest well, shalt thou not be accepted? and if
thou doest not well, sin lieth at the door: and unto thee shall be his desire,
and thou shalt rule over him.

8 And Cain talked with Abel his brother: and it came to pass, when they
were in the field, that Cain rose up against Abel his brother, and slew him.

9 And the Lord said unto Cain, Where is Abel thy brother? And he said,
I know not: Am I my brother's keeper?

10 And he said, What hast thou done? the voice of thy brother's blood crieth
11 unto me from the ground. And now art thou cursed from the earth, which
12 hath opened her mouth to receive thy brother's blood from thy hand. When
thou tillest the ground, it shall not henceforth yield unto thee her strength;
a fugitive and a vagabond shalt thou be in the earth.

13 And Cain said unto the Lord, My punishment is greater than I can bear.
14 Behold, thou hast driven me out this day from the face of the earth; and from
thy face shall I be hid; and I shall be a fugitive and a vagabond in the earth;
and it shall come to pass, that every one that findeth me shall slay me.

15 And the Lord said unto him, Therefore whosoever slayeth Cain, vengeance shall be taken on him sevenfold. And the Lord set a mark upon Cain,
lest any finding him should kill him.

16 And Cain went out from the presence of the Lord, and dwelt in the land
17 of Nod, on the east of Eden. And Cain knew his wife; and she conceived,
and bare Enoch: and he builded a city, and called the name of the city, after
the name of his son, Enoch.

Considerations and Questions

1. We are accustomed to such widely inclusive metaphorical expressions as "the brotherhood of man," and "soul brother," and "brother, can you spare a dime." It has seemed to many that Cain's crime represents the murder of any human being by another. Yet in the story itself we should see that the literal family relationship is insistently present. Consider the acts and circumstances with which the story begins. Consider how often and in what contexts the word *brother* appears as the tale goes on.
2. When Cain asks his famous question, "Am I my brother's keeper?" he evidently assumes the answer "No." God and the story in effect answer "Yes." Cain kills the very person whom he ought most to protect, his own flesh and blood. This may seem too special a case to be symbolic of murder in general. Do you find in it any implication that killing strangers or aliens is acceptable? In Cain's fears for his own safety what can you recognize as an inevitable part of murder in general?
3. Does Cain kill Abel because God likes meat better than vegetables? What is his motive? The Lord asks him why he is angry and frowning, but Cain does not answer. Why not? What light does the Lord's psychological counseling of Cain in verse 7 shed on these questions? What about Cain's immediate response to this counseling?
4. The mark which the Lord sets on Cain, often alluded to as "the brand of Cain," obviously identifies him as a murderer. What, however, is the reason given in the story for Cain's label?

4. Noah

Allas, now cometh Noweles flood!
GEOFFREY CHAUCER, *The Miller's Tale*

The cartoon image of the great tubby Ark, miles of animals two by two stretching away into the distance from the side hatch, the bearded skipper leaning over the rail, is familiar to countless people who have not actually read Genesis. Medieval audiences laughed at "miracle plays" about Noah, his family, his Ark, and his animals. The popular modern American stand-up comic, Bill Cosby, has an extremely funny monologue about Noah's dealings with the Lord.

These things remind us that the Noah story is, among other things, comedy. In Genesis it is not told, of course, just for the laughs. To the extent that Noah's story is comedy, it is so in a serious literary sense. That is, it is a work of art depicting and accepting the real follies and foibles of humanity.

The story involves the destruction of the world, and that is not for most people an immediately amusing idea. But such comedy as I find in the Noah story is not primarily concerned with light amusement or jolly irrelevancies, but with frail humanity facing harsh realities.

While, at this writing, the end of the world is not a *historical* reality, it is a *mythic* reality. The harsh fact is that we all carry an idea of the end of the world around with us. Not that we all pass our conscious moments brooding about universal destruction. On the contrary, most of us commonly go about our business as though we and our world were permanent. But every once in a while something calls the idea up out of our depths and reminds us that it is really there. The prophetic words of scientists, philosophers, theologians, and priests may trigger such an emergence. So may pictures or accounts of vast batteries of hydrogen war-heads. So may the work of all sorts of imaginative artists. All of these can operate with the force of myth. If we are convinced of their truth it is because we recognize in them something we have somehow always known.

The Lord's threat to destroy the world in the Noah story is the result of mankind's wickedness and corruption. Such destruction occurs on various scales frequently in the literature of the Bible. Later in Genesis, for example, we encounter the destruction of the evil cities of Sodom and Gomorrah. The Book of Jonah is a short story in which the Lord threatens to demolish the great city of Nineveh. Besides a simple religious idea of divine justice in this pattern, we may note a rather overpowering comic paradox. The cities or empires threatened or destroyed by the hand of the Lord are always great and powerful. The people drowned by the flood in Noah's story are described as "giants in the earth," "mighty men," and "men of renown." In Biblical literature, as in a great deal of other literature, for man to achieve the goods of wealth and power is frequently for him to achieve the evils of corruption and vulnerability.

When the Cold War between the United States and Russia was at, I trust, its coldest, back in the late forties and early fifties, a comic and curious analogy to the Noah story was visible in our land. A good many people, expecting the mushroom cloud of a nuclear bomb to signal the destruction of the world, got to work on stationary arks—bomb shelters in the backyard. Whether, like Noah, these were the righteous portion of the population is hard to establish now. Noah himself says nothing in the story about his peculiar worthiness, but like the shelter-owners he believes the end to be coming and like them works hard at being a survivor. Don't underestimate the extent and detail of his efforts: that gopher-wood ark, about 450 feet long, pitched within and without, with rooms, windows, and hatches specified by the Designer, is quite a project for one man and his immediate family. Noah's job has a kind of dignity that the bustle of his twentieth-century successors with their structural steel, concrete, air shafts, and stockpiles of canned food fell short of. He does have a divinely appointed mission to save not only himself and his family but to ensure the continuation of the animal kingdom. Yet both sets of survivors remind us of comic aspects in mortal life: there they all are, little men, busy as squirrels, pitting their amateur skills against cosmic disaster.

Like some, but not all comedy, Noah's story ends more or less happily. I say "more or less" because we find at the end of the tale not a grand Conclusion, but merely an illustration of that basic comic principle: human life goes on somehow, and, being human, it is not perfect.

If Noah is the only righteous father on the face of the earth and a heroic leader of survivors, he still gets blind drunk and lies around in an unseemly manner after the flood. His family includes a peeping Tom whom the righteous but boozy father curses ill-temperedly for his nasty curiosity. The spectacle of the two righteous brothers, Shem and Japheth, solemnly backing up to their naked father with a modest covering draped over their shoulders is a classic bit of comic action which reminds us that even winners in the game of life often look somewhat absurd.

Some Sunday School lessons find a perfect conclusion to the Noah story in God's promise not to destroy the world again and in the lovely rainbow with which He seals that promise. On the other hand we might note that the Lord as a character in the story gives reasons for his intended forebearance which do not suggest that everything is now all right. In 8:21 He says: "I will not again curse the ground for man's sake; for the imagination of man's heart is evil from his youth." God's promise is not, then, a reward for the total reform of the human species. Rather it appears based on a wry willingness to put up with Man, such as Man is . . . which is somewhat wicked.

Genesis

6   And it came to pass, when men began to multiply on the face of the earth,
2 and daughters were born unto them, That the sons of God saw the daughters of men that they were fair; and they took them wives of all which they
3 chose. And the Lord said, My Spirit shall not always strive with man, for
4 that he also is flesh: yet his days shall be a hundred and twenty years. There were giants in the earth in those days; and also after that, when the sons of God came in unto the daughters of men, and they bare children to them, the same became mighty men which were of old, men of renown.

5   And God saw that the wickedness of man was great in the earth, and that
6 every imagination of the thoughts of his heart was only evil continually. And it repented the Lord that he had made man on the earth, and it grieved him
7 at his heart. And the Lord said, I will destroy man whom I have created from the face of the earth; both man, and beast, and the creeping thing, and
8 the fowls of the air; for it repenteth me that I have made them. But Noah found grace in the eyes of the Lord.

12   And God looked upon the earth, and, behold, it was corrupt; for all flesh
13 had corrupted his way upon the earth. And God said unto Noah, The end of all flesh is come before me; for the earth is filled with violence through
14 them; and, behold, I will destroy them with the earth. Make thee an ark of gopher wood; rooms shalt thou make in the ark, and shalt pitch it within
15 and without with pitch. And this is the fashion which thou shalt make it of: The length of the ark shall be three hundred cubits, the breadth of it fifty
16 cubits, and the height of it thirty cubits. A window shalt thou make to the ark, and in a cubit shalt thou finish it above; and the door of the ark shalt thou set in the side thereof; with lower, second, and third stories shalt thou make it.

17   And, behold, I, even I, do bring a flood of waters upon the earth, to destroy all flesh, wherein is the breath of life, from under heaven; and every
18 thing that is in the earth shall die. But with thee will I establish my covenant; and thou shalt come into the ark, thou, and thy sons, and thy wife, and thy
19 sons' wives with thee. And of every living thing of all flesh, two of every sort shalt thou bring into the ark, to keep them alive with thee; they shall be
21 male and female. And take thou unto thee of all food that is eaten, and thou
22 shalt gather it to thee; and it shall be for food for thee, and for them. Thus did Noah; according to all that God commanded him, so did he.

7   And the Lord said unto Noah, Come thou and all thy house into the ark;
2 for thee have I seen righteous before me in this generation. Of every clean beast thou shalt take to thee by sevens, the male and his female: and of
3 beasts that are not clean by two, the male and his female. Of fowls also of the air by sevens, the male and the female; to keep seed alive upon the face
4 of all the earth. For yet seven days, and I will cause it to rain upon the earth forty days and forty nights; and every living substance that I have made will I destroy from off the face of the earth.

5,7   And Noah did according unto all that the Lord commanded him. And Noah went in, and his sons, and his wife, and his sons' wives with him, into
8 the ark, because of the waters of the flood. Of clean beasts, and of beasts

purification

that are not clean, and of fowls, and of every thing that creepeth upon the
9 earth, There went in two and two unto Noah into the ark, the male and
the female, as God had commanded Noah.

10 And it came to pass after seven days, that the waters of the flood were
11 upon the earth. In the six hundredth year of Noah's life, in the second month,
the seventeenth day of the month, the same day were all the fountains of the
12 great deep broken up, and the windows of heaven were opened. And the
16 rain was upon the earth forty days and forty nights. . . . and the Lord shut
17 him in. And the flood was forty days upon the earth; and the waters in-
18 creased, and bare up the ark, and it was lifted up above the earth. And the
waters prevailed, and were increased greatly upon the earth; and the ark
19 went upon the face of the waters. And the waters prevailed exceedingly
upon the earth; and all the high hills, that were under the whole heaven,
20 were covered. Fifteen cubits upward did the waters prevail; and the mountains were covered.

21 And all flesh died that moved upon the earth, both of fowl, and of cattle,
and of beast, and of every creeping thing that creepeth upon the earth, and
22 every man: All in whose nostrils was the breath of life, of all that was in
23 the dry land, died. . . . and Noah only remained alive, and they that were
24 with him in the ark. And the waters prevailed upon the earth a hundred and
fifty days.

8 And God remembered Noah, and every living thing, and all the cattle
that was with him in the ark: and God made a wind to pass over the earth,
2 and the waters assuaged. The fountains also of the deep and the windows
3 of heaven were stopped, and the rain from heaven was restrained. And the
waters returned from off the earth continually: . . .

6 And it came to pass at the end of forty days, that Noah opened the window
7 of the ark which he had made: And he sent forth a raven, which went forth
8 to and fro, until the waters were dried up from off the earth. Also he sent
forth a dove from him, to see if the waters were abated from off the face of
9 the ground. But the dove found no rest for the sole of her foot, and she returned unto him into the ark; for the waters were on the face of the whole
earth. Then he put forth his hand, and took her, and pulled her in unto him
into the ark.

10 And he stayed yet other seven days; and again he sent forth the dove out
11 of the ark. And the dove came in to him in the evening, and, lo, in her mouth
was an olive leaf plucked off: so Noah knew that the waters were abated
12 from off the earth. And he stayed yet other seven days, and sent forth the
dove, which returned not again unto him any more.

13 . . . and Noah removed the covering of the ark, and looked, and, behold,
15,16 the face of the ground was dry. And God spake unto Noah, saying, Go
forth of the ark, thou, and thy wife, and thy sons, and thy sons' wives with
17 thee. Bring forth with thee every living thing that is with thee, . . . that they
may breed abundantly in the earth, and be fruitful, and multiply upon the
18 earth. And Noah went forth, and his sons, and his wife, and his sons' wives
19 with him: Every beast, every creeping thing, and every fowl, and whatsoever creepeth upon the earth, after their kinds, went forth out of the ark.
20 And Noah built an altar unto the Lord; and took of every clean beast,
21 and of every clean fowl, and offered burnt offerings on the altar. And the

Lord smelled a sweet savor; and the Lord said in his heart, I will not again curse the ground any more for man's sake; for the imagination of man's heart is evil from his youth: neither will I again smite any more every thing

22 living, as I have done. While the earth remaineth, seedtime and harvest, and cold and heat, and summer and winter, and day and night shall not cease.

9 And God blessed Noah and his sons, and said unto them, Be fruitful, and
2 multiply, and replenish the earth. And the fear of you and the dread of you shall be upon every beast of the earth, and upon every fowl of the air, upon all that moveth upon tne earth, and upon all the fishes of the sea; into your
3 hand are they delivered. Every moving thing that liveth shall be meat for you; even as the green herb have I given you all things.

8,12 And God spake unto Noah, and to his sons with him, saying, . . . This is the token of the covenant which I make between me and you, and every
13 living creature that is with you, for perpetual generations: I do set my bow in the cloud, and it shall be for a token of a covenant between me and the
14 earth. And it shall come to pass, when I bring a cloud over the earth, that the
15 bow shall be seen in the cloud: And I will remember my covenant, which is between me and you and every living creature of all flesh; and the waters
16 shall no more become a flood to destroy all flesh. And the bow shall be in the cloud; and I will look upon it, that I may remember the everlasting covenant between God and every living creature of all flesh that is upon the earth.

18 And the sons of Noah, that went forth of the ark, were Shem, and Ham,
19 and Japheth: and Ham is the father of Canaan. These are the three sons of Noah: and of them was the whole earth overspread.

20,21 And Noah began to be a husbandman, and he planted a vineyard: And he drank of the wine, and was drunken; and he was uncovered within his tent.
22 And Ham, the father of Canaan, saw the nakedness of his father, and told
23 his two brethren without. And Shem and Japheth took a garment, and laid it upon both their shoulders, and went backward, and covered the nakedness of their father; and their faces were backward, and they saw not their father's nakedness.

24 And Noah awoke from his wine, and knew what his younger son had
25 done unto him. And he said,

> Cursed be Canaan;
> a servant of servants shall he be unto his brethren.

26 And he said,

> Blessed be the Lord God of Shem;
> and Canaan shall be his servant.
27 God shall enlarge Japheth,
> and he shall dwell in the tents of Shem;
> and Canaan shall be his servant.

28,29 And Noah lived after the flood three hundred and fifty years. And all the days of Noah were nine hundred and fifty years: and he died.

Considerations and Questions

1. Parts of the Noah story are similar to other, non-Biblical mythologies. Consider that rather perplexing business about the "sons of God" early in the story (chapter 6). Like the family of Olympian Zeus in Homer, these "sons of God" cohabit with mortal women, apparently leaping with immortal vigor through the bedroom windows of the world. Neither as literal nor symbolic beings do they seem to fit in with Judaic theology as the Old Testament reflects its development. Just who or what are these "sons of God" as they figure in the Noah story?

2. Here are some notes on these "sons of God" which may help us to some sort of theory about them.

   (a) They are sexually vulnerable in the mortal fashion. They "saw the daughters of men that they were fair; and they took them wives of all which they chose."

   (b) The children they sire on mortal women are not divine or semi-divine. They are "giants" and "mighty men" and they are wicked. Their wickedness is not an idea relevant to the similar set of circumstances generally found in pagan mythologies.

   (c) The results, and so perhaps the perpetrators, of this adventure in mixed breeding have anything but the approval of the Lord.

   (d) The race of progeny produced by the "sons of God" is wiped out by the flood. Chapter 5 of Genesis (not included in this text) establishes the family of Noah as having purely human genealogical credentials back to Adam.

3. The divine decision to destroy a wicked world but to except a particular worthy family is also to be found in Greek mythology. Zeus, the father of men and gods, produces a flood after an "Iron Age" of human misbehavior. He directs the good man Deucalion and his wife Pyrrha to find refuge from the waters on the peak of Mount Parnassus. Other mythologies supply the same general story. Does this lead you to suppose that there must have been some early contact between the peoples from whom these mythologies sprung? What other explanations for the repetitions of the pattern occur to you?

4. There are significant likenesses between what happens in the Noah story and what happens in the first three chapters of Genesis. In both sequences the Lord tells the only people on earth to be fruitful and multiply and delivers into their hands dominance over all flora and fauna. In the Noah story, as in chapter 1, appears the idea that God created man in His own image. In the Noah story, as in chapters 2 and 3, the Lord restricts man from certain actions and assigns him certain duties. Yet here specifically we find certain differences between the situations of Adam and of Noah. How do the restrictions and duties differ in the two cases?

5. Babel

They built to last, for they thought their city
would last forever.

KENNETH GRAHAME, *The Wind in the Willows*

The Babel story is about the beginning of urban civilization. It is also about the fact that the peoples of the world speak different languages and do not live and work in cooperative harmony. It is about human idealism and moral aspirations. It is about the thought and technology mankind applies towards realizing its goals. It is about that frequently observed paradox that the most strenuous human efforts in one direction often propel humanity in the opposite direction. It is, above all, about mortal limits and the inexorable nonmortal Necessity which establishes them. If the Babel story is not in itself a tragedy, it contains all the general ingredients of tragic literature. There is all this and more in a mere nine verses.

The mythic proposition with which the story begins is a time when there is only one language on all the earth. This is not so fanciful a notion as it might first appear. If one believes that humankind has in some way evolved from more primitive forms of animal life, one also has to believe that there was a time in that process when there was no language beyond blows, grunts, snarls, nods, shakes, and other basic noises and gestures, and that only with the development and sophistication of words and syntax came differences in the kind of communication employed by various tribes of the species. Moreover, the theories of etymologists based on prehistoric "families of language" (like Indo-European) orient us to the acceptance of a "world" with common speech.

You will see that there is only one individual character in the Babel story. The people, the Babel-builders, have a kind of collective personality, but the Lord is a single identifiable person. Nevertheless, one of the things that does *not* go on in the Babel story is the attempt of a theologian to describe the nature of God. The Lord here is a character in a work of literature, mythic literature. While the writer obviously believes in God, he is in no sense seriously reporting what God literally did or said in some time or place. How could he? The character of the Lord in the Babel story gives flesh to the force of Necessity, that intangible mysterious principle which continually over-rules the plans of mankind.

The story, then, is about the human circumstance, not about God, even though God is the only important character in the story. I emphasize this partly because the Lord's personality in this myth is one which our humanistic modern viewpoint is likely to find unsympathetic. If a President of the United States were to behave as the Lord does in the Babel story (and some Presidents have been accused of doing so), moral outrage would rock the land. As a character, the Lord appears bent on thwarting progress, peace, prosperity, and universal understanding. The reason He gives for being so disposed may seem that of a rather petty and very human tyrant.

Genesis

11:1,2   And the whole earth was of one language, and of one speech. And it came to pass, as they journeyed from the east, that they found a plain in the land
3 of Shinar; and they dwelt there. And they said one to another, Go to, let us make brick, and burn them thoroughly. And they had brick for stone, and
4 slime had they for mortar. And they said, Go to, let us build us a city, and a tower, whose top may reach unto heaven; and let us make us a name, lest we be scattered abroad upon the face of the whole earth.
5   And the Lord came down to see the city and the tower, which the children
6 of men builded. And the Lord said, Behold, the people is one, and they have all one language; and this they begin to do: and now nothing will be re-
7 strained from them, which they have imagined to do. Go to, let us go down, and there confound their language, that they may not understand one an-
8 other's speech. So the Lord scattered them abroad from thence upon the face
9 of all the earth: and they left off to build the city. Therefore is the name of it called Babel; because the Lord did there confound the language of all the earth: and from thence did the Lord scatter them abroad upon the face of all the earth.

Considerations and Questions

1. Are peoples separated from other peoples because of language differences? Or are there language differences because peoples are separated from other peoples? How does the writer of the Babel story treat this pair of questions?

2. Some cities, perhaps most cities, just seem to happen without the conscious plan of the people who build them. Historians have explained the existence of cities by citing such impersonal forces as routes of trade, military convenience, proximity of natural resources, or the fact that groups of migratory people finally became too tired to wander further. What is the formal plan and purpose of the Babel-builders? Is there some implication in the story that the historical kind of explanation may also be pertinent to the founding of Babel?

3. Most of us have heard people contrasting life in school or college with something ahead called "the real world." The practical fact is that wherever you are living is the real world, just as real as any other you will encounter under the sun. Something like this is the point of view of mythic literature. In the Babel story, for example, there is no attempt to explain why all living people speak the same language and also appear to have made a single journey from the east to the plain of Shinar for the purpose of building a single city. These circumstances are casual assumptions about how things are in the real world of the story. With arguing how such things can be in the terms of another real world, the reader's for example, the story teller has nothing to do.

4. What is the function and effect of the connective words with which the nine verses of this reading start? (Note that there are six "Ands," a "Go to," a "So," and a "Therefore.")

5. The Babel story is one of those events in the Bible which is continually alluded to in order to illuminate events in human history. Dostoyevsky, among many others, compared the social revolutions he saw and foresaw to the building of Babel. I have heard people refer to the United Nations as a new attempt to "build Babel." Communes and other utopian projects have often been compared to Babel. What do such allusions indicate about their users' attitudes towards these specific attempts to improve life? What do they suggest about their view of the human condition in general?

III

Legendary Heroes
Of Genesis

"Let us now praise famous men. . . ."

Ecclesiasticus, XLIV

1. A Note on Legend

. . . asleep in the lap of legends old.
JOHN KEATS, *The Eve of St. Agnes*

Mythic literature is essentially symbolic literature. The main importance of the people and events in mythic narrative is not that they occurred at some specific place and time in the story of mankind, but they embody realities that we somehow know but cannot see without symbolic help. Although it might be argued that all literature is to some extent symbolic, and thus mythic, history and legend are, in contrast to what we have called myth, essentially concerned with people and events as literal occurrences in space and time.

We call the narratives to be considered in this section of our Introduction *legends,* and their characters *legendary,* although you will see that both mythic and historical literary components are also present in them. Like myth, legend has picked up a shabby reputation in loose popular speech. For many people, it is simply a synonym for falsehood as contrasted with the "truth" of history. It is true, of course, that like mythic literature and historical literature, legendary literature may fail as a means to the truth, may simply be wrong or phoney. But when legendary literature is successful, true to its own terms, it is as much a reflection of reality as any other kind of literature.

Legends express and preserve *attitudes* towards the past. Legends are the sustainers of the traditional reactions of a group or culture towards itself. Such attitudes or traditional reactions are as much facts of life as the last election returns.

Legends are stories about important people and events in the past. The importance of such people and events is in their hold on the hearts and minds of the people in whose legends they appear. It follows that legends are local or cultural in a sense that history tries not to be. Most of us, for example, have a stock of stories about our own families. These may be about how grandfather met grandmother, what Uncle Mike did in the war, why we don't talk much about Aunt Lavinia, or a fist fight on the playground. Perhaps there are documents somewhere which would substantiate these occasions and their consequences so that historical literature could be made of them. Generally, however, they survive and thrive because our family thinks them important and accepts their literal truth in space and time. They survive and thrive as legend, transmitted orally among the group concerned with them. It is just barely conceivable that as historical subjects the stuff of our family legends might be interesting to some unknown family in another town, but as legends they are pretty much the exclusive concern of the clan whose traditions they reflect.

Lest this example imply that legend is too small or parochial a matter to be real literature, let us remember that the family is only one of the groups to which most members of our species belong. Bodies of legend inevitably occur in our circles of friends, our schools, our clubs, our jobs, our regions, our nations, our civilizations, and perhaps, the human race itself.

Unlike myth, legend assumes the literal reality in space and time of its people and events. But unlike history, legend does not labor to establish or document that literal reality. Legend is almost by definition undocumented. Often it is so because such evidence is unavailable, but even if it were, the business of legend is not to prove the past but to express our mutual attitude towards it.

No documents contemporary with their times survive to "prove" that Abraham, Isaac, Jacob, and Joseph actually existed. In that sense they are not historical characters. Yet long before the first versions of their stories were written down they were real parts of the past, parts of the language of that extraordinary family we call Israel.

As legendary literature, the primary goal of these narratives is not, as in the case of mythic literature, to make us recognize an embodiment of what we have always somehow known. They deal with special events rather than with universal human conditions. As legendary literature, their goal is not like history's, to declare that something happened at a particular time and place. They assume their happenings without insistence. As legendary literature, the stories of Abraham, Isaac, Jacob and Joseph emphasize above all to their audience, "This is how we see ourselves as people." That audience begins with a legendary family, expands to a historical nation, and continues today as a current of the civilization in which we swim.

2. Abraham

Charles Darwin, the Abraham of scientific men
—a searcher as obedient to the command of truth
as was the patriarch to the command of God.
                    JOHN TYNDALL, *Science and Man*

Before the appearance of Abraham in the Biblical narrative its stories are about the mythic "peoples of the earth." There are good men like Noah and bad men like Cain; there are cities of the peoples of earth like Babel. But these stories are not concerned with particular nations, or with particular families within the universal mythic family of Adam. With Abraham we first encounter the idea of a special people among peoples, selected by God for certain obligations and certain advantages. The special people are, of course, the seed of Abraham, the children of Israel, the Jews, and all the various inheritors of their advantages and obligations.

Abraham is the founding father, the legendary first patriarch, or high father, of Israel. In telling his story, the Bible begins to concentrate on the chosen people as they deal with other peoples and with the God who has picked them out from among all others.

The story of Abraham simply as the biography of a tough and wily desert chieftain who wrings success from a hard world is a good one. The details of his adventures, domestic problems, and of his remarkable personality are the stuff of first-rate literature. If his story were this and no more, we might admire it as the legend of his immediate family about the founding of their fortune. He might remind us of any number of fascinating grandfathers who with more bold imagination than scruples have made something of themselves and their own. But the legend of Abraham is on a much larger scale than this. His story is above all the story of the man with whom God makes a contract, a Covenant, and who serves as the first agent for all future generations of special people bound by that Covenant. All the other interesting things that Abraham is and does are related by the sure hands of the writers and translators of Genesis to the theme of the Covenant.

Genesis

11:27 Now these are the generations of Terah: Terah begat Abram, Nahor, and
28 Haran; and Haran begat Lot. And Haran died before his father Terah in
29 the land of his nativity, in Ur of the Chaldees. And Abram° and Nahor took
them wives: the name of Abram's wife was Sarai;° and the name of Nahor's
wife, Milcah, the daughter of Haran, the father of Milcah, and the father of
30 Iscah. But Sarai was barren; she had no child.
31 And Terah took Abram his son, and Lot the son of Haran his son's son,
and Sarai his daughter-in-law, his son Abram's wife; and they went forth
with them from Ur of the Chaldees, to go into the land of Canaan; and they
32 came unto Haran, and dwelt there. And the days of Terah were two hundred
and five years: and Terah died in Haran.
12 Now the Lord had said unto Abram, Get thee out of thy country, and
from thy kindred, and from thy father's house, unto a land that I will show
2 thee: And I will make of thee a great nation, and I will bless thee, and make
3 thy name great; and thou shalt be a blessing: And I will bless them that bless
thee, and curse him that curseth thee: and in thee shall all families of the
earth be blessed.
4 So Abram departed, as the Lord had spoken unto him; and Lot went
with him: and Abram was seventy and five years old when he departed out
5 of Haran. And Abram took Sarai his wife, and Lot his brother's son, and
all their substance that they had gathered, and the souls that they had
gotten in Haran; and they went forth to go into the land of Canaan; and
6 into the land of Canaan they came. And Abram passed through the land unto
the place of Sichem, unto the plain of Moreh. And the Canaanite was then
in the land.
7 And the Lord appeared unto Abram, and said, Unto thy seed will I give
this land: and there builded he an altar unto the Lord, who appeared unto
8 him. And he removed from thence unto a mountain on the east of Beth-el,
and pitched his tent, having Beth-el on the west, and Hai on the east; and
there he builded an altar unto the Lord, and called upon the name of the
9 Lord. And Abram journeyed, going on still toward the south.
10 And there was a famine in the land: and Abram went down into Egypt
11 to sojourn there; for the famine was grievous in the land. And it came to
pass, when he was come near to enter into Egypt, that he said unto Sarai
his wife, Behold now, I know that thou art a fair woman to look upon:
12 Therefore it shall come to pass, when the Egyptians shall see thee, that they
shall say, This is his wife: and they will kill me, but they will save thee alive.
13 Say, I pray thee, thou art my sister: that it may be well with me for thy
sake; and my soul shall live because of thee.
14 And it came to pass, that, when Abram was come into Egypt, the Egyp-
15 tians beheld the woman that she was very fair. The princes also of Pharaoh
saw her, and commended her before Pharaoh: and the woman was taken
16 into Pharaoh's house. And he entreated Abram well for her sake: and he

---

° The names of Abram and Sarai change, by God's command, to Abraham (17:5)
and Sarah (17:15). The reasons for the changes are unknown.

had sheep, and oxen, and he asses, and menservants, and maidservants, and
17 she asses, and camels. And the Lord plagued Pharaoh and his house with
great plagues, because of Sarai, Abram's wife.

18 And Pharaoh called Abram, and said, What is this that thou hast done
19 unto me? why didst thou not tell me that she was thy wife? Why saidst
thou, She is my sister? so I might have taken her to me to wife: now there-
20 fore behold thy wife, take her, and go thy way. And Pharaoh commanded
his men concerning him: and they sent him away, and his wife, and all that
he had.

13 And Abram went up out of Egypt, he, and his wife, and all that he had,
2 and Lot with him, into the south. And Abram was very rich in cattle, in
3 silver, and in gold. And he went on his journeys from the south even to
Beth-el, unto the place where his tent had been at the beginning, between
4 Beth-el and Hai; Unto the place of the altar, which he had made there at
the first: and there Abram called on the name of the Lord.

5 And Lot also, which went with Abram, had flocks, and herds, and tents.
6 And the land was not able to bear them, that they might dwell together: for
7 their substance was great, so that they could not dwell together. And there
was a strife between the herdmen of Abram's cattle and the herdmen of
Lot's cattle: and the Canaanite and the Perizzite dwelt then in the land.

8 And Abram said unto Lot, Let there be no strife, I pray thee, between me
9 and thee, and between my herdmen and thy herdmen; for we be brethren. Is
not the whole land before thee? separate thyself, I pray thee, from me: if
thou wilt take the left hand, then I will go to the right; or if thou depart to
the right hand, then I will go to the left.

10 And Lot lifted up his eyes, and beheld all the plain of Jordan, that it was
11 well watered every where, . . . even as the garden of the Lord . . . Then
Lot chose him all the plain of Jordan; and Lot journeyed east: and they
12 separated themselves the one from the other. Abram dwelt in the land of
Canaan, and Lot dwelt in the cities of the plain, and pitched his tent toward
13 Sodom. But the men of Sodom were wicked and sinners before the Lord exceedingly.

14 And the Lord said unto Abram, after that Lot was separated from him,
Lift up now thine eyes, and look from the place where thou art northward,
15 and southward, and eastward, and westward: For all the land which thou
16 seest, to thee will I give it, and to thy seed for ever. And I will make thy
seed as the dust of the earth: so that if a man can number the dust of the
17 earth, then shall thy seed also be numbered. Arise, walk through the land
18 in the length of it and in the breadth of it; for I will give it unto thee. Then
Abram removed his tent, and came and dwelt in the plain of Mamre, which
is in Hebron, and built there an altar unto the Lord.

15 After these things the word of the Lord came unto Abram in a vision,
saying, Fear not, Abram: I am thy shield, and thy exceeding great reward.
2 And Abram said, Lord God, what wilt thou give me, seeing I go child-
5 less, . . . And he brought him forth abroad, and said, Look now toward
heaven, and tell the stars, if thou be able to number them: and he said unto
him, So shall thy seed be.

12 And when the sun was going down, a deep sleep fell upon Abram; and,
13 lo, a horror of great darkness fell upon him. And he said unto Abram, Know

of a surety that thy seed shall be a stranger in a land that is not theirs, and
14 shall serve them; and they shall afflict them four hundred years; And also
that nation, whom they shall serve, will I judge: and afterward shall they
15 come out with great substance. And thou shalt go to thy fathers in peace;
16 thou shalt be buried in a good old age. But in the fourth generation they
shall come hither again: for the iniquity of the Amorites is not yet full.
17 And it came to pass, that, when the sun went down, and it was dark, behold a smoking furnace, and a burning lamp that passed between those
18 pieces. In that same day the Lord made a covenant with Abram, saying,
Unto thy seed have I given this land, from the river of Egypt unto the great
river, the river Euphrates:

16 Now Sarai, Abram's wife, bare him no children: and she had a handmaid,
2 an Egyptian, whose name was Hagar. And Sarai said unto Abram, Behold
now, the Lord hath restrained me from bearing: I pray thee, go in unto my
maid; it may be that I may obtain children by her. And Abram hearkened to
3 the voice of Sarai. And Sarai, Abram's wife, took Hagar her maid the
Egyptian, after Abram had dwelt ten years in the land of Canaan, and gave
4 her to her husband Abram to be his wife. And he went in unto Hagar, and
she conceived: and when she saw that she had conceived, her mistress was
despised in her eyes.

There are two stories of Hagar in Genesis, the second beginning at 21:9. These are thought to be variants of the same account. This later story introduces refinements in style and content, such as Abraham's com-passion for Hagar, God's reassurance to him, the greater artistry in depicting her grief, and the happy ending. To facilitate comparison the two are presented in parallel columns.

16: 5 And Sarai said unto Abram, My wrong be upon thee: I have given my maid into thy bosom; and when she saw that she had
6 conceived, I was despised in her eyes: the Lord judge between me and thee. But Abram said unto Sarai, Behold, thy maid is in thy hand; do to her as it pleaseth thee. And when Sarai dealt hardly with her, she fled from her face.
7 And the angel of the Lord found her by a fountain of water in the wilderness, by the fountain
8 in the way to Shur. And he said, Hagar, Sarai's maid, whence camest thou? and whither wilt thou go? And she said, I flee from
9 the face of my mistress Sarai. And the angel of the Lord said unto her, Return to thy mistress, and submit thyself under her hands.

21: 9 And Sarah saw the son of Hagar the Egyptian, which she had borne unto Abraham, mock-
10 ing. Wherefore she said unto Abraham, Cast out this bond-woman and her son: for the son of this bondwoman shall not be heir with my son, even with Isaac.
11 And the thing was very grievous in Abraham's sight because of his son.
12 And God said unto Abraham, Let it not be grievous in thy sight because of the lad, and because of thy bondwoman; in all that Sarah hath said unto thee, hearken unto her voice; for in Isaac shall thy
13 seed be called. And also of the son of the bondwoman will I make a nation, because he is thy seed.
14 And Abraham rose up early in the morning, and took bread, and

16:10 And the angel of the Lord said unto her, I will multiply thy seed exceedingly, that it shall not be numbered for multitude.

11 And the angel of the Lord said unto her, Behold, thou art with child, and shalt bear a son, and shalt call his name Ishmael; because the Lord hath heard thy
12 affliction. And he will be a wild man; his hand will be against every man, and every man's hand against him: and he shall dwell in the presence of all his brethren.

15 And Hagar bare Abram a son: and Abram called his son's name,
16 which Hagar bare, Ishmael. And Abram was fourscore and six years old, when Hagar bare Ishmael to Abram.

a bottle of water, and gave it unto Hagar, putting it on her shoulder, and the child, and sent her away: and she departed, and wandered in the wilderness of
21:15 Beer-sheba. And the water was spent in the bottle, and she cast the child under one of the shrubs.

16 And she went, and sat her down over against him a good way off, as it were a bowshot: for she said, Let me not see the death of the child. And she sat over against him, and lifted up her voice, and wept.

17 And God heard the voice of the lad; and the angel of God called to Hagar out of heaven, and said unto her, What aileth thee, Hagar? fear not; for God hath heard the voice of the lad where
18 he is. Arise, lift up the lad, and hold him in thine hand; for I will
19 make him a great nation. And God opened her eyes, and she saw a well of water; and she went, and filled the bottle with water, and gave the **lad** drink.
20 And God was with the lad; and he grew, and dwelt in the wilderness, and became an archer.

17 And when Abram was ninety years old and nine, the Lord appeared to Abram, and said unto him, I am the Almighty God; walk before me, and be
2 thou perfect. And I will make my covenant between me and thee, and will multiply thee exceedingly.
3,4 And Abram fell on his face: and God talked with him, saying, As for me, behold, my covenant is with thee, and thou shalt be a father of many
5 nations. Neither shall thy name any more be called Abram, but thy name
6 shall be Abraham; for a father of many nations have I made thee. And I will make thee exceeding fruitful, and I will make nations of thee, and
7 kings shall come out of thee. And I will establish my covenant between me and thee and thy seed after thee in their generations, for an everlasting
8 covenant, to be a God unto thee and to thy seed after thee. And I will give unto thee, and to thy seed after thee, the land wherein thou art a stranger, all the land of Canaan, for an everlasting possession; and I will be their God.
9 And God said unto Abraham, Thou shalt keep my covenant therefore,
10 thou, and thy seed after thee in their generations. This is my covenant, which ye shall keep, between me and you and thy seed after thee; Every

11 man child among you shall be circumcised. And ye shall circumcise the flesh of your foreskin; and it shall be a token of the covenant betwixt me
12 and you. And he that is eight days old shall be circumcised among you, every man child in your generations, he that is born in the house, or bought
13 with money of any stranger, which is not of thy seed. He that is born in thy house, and he that is bought with thy money, must needs be circumcised:
14 and my covenant shall be in your flesh for an everlasting covenant. And the uncircumcised man child whose flesh of his foreskin is not circumcised, that soul shall be cut off from his people; he hath broken my covenant.

15 And God said unto Abraham, As for Sarai thy wife, thou shalt not call
16 her name Sarai, but Sarah shall her name be. And I will bless her, and give thee a son also of her: yea, I will bless her, and she shall be a mother of nations; kings of people shall be of her.

17 Then Abraham fell upon his face, and laughed, and said in his heart, Shall a child be born unto him that is a hundred years old? and shall Sarah, that is ninety years old, bear?

18 And the Lord appeared unto him in the plains of Mamre: and he sat in
2 the tent door in the heat of the day; And he lifted up his eyes and looked, and, lo, three men stood by him: and when he saw them, he ran to meet them
3 from the tent door, and bowed himself toward the ground, And said, My Lord, if now I have found favor in thy sight, pass not away, I pray thee,
4 from thy servant: Let a little water, I pray you, be fetched, and wash your
5 feet, and rest yourselves under the tree: And I will fetch a morsel of bread, and comfort ye your hearts; after that ye shall pass on: for therefore are ye come to your servant. And they said, So do, as thou hast said.

6 And Abraham hastened into the tent unto Sarah, and said, Make ready quickly three measures of fine meal, knead it, and make cakes upon the
7 hearth. And Abraham ran unto the herd, and fetched a calf tender and good,
8 and gave it unto a young man; and he hasted to dress it. And he took butter, and milk, and the calf which he had dressed, and set it before them; and he stood by them under the tree, and they did eat.

9 And they said unto him, Where is Sarah thy wife? And he said, Behold, in
10 the tent. And he said, I will certainly return unto thee according to the time of life; and, lo, Sarah thy wife shall have a son. And Sarah heard it in the
11 tent door, which was behind him. Now Abraham and Sarah were old and well stricken in age; and it ceased to be with Sarah after the manner of
12 women. Therefore Sarah laughed within herself, saying, After I am waxed old shall I have pleasure, my lord being old also?

13 And the Lord said unto Abraham, Wherefore did Sarah laugh, saying,
14 Shall I of a surety bear a child, which am old? Is any thing too hard for the Lord? At the time appointed I will return unto thee, according to the time
15 of life, and Sarah shall have a son. Then Sarah denied, saying, I laughed not; for she was afraid. And he said, Nay; but thou didst laugh.

16 And the men rose up from thence, and looked toward Sodom: and Abra-
20 ham went with them to bring them on the way. And the Lord said, Because the cry of Sodom and Gomorrah is great, and because their sin is very griev-
21 ous, I will go down now, and see whether they have done altogether accord-
22 ing to the cry of it, which is come unto me; and if not, I will know. And the men turned their faces from thence, and went toward Sodom: but Abraham stood yet before the Lord.

Legendary Heroes of Genesis

23 And Abraham drew near, and said, Wilt thou also destroy the righteous
24 with the wicked? Peradventure there be fifty righteous within the city: wilt
thou also destroy and not spare the place for the fifty righteous that are
25 therein? That be far from thee to do after this manner, to slay the righteous
with the wicked; and that the righteous should be as the wicked, that be far
from thee: Shall not the Judge of all the earth do right?
26 And the Lord said, If I find in Sodom fifty righteous within the city, then
I will spare all the place for their sakes.
27 And Abraham answered and said, Behold now, I have taken upon me to
28 speak unto the Lord, which am but dust and ashes: Peradventure there shall
lack five of the fifty righteous: wilt thou destroy all the city for lack of five?
And he said, If I find there forty and five, I will not destroy it.
29 And he spake unto him yet again, and said, Peradventure there shall be
30 forty found there. And he said, I will not do it for forty's sake. And he said
unto him, Oh let not the Lord be angry, and I will speak: Peradventure there
shall thirty be found there. And he said, I will not do it, if I find thirty there.
31 And he said, Behold now, I have taken upon me to speak unto the Lord:
Peradventure there shall be twenty found there. And he said, I will not
destroy it for twenty's sake.
32 And he said, Oh let not the Lord be angry, and I will speak yet but this
once: Peradventure ten shall be found there. And he said, I will not destroy
33 it for ten's sake. And the Lord went his way, as soon as he had left commun-
ing with Abraham: and Abraham returned unto his place.

19 And there came two angels to Sodom at even; and Lot sat in the gate of
Sodom: and Lot seeing them rose up to meet them; and he bowed himself
2 with his face toward the ground; And he said, Behold now, my lords, turn
in, I pray you, into your servant's house, and tarry all night, and wash your
feet, and ye shall rise up early, and go on your ways. And they said, Nay;
3 but we will abide in the street all night. And he pressed upon them greatly;
and they turned in unto him, and entered into his house; and he made them
a feast, and did bake unleavened bread, and they did eat.
4 But before they lay down, the men of the city, even the men of Sodom,
compassed the house round, both old and young, all the people from every
5 quarter: And they called unto Lot, and said unto him, Where are the men
which came in to thee this night? bring them out unto us, that we may know
them.
6 And Lot went out at the door unto them, and shut the door after him,
7,8 And said, I pray you, brethren, do not so wickedly. Behold now, I have two
daughters which have not known man; let me, I pray you, bring them out
unto you, and do ye to them as is good in your eyes; only unto these men
do nothing; for therefore came they under the shadow of my roof.
9 And they said, Stand back. And they said again, This one fellow came in
to sojourn, and he will needs be a judge: now will we deal worse with thee
than with them. And they pressed sore upon the man, even Lot, and came
10 near to break the door. But the men put forth their hand, and pulled Lot into
11 the house to them, and shut to the door. And they smote the men that were
at the door of the house with blindness, both small and great: so that they
wearied themselves to find the door.
12 And the men said unto Lot, Hast thou here any besides? son-in-law, and
thy sons, and thy daughters, and whatsoever thou hast in the city, bring them

13 out of this place: For we will destroy this place, because the cry of them is waxen great before the face of the Lord; and the Lord hath sent us to destroy

14 it. And Lot went out, and spake unto his sons-in-law, which married his daughters, and said, Up, get you out of this place; for the Lord will destroy this city. But he seemed as one that mocked unto his sons-in-law.

15 And when the morning arose, then the angels hastened Lot, saying, Arise, take thy wife, and thy two daughters, which are here; lest thou be consumed

17 in the iniquity of the city. . . . Escape for thy life; look not behind thee, neither stay thou in all the plain; escape to the mountain, lest thou be consumed.

18,19 And Lot said unto them, Oh, not so, my Lord: Behold now, thy servant hath found grace in thy sight, and thou hast magnified thy mercy, which thou hast showed unto me in saving my life; and I cannot escape to the

20 mountain, lest some evil take me, and I die: Behold now, this city is near to flee unto, and it is a little one: O, let me escape thither, (is it not a little one?) and my soul shall live.

21 And he said unto him, See, I have accepted thee concerning this thing also, that I will not overthrow this city, for the which thou hast spoken.

22 Haste thee, escape thither; for I cannot do any thing till thou be come thither. Therefore the name of the city was called Zoar.

23,24 The sun was risen upon the earth when Lot entered into Zoar. Then the Lord rained upon Sodom and upon Gomorrah brimstone and fire from the

25 Lord out of heaven; And he overthrew those cities, and all the plain, and all the inhabitants of the cities, and that which grew upon the ground.

26 But his wife looked back from behind him, and she became a pillar of salt.

27 And Abraham gat up early in the morning to the place where he stood

28 before the Lord: And he looked toward Sodom and Gomorrah, and toward all the land of the plain, and beheld, and, lo, the smoke of the country went

29 up as the smoke of a furnace. And it came to pass, when God destroyed the cities of the plain, that God remembered Abraham, and sent Lot out of the midst of the overthrow, when he overthrew the cities in the which Lot dwelt.

30 And Lot went up out of Zoar, and dwelt in the mountain, and his two daughters with him; for he feared to dwell in Zoar: and he dwelt in a cave,

31 he and his two daughters. And the firstborn said unto the younger, Our father is old, and there is not a man in the earth to come in unto us after

32 the manner of all the earth: Come, let us make our father drink wine, and

33 we will lie with him, that we may preserve seed of our father. And they made their father drink wine that night: and the firstborn went in, and lay with her father; and he perceived not when she lay down, nor when she arose.

34 And it came to pass on the morrow, that the firstborn said unto the younger, Behold, I lay yesternight with my father: let us make him drink wine this night also; and go thou in, and lie with him, that we may preserve

35 seed of our father. And they made their father drink wine that night also: and the younger arose, and lay with him; and he perceived not when she lay down, nor when she arose.

36,37 Thus were both the daughters of Lot with child by their father. And the firstborn bare a son, and called his name Moab: the same is the father of the

38 Moabites unto this day. And the younger, she also bare a son, and called

his name Ben-ammi: the same is the father of the children of Ammon unto this day.

21 And the Lord visited Sarah as he had said, and the Lord did unto Sarah
2 as he had spoken. For Sarah conceived, and bare Abraham a son in his old
3 age, at the set time of which God had spoken to him. And Abraham called
the name of his son that was born unto him, whom Sarah bare to him, Isaac.
4 And Abraham circumcised his son Isaac being eight days old, as God had
5 commanded him. And Abraham was a hundred years old, when his son
Isaac was born unto him.
6 And Sarah said, God hath made me to laugh, so that all that hear will
7 laugh with me. And she said, Who would have said unto Abraham, that
Sarah should have given children suck? for I have borne him a son in his old
8 age. And the child grew, and was weaned: and Abraham made a great feast
the same day that Isaac was weaned.

22 And it came to pass after these things, that God did tempt Abraham, and
2 said unto him, Abraham: and he said, Behold, here I am. And he said, Take
now thy son, thine only son Isaac, whom thou lovest, and get thee into the
land of Moriah; and offer him there for a burnt offering upon one of the
mountains which I will tell thee of.
3 And Abraham rose up early in the morning, and saddled his ass, and took
two of his young men with him, and Isaac his son, and clave the wood for
the burnt offering, and rose up, and went unto the place of which God had
4 told him. Then on the third day Abraham lifted up his eyes, and saw the
5 place afar off. And Abraham said unto his young men, Abide ye here with
the ass; and I and the lad will go yonder and worship, and come again to
6 you. And Abraham took the wood of the burnt offering, and laid it upon
Isaac his son; and he took the fire in his hand, and a knife; and they went
both of them together.
7 And Isaac spake unto Abraham his father, and said, My father: and he
said, Here am I, my son. And he said, Behold the fire and the wood: but
8 where is the lamb for a burnt offering? And Abraham said, My son, God
will provide himself a lamb for a burnt offering: so they went both of them
together.
9 And they came to the place which God had told him of; and Abraham
built an altar there, and laid the wood in order, and bound Isaac his son,
10 and laid him on the altar upon the wood. And Abraham stretched forth his
hand, and took the knife to slay his son.
11 And the Angel of the Lord called unto him out of heaven, and said, Abra-
12 ham, Abraham: and he said, Here am I. And he said, Lay not thine hand
upon the lad, neither do thou any thing unto him: for now I know that thou
fearest God, seeing thou hast not withheld thy son, thine only son, from me.
13 And Abraham lifted up his eyes, and looked, and behold behind him a ram
caught in a thicket by his horns: and Abraham went and took the ram and
14 offered him up for a burnt offering in the stead of his son. And Abraham
called the name of that place Jehovah-jireh: as it is said to this day, In the
mount of the Lord it shall be seen.
15 And the Angel of the Lord called unto Abraham out of heaven the second
16 time, And said, By myself have I sworn, saith the Lord, for because thou

17 hast done this thing, and hast not withheld thy son, thine only son, That in blessing I will bless thee, and in multiplying I will multiply thy seed as the stars of the heaven, and as the sand which is upon the seashore; and thy

18 seed shall possess the gate of his enemies; And in thy seed shall all the nations of the earth be blessed; because thou hast obeyed my voice.

19 So Abraham returned unto his young men, and they rose up and went together to Beer-sheba; and Abraham dwelt at Beer-sheba.

24 And Abraham was old, and well stricken in age: and the Lord had blessed
2 Abraham in all things. And Abraham said unto his eldest servant of his house, that ruled over all that he had, Put, I pray thee, thy hand under my
3 thigh: And I will make thee swear by the Lord, the God of heaven, and the God of the earth, that thou shalt not take a wife unto my son of the daughters
4 of the Canaanites, among whom I dwell: But thou shalt go unto my country, and to my kindred, and take a wife unto my son Isaac.

5 And the servant said unto him, Peradventure the woman will not be willing to follow me unto this land: must I needs bring thy son again unto the land from whence thou camest?

6 And Abraham said unto him, Beware thou that thou bring not my son
7 thither again. The Lord God of heaven, which took me from my father's house, and from the land of my kindred, and which spake unto me, and that sware unto me, saying, Unto thy seed will I give this land; he shall send his angel before thee, and thou shalt take a wife unto my son from thence.

8 And if the woman will not be willing to follow thee, then thou shalt be clear from this my oath: only bring not my son thither again.

9 And the servant put his hand under the thigh of Abraham his master, and
10 sware to him concerning that matter. And the servant took ten camels of the camels of his master, and departed; for all the goods of his master were in his hand: and he arose, and went to Mesopotamia, unto the city of Nahor.

11 And he made his camels to kneel down without the city by a well of water at the time of the evening, even the time that women ˊ out to draw water.

12 And he said, O Lord God of my master Abraham, I pray thee, send me
13 good speed this day, and show kindness unto my master Abraham. Behold, I stand here by the well of water; and the daughters of the men of the city
14 come out to draw water: And let it come to pass, that the damsel to whom I shall say, Let down thy pitcher, I pray thee, that I may drink; and she shall say, Drink, and I will give thy camels drink also: let the same be she that thou hast appointed for thy servant Isaac; and thereby shall I know that thou hast showed kindness unto my master.

15 And it came to pass, before he had done speaking, that, behold, Rebekah came out, who was born to Bethuel, son of Milcah, the wife of Nahor,
16 Abraham's brother, with her pitcher upon her shoulder. And the damsel was very fair to look upon, a virgin, neither had any man known her: and she
17 went down to the well, and filled her pitcher, and came up. And the servant ran to meet her, and said, Let me, I pray thee, drink a little water of thy pitcher.

18 And she said, Drink, my lord: and she hasted, and let down her pitcher
19 upon her hand, and gave him drink. And when she had done giving him drink, she said, I will draw water for thy camels also, until they have done
20 drinking. And she hasted, and emptied her pitcher into the trough, and ran

21 again unto the well to draw water, and drew for all his camels. And the man wondering at her held his peace, to wit whether the Lord had made his journey prosperous or not.

22 And it came to pass, as the camels had done drinking, that the man took a golden earring of half a shekel weight, and two bracelets for her hands of

23 ten shekels weight of gold; And said, Whose daughter art thou? tell me, I pray thee: is there room in thy father's house for us to lodge in?

24 And she said unto him, I am the daughter of Bethuel the son of Milcah,

25 which she bare unto Nahor. She said moreover unto him, We have both

26 straw and provender enough, and room to lodge in. And the man bowed

27 down his head, and worshipped the Lord. And he said, Blessed be the Lord God of my master Abraham, who hath not left destitute my master of his mercy and his truth: I being in the way, the Lord led me to the house of my

28 master's brethren. And the damsel ran, and told them of her mother's house these things.

29 And Rebekah had a brother, and his name was Laban: and Laban ran out

30 unto the man, unto the well. And it came to pass, when he saw the earring, and bracelets upon his sister's hands, and when he heard the words of Rebekah his sister, saying, Thus spake the man unto me, that he came unto

31 the man; and, behold, he stood by the camels at the well. And he said, Come in, thou blessed of the Lord; wherefore standest thou without? for I have prepared the house, and room for the camels.

32 And the man came into the house: and he ungirded his camels, and gave straw and provender for the camels, and water to wash his feet, and the

33 men's feet that were with him. And there was set meat before him to eat: but he said, I will not eat, until I have told mine errand. And he said, Speak on.

34,35 And he said, I am Abraham's servant. And the Lord hath blessed my master greatly, and he is become great: and he hath given him flocks, and herds, and silver, and gold, and menservants, and maidservants, and camels,

36 and asses. And Sarah my master's wife bare a son to my master when she

37 was old: and unto him hath he given all that he hath. And my master made me swear, saying, Thou shalt not take a wife to my son of the daughters of

38 the Canaanites, in whose land I dwell: But thou shalt go unto my father's house, and to my kindred, and take a wife unto my son.

42,45 And I came this day unto the well, and . . . behold, Rebekah came forth with her pitcher on her shoulder; and she went down unto the well, and drew

46 water: and I said unto her, Let me drink, I pray thee. And she made haste, and let down her pitcher from her shoulder, and said, Drink, and I will give thy camels drink also: so I drank, and she made the camels drink also.

47 And I asked her, and said, Whose daughter art thou? And she said, The daughter of Bethuel, Nahor's son, whom Milcah bare unto him: and I put

48 the earring upon her face, and the bracelets upon her hands. And I bowed down my head, and worshipped the Lord, and blessed the Lord God of my master Abraham, which had led me in the right way to take my master's

49 brother's daughter unto his son. And now, if ye will deal kindly and truly with my master, tell me: and if not, tell me; that I may turn to the right hand, or to the left.

50 Then Laban and Bethuel answered and said, The thing proceedeth from

51 the Lord: we cannot speak unto thee bad or good. Behold, Rebekah is before thee; take her, and go, and let her be thy master's son's wife, as the Lord hath spoken.

52 And it came to pass, that, when Abraham's servant heard their words,
53 he worshipped the Lord, bowing himself to the earth. And the servant brought forth jewels of silver, and jewels of gold, and raiment, and gave them to Rebekah: he gave also to her brother and to her mother precious things.

54 And they did eat and drink, he and the men that were with him, and tarried all night; and they rose up in the morning, and he said, Send me away
55 unto my master. And her brother and her mother said, Let the damsel abide with us a few days, at the least ten; after that she shall go.

56 And he said unto them, Hinder me not, seeing the Lord hath prospered
57 my way; send me away that I may go to my master. And they said, We will call the damsel, and inquire at her mouth.

58 And they called Rebekah, and said unto her, Wilt thou go with this man?
59 And she said, I will go. And they sent away Rebekah their sister, and her
60 nurse, and Abraham's servant, and his men. And they blessed Rebekah, and said unto her, Thou art our sister; be thou the mother of thousands of
61 millions, and let thy seed possess the gate of those which hate them. And Rebekah arose, and her damsels, and they rode upon the camels, and followed the man: and the servant took Rebekah, and went his way.

62 And Isaac came from the way of the well Lahai-roi; for he dwelt in the
63 south country. And Isaac went out to meditate in the field at the eventide: and he lifted up his eyes, and saw, and, behold, the camels were coming.
64 And Rebekah lifted up her eyes, and when she saw Isaac, she lighted off
65 the camel. For she had said unto the servant, What man is this that walketh in the field to meet us? And the servant had said, It is my master: therefore
66 she took a veil, and covered herself. And the servant told Isaac all things that he had done.

67 And Isaac brought her into his mother Sarah's tent, and took Rebekah, and she became his wife; and he loved her: and Isaac was comforted after his mother's death.

Considerations and Questions

1. According to the last verses of chapter 11, Abraham is born and grows to manhood in Ur of the Chaldees. (Historical evidence indicates that in 2000 B.C., which is about the legendary time of Abraham, Ur was a prosperous and sophisticated city in what is now Iran.) For no reported reason, Terah, Abraham's father, packs up his family and undertakes a long wilderness trek towards what is now Israel, the land of Canaan. From this early point in his story, then, we see Abraham separated from the customary courses of his world by circumstance. He is, as we see later, a decisive man, but is it not suggested from the beginning that certain decisions are made for him? As the story goes on, is it Abraham who approaches God with the proposal for a Covenant?

2. What detail about the married life of Abraham and Sarah should we note in those verses of chapter 11 which deal with their life in Ur of the Chaldees?

3. What references to God or religion appear in the story up to the point of Terah's death in Haran? How does the answer to this question contribute to our understanding that it is Abraham who is the patriarch of Israel?

4. Abraham's legendary stature is heroic, but he is neither morally nor physically a superman. Consider how he must scuffle for his life, tell a few lies, maneuver for wealth. Note how he diversifies his sex life and trades the use of his wife for his own advantage and safety. Where, on the other hand, do we see examples of his generosity and magnanimity, and of his loyalty to his kinfolk? Does it still appear that these virtues pay him material dividends?

5. In the first verse of chapter 12 begins the experience of Abraham as a mystic, a man to whom God speaks directly. The Lord commands Abraham to continue the interrupted family migration to the land of Canaan. From this early stage there is a businesslike quality to God's dealings with the patriarch. Along with the divine command, what explicit promises for payment or, in contractual terms, "considerations" are made for obeying it? Does it appear that Abraham bargains with God? Explain.

6. Abraham and his family do, of course, obey God's command and move on from Haran to Canaan. While they are in that country, two significant things occur in the religious life of Abraham: (1) the Lord promises that Canaan will belong to Abraham's descendants; and (2) for the first recorded time Abraham builds an altar unto the Lord. How do these events depict Abraham's developing idea of what his God is like?

7. Abraham and his family do not stay in Canaan long. The story does not indicate that they are disobeying the Lord in leaving, but their reasons for doing so are not in the least mystical. They are matters of immediate survival. What are they? (See verses 6 and 10 of chapter 12.)

8. Abraham tells the Egyptians that his wife Sarah is his sister; and when Abraham leaves Egypt he is rich. What is the connection between these two events in the narrative? Granted that Abraham is the hero of our legend, how do you feel his behavior compares with Pharaoh's in this episode?

9. Sodom and Gomorrah and Lot's backward-glancing wife are common allusions among people who may not associate them with the legend of Abraham, but Lot is, in fact, part of the literary structure of Abraham's story. Until shortly after Abraham & Co. leave Egypt, Lot appears to be an obedient family follower. At this point there is still no personal friction between the patriarch and his nephew. Abraham's proposal that they now go their separate ways is evidently made to keep things amicable. In Egypt we have seen Abraham's perhaps less attractive side, but how do his magnanimous qualities now appear as he deals with Lot? What is Lot's response to his uncle's generosity?

10. What sequence of events leads to Lot's residence in the city of Sodom? How does Abraham figure in each of these events?

11. Compared with Abraham, Lot appears to be a man to whom things happen rather than one who makes them happen. Yet how do we also see in him a man of courage, integrity, and unyielding devotion to a primitive code of ethics?

12. Note how the balance between Abraham as a mystic and Abraham as a man of the world is maintained throughout his story. His interviews with the Lord and his worship of Him increase as the legend progresses, but these are juxtaposed to and interrelated with his secular problems as a father, a husband, and a ruler: an important man of flesh and blood.

   One of these problems is that of Sarah's barren womb. The basic social and political unit of Abraham's world is the family; without children, of course, families decline and disappear. Furthermore, the only continuing identity Abraham can imagine must be in terms of his own offspring. (Neither the Lord nor anyone else mentions life after death in Genesis.) So Abraham is caught between his obviously passionate love of Sarah (who, though barren, is attractive enough to catch the eye of at least two kings) and an equally passionate need to reproduce himself.

   What plan does Sarah herself propose in order to resolve this dilemma? To what extent is the undertaking successful? What are Sarah's reactions to its limited success? What are Abraham's reactions to *her* reactions? What picture of these two people and their marriage emerges?

13. Like the rest of us struggling in the currents of this world, Abraham must often act against his own desires and accept what appear to be lesser evils. Only in the central matter of the Covenant with his God is Abraham's power of decision simple and absolute, although his grasp of all its implications is gradual and at times painful.

It is important that we understand the details of the Covenant. In chapter 17 we find a sort of formal "signing" of the completed basic contract which the Lord has been telling Abraham about over many years.

Note that the Lord, the party-of-the-first-part, begins the session with a clear identification of those involved. In the first verse He says "I am the Almighty God." In the fifth verse He changes the former "Abram" to Abraham, as He will shortly change "Sarai" to Sarah. "Almighty" is a key term in this preamble. Everything that follows in the transaction depends on Abraham's understanding of its implications. The ancient world is well-populated with gods, but only the *Almighty* God can make this Covenant and provide the "considerations" it stipulates. What are these considerations?

From the party-of-the-second-part, Abraham, the Covenant requires that he "walk before me and be . . . perfect." Very clearly neither Abraham nor his descendants have been perfect by *every* standard since the Covenant. What particular kind of perfection does the Lord require here? Try reading the Lord's speech aloud with an emphasis on the italicized words: "I am the *Almighty* God; walk before *me* and be thou perfect." Does it seem that perfect means absolute and exclusive? That Abraham and his seed are to "walk before" or serve this Almighty God and no other God? Or do you think that this is a conditional statement: "Serve me and by the only standard that matters you will be perfect"?

The other requirement of the Covenant is direct, explicit, and stated in crude detail. It does not provoke the question, "What does He mean?" Rather, the reader might be inclined to wonder, "Why does He mean it?"

14. Up to a late point in the Covenant meeting of chapter 17, Abraham obviously assumes that the descendants or "seed" which the Lord will bless him with will be his only through his illegitimate son Ishmael. As holy patriarch, covenanted to walk before the Lord, he accepts and obeys God's orders, but as a natural man whose experience with sex is rather extensive, he collapses with laughter at the Lord's announcement that he will have a legitimate son at the age of a hundred born by his ninety-year-old Sarah. Then, passing over God's little joke, he earnestly recommends Ishmael. Although there seem to be humorous aspects to the Lord's treatment of the patriarch at times, He is not, of course, having His little joke. God tells Abraham explicitly that Sarah will bear him a son, when she will do so, what the son's name will be, and that the son, Isaac, will be the inheritor of the Covenant. Like Lot, Ishmael will be the ancestor of nations, but his children will not carry on the special terms of God's contract with Abraham. Can you see here an instance of how the Abraham

legend binds together the life of its hero as mystical man of God and his life as mortal flesh and blood?

15. Sarah also laughs when, eavesdropping, she hears her husband's mysterious visitors repeat the information about her future child-bearing in chapter 18. How is her laughter different from Abraham's? Is it significant that in this instance, the Lord, who has spoken to Abraham directly in the spirit, arrives as a human traveler with two companions? Note that there is more of what writers call "scene" in this episode than in many other parts of the Abraham story. There is a sense of place and movement, tents and cookery. We see physical things happening, hear real voices as Abraham meets, entertains, and sees his guests on their way. Does all this suggest something about the differing characters of Abraham and Sarah?

3. Abraham's Heirs: Isaac and Jacob

*But God, who is able to prevail, wrestled with
him, as the Angel did with Jacob, and marked
him; marked him for his own.*

IZAAK WALTON, *Life of Donne*

Through Ishmael and other children, legendary Abraham is
father to various nations, but the legend insists that only his seed through
Sarah's son Isaac will form the people of the Covenant. And of Isaac's
children, only Jacob, later to be named Israel, will continue the line. It
follows that the chosen people are, in the times of Isaac and Jacob, few in
number. They are, in fact, simply the members, servants, and immediate
followers of a single family of tough, wandering sheepherders. The family
has been and continues to be prosperous by the standards of its time and
place, but its prosperity and its survival are precarious matters. The father
of the clan must keep it on the move in search of grazing land and grain
and water, and must somehow deal with the often larger and stronger
groups who claim that same grazing land, grain, and water. Although there
are occasional acts and threats of violence in the life of this family of
Isaac and Jacob, they are not at this point warlike. As they are much too
few in number to cut any military figure in the ancient world, their tendency
is to meet the dangers of life with trickery and strategic withdrawal.

We see at this point no particular indication that the central
line of Abraham's seed is made up of people more attractive, honest, or
better behaved than other people. They are signed up to walk before the
Almighty God and to be perfect—that is, complete in their allegiance to
Him only. Their painful symbol of this simple commitment is circum-
cision.

But besides the commitment and its symbol, they do main-
tain, in their patriarchs, the heavy personal stamp of the first patriarch,
Abraham.

Isaac and Jacob are, like Abraham, somewhat devious, practical
men of deeply religious temperaments. Unlike their thoughtless, violent
brothers, Ishmael and Esau (who are excluded from the line of the
Covenant), and again like Abraham, they are peaceful men and careful
men. They choose their paths with their eyes on the distance. And they are
determined men who will not leave those paths once chosen.

The stories of Isaac and Jacob emphasize the personal stamp
of Abraham most specifically by the inclusion of circumstances in their lives

that remind us of Abraham's life. Abraham's Sarah appears to be barren; so do Isaac's Rebekah and Jacob's Rachael. Each barren wife is intensely loved by her husband. Each does give birth to a favored son who will be the major leader of the Covenant line in the sequence to follow. Isaac, like his father, pretends that his beautiful wife is his sister and makes her available to a powerful king in order to preserve his life and property. To Isaac and Jacob, the Lord clearly identifies Himself as the God of Abraham, and like Abraham, they build altars unto Him. As Abraham must sorrowfully send his first-born, Ishmael, away, Isaac must reluctantly dispossess his eldest, Esau. Although he does not exclude him, Jacob too is disappointed with his promising eldest son, whom he judges in the end as "unstable as water."

Genesis

And Isaac was forty years old when he took Rebekah to wife, the daughter of Bethuel the Syrian of Padan-aram, the sister to Laban the Syrian.
21 And Isaac entreated the Lord for his wife, because she was barren: and the
22 Lord was entreated of him, and Rebekah his wife conceived. And the children struggled together within her; and she said, If it be so, why am I
23 thus? And she went to inquire of the Lord. And the Lord said unto her,

> Two nations are in thy womb,
>> and two manner of people shall be separated from thy bowels;
> and the one people shall be stronger than the other people;
>> and the elder shall serve the younger.

24 And when her days to be delivered were fulfilled, behold, there were
25 twins in her womb. And the first came out red, all over like a hairy garment;
26 and they called his name Esau. And after that came his brother out, and his hand took hold on Esau's heel; and his name was called Jacob: and Isaac was
27 threescore years old when she bare them. And the boys grew: and Esau was a cunning hunter, a man of the field; and Jacob was a plain man, dwelling in
28 tents. And Isaac loved Esau, because he did eat of his venison: but Rebekah loved Jacob.
29 And Jacob sod pottage: and Esau came from the field, and he was faint:
30 And Esau said to Jacob, Feed me, I pray thee, with that same red pottage;
31 for I am faint: therefore was his name called Edom. And Jacob said, Sell me
32 this day thy birthright. And Esau said, Behold, I am at the point to die:
33 and what profit shall this birthright do to me? And Jacob said, Swear to me
34 this day; and he sware unto him: and he sold his birthright unto Jacob. Then Jacob gave Esau bread and pottage of lentils; and he did eat and drink, and rose up, and went his way. Thus Esau despised his birthright.
26:34 And Esau was forty years old when he took to wife Judith the daughter of Beeri the Hittite, and Bashemath the daughter of Elon the Hittite:
35 Which were a grief of mind unto Isaac and to Rebekah.
27 And it came to pass, that when Isaac was old, and his eyes were dim, so that he could not see, he called Esau his eldest son, and said unto him, My
2 son: and he said unto him, Behold, here am I. And he said, Behold now, I
3 am old, I know not the day of my death: Now therefore take, I pray thee, thy weapons, thy quiver and thy bow, and go out to the field, and take me
4 some venison; And make me savory meat, such as I love, and bring it to me,
5 that I may eat; that my soul may bless thee before I die. And Rebekah heard when Isaac spake to Esau his son. And Esau went to the field to hunt for venison, and to bring it.
6 And Rebekah spake unto Jacob her son, saying, Behold, I heard thy father
7 speak unto Esau thy brother, saying, Bring me venison, and make me savory meat, that I may eat, and bless thee before the Lord before my death.
8 Now therefore, my son, obey my voice according to that which I command
9 thee. Go now to the flock, and fetch me from thence two good kids of the goats; and I will make them savory meat for thy father, such as he loveth:

10 And thou shalt bring it to thy father, that he may eat, and that he may bless thee before his death.

11 And Jacob said to Rebekah his mother, Behold, Esau my brother is a
12 hairy man, and I am a smooth man: My father peradventure will feel me, and I shall seem to him as a deceiver; and I shall bring a curse upon me, and
13 not a blessing. And his mother said unto him, Upon me be thy curse, my son:
14 only obey my voice, and go fetch me them. And he went, and fetched, and brought them to his mother: and his mother made savory meat, such as his father loved.

15 And Rebekah took goodly raiment of her eldest son Esau, which were
16 with her in the house, and put them upon Jacob her younger son: And she put the skins of the kids of the goats upon his hands, and upon the smooth
17 of his neck: And she gave the savory meat and the bread, which she had prepared, into the hand of her son Jacob.

18 And he came unto his father, and said, My father: and he said, Here am
19 I; who art thou, my son? And Jacob said unto his father, I am Esau thy firstborn; I have done according as thou badest me: arise, I pray thee, sit and eat of my venison, that thy soul may bless me.

20 And Isaac said unto his son, How is it that thou hast found it so quickly, my son? And he said, Because the Lord thy God brought it to me.

21 And Isaac said unto Jacob, Come near, I pray thee, that I may feel thee,
22 my son, whether thou be my very son Esau or not. And Jacob went near unto Isaac his father; and he felt him, and said, The voice is Jacob's voice,
23 but the hands are the hands of Esau. And he discerned him not, because his hands were hairy, as his brother Esau's hands: so he blessed him.

24,25 And he said, Art thou my very son Esau? And he said, I am. And he said, Bring it near to me, and I will eat of my son's venison, that my soul may bless thee. And he brought it near to him, and he did eat: and he brought him wine, and he drank.

26 And his father Isaac said unto him, Come near now, and kiss me, my son.
27 And he came near, and kissed him: and he smelled the smell of his raiment, and blessed him, and said,

> See, the smell of my son is as the smell of a field
> which the Lord hath blessed:

28
> Therefore God give thee of the dew of heaven,
> and the fatness of the earth,
> and plenty of corn and wine:

29
> Let people serve thee,
> and nations bow down to thee:
> be lord over thy brethren,
> and let thy mother's sons bow down to thee:
> cursed be every one that curseth thee,
> and blessed be he that blesseth thee.

30 And it came to pass, as soon as Isaac had made an end of blessing Jacob, and Jacob was yet scarce gone out from the presence of Isaac his father,
31 that Esau his brother came in from his hunting. And he also had made savory meat, and brought it unto his father, and said unto his father, Let my father arise, and eat of his son's venison, that thy soul may bless me.

32 And Isaac his father said unto him, Who art thou? And he said, I am thy
33 son, thy firstborn, Esau. And Isaac trembled very exceedingly, and said, Who? where is he that hath taken venison, and brought it me, and I have eaten of all before thou camest, and have blessed him? yea, and he shall be blessed.

34 And when Esau heard the words of his father, he cried with a great and exceeding bitter cry, and said unto his father, Bless me, even me also, O my
35 father. And he said, Thy brother came with subtilty, and hath taken away
36 thy blessing. And he said, Is not he rightly named Jacob? for he hath supplanted me these two times: he took away my birthright; and, behold, now he hath taken away my blessing. And he said, Hast thou not reserved a blessing for me?

37 And Isaac answered and said unto Esau, Behold, I have made him thy lord, and all his brethren have I given to him for servants; and with corn and wine have I sustained him: and what shall I do now unto thee, my son?

38 And Esau said unto his father, Hast thou but one blessing, my father? bless me, even me also, O my father. And Esau lifted up his voice, and wept.

39 And Isaac his father answered and said unto him,

> Behold, thy dwelling shall be the fatness of the earth,
> and of the dew of heaven from above;

40 And by thy sword shalt thou live,
> and shalt serve thy brother:
> and it shall come to pass when thou shalt have the dominion,
> that thou shalt break his yoke from off thy neck.

41 And Esau hated Jacob because of the blessing wherewith his father blessed him: and Esau said in his heart, The days of mourning for my father are at hand; then will I slay my brother Jacob.

42 And these words of Esau her elder son were told to Rebekah: and she sent and called Jacob her younger son, and said unto him, Behold, thy brother Esau, as touching thee, doth comfort himself, purposing to kill thee.

43 Now therefore, my son, obey my voice; and arise, flee thou to Laban my
44 brother to Haran; And tarry with him a few days, until thy brother's fury
45 turn away; Until thy brother's anger turn away from thee, and he forget that which thou hast done to him: then I will send, and fetch thee from thence: why should I be deprived also of you both in one day?

46 And Rebekah said to Isaac, I am weary of my life because of the daughters of Heth: if Jacob take a wife of the daughters of Heth, such as these which are of the daughters of the land, what good shall my life do me?

28 And Isaac called Jacob, and blessed him, and charged him, and said unto
2 him, Thou shalt not take a wife of the daughters of Canaan. Arise, go to Padan-aram, to the house of Bethuel thy mother's father; and take thee a
3 wife from thence of the daughters of Laban thy mother's brother. And God Almighty bless thee, and make thee fruitful, and multiply thee, that thou
4 mayest be a multitude of people; And give thee the blessing of Abraham, to thee, and to thy seed with thee; that thou mayest inherit the land wherein
5 thou art a stranger, which God gave unto Abraham. And Isaac sent away Jacob: and he went to Padan-aram unto Laban, son of Bethuel the Syrian, the brother of Rebekah, Jacob's and Esau's mother.

Introduction to Biblical Literature

6 When Esau saw that Isaac had blessed Jacob, and sent him away to Padan-aram, to take him a wife from thence; and that as he blessed him he gave him a charge, saying, Thou shalt not take a wife of the daughters of 7 Canaan; And that Jacob obeyed his father and his mother, and was gone 8 to Padan-aram; And Esau seeing that the daughters of Canaan pleased not 9 Isaac his father; Then went Esau unto Ishmael, and took unto the wives which he had Mahalath the daughter of Ishmael Abraham's son, the sister of Nebajoth, to be his wife.

10,11 And Jacob went out from Beer-sheba, and went toward Haran. And he lighted upon a certain place, and tarried there all night, because the sun was set; and he took of the stones of that place, and put them for his pillows, and lay down in that place to sleep.

12 And he dreamed, and behold a ladder set up on the earth, and the top of it reached to heaven: and behold the angels of God ascending and descending 13 on it. And, behold, the Lord stood above it, and said, I am the Lord God of Abraham thy father, and the God of Isaac: the land whereon thou liest, to 14 thee will I give it, and to thy seed; And thy seed shall be as the dust of the earth; and thou shalt spread abroad to the west, and to the east, and to the north, and to the south: and in thee and in thy seed shall all the families 15 of the earth be blessed. And, behold, I am with thee, and will keep thee in all places whither thou goest, and will bring thee again into this land; for I will not leave thee, until I have done that which I have spoken to thee of.

16 And Jacob awaked out of his sleep, and he said, Surely the Lord is in this 17 place; and I knew it not. And he was afraid, and said, How dreadful is this place! this is none other but the house of God, and this is the gate of heaven. 18 And Jacob rose up early in the morning, and took the stone that he had put for his pillows, and set it up for a pillar, and poured oil upon the top of it. 19 And he called the name of that place Beth-el: but the name of that city was called Luz at the first.

20 And Jacob vowed a vow, saying, If God will be with me, and will keep me in this way that I go, and will give me bread to eat, and raiment to put on, 21 So that I come again to my father's house in peace; then shall the Lord be 22 my God: And this stone, which I have set for a pillar, shall be God's house: and of all that thou shalt give me I will surely give the tenth unto thee.

29 Then Jacob went on his journey, and came into the land of the people of 2 the east. And he looked, and behold a well in the field, and, lo, there were three flocks of sheep lying by it; for out of that well they watered the flocks: 3 and a great stone was upon the well's mouth. And thither were all the flocks gathered: and they rolled the stone from the well's mouth, and watered the sheep, and put the stone again upon the well's mouth in his place.

4 And Jacob said unto them, My brethren, whence be ye? And they said, 5 Of Haran are we. And he said unto them, Know ye Laban the son of 6 Nahor? And they said, We know him. And he said unto them, Is he well? And they said, He is well: and, behold, Rachel his daughter cometh with the 7 sheep. And he said, Lo, it is yet high day, neither is it time that the cattle should be gathered together: water ye the sheep, and go and feed them. 8 And they said, We cannot, until all the flocks be gathered together, and till they roll the stone from the well's mouth; then we water the sheep.

9 And while he yet spake with them, Rachel came with her father's sheep:
10 for she kept them. And it came to pass, when Jacob saw Rachel the daughter of Laban his mother's brother, and the sheep of Laban his mother's brother, that Jacob went near, and rolled the stone from the well's mouth, and
11 watered the flock of Laban his mother's brother. And Jacob kissed Rachel,
12 and lifted up his voice, and wept. And Jacob told Rachel that he was her father's brother, and that he was Rebekah's son: and she ran and told her father.
13 And it came to pass, when Laban heard the tidings of Jacob his sister's son, that he ran to meet him, and embraced him, and kissed him, and
14 brought him to his house. And he told Laban all these things. And Laban said to him, Surely thou art my bone and my flesh. And he abode with him
15 the space of a month. And Laban said unto Jacob, Because thou art my brother, shouldest thou therefore serve me for nought? tell me, what shall thy wages be?
16 And Laban had two daughters: the name of the elder was Leah, and the
17 name of the younger was Rachel. Leah was tender eyed; but Rachel was
18 beautiful and well-favored. And Jacob loved Rachel; and said, I will serve
19 thee seven years for Rachel thy younger daughter. And Laban said, It is better that I give her to thee, than that I should give her to another man:
20 abide with me. And Jacob served seven years for Rachel; and they seemed unto him but a few days, for the love he had to her.
21 And Jacob said unto Laban, Give me my wife, for my days are fulfilled,
22 that I may go in unto her. And Laban gathered together all the men of the
23 place, and made a feast. And it came to pass in the evening, that he took
24 Leah his daughter, and brought her to him; and he went in unto her. And Laban gave unto his daughter Leah Zilpah his maid for a handmaid.
25 And it came to pass, that in the morning, behold, it was Leah: and he said to Laban, What is this thou hast done unto me? did not I serve with thee for Rachel? wherefore then hast thou beguiled me?
26 And Laban said, It must not be so done in our country, to give the
27 younger before the firstborn. Fulfill her week, and we will give thee this also for the service which thou shalt serve with me yet seven other years.
28 And Jacob did so, and fulfilled her week: and he gave him Rachel his
29 daughter to wife also. And Laban gave to Rachel his daughter Bilhah his
30 handmaid to be her maid. And he went in also unto Rachel, and he loved also Rachel more than Leah, and served with him yet seven other years.
31 And when the Lord saw that Leah was hated, he opened her womb: but Rachel was barren.

30:22 And God remembered Rachel, and God hearkened to her, and opened
23 her womb. And she conceived, and bare a son; and said, God hath taken
24 away my reproach: And she called his name Joseph; and said, The Lord shall add to me another son.
25 And it came to pass, when Rachel had borne Joseph, that Jacob said unto Laban, Send me away, that I may go unto mine own place, and to my
26 country. Give me my wives and my children, for whom I have served thee, and let me go: for thou knowest my service which I have done thee.
27 And Laban said unto him, I pray thee, if I have found favor in thine eyes,

tarry: for I have learned by experience that the Lord hath blessed me for
28 thy sake. And he said, Appoint me thy wages, and I will give it.
29   And he said unto him, Thou knowest how I have served thee, and how
30 thy cattle was with me. For it was little which thou hadst before I came, and
it is now increased unto a multitude; and the Lord hath blessed thee since
my coming: and now, when shall I provide for mine own house also?
31   And he said, What shall I give thee? And Jacob said, Thou shalt not give
me any thing: if thou wilt do this thing for me, I will again feed and keep
32 thy flock. I will pass through all thy flock to-day, removing from thence all
the speckled and spotted cattle, and all the brown cattle among the sheep,
and the spotted and speckled among the goats: and of such shall be my hire.
33 So shall my righteousness answer for me in time to come, when it shall come
for my hire before thy face: every one that is not speckled and spotted
among the goats, and brown among the sheep, that shall be counted stolen
with me.
34   And Laban said, Behold, I would it might be according to thy word.
35 And he removed that day the he goats that were ring-streaked and spotted,
and all the she goats that were speckled and spotted, and every one that
had some white in it, and all the brown among the sheep, and gave them
36 into the hand of his sons. And he set three days' journey betwixt himself
and Jacob: and Jacob fed the rest of Laban's flocks.
37   And Jacob took him rods of green poplar, and of the hazel and chestnut
tree; and pilled white streaks in them, and made the white appear which
38 was in the rods. And he set the rods which he had pilled before the flocks in
the gutters in the watering troughs when the flocks came to drink, that they
39 should conceive when they came to drink. And the flocks conceived before
the rods, and brought forth cattle ring-streaked, speckled, and spotted.
40 And Jacob did separate the lambs, and set the faces of the flocks toward the
ring-streaked, and all the brown in the flock of Laban; and he put his own
41 flocks by themselves, and put them not unto Laban's cattle. And it came to
pass, whensoever the stronger cattle did conceive, that Jacob laid the rods
before the eyes of the cattle in the gutters, that they might conceive among
42 the rods. But when the cattle were feeble, he put them not in: so the feebler
43 were Laban's, and the stronger Jacob's. And the man increased exceedingly,
and had much cattle, and maidservants, and menservants, and camels, and
asses.

31   And he heard the words of Laban's sons, saying, Jacob hath taken away
all that was our father's; and of that which was our father's hath he gotten
2 all this glory. And Jacob beheld the countenance of Laban, and, behold, it
3 was not toward him as before. And the Lord said unto Jacob, Return unto
the land of thy fathers, and to thy kindred; and I will be with thee.
4   And Jacob sent and called Rachel and Leah to the field unto his flock,
5 And said unto them, I see your father's countenance, that it is not toward me
6 as before; but the God of my father hath been with me. And ye know that
7 with all my power I have served your father. And your father hath deceived
me, and changed my wages ten times; but God suffered him not to hurt me.
8 If he said thus, The speckled shall be thy wages; then all the cattle bare
speckled: and if he said thus, The ring-streaked shall be thy hire; then bare

9 all the cattle ring-streaked. Thus God hath taken away the cattle of your father, and given them to me.

10 And it came to pass at the time that the cattle conceived, that I lifted up mine eyes, and saw in a dream, and, behold, the rams which leaped upon the
11 cattle were ring-streaked, speckled, and grizzled. And the angel of God
12 spake unto me in a dream, saying, Jacob: and I said, Here am I. And he said, Lift up now thine eyes, and see, all the rams which leap upon the cattle are ring-streaked, speckled, and grizzled: for I have seen all that
13 Laban doeth unto thee. I am the God of Beth-el, where thou anointedst the pillar, and where thou vowedst a vow unto me: now arise, get thee out from this land, and return unto the land of thy kindred.

14 And Rachel and Leah answered and said unto him, Is there yet any portion
15 or inheritance for us in our father's house? Are we not counted of him
16 strangers? for he hath sold us, and hath quite devoured also our money. For all the riches which God hath taken from our father, that is ours, and our children's: now then, whatsoever God hath said unto thee, do.

17,18 Then Jacob rose up, and set his sons and his wives upon camels; And he
19 carried away all his cattle, and all his goods which he had gotten, . . . And Laban went to shear his sheep: and Rachel had stolen the images that were
20 her father's. And Jacob stole away unawares to Laban the Syrian, in that he
21 told him not that he fled. So he fled with all that he had; and he rose up, and passed over the river, and set his face toward the mount Gilead.

22,23 And it was told Laban on the third day, that Jacob was fled. And he took his brethren with him, and pursued after him seven days' journey; and they
24 overtook him in the mount Gilead. And God came to Laban the Syrian in a dream by night, and said unto him, Take heed that thou speak not to Jacob either good or bad.

25 Then Laban overtook Jacob. Now Jacob had pitched his tent in the mount:
26 and Laban with his brethren pitched in the mount of Gilead. And Laban said to Jacob, What hast thou done, that thou hast stolen away unawares to me, and carried away my daughters, as captives taken with the sword?
27 Wherefore didst thou flee away secretly, and steal away from me; and didst not tell me, that I might have sent thee away with mirth, and with
28 songs, with tabret, and with harp? And hast not suffered me to kiss my sons
29 and my daughters? thou hast now done foolishly in so doing. It is in the power of my hand to do you hurt: but the God of your father spake unto me yesternight, saying, Take thou heed that thou speak not to Jacob either good
30 or bad. And now, though thou wouldest needs be gone, because thou sore longedst after thy father's house, yet wherefore hast thou stolen my gods?
31 And Jacob answered and said to Laban, Because I was afraid: for I said,
32 Peradventure thou wouldest take by force thy daughters from me. With whomsoever thou findest thy gods, let him not live: before our brethren discern thou what is thine with me, and take it to thee. For Jacob knew not that Rachel had stolen them.
33 And Laban went into Jacob's tent, and into Leah's tent, and into the two maidservants' tents; but he found them not. Then went he out of Leah's
34 tent, and entered into Rachel's tent. Now Rachel had taken the images, and put them in the camel's furniture, and sat upon them. And Laban searched
35 all the tent, but found them not. And she said to her father, Let it not dis-

please my lord that I cannot rise up before thee; for the custom of women is upon me. And he searched, but found not the images.

36 And Jacob was wroth, and chode with Laban: and Jacob answered and said to Laban, What is my trespass? what is my sin, that thou hast so hotly
37 pursued after me? Whereas thou hast searched all my stuff, what hast thou found of all thy household stuff? set it here before my brethren and thy
38 brethren, that they may judge betwixt us both. This twenty years have I been with thee; thy ewes and thy she goats have not cast their young, and
39 the rams of thy flock have I not eaten. That which was torn of beasts I brought not unto thee; I bare the loss of it; of my hand didst thou require it,
40 whether stolen by day, or stolen by night. Thus I was; in the day the drought consumed me, and the frost by night; and my sleep departed from
41 mine eyes. Thus have I been twenty years in thy house: I served thee four-teen years for thy two daughters, and six years for thy cattle; and thou hast
42 changed my wages ten times. Except the God of my father, the God of Abraham, and the fear of Isaac, had been with me, surely thou hadst sent me away now empty. God hath seen mine affliction and the labor of my hands, and rebuked thee yesternight.
43 And Laban answered and said unto Jacob, These daughters are my daughters, and these children are my children, and these cattle are my cattle, and all that thou seest is mine: and what can I do this day unto these my
44 daughters, or unto their children which they have borne? Now therefore come thou, let us make a covenant, I and thou; and let it be for a witness
45 between me and thee. And Jacob took a stone, and set it up for a pillar.
46 And Jacob said unto his brethren, Gather stones; and they took stones, and
47 made a heap: and they did eat there upon the heap. And Laban called it Jegar-sahadutha: but Jacob called it Galeed.
48 And Laban said, This heap is a witness between me and thee this day.
49 Therefore was the name of it called Galeed, And Mizpah; for he said, The
50 Lord watch between me and thee,   when we are absent one from another. If thou shalt afflict my daughters, or if thou shalt take other wives beside my
51 daughters, no man is with us; see, God is witness betwixt me and thee. And Laban said to Jacob, Behold this heap, and behold this pillar, which I have
52 cast betwixt me and thee; This heap be witness, and this pillar be witness, that I will not pass over this heap to thee, and that thou shalt not pass over
53 this heap and this pillar unto me, for harm. The God of Abraham, and the God of Nahor, the God of their father, judge betwixt us. And Jacob sware by the fear of his father Isaac.
54 Then Jacob offered sacrifice upon the mount, and called his brethren to
55 eat bread: and they did eat bread, and tarried all night in the mount. And early in the morning Laban rose up, and kissed his sons and his daughters, and blessed them: and Laban departed, and returned unto his place.

32: 3 And Jacob sent messengers before him to Esau his brother unto the land
4 of Seir, the country of Edom. And he commanded them, saying, Thus shall ye speak unto my lord Esau; Thy servant Jacob saith thus, I have sojourned
5 with Laban, and stayed there until now: And I have oxen, and asses, flocks, and menservants, and womenservants: and I have sent to tell my lord, that I may find grace in thy sight.
6 And the messengers returned to Jacob, saying, We came to thy brother

Esau, and also he cometh to meet thee, and four hundred men with him.
7 Then Jacob was greatly afraid and distressed: and he divided the people
that was with him, and the flocks, and herds, and the camels, into two bands;
8 And said, If Esau come to the one company, and smite it, then the other
company which is left shall escape.
9 And Jacob said, O God of my father Abraham, and God of my father
Isaac, the Lord which saidst unto me, Return unto thy country, and to thy
10 kindred, and I will deal well with thee: I am not worthy of the least of all
the mercies, and of all the truth, which thou hast showed unto thy servant;
for with my staff I passed over this Jordan; and now I am become two bands.
11 Deliver me, I pray thee, from the hand of my brother, from the hand of
Esau: for I fear him, lest he will come and smite me, and the mother with the
12 children. And thou saidst, I will surely do thee good, and make thy seed as
the sand of the sea, which cannot be numbered for multitude.
13 And he lodged there that same night; and took of that which came to his
14 hand a present for Esau his brother; Two hundred she goats and twenty he
15 goats, two hundred ewes and twenty rams, Thirty milch camels with their
16 colts, forty kine and ten bulls, twenty she asses and ten foals. And he
delivered them into the hand of his servants, every drove by themselves;
and said unto his servants, Pass over before me, and put a space betwixt
drove and drove.
17 And he commanded the foremost, saying, When Esau my brother meeteth
thee, and asketh thee, saying, Whose art thou? and whither goest thou? and
18 whose are these before thee? Then thou shalt say, They be thy servant
Jacob's; it is a present sent unto my lord Esau: and, behold, also he is behind
19 us. And so commanded he the second, and the third, and all that followed
the droves, saying, On this manner shall ye speak unto Esau, when ye find
20 him. And say ye moreover, Behold, thy servant Jacob is behind us. For he
said, I will appease him with the present that goeth before me, and afterward
21 I will see his face; peradventure he will accept of me. So went the present
over before him; and himself lodged that night in the company.
22 And he rose up that night, and took his two wives, and his two women-
23 servants, and his eleven sons, and passed over the ford Jabbok. And he took
them, and sent them over the brook, and sent over that he had.
24 And Jacob was left alone; and there wrestled a man with him until the
25 breaking of the day. And when he saw that he prevailed not against him, he
touched the hollow of his thigh; and the hollow of Jacob's thigh was out of
26 joint, as he wrestled with him. And he said, Let me go, for the day breaketh.
27 And he said, I will not let thee go, except thou bless me. And he said unto
28 him, What is thy name? And he said, Jacob. And he said, Thy name shall be
called no more Jacob, but Israel: for as a prince hast thou power with God
29 and with men, and hast prevailed. And Jacob asked him, and said, Tell me,
I pray thee, thy name. And he said, Wherefore is it that thou dost ask after
30 my name? And he blessed him there. And Jacob called the name of the place
Peniel: for I have seen God face to face, and my life is preserved.

33 And Jacob lifted up his eyes, and looked, and, behold, Esau came, and
with him four hundred men. And he divided the children unto Leah, and
2 unto Rachel, and unto the two handmaids. And he put the handmaids and

their children foremost, and Leah and her children after, and Rachel and
3 Joseph hindermost. And he passed over before them, and bowed himself to
the ground seven times, until he came near to his brother.

4 And Esau ran to meet him, and embraced him, and fell on his neck, and
5 kissed him: and they wept. And he lifted up his eyes, and saw the women
and the children, and said, Who are those with thee? And he said, The
33: 6 children which God hath graciously given thy servant. Then the handmaidens came near, they and their children, and they bowed themselves.
7 And Leah also with her children came near, and bowed themselves: and
after came Joseph near and Rachel, and they bowed themselves.

8 And he said, What meanest thou by all this drove which I met? And he
9 said, These are to find grace in the sight of my lord. And Esau said, I have
10 enough, my brother; keep that thou hast unto thyself. And Jacob said, Nay,
I pray thee, if now I have found grace in thy sight, then receive my present
at my hand: for therefore I have seen thy face, as though I had seen the
11 face of God, and thou wast pleased with me. Take, I pray thee, my blessing
that is brought to thee; because God hath dealt graciously with me, and
because I have enough. And he urged him, and he took it.

13 And he said unto him, My lord knoweth that the children are tender,
and the flocks and herds with young are with me; and if men should over-
14 drive them one day, all the flock will die. Let my lord, I pray thee, pass over
before his servant; and I will lead on softly, according as the cattle that goeth
before me and the children be able to endure, until I come unto my lord unto
15 Seir. And Esau said, Let me now leave with thee some of the folk that are
with me. And he said, What needeth it? let me find grace in the sight of my
lord.

16,18 So Esau returned that day on his way unto Seir. And Jacob came to
Shalem, a city of Shechem, which is in the land of Canaan, when he came
19 from Padan-aram; and pitched his tent before the city. And he bought a
parcel of a field, where he had spread his tent, at the hand of the children
20 of Hamor, Shechem's father, for a hundred pieces of money. And he erected
there an altar, and called it El-Elohe-Israel.

35 And God said unto Jacob, Arise, go up to Beth-el, and dwell there: and
make there an altar unto God, that appeared unto thee when thou fleddest
2 from the face of Esau thy brother. Then Jacob said unto his household, and
to all that were with him, Put away the strange gods that are among you,
3 and be clean, and change your garments: And let us arise, and go up to
Beth-el; and I will make there an altar unto God, who answered me in the
4 day of my distress, and was with me in the way which I went. And they
gave unto Jacob all the strange gods which were in their hand, and all their
earrings which were in their ears; and Jacob hid them under the oak which
5 was by Shechem. And they journeyed: and the terror of God was upon the
cities that were round about them, and they did not pursue after the sons
of Jacob.

6 So Jacob came to Luz which is in the land of Canaan, that is, Beth-el,
7 he and all the people that were with him. And he built there an altar, and
called the place El-beth-el; because there God appeared unto him, when he
35:14 fled from the face of his brother. And Jacob set up a pillar in the place where

he talked with him, even a pillar of stone: and he poured a drink offering
15 thereon, and he poured oil thereon. And Jacob called the name of the place where God spake with him, Beth-el.

16 And they journeyed from Beth-el; and there was but a little way to come
17 to Ephrath; and Rachel travailed, and she had hard labor. And it came to pass, when she was in hard labor, that the midwife said unto her, Fear not;
18 thou shalt have this son also. And it came to pass, as her soul was in departing, (for she died,) that she called his name Ben-oni: but his father called him
19 Benjamin. And Rachel died, and was buried in the way to Ephrath, which is
20 Bethlehem. And Jacob set a pillar upon her grave: that is the pillar of Rachel's grave unto this day.

22,23 . . . Now the sons of Jacob were twelve: The sons of Leah; Reuben, Jacob's firstborn, and Simeon, and Levi, and Judah, and Issachar, and
24,25 Zebulun: The sons of Rachel; Joseph, and Benjamin: And the sons of Bilhah,
26 Rachel's handmaid; Dan, and Naphtali: And the sons of Zilpah, Leah's handmaid: Gad, and Asher. . . .

27 And Jacob came unto Isaac his father unto Mamre, unto the city of Arba,
28 which is Hebron, where Abraham and Isaac sojourned. And the days of
29 Isaac were a hundred and fourscore years. And Isaac gave up the ghost, and died, and was gathered unto his people, being old and full of days: and his sons Esau and Jacob buried him.

Considerations and Questions

1. There are few descriptions of personal appearance in the Bible. In the stories about Abraham and his family we read that Sarah and Rebekah are very fair to look upon; that Rachael is beautiful and well-favored but that her sister Leah has "tender eyes" (presumably a rather unattractive infection still common in the Near East). Esau is hairy and Jacob is smooth. What else can you find about how these people and other characters in the story look?

   Granting that such details of description are most economically offered in the Biblical style as we have seen it to this point, what do you think to be the basic criteria for the inclusion of any of them at all? Why should we have it spelled out that Jacob is smooth and Esau hairy? That Rachael is "well-favored" and that Leah has gummy eyes?

   (We may note, by the way, that this descriptive economy seems to be a stylistic characteristic of the early Hebrew writers. The scholars who produced the early English translations, certainly the King James Version, worked in a literary tradition very much addicted to visual descriptions of people.)

2. Do your reflections on the preceding question lead you to the notion that the style of the Abraham family legend lacks concreteness or explicitness? If that is the case, consider the intensely *physical* way in which these stories are told. There is very little, if any, direct philosophical or theological generalization. God speaks to His patriarchs, but note that He does not explain much to them. What are some of the events, things, and relationships that make the stories go? What are the exact terms of Jacob's mystical visions? What parts do the physical details of taking care of animals, preparing food, moving from one place to another, getting along in the family, play in these tales? With what "things" is the world of these stories furnished?

3. From my reading of these stories, Abraham emerges as the greatest, the most "heroic" of the three, and Jacob as the most interesting. Isaac seems to me to suffer by comparison with his father and with his son. I do not think that we find in the lives of either of Abraham's descendants such high-souled moments as his rescues of his nephew Lot or his resolute willingness to sacrifice his son at his God's command. I find also a kind of unique greatness in Abraham's patient acceptance of the curse of barrenness in his beloved Sarah as well as in his capacity to laugh (however wryly) at what he thinks is the Lord's joke about it. Neither of the following patriarchs put themselves or their feelings on the line with the largeness of Father Abraham. Of course, his story gives Isaac a relatively easy life (as the lives of the early patriarchs go) and one might argue that Jacob's long labors for Laban in order to marry Rachael suggest a readiness for sacrifice. What do you think?

Consider as an example of how the legend treats its three heroes their respective responses to the infertility of their wives. Note that Isaac merely prays that Rebekah's womb be opened—and it is. The event is begun, summarized, and completed in a single verse. When Rachael complains to Jacob of her childless state, he snaps at her, "Do you think I'm God? I can't make you fertile." And there follows an extended baby-bearing competition between Jacob's two wives.

4. Compare the marriage of Isaac and Rebekah with the courtship of Jacob and Rachael. How often do we hear (or see in direct speech) the words of Isaac? Compare the relationships between Isaac and Ishmael with those between Jacob and Esau. Consider Isaac's two striking "scenic" episodes: when his father leads him up the mountain to sacrifice him to the Lord, and when, old and blind, he is duped by Jacob and Rebekah. Do you find indications here of a more "passive" literary character than Jacob or Abraham?

5. Ishmael and Esau, the dispossessed brothers of Isaac and Jacob, respectively, are similar not only in their experiences but in their personalities. In Genesis 21:9 we find young Ishmael "mocking" at a feast in honor of Isaac. Whatever his feelings may have been on that occasion, he would have done better to keep them to himself. Sarah observes him and persuades her husband to send Ishmael and his mother out to die in the desert. What instances can you cite of Esau's careless or unwise behavior? Are these men inclined to expose themselves on thoughtless impulse? What other qualities seem alike in their characters? How do they compare as types with the Covenant patriarchs, Isaac and Jacob? Both Ishmael and Esau appear to be on good terms with their respective brothers in later life, although the expectations of both have been disappointed by those brothers. Does this suggest anything about their personalities?

6. Like his grandfather, Jacob is renamed by the Lord. As the writer of the story knows, and we know, the name he receives, Israel, is the name of the nation yet to come. Whatever its other significance, this detail of Jacob's story supplies him with an exclusive emphasis. It is the God of Abraham who makes the Covenant with the first patriarch and maintains it through the relatively colorless administration of Isaac, but it is Jacob who is labeled father of the Children of Israel. Their distinction from other peoples in Biblical literature is chiefly a matter of their religion. Just what do we learn in the story of Jacob's life about *his* religion? His dealings with his God come through more vividly than those of his forebears, but may this not be more because of the highly original and concrete terms (like the ladder and the wrestler) in which they are related than of their profounder moral and spiritual meanings? Is he in any sense a better man than the former patriarchs?

4. Joseph

If to be fat be to be hated, then Pharaoh's lean kine are to be loved.

WILLIAM SHAKESPEARE, *Henry IV, Part I*

The fourth hero of Abraham's patriarchal line is the eleventh son of Jacob, by name, Joseph. He is not in his generation the sole carrier of the Covenant tradition nor of the family identity so that he is perhaps not really a patriarch of Israel. Furthermore, the patriarch Jacob, his father, is alive and well during almost all of Joseph's story. Yet in these final episodes of Genesis it is Joseph who is clearly the leader, benefactor, and protector of his family. He is the outstanding man of his people, and his remarkable career effects one of the most significant events in the Israelites' history, their sojourn in Egypt. There is legendary and mythic importance to that sojourn, but we also encounter it in this story as a historical event. When the family of Israel enters Egypt this time, it enters world history.

The narrative about Joseph is among the most popular of "Bible stories." From it we have such common sayings as "a coat of many colors," and "Potiphar's wife," and "Pharaoh's lean kine," and "sold into Egypt." Significantly, these allusions are not generally made with any direct religious reference. The story is not, taken out of context, about God or religion. Although Joseph himself is a faithful son of Israel, circumcised and walking before the Lord, and although we may find him of rather more impressive ethical character than his father, he is neither saint nor mystic. He does not talk with God. He believes in God; he trusts in God; he gives God the credit for his fortunes and his talents; but the Lord is not a character in the story of his life as He is in those of Abraham, Isaac, and Jacob.

The style and construction of the Joseph story is surely one reason for its lasting popularity. It is a beautiful piece of literary work. There are many other appeals, of course, some more important to one reader than to another. Three explanations for the tale's success which are perhaps most evident and interesting are its mythic quality, its depiction of Joseph, and its adventurousness.

As myth, the Joseph story manifests a very familiar pattern. Countless fairy tales, "Cinderella" and "The Ugly Duckling" among them, are based on it. Tales about younger and oppressed brothers or sisters who rise to eminence are found, in fact, just about everywhere in the known world. The appeal of this pattern does not appear to diminish with repetition, and its variations appear on virtually every literary level. It is part of Shakespeare's *King Lear* and it is part of Puzo's *The Godfather*.

69

Somewhere within us, we seem convinced that the last may be first, and we continue to be fascinated by divers embodiments of that idea.

Joseph is an admirable man. He is generous, chaste, loyal, patient, industrious, reverent, discreet, intelligent, and kind. If these qualities, unqualified by any other personality traits, made up the whole Joseph of the story, I am afraid that few readers would find him an interesting character, however admirable as a man. But although he genuinely possesses all of these virtues, he does not come through as an impossible pasteboard silhouette of goodness. For one thing, his intelligence embraces a remarkable gift: he can, long before Dr. Freud and Dr. Jung, interpret dreams. For another, his impressive array of fine qualities contributes to an ironically inauspicious boyhood. When he is seventeen, he is such a tactless prig, so conscious of the approval of his father, that his elder brothers cannot speak civilly to him. (As we learn of his smug interpretations of his own dreams, it is hard to blame them.) His generosity to the brothers who have wronged him is genuine, but it is somewhat tempered by the tests and humiliations he puts them through before he openly bestows it. Indeed, in his maturity he appears to take a rather petty but very human private satisfaction in fulfilling his boyhood dreams to the very letter.

As all this may suggest, there is a deep strain of ambition in Joseph's personality. Ambition is an ambiguous trait; we may admire it in our children and deplore it in Macbeth. The young man who has the drive and the capacity to get ahead is often not an admirable character in our view, but he is generally an interesting one, if only because he is in motion. Things happen where he is. In Joseph, however, we have a man who is both admirable and ambitious. He rises to the top of every situation he enters, but he will not do *any*thing for a buck. Moral and emotional scruples are, of course, limitations on ambition, but Joseph manages to maintain his scruples and yet achieve complete material success. He is resourceful and he has style. He is like Odysseus, without that crafty Greek warrior's violence, and also like what Tom Sawyer wants to be. Joseph is practical without being immoral, emotional without being sentimental, and when he cuts a fine figure in the world, it is as a sophisticated gentleman, not a popinjay.

Unlike a great many popular historical and legendary tales from antiquity, Joseph's story is not a war story, nor a story that depends in any measure on violence among people or between people and nature. Yet it might well be called *The Adventures of Joseph in Egypt,* for much of its appeal is that of an adventure story. Adventure in literature (and I suppose in life) might be described as exhilarating changes of fortune. Escapes from death, slavery, and prison are adventures in this sense. So, in most cases, are sexual overtures from the boss's wife, sudden promotions, being put in jail, changing the political and economic structures of nations, and becoming accepted by strangers in a strange land.

The plot of the chapters about Joseph moves briskly from one adventure to the next. They are exciting and interesting, as adventures ought to be, but note that they do not essentially violate the limits of human experience as we think we know it. Joseph is not Captain Marvel and he is not James Bond. The kind of story inhabited by men of those sorts depends for its adventurous appeal on our sense that what happens in it has no relationship to reality. We call such stories "escape literature." The story of Joseph is not escape literature. Like other serious tales of adventure, it excites our interest partly by the remarkableness (not impossibility) of its events, and partly by how it leads us to relate those events to our vision of real possibilities.

Genesis

37: 2 . . . Joseph, being seventeen years old, was feeding the flock with his brethren; and the lad was with the sons of Bilhah, and with the sons of Zilpah, his father's wives: and Joseph brought unto his father their evil

3 report. *Now Israel loved Joseph more than all his children, because he was the son*

4 *of his old age: and he made him a coat of many colors. And when his brethren saw that their father loved him more than all his brethren, they hated him, and could not speak peaceably unto him.*

5 And Joseph dreamed a dream, and he told it his brethren: and they hated

6 him yet the more. And he said unto them, Hear, I pray you, this dream

7 which I have dreamed: For, behold, we were binding sheaves in the field, and, lo, my sheaf arose, and also stood upright; and, behold, your sheaves

8 stood round about, and made obeisance to my sheaf. And his brethren said to him, Shalt thou indeed reign over us? or shalt thou indeed have dominion over us? And they hated him yet the more for his dreams, and for his words.

9 And he dreamed yet another dream, and told it his brethren, and said, Behold, I have dreamed a dream more; and, behold, the sun and the moon

10 and the eleven stars made obeisance to me. And he told it to his father, and to his brethren: and his father rebuked him, and said unto him, What is this dream that thou hast dreamed? Shall I and thy mother and thy brethren

11 indeed come to bow down ourselves to thee to the earth? And his brethren envied him; but his father observed the saying.

12,13 *And his brethren went to feed their father's flock in Shechem. And Israel said unto Joseph, Do not thy brethren feed the flock in Shechem? come, and I will send*

14 *thee unto them. And he said to him, Here am I.* And he said to him, Go, I pray thee, see whether it be well with thy brethren, and well with the flocks; and bring me word again. *So he sent him out of the vale of Hebron, and he came to Shechem.*

15 *And a certain man found him, and, behold, he was wandering in the field:*

16 *and the man asked him, saying, What seekest thou? And he said, I seek my breth-*

17 *ren: tell me, I pray thee, where they feed their flocks. And the man said, They are departed hence; for I heard them say, Let us go to Dothan. And Joseph went after his brethren, and found them in Dothan.*

18 And when they saw him afar off, *even before he came near unto them, they*

19 *conspired against him to slay him.* And they said one to another, Behold, this

20 dreamer cometh. Come now therefore, and let us slay him, and cast him into some pit, and we will say, Some evil beast hath devoured him; and we shall see what will become of his dreams.

21 *And Reuben heard it, and he delivered him out of their hands; and said, Let*

22 *us not kill him.* And Reuben said unto them, Shed no blood, but cast him into this pit that is in the wilderness, and lay no hand upon him; that he might rid him out of their hands, to deliver him to his father again.

23 *And it came to pass, when Joseph was come unto his brethren, that they stripped*

24 *Joseph out of his coat, his coat of many colors that was on him;* And they took him, and cast him into a pit: and the pit was empty, there was no water in it.

25 *And they sat down to eat bread: and they lifted up their eyes and looked, and, behold, a company of Ishmaelites came from Gilead, with their camels bearing*

26 *spicery and balm and myrrh, going to carry it down to Egypt. And Judah said unto his brethren, What profit is it if we slay our brother, and conceal his blood?*

27 *Come, and let us sell him to the Ishmaelites, and let not our hand be upon him; for he is our brother and our flesh: and his brethren were content.*

28 Then there passed by Midianites merchantmen; and they drew and lifted up Joseph out of the pit, *and sold Joseph to the Ishmaelites for twenty pieces of silver: and they brought Joseph into Egypt.*

29 And Reuben returned unto the pit; and, behold, Joseph was not in the pit;
30 and he rent his clothes. And he returned unto his brethren, and said, The
31 child is not; and I, whither shall I go? *And they took Joseph's coat, and killed a*
32 *kid of the goats, and dipped the coat in the blood; And they sent the coat of many colors, and they brought it to their father;* and said, This have we found: know now whether it be thy son's coat or no.

33 *And he knew it, and said, It is my son's coat;* an evil beast hath devoured him;
34 *Joseph is without doubt rent in pieces.* And Jacob rent his clothes, and put
35 sackcloth upon his loins, *and mourned for his son many days.* And all his sons and all his daughters rose up to comfort him; but he refused to be comforted; and he said, For I will go down into the grave unto my son mourning. Thus his father wept for him.

36 And the Midianites sold him into Egypt unto Potiphar, an officer of Pharaoh's, and captain of the guard.

9 And Joseph was brought down to Egypt; and Potiphar, an officer of Pharaoh, captain of the guard, an Egyptian, bought him of the hands of the
2 Ishmaelites, which had brought him down thither. And the Lord was with Joseph, and he was a prosperous man; and he was in the house of his
3 master the Egyptian. And his master saw that the Lord was with him, and
4 that the Lord made all that he did to prosper in his hand. And Joseph found grace in his sight, and he served him: and he made him overseer over his
6 house, and all that he had he put into his hand. And he left all that he had in Joseph's hand; and he knew not aught he had, save the bread which he did eat. And Joseph was a goodly person, and well-favored.

7 And it came to pass after these things, that his master's wife cast her
8 eyes upon Joseph; and she said, Lie with me. But he refused, and said unto his master's wife, Behold, my master wotteth not what is with me in the
9 house, and he hath committed all that he hath to my hand; There is none greater in this house than I; neither hath he kept back any thing from me but thee, because thou art his wife: how then can I do this great wickedness,
10 and sin against God? And it came to pass, as she spake to Joseph day by day, that he hearkened not unto her, to lie by her, or to be with her.

11 And it came to pass about this time, that Joseph went into the house to do
12 his business; and there was none of the men of the house there within. And she caught him by his garment, saying, Lie with me: and he left his garment in her hand, and fled, and got him out.

13 And it came to pass, when she saw that he had left his garment in her
14 hand, and was fled forth, That she called unto the men of her house, and spake unto them, saying, See, he hath brought in a Hebrew unto us to mock
15 us; he came in unto me to lie with me, and I cried with a loud voice: And it came to pass, when he heard that I lifted up my voice and cried, that he left his garment with me, and fled, and got him out.

16,17 And she laid up his garment by her, until his lord came home. And she
spake unto him according to these words, saying, The Hebrew servant,
18 which thou hast brought unto us, came in unto me to mock me: And it
came to pass, as I lifted up my voice and cried, that he left his garment with
me, and fled out.
19 And it came to pass, when his master heard the words of his wife, which
she spake unto him, saying, After this manner did thy servant to me; that
20 his wrath was kindled. And Joseph's master took him, and put him into the
prison, a place where the king's prisoners were bound: and he was there in
the prison.
21 But the Lord was with Joseph, and showed him mercy, and gave him
22 favor in the sight of the keeper of the prison. And the keeper of the prison
committed to Joseph's hand all the prisoners that were in the prison; and
23 whatsoever they did there, he was the doer of it. The keeper of the prison
looked not to any thing that was under his hand; because the Lord was with
him, and that which he did, the Lord made it to prosper.
40 And it came to pass after these things, that the butler of the king of
2 Egypt and his baker had offended their lord the king of Egypt. And Pharaoh
was wroth against two of his officers, against the chief of the butlers, and
3 against the chief of the bakers. And he put them in ward in the house of the
captain of the guard, into the prison, the place where Joseph was bound.
4 And the captain of the guard charged Joseph with them, and he served them:
and they continued a season in ward.
5 And they dreamed a dream both of them, each man his dream in one
night, each man according to the interpretation of his dream, the butler and
6 the baker of the king of Egypt, which were bound in the prison. And Joseph
came in unto them in the morning, and looked upon them, and, behold, they
7 were sad. And he asked Pharaoh's officers that were with him in the ward
8 of his lord's house, saying, Wherefore look ye so sadly to-day? And they
said unto him, We have dreamed a dream, and there is no interpreter of it.
And Joseph said unto them, Do not interpretations belong to God? tell me
them, I pray you.
9 And the chief butler told his dream to Joseph, and said to him, In my
10 dream, behold, a vine was before me; And in the vine were three branches:
and it was as though it budded, and her blossoms shot forth; and the clusters
11 thereof brought forth ripe grapes: And Pharaoh's cup was in my hand: and
I took the grapes, and pressed them into Pharaoh's cup, and I gave the cup
into Pharaoh's hand.
12 And Joseph said unto him, This is the interpretation of it: The three
13 branches are three days: Yet within three days shall Pharaoh lift up thine
head, and restore thee unto thy place; and thou shalt deliver Pharaoh's cup
14 into his hand, after the former manner when thou wast his butler. But think
on me when it shall be well with thee, and show kindness, I pray thee, unto
me, and make mention of me unto Pharaoh, and bring me out of this house:
15 For indeed I was stolen away out of the land of the Hebrews: and here also
have I done nothing that they should put me into the dungeon.
16 When the chief baker saw that the interpretation was good, he said unto
Joseph, I also was in my dream, and, behold, I had three white baskets on
17 my head: And in the uppermost basket there was of all manner of bakemeats
for Pharaoh; and the birds did eat them out of the basket upon my head.

18 And Joseph answered and said, This is the interpretation thereof: The
19 three baskets are three days: Yet within three days shall Pharaoh lift up
thy head from off thee, and shall hang thee on a tree; and the birds shall eat
thy flesh from off thee.

20 And it came to pass the third day, which was Pharaoh's birthday, that he
made a feast unto all his servants: and he lifted up the head of the chief
21 butler and of the chief baker among his servants. And he restored the chief
butler unto his butlership again; and he gave the cup into Pharaoh's hand:
22,23 But he hanged the chief baker: as Joseph had interpreted to them. Yet did
not the chief butler remember Joseph, but forgat him.

41 And it came to pass at the end of two full years, that Pharaoh dreamed: . . .
8 And it came to pass in the morning that his spirit was troubled; and he sent
and called for all the magicians of Egypt, and all the wise men thereof: and
Pharaoh told them his dream; but there was none that could interpret them
unto Pharaoh.

9 Then spake the chief butler unto Pharaoh, saying, I do remember my
10 faults this day: Pharaoh was wroth with his servants, and put me in ward
11 in the captain of the guard's house, both me and the chief baker: And we
dreamed a dream in one night, I and he; we dreamed each man according to
12 the interpretation of his dream. And there was there with us a young man,
a Hebrew, servant to the captain of the guard; and we told him, and he interpreted to us our dreams; to each man according to his dream he did interpret.
13 And it came to pass, as he interpreted to us, so it was; me he restored unto
mine office, and him he hanged.

14 Then Pharaoh sent and called Joseph, and they brought him hastily out
of the dungeon: and he shaved himself, and changed his raiment, and came
15 in unto Pharaoh. And Pharaoh said unto Joseph, I have dreamed a dream, and
there is none that can interpret it: and I have heard say of thee, that thou
16 canst understand a dream to interpret it. And Joseph answered Pharaoh,
saying, It is not in me: God shall give Pharaoh an answer of peace.

17 And Pharaoh said unto Joseph, In my dream, behold, I stood upon the
18 bank of the river: And, behold, there came up out of the river seven kine,
19 fat-fleshed and well-favored; and they fed in a meadow: And, behold, seven
other kine came up after them, poor and very ill-favored and lean-fleshed,
20 such as I never saw in all the land of Egypt for badness: And the lean and
21 the ill-favored kine did eat up the first seven fat kine: And when they had
eaten them up, it could not be known that they had eaten them; but they
22 were still ill-favored, as at the beginning. So I awoke. And I saw in my
23 dream, and, behold, seven ears came up in one stalk, full and good: And,
behold, seven ears, withered, thin, and blasted with the east wind, sprung up
24 after them: And the thin ears devoured the seven good ears: and I told this
unto the magicians; but there was none that could declare it to me.

25 And Joseph said unto Pharaoh, The dream of Pharaoh is one: God hath
26 showed Pharaoh what he is about to do. The seven good kine are seven
27 years; and the seven good ears are seven years: the dream is one. And the
seven thin and ill-favored kine that came up after them are seven years; and
the seven empty ears blasted with the east wind shall be seven years of
28 famine. This is the thing which I have spoken unto Pharaoh: What God is
about to do he showeth unto Pharaoh.

29 Behold, there come seven years of great plenty throughout all the land of

30 Egypt: And there shall arise after them seven years of famine; and all the plenty shall be forgotten in the land of Egypt; and the famine shall consume
31 the land; And the plenty shall not be known in the land by reason of that
32 famine following; for it shall be very grievous. And for that the dream was doubled unto Pharaoh twice; it is because the thing is established by God, and God will shortly bring it to pass.

33 Now therefore let Pharaoh look out a man discreet and wise, and set him
34 over the land of Egypt. Let Pharaoh do this, and let him appoint officers over the land, and take up the fifth part of the land of Egypt in the seven
35 plenteous years. And let them gather all the food of those good years that come, and lay up corn under the hand of Pharaoh, and let them keep food in
36 the cities. And that food shall be for store to the land against the seven years of famine, which shall be in the land of Egypt; that the land perish not through the famine.

37 And the thing was good in the eyes of Pharaoh, and in the eyes of all his
38 servants. And Pharaoh said unto his servants, Can we find such a one as this is, a man in whom the Spirit of God is?

39 And Pharaoh said unto Joseph, Forasmuch as God hath showed thee all
40 this, there is none so discreet and wise as thou art: Thou shalt be over my house, and according unto thy word shall all my people be ruled: only in the
41 throne will I be greater than thou. And Pharaoh said unto Joseph, See, I have
42 set thee over all the land of Egypt. And Pharaoh took off his ring from his hand, and put it upon Joseph's hand, and arrayed him in vestures of fine linen,
43 and put a gold chain about his neck; And he made him to ride in the second chariot which he had; and they cried before him, Bow the knee: and he made him ruler over all the land of Egypt.

44 And Pharaoh said unto Joseph, I am Pharaoh, and without thee shall no
45 man lift up his hand or foot in all the land of Egypt. And Pharaoh called Joseph's name Zaphnath-paaneah; and he gave him to wife Asenath the daughter of Poti-pherah priest of On. And Joseph went out over all the land of
46 Egypt. And Joseph was thirty years old when he stood before Pharaoh king of Egypt. And Joseph went out from the presence of Pharaoh, and went throughout all the land of Egypt.

47 And in the seven plenteous years the earth brought forth by handfuls.
48 And he gathered up all the food of the seven years, which were in the land of Egypt, and laid up the food in the cities: the food of the field, which was
49 round about every city, laid he up in the same. And Joseph gathered corn as the sand of the sea, very much, until he left numbering; for it was without number.

50 And unto Joseph were born two sons, before the years of famine came: which Asenath the daughter of Poti-pherah priest of On bare unto him.
51 And Joseph called the name of the firstborn Manasseh: For God, said he,
52 hath made me forget all my toil, and all my father's house. And the name of the second called he Ephraim: For God hath caused me to be fruitful in the land of my affliction.

53 And the seven years of plenteousness, that was in the land of Egypt, were
54 ended. And the seven years of dearth began to come, according as Joseph had said: and the dearth was in all lands; but in all the land of Egypt there
55 was bread. And when all the land of Egypt was famished, the people cried to Pharaoh for bread: and Pharaoh said unto all the Egyptians, Go unto

56 Joseph; what he saith to you, do. And the famine was over all the face of the earth: and Joseph opened all the storehouses, and sold unto the Egyptians;
57 and the famine waxed sore in the land of Egypt. And all countries came into Egypt to Joseph for to buy corn; because that the famine was so sore in all lands.

42 Now when Jacob saw that there was corn in Egypt, Jacob said unto his
2 sons, Why do ye look one upon another? And he said, Behold, I have heard that there is corn in Egypt: get you down thither, and buy for us from thence;
3 that we may live, and not die. And Joseph's ten brethren went down to buy
4 corn in Egypt. But Benjamin, Joseph's brother, Jacob sent not with his brethren; for he said, Lest peradventure mischief befall him.
6 And Joseph was the governor over the land, and he it was that sold to all the people of the land: and Joseph's brethren came, and bowed down them-
7 selves before him with their faces to the earth. And Joseph saw his brethren, and he knew them, but made himself strange unto them, and spake roughly unto them; and he said unto them, Whence come ye? And they said, From
8 the land of Canaan to buy food. And Joseph knew his brethren, but they
9 knew not him. And Joseph remembered the dreams which he dreamed of them, and said unto them, Ye are spies; to see the nakedness of the land
13 ye are come. And they said, Thy servants are twelve brethren, the sons of one man in the land of Canaan; and, behold, the youngest is this day with our father, and one is not.
14 And Joseph said unto them, That is it that I spake unto you, saying, Ye
15 are spies: Hereby ye shall be proved: By the life of Pharaoh ye shall not
16 go forth hence, except your youngest brother come hither. Send one of you, and let him fetch your brother, and ye shall be kept in prison, that your words may be proved, whether there be any truth in you: or else by
17 the life of Pharaoh surely ye are spies. And he put them all together into ward three days.
18 And Joseph said unto them the third day, This do, and live; for I fear God:
19 If ye be true men, let one of your brethren be bound in the house of your
20 prison: go ye, carry corn for the famine of your houses: But bring your youngest brother unto me; so shall your words be verified, and ye shall not die. And they did so.
21 And they said one to another, We are verily guilty concerning our brother, in that we saw the anguish of his soul, when he besought us, and we
22 would not hear; therefore is this distress come upon us. And Reuben answered them, saying, Spake I not unto you, saying, Do not sin against the child; and ye would not hear? therefore, behold, also his blood is required.
23 And they knew not that Joseph understood them; for he spake unto them
24 by an interpreter. And he turned himself about from them, and wept; and returned to them again, and communed with them, and took from them Simeon, and bound him before their eyes.
25 Then Joseph commanded to fill their sacks with corn, and to restore every man's money into his sack, and to give them provision for the way: and
26 thus did he unto them. And they laded their asses with the corn, and departed thence.
29 And they came unto Jacob their father unto the land of Canaan, and told
30 him all that befell unto them; saying, The man, who is the lord of the land, spake roughly to us, and took us for spies of the country.

35 And it came to pass as they emptied their sacks, that, behold, every man's bundle of money was in his sack: and when both they and their father saw the bundles of money, they were afraid.

36 And Jacob their father said unto them, Me have ye bereaved of my children: Joseph is not, and Simeon is not, and ye will take Benjamin away: all

37 these things are against me. And Reuben spake unto his father, saying, Slay my two sons, if I bring him not to thee: deliver him into my hand, and I will

38 bring him to thee again. And he said, My son shall not go down with you; for his brother is dead, and he is left alone: if mischief befall him by the way in the which ye go, then shall ye bring down my gray hairs with sorrow to the grave.

43:1,2 And the famine was sore in the land. And it came to pass, when they had eaten up the corn which they had brought out of Egypt, their father said unto them, Go again, buy us a little food.

3 And Judah spake unto him, saying, The man did solemnly protest unto us,

4 saying, Ye shall not see my face, except your brother be with you. If thou wilt send our brother with us, we will go down and buy thee food:

6 And Israel said, Wherefore dealt ye so ill with me, as to tell the man

7 whether ye had yet a brother? And they said, The man asked us straitly of our state, and of our kindred, saying, Is your father yet alive? have ye another brother? and we told him according to the tenor of these words: Could we certainly know that he would say, Bring your brother down?

8 And Judah said unto Israel his father, Send the lad with me, and we will arise and go; that we may live, and not die, both we, and thou, and also our

9 little ones. I will be surety for him; of my hand shalt thou require him: if I bring him not unto thee, and set him before thee, then let me bear the blame

10 for ever: For except we had lingered, surely now we had returned this second time.

11 And their father Israel said unto them, If it must be so now, do this; take of the best fruits in the land in your vessels, and carry down the man a present, a little balm, and a little honey, spices and myrrh, nuts and almonds:

12 And take double money in your hand; and the money that was brought again in the mouth of your sacks, carry it again in your hand; peradventure it was

13 an oversight. Take also your brother, and arise, go again unto the man:

14 And God Almighty give you mercy before the man, . . .

15 And the men took that present, and they took double money in their hand, and Benjamin; and rose up, and went down to Egypt, and stood before

16 Joseph. And when Joseph saw Benjamin with them, he said to the ruler of his house, Bring these men home, and slay, and make ready; for these men

17 shall dine with me at noon. And the man did as Joseph bade; and the man brought the men into Joseph's house.

18 And the men were afraid, because they were brought into Joseph's house; and they said, Because of the money that was returned in our sacks at the first time are we brought in; that he may seek occasion against us, and fall upon us, and take us for bondmen, and our asses.

19 And they came near to the steward of Joseph's house, and they com-

20 muned with him at the door of the house, And said, O sir, we came indeed

21 down at the first time to buy food: And it came to pass, when we came to the inn, that we opened our sacks, and, behold, every man's money was in

the mouth of his sack, our money in full weight: and we have brought it
22 again in our hand. And other money have we brought down in our hands to buy food: we cannot tell who put our money in our sacks.
23 And he said, Peace be to you, fear not: your God, and the God of your father, hath given you treasure in your sacks: I had your money. And he
24 brought Simeon out unto them. And the man brought the men into Joseph's house, and gave them water, and they washed their feet; and he gave their
25 asses provender. And they made ready the present against Joseph came at noon: for they heard that they should eat bread there.
26 And when Joseph came home, they brought him the present which was in their hand into the house, and bowed themselves to him to the earth.
27 And he asked them of their welfare, and said, Is your father well, the old
28 man of whom ye spake? Is he yet alive? And they answered, Thy servant our father is in good health, he is yet alive. And they bowed down their heads, and made obeisance.
29 And he lifted up his eyes, and saw his brother Benjamin, his mother's son, and said, Is this your younger brother, of whom ye spake unto me? And he
30 said, God be gracious unto thee, my son. And Joseph made haste; for his bowels did yearn upon his brother: and he sought where to weep; and he entered into his chamber, and wept there.
31 And he washed his face, and went out, and refrained himself, and said,
32 Set on bread. And they set on for him by himself, and for them by themselves, and for the Egyptians, which did eat with him, by themselves: because the Egyptians might not eat bread with the Hebrews; for that is an abomination
33 unto the Egyptians. And they sat before him, the firstborn according to his birthright, and the youngest according to his youth: and the men marveled
34 one at another. And he took and sent messes unto them from before him: but Benjamin's mess was five times so much as any of theirs. And they drank, and were merry with him.

45 Then Joseph could not refrain himself before all them that stood by him; and he cried, Cause every man to go out from me. And there stood no man
2 with him, while Joseph made himself known unto his brethren. And he wept
3 aloud: and the Egyptians and the house of Pharaoh heard. And Joseph said unto his brethren, I am Joseph; doth my father yet live? And his brethren could not answer him; for they were troubled at his presence.
4 And Joseph said unto his brethren, Come near to me, I pray you. And they came near. And he said, I am Joseph your brother, whom ye sold into
5 Egypt. Now therefore be not grieved, nor angry with yourselves, that ye
7 sold me hither: for God did send me before you to preserve life. And God sent me before you to preserve you a posterity in the earth, and to save your
8 lives by a great deliverance. So now it was not you that sent me hither, but God: and he hath made me a father to Pharaoh, and lord of all his house, and a ruler throughout all the land of Egypt.
9 Haste ye, and go up to my father, and say unto him, Thus saith thy son Joseph, God hath made me lord of all Egypt: come down unto me, tarry not:
10 And thou shalt dwell in the land of Goshen, and thou shalt be near unto me, thou, and thy children, and thy children's children, and thy flocks, and thy
11 herds, and all that thou hast: And there will I nourish thee; for yet there are five years of famine; lest thou, and thy household, and all that thou hast,

13 come to poverty. And ye shall tell my father of all my glory in Egypt, and
of all that ye have seen; and ye shall haste and bring down my father hither.

14 And he fell upon his brother Benjamin's neck, and wept; and Benjamin
15 wept upon his neck. Moreover he kissed all his brethren, and wept upon
them: and after that his brethren talked with him.

16 And the fame thereof was heard in Pharaoh's house, saying, Joseph's
17 brethren are come: and it pleased Pharaoh well, and his servants. And
Pharaoh said unto Joseph, Say unto thy brethren, This do ye; lade your
18 beasts, and go, get you unto the land of Canaan; And take your father and
your households, and come unto me: and I will give you the good of the
19 land of Egypt, and ye shall eat the fat of the land. Now thou art commanded,
this do ye; take you wagons out of the land of Egypt for your little ones,
20 and for your wives, and bring your father, and come. Also regard not your
stuff; for the good of all the land of Egypt is yours.

21 And the children of Israel did so: and Joseph gave them wagons, according to the commandment of Pharaoh, and gave them provision for the way.
22 To all of them he gave each man changes of raiment; but to Benjamin he gave
23 three hundred pieces of silver, and five changes of raiment. And to his father
he sent after this manner; ten asses laden with the good things of Egypt,
and ten she asses laden with corn and bread and meat for his father by the
24 way. So he sent his brethren away, and they departed: and he said unto
them, See that ye fall not out by the way.

25 And they went up out of Egypt, and came into the land of Canaan unto
26 Jacob their father, And told him, saying, Joseph is yet alive, and he is
governor over all the land of Egypt. And Jacob's heart fainted, for he be-
27 lieved them not. And they told him all the words of Joseph, which he had
said unto them: and when he saw the wagons which Joseph had sent to carry
28 him, the spirit of Jacob their father revived. And Israel said, It is enough;
Joseph my son is yet alive: I will go and see him before I die.

46 And Israel took his journey with all that he had, and came to Beer-sheba,
2 and offered sacrifices unto the God of his father Isaac. And God spake unto
Israel in the visions of the night, and said, Jacob, Jacob. And he said, Here
3 am I. And he said, I am God, the God of thy father: fear not to go down into
4 Egypt; for I will there make of thee a great nation. I will go down with thee
into Egypt; and I will also surely bring thee up again: and Joseph shall put
his hand upon thine eyes.

5 And Jacob rose up from Beer-sheba: and the sons of Israel carried Jacob
their father, and their little ones, and their wives, in the wagons which
6 Pharaoh had sent to carry him. And they took their cattle, and their goods,
which they had gotten in the land of Canaan, and came into Egypt, Jacob,
7 and all his seed with him: His sons, and his sons' sons with him, his daughters, and his sons' daughters, and all his seed brought he with him into
26 Egypt. All the souls that came with Jacob into Egypt, which came out of his
loins, besides Jacob's sons' wives, all the souls were threescore and six;
28 And he sent Judah before him unto Joseph, to direct his face unto Goshen;
29 and they came into the land of Goshen. And Joseph made ready his chariot,
and went up to meet Israel his father, to Goshen, and presented himself unto
30 him; and he fell on his neck, and wept on his neck a good while. And Israel
said unto Joseph, Now let me die, since I have seen thy face, because thou
art yet alive.

31 And Joseph said unto his brethren, and unto his father's house, I will go up, and show Pharaoh, and say unto him, My brethren, and my father's house,
32 which were in the land of Canaan, are come unto me; And the men are shepherds, for their trade hath been to feed cattle; and they have brought
33 their flocks, and their herds, and all that they have. And it shall come to pass, when Pharaoh shall call you, and shall say, What is your occupation?
34 That ye shall say, Thy servants' trade hath been about cattle from our youth even until now, both we, and also our fathers: that ye may dwell in the land of Goshen; for every shepherd is an abomination unto the Egyptians.

47 Then Joseph came and told Pharaoh, and said, My father and my brethren, and their flocks, and their herds, and all that they have, are come out
2 of the land of Canaan; and, behold, they are in the land of Goshen. And he took some of his brethren, even five men, and presented them unto Pharaoh.
3 And Pharaoh said unto his brethren, What is your occupation? And they said unto Pharaoh, Thy servants are shepherds, both we, and also our
4 fathers. They said moreover unto Pharaoh, For to sojourn in the land are we come; for thy servants have no pasture for their flocks; for the famine is sore in the land of Canaan: now therefore, we pray thee, let thy servants dwell in the land of Goshen.
5 And Pharaoh spake unto Joseph, saying, Thy father and thy brethren
6 are come unto thee: The land of Egypt is before thee; in the best of the land make thy father and brethren to dwell; in the land of Goshen let them dwell: and if thou knowest any men of activity among them, then make them rulers over my cattle.
7 And Joseph brought in Jacob his father, and set him before Pharaoh: and
8 Jacob blessed Pharaoh. And Pharaoh said unto Jacob, How old art thou?
9 And Jacob said unto Pharaoh, The days of the years of my pilgrimage are a hundred and thirty years: few and evil have the days of the years of my life been, and have not attained unto the days of the years of the life of my
10 fathers in the days of their pilgrimage. And Jacob blessed Pharaoh, and went out from before Pharaoh.
11 And Joseph placed his father and his brethren, and gave them a possession in the land of Egypt, in the best of the land, in the land of Rameses, as
12 Pharaoh had commanded. And Joseph nourished his father, and his brethren, and all his father's household, with bread, according to their families.
13 And there was no bread in all the land; for the famine was very sore, so that the land of Egypt and all the land of Canaan fainted by reason of the
14 famine. And Joseph gathered up all the money that was found in the land of Egypt, and in the land of Canaan, for the corn which they bought: and Joseph brought the money into Pharaoh's house.
15 And when money failed in the land of Egypt, and in the land of Canaan, all the Egyptians came unto Joseph, and said, Give us bread: for why should
16 we die in thy presence? for the money faileth. And Joseph said, Give your
17 cattle; and I will give you for your cattle, if money fail. And they brought their cattle unto Joseph: and Joseph gave them bread in exchange for horses, and for the flocks, and for the cattle of the herds, and for the asses; and he fed them with bread for all their cattle for that year.
18 When that year was ended, they came unto him the second year, and said unto him, We will not hide it from my lord, how that our money is spent;

my lord also hath our herds of cattle; there is not aught left in the sight of
19 my lord, but our bodies, and our lands: Wherefore shall we die before thine
eyes, both we and our land? buy us and our land for bread, and we and our
land will be servants unto Pharaoh: and give us seed, that we may live, and
20 not die, that the land be not desolate. And Joseph bought all the land of
Egypt for Pharaoh; for the Egyptians sold every man his field, because the
21 famine prevailed over them: so the land became Pharaoh's. And as for the
people, he removed them to cities from one end of the borders of Egypt even
22 to the other end thereof. Only the land of the priests bought he not; for the
priests had a portion assigned them of Pharaoh, and did eat their portion
which Pharaoh gave them: wherefore they sold not their lands.

13 Then Joseph said unto the people, Behold, I have bought you this day and
your land for Pharaoh: lo, here is seed for you, and ye shall sow the land.
24 And it shall come to pass in the increase, that ye shall give the fifth part
unto Pharaoh, and four parts shall be your own, for seed of the field, and for
your food, and for them of your households, and for food for your little ones.
25 And they said, Thou hast saved our lives: let us find grace in the sight of
26 my lord, and we will be Pharaoh's servants. And Joseph made it a law over
the land of Egypt unto this day, that Pharaoh should have the fifth part;
except the land of the priests only, which became not Pharaoh's.

27 And Israel dwelt in the land of Egypt, in the country of Goshen; and they
28 had possessions therein, and grew, and multiplied exceedingly. And Jacob
lived in the land of Egypt seventeen years: so the whole age of Jacob was a
hundred forty and seven years.

29 And the time drew nigh that Israel must die: and he called his son Joseph,
and said unto him, If now I have found grace in thy sight, put, I pray thee,
thy hand under my thigh, and deal kindly and truly with me; bury me not,
30 I pray thee, in Egypt: But I will lie with my fathers, and thou shalt carry
me out of Egypt, and bury me in their buryingplace. And he said, I will do
31 as thou hast said. And he said, Swear unto me. And he sware unto him.
And Israel bowed himself upon the bed's head.

49 And Jacob called unto his sons, and said, Gather yourselves together, that
I may tell you that which shall befall you in the last days.

2 Gather yourselves together, and hear, ye sons of Jacob;
and hearken unto Israel your father.

3 Reuben, thou art my firstborn,
my might, and the beginning of my strength,
the excellency of dignity, and the excellency of power:
4 Unstable as water, thou shalt not excel;
because thou wentest up to thy father's bed;
then defiledst thou it: he went up to my couch.

5 Simeon and Levi are brethren;
instruments of cruelty are in their habitations.
6 O my soul, come not thou into their secret;
unto their assembly, mine honor, be not thou united:
for in their anger they slew a man,
and in their self-will they digged down a wall.

7   Cursed be their anger, for it was fierce;
        and their wrath, for it was cruel:
    I will divide them in Jacob,
        and scatter them in Israel.

8   Judah, thou art he whom thy brethren shall praise:
        thy hand shall be in the neck of thine enemies;
        thy father's children shall bow down before thee.

9   Judah is a lion's whelp:
        from the prey, my son, thou art gone up:
    he stooped down, he couched as a lion, and as an old lion;
        who shall rouse him up?

10 The sceptre shall not depart from Judah,
        nor a lawgiver from between his feet,
        until Shiloh come;
    and unto him shall the gathering of the people be.

11   Binding his foal unto the vine,
        and his ass's colt unto the choice vine;
    he washed his garments in wine,
        and his clothes in the blood of grapes:

12 His eyes shall be red with wine,
        and his teeth white with milk.

13 Zebulun shall dwell at the haven of the sea;
        and he shall be for a haven of ships;
        and his border shall be unto Zidon.

14 Issachar is a strong ass
        couching down between two burdens:

15 And he saw that rest was good,
        and the land that it was pleasant;
    and bowed his shoulder to bear,
        and became a servant unto tribute.

16 Dan shall judge his people,
        as one of the tribes of Israel.

17 Dan shall be a serpent by the way,
        an adder in the path, that biteth the horse heels,
        so that his rider shall fall backward.

18 I have waited for thy salvation, O Lord.

19 Gad, a troop shall overcome him:
        but he shall overcome at the last.

20 Out of Asher his bread shall be fat,
        and he shall yield royal dainties.

21 Naphtali is a hind let loose:
        he giveth goodly words.

22 Joseph is a fruitful bough,
        even a fruitful bough by a well;
        whose branches run over the wall:

23 The archers have sorely grieved him,

Legendary Heroes of Genesis

and shot at him, and hated him:

24   But his bow abode in strength,
      and the arms of his hands were made strong
      by the hands of the mighty God of Jacob;
      (from thence is the shepherd, the stone of Israel;)

25   Even by the God of thy father, who shall help thee;
      and by the Almighty, who shall bless thee
      with blessings of heaven above,
      blessings of the deep that lieth under,
      blessings of the breasts, and of the womb:

26   The blessings of thy father have prevailed above the blessings
      of my progenitors
      unto the utmost bound of the everlasting hills:
    they shall be on the head of Joseph,
      and on the crown of the head of him that was separate from
      his brethren.

27   Benjamin shall raven as a wolf:
      in the morning he shall devour the prey,
      and at night he shall divide the spoil.

28   All these are the twelve tribes of Israel: and this is it that their father spake unto them, and blessed them; every one according to his blessing he 29 blessed them. And he charged them, and said unto them, I am to be gathered unto my people: bury me with my fathers in the cave that is in the field of 30 Ephron the Hittite, In the cave that is in the field of Machpelah, which is before Mamre, in the land of Canaan, which Abraham bought with the field of Ephron the Hittite for a possession of a buryingplace.

31   There they buried Abraham and Sarah his wife; there they buried Isaac 33 and Rebekah his wife; and there I buried Leah. And when Jacob had made an end of commanding his sons, he gathered up his feet into the bed, and yielded up the ghost, and was gathered unto his people.

50   And Joseph fell upon his father's face, and wept upon him, and kissed him.
2 And Joseph commanded his servants the physicians to embalm his father:
3 and the physicians embalmed Israel. And forty days were fulfilled for him; for so are fulfilled the days of those which are embalmed: and the Egyptians mourned for him threescore and ten days.

4   And when the days of his mourning were past, Joseph spake unto the house of Pharaoh, saying, If now I have found grace in your eyes, speak, I 5 pray you, in the ears of Pharaoh, saying, My father made me swear, saying, Lo, I die: in my grave which I have digged for me in the land of Canaan, there shalt thou bury me. Now therefore let me go up, I pray thee, and bury 6 my father, and I will come again. And Pharaoh said, Go up, and bury thy father, according as he made thee swear.

7   And Joseph went up to bury his father: and with him went up all the servants of Pharaoh, the elders of his house, and all the elders of the land of 8 Egypt, And all the house of Joseph, and his brethren, and his father's house: only their little ones, and their flocks, and their herds, they left in the land 9 of Goshen. And there went up with him both chariots and horsemen: and it was a very great company.

10 And they came to the threshing-floor of Atad, which is beyond Jordan; and there they mourned with a great and very sore lamentation: and he made

11 a mourning for his father seven days. And when the inhabitants of the land, the Canaanites, saw the mourning in the floor of Atad, they said, This is a grievous mourning to the Egyptians: wherefore the name of it was called Abel-mizraim, which is beyond Jordan.

12,13 And his sons did unto him according as he commanded them: For his sons carried him into the land of Canaan, and buried him in the cave of the field of Machpelah, which Abraham bought with the field for a possession of a

14 buryingplace of Ephron the Hittite, before Mamre. And Joseph returned into Egypt, he, and his brethren, and all that went up with him to bury his father, after he had buried his father.

15 And when Joseph's brethren saw that their father was dead, they said, Joseph will peradventure hate us, and will certainly requite us all the evil

16 which we did unto him. And they sent a messenger unto Joseph, saying,

17 Thy father did command before he died, saying, So shall ye say unto Joseph, Forgive, I pray thee now, the trespass of thy brethren, and their sin; for they did unto thee evil: and now, we pray thee, forgive the trespass of the servants of the God of thy father. And Joseph wept when they spake unto him.

18 And his brethren also went and fell down before his face; and they said, Behold, we be thy servants.

19 And Joseph said unto them, Fear not: for am I in the place of God?

20 But as for you, ye thought evil against me; but God meant it unto good, to

21 bring to pass, as it is this day, to save much people alive. Now therefore fear ye not: I will nourish you, and your little ones. And he comforted them, and spake kindly unto them.

22 And Joseph dwelt in Egypt, he, and his father's house: and Joseph lived

23 a hundred and ten years. And Joseph saw Ephraim's children of the third generation: the children also of Machir the son of Manasseh were brought up upon Joseph's knees.

24 And Joseph said unto his brethren, I die; and God will surely visit you, and bring you out of this land unto the land which he sware to Abraham, to

25 Isaac, and to Jacob. And Joseph took an oath of the children of Israel, saying,

26 God will surely visit you, and ye shall carry up my bones from hence. So Joseph died, being a hundred and ten years old: and they embalmed him, and he was put in a coffin in Egypt.

Considerations and Questions

1. Along with all the other things going for him, Joseph has what some people these days call "charisma." People appear drawn to him personally by some magnetic force in his personality. What examples of this built-in attractiveness do you find in his story? How do you explain the major exception represented in his brothers' dislike of him?

2. Joseph's brothers, early in the story, refer to him as "the dreamer," and not with admiration. His own boyhood dreams come true, of course, but even his doting old father considers them ridiculously impossible when Joseph recounts them. Do you find this part of the story too magical or unbelievable? Or do you see these dreams as pretty obvious reflections of Joseph's particular character and the probable direction such a character will take?

3. In Egypt people applaud and reward Joseph's interest in dreams. At that point of the story, however, someone else is doing the dreaming and Joseph acts as analyst. If you find the accuracy of his work hard to accept, check in with Dr. Carl G. Jung and other twentieth-century depth psychologists. Simply put, their convincing proposition is that human beings observe more evidence of what is to come than they realize they do. The human subconscious self often draws accurate conclusions from that "unknown" evidence and presents such conclusions in dream symbols. Apply this theory to the dreams of Pharaoh's butler, his baker, and of Pharaoh himself.

4. Joseph, the hero, is a superior man. He rises above his family in certain important ways, and in other ways he is clearly far ahead of the Egyptians. To what extent does it appear that his superiority to the Egyptians is because he is an Israelite?

5. Two places where the roster of Jacob's sons can be easily reviewed are chapter 37:22–26, and chapter 49, where Jacob gives his death-bed blessing to the twelve. Which of these sons thwart the plot to kill Joseph? What are their apparent reasons for doing so? Which son has nothing at all to do with that plot? Why?

6. Potiphar's wife casts her eyes upon Joseph; he is "of a fair person and well-favored." She says to him, "Lie with me." He won't, and gives reasons. Day after day she insists. Finally, when the house is empty, she catches him by his garment; he flies, leaving it with her, and he is in trouble. In the thrifty style to which we have become accustomed in the narratives of Genesis, this episode moves quickly and clearly. Yet there is more to the episode for our speculative attention than its apparent simplicity and its brevity suggest. Is the reader, for example, to assume that Potiphar's wife is sexually attractive? The story does not say so directly, but are there implications that she is? Does her physical desirability make any difference? What do you make of her three-word ap-

proach to Joseph? What practical results might Joseph foresee as a consequence to his agreeing to the liaison? How does the probability of such consequences compare with what does happen because he does not agree? Why does Potiphar's wife finally frame Joseph? If Potiphar believes his wife's story, why is his reaction so relatively mild?

7. Why do you suppose that Pharaoh does not administer his own famine control program? Why should he hire and empower a foreign dreamer? What considerable political changes does Joseph's administration of agriculture and economy in Egypt bring about? Do such changes apparently represent Joseph's political ideology?

8. What indications are there in the Joseph story of family loyalty among the members of the house of Israel? What causes can you ascribe to this loyalty? What pressures challenge its solidarity? How does this principle of loyalty become more explicit in the course of the narrative?

9. At the beginning of chapter 46 we note that Jacob does not make the move to Egypt without the spoken approval of the Lord. No such religious visions are in Joseph's experience as we read of it. What is the effect of Joseph's religious commitment on what happens to him, what he is, and what he does? How does it appear that he is aware of this force in his life?

10. Joseph's removal of his family to Egypt seems to represent a distinct rise in that family's worldly fortunes. What is the special status of the Israelites in Egypt at the end of the story? On what grounds do they enjoy that status? What effects do you think that this migration is likely to have on the family's commitment to the terms of the Covenant? Remember that the Lord has promised them the land of Canaan.

5. Another Investigation

Here are some quotations from what we have covered in Genesis. If you can identify the people and circumstances pertinent to each passage, you have apparently retained your reading pretty well. If you can respond to the questions with information, imagination, and understanding, your introduction to Biblical literature is showing symptoms of eventual success.

1. "My wrong be upon thee: I have given my maid into thy bosom; and when she saw that she had conceived, I was despised in her eyes: the Lord judge between me and thee."

(a) What exactly does the speaker mean by *wrong* here?
(b) How do the first and last clauses of this passage indicate the speaker's attitude towards the person addressed?
(c) What are the narrative facts summarized concisely between that first clause and that last clause?
(d) How does the quotation taken as a whole characterize the particular speaker?

2. "If God will be with me, and will keep me in this way that I go, and will give me bread to eat, and raiment to put on, so that I come again to my father's house in peace; then shall the Lord be my God."

(a) The speaker is *not* Joseph. In what respects is the passage inappropriate to his life and personality?
(b) A great many modern religious people would disapprove of the kind of proposition the speaker makes here. Why?
(c) Is this passage about *belief* in God?
(d) The speaker of these words is a very shrewd worldly man who is also a mystic. How is his personality reflected in the passage?

3. "And he drank of the wine and was drunken; and he was uncovered within his tent."

(a) Is the effect of this sentence one of moral recrimination? Does the writer focus our attention on the man's flaws of character or behavior? Compare the phrasing of the sentence with "He got drunk and passed out naked in the tent."
(b) "Wine" and "tent" are the only concrete nouns in the sentence. How do they provide fixed points on which the episode is established?

4. "And tarry with him a few days until thy brother's fury turns away, until thy brother's anger turns away from thee, and he forget

that which thou hast done to him: then will I send, and fetch thee from thence: why should I be deprived also of you both in one day?"

- (a) What does "a few days" suggest about the speaker's opinion of the brother? What other terms in the sentence help make that opinion evident?
- (b) The sentence begins with an instruction or even a command. It ends with a request for an explanation. What do these approaches, taken singly and together, indicate to us about the speaker?
- (c) If you have identified this passage accurately, the words "that which thou hast done to him" may strike you as unfair. Why?

5. "The woman whom thou gavest to be with me, she gave me of the tree, and I did eat."

- (a) Three people appear to be responsible for something as the speaker expresses it here. What is significant about the order in which he mentions them?
- (b) What major change in the life of humankind does this sentence represent? How?

6. "And he made him to ride in the second chariot which he had; and they cried before him, Bow the knee: and he made him ruler over all the land of Egypt."

- (a) Every society has symbols of power and authority. These may be official cars, uniforms, salutes, titles, or any number of other outward signs. Of course, such emblems indicate various kinds or degrees of power and authority. What do you make of the ones in this sentence?
- (b) What in this sentence does "ruler" mean, and not mean?
- (c) "Which he had" and "all the land of" may strike some casual readers as unnecessary, wordy elements in this sentence. Consider them carefully. What weight do they actually carry?

7. "And the water was spent in the bottle, and she cast the child under one of the shrubs. And she went, and sat her down over against him a good way off, as it were a bowshot: for she said, Let me not see the death of the child."

- (a) Although "over against him" is an unfamiliar idiom to us, what can we see that it means in physical terms here? How do "as it were a bowshot" and "Let me not see" help?
- (b) What material things are mentioned in this passage? What is their contribution to picturing a situation of despair?
- (c) How do the woman's actions (rather than her words) indicate

her state of mind? Do they in some way compromise the apparently total despondency of what she says?

8. "Behold now, I have two daughters which have not known man; let me, I pray you, bring them out unto you, and do ye to them as is good in your eyes: only unto these men do nothing; for therefore came they under the shadow of my roof."

(a) In this passage what is the measure of how desperate the situation is for the speaker?

(b) The last clause means that these men have come into the speaker's house for their own safety. What part of a primitive ethical code is implicit here? Is it part of the specific Covenant between the Lord and the children of Abraham?

(c) In this passage we find the characteristic use of "know" or "known" to mean sexual relationships. What exactly is the speaker offering to the people he addresses? How does this indicate what he is trying to dissuade them from?

(d) What is the personal approach of the speaker? Is he threatening? Moralistic? How is his approach made evident in the passage? Can you explain why he takes the line that he does?

9. "Let us make man in our image, after our likeness: and let them have dominion over the fish of the sea, and over the fowl of the air, and over the cattle, and over all the earth, and over every creeping thing that creepeth upon the earth."

(a) Does the wording of this passage indicate that man is to be the exact duplicate of the speaker?

(b) To what specific role does the writer of this passage assign man in the order of nature?

(c) Accepting this mythic statement as true, and validated by experience, some people these days have suggested that part of it at least is a very unfortunate truth. They have pointed out that man's "dominion" has resulted in the ecological pillage of the earth. What do you think?

(d) Other people, and for a long time, have speculated that for man to think of himself as having been created in the image of this particular speaker has had disastrous effects. What do you think about that?

10. "Lift up now thine eyes, and look from the place where thou art northward, and southward, and eastward, and westward: For all the land which thou seest, to thee will I give it, and to thy seed for ever. And I will make thy seed as the dust of the earth: so that if a man can number the dust of the earth, then shall thy seed also be numbered."

What are the two specific promises made in this passage?

IV

From The History
Of Ancient Israel

"The people will live on.
The learning and blundering people will live on."
Carl Sandburg, "The People, Yes"

1. A Note on History

It may be that universal history is the history of a handful of metaphors.

JORGE LUIS BORGES, *The Fearful Sphere of Pascal*

I call this section of the book "From the *History* of Ancient Israel" because I want to emphasize a distinction between what we have already studied and what we are about to study. As you know, I believe the central literary methods of the Genesis writers to be mythic and legendary. The author of the Eden story, for example, seems to me far more concerned with bringing to our conscious recognition an idea about the nature of mankind than with recording literal occurrences in a particular time and place. The teller or tellers of the tales of the patriarchs seem to me more concerned with perpetuating the attitudes of a people towards its own identity than with presenting a series of events in time and space.

The writers of the literature we are now approaching, however, *are* primarily concerned with a series of literal events in time and space. If these writers acknowledge and contrive to impart a mythic and legendary significance to Israel's exodus from Egypt or David's defeat of Goliath, their first concern is to record that these occurrences actually happened and are parts of a pattern of strict cause and effect which extends to this very day.

When we use such classifications as myth, legend, and history, it is important to remember that we are referring to literary intentions and resulting methods only. No one of these approaches, as such, makes its subject matter "true" or "false." Our immediate business as students of literature is to grasp what certain writers are telling us. To recognize why and how they write as they do is an essential step to that understanding. When we do have the best grasp we can manage of what writers are actually saying to us, then, perhaps, as individual human beings we will be in some sort of shape to assess the extent to which we accept their work.

I think that the Biblical literature represented in this section is intended to be an account of the emergence and early development of the nation of Israel. Although all writers of all eras have had various motivations for their work, such a view of this literature clearly seems to be the encompassing one on which we should fix our focus here. We will start with a few tribes of Hebrews, the legendary "children of Israel," oppressed aliens living in the powerful Egyptian kingdom of about 1500 B.C. We will conclude with a kingdom called Israel which occupies its own territories, maintains its own unique cultural patterns, and is a significant force in the affairs of its world. This transition takes approximately five very tough centuries.

Writers of historical literature are, almost without exception, especially committed to concrete detail. This is reasonable, since the historical intent assumes that the exact events of the literal past lead truthfully to the present. Like other works of historical intent, what we are about to study will include a great deal of detail: of national and international events, of legal organization and codes, of economic circumstances, of military policies, of political organization, of cultural practices, of agreements and disagreements. In the Old Testament the details of the national religion of the Jews and its development are of unusual importance, for almost all the other details unique to Israel depend on them.

2. The Escape from Egypt: Moses

*After supper she got our her book and learned
me about Moses and the Bulrushers, and I was in
a sweat to find out all about him; but by and by
she let it out that Moses had been dead a considerable long time; so then I didn't care no more
about him, because I don't take no stock in dead
people.*

MARK TWAIN, *Huckleberry Finn*

The book called Exodus begins with a geographical location
and a social condition. The geographical location is ancient Egypt (probably about the time of the reign of Rameses II) and, within that kingdom,
the fertile section of Goshen where an alien group of Hebrews lives. Their
legendary view of themselves includes, as we know, that they are "the
children of Israel," the descendants of Jacob's twelve sons. They believe
that their ancestors were brought into Egypt by a remarkable family hero
named Joseph, a figure whose deeds and words embody some of the best
qualities of their race. They apparently look back to the times of Joseph
as times when there was peaceful and mutually advantageous co-existence
between themselves and the Egyptians. They also maintain a dim but stubborn belief that they are under the special protection of an exclusive god
who has made specific promises to and demands of certain of their ancestors back to a legendary founding father, Abraham. As part of their
cultural self-portrait this racial and religious identity is the stuff of legend,
but in the narrative of Exodus it also becomes a historical fact with historical effects.

For one thing, their collective picture of themselves must
contribute to their condition of separateness from the Egyptians among
whom they dwell. In a great many countries (the United States, for example) immigrants are likely to take on the patterns of behavior and belief native to their new homes. As generations go by, the children and
grandchildren of the new Americans become more or less indistinguishable
from those of most older Americans. At the beginning of Exodus, however,
the children of Israel have not become Egyptians.

For another, the value which they traditionally (or legend-
arily) set upon themselves as a special group seems to encourage them to
work harder and breed faster than do the native Egyptians. We see early
that their survival as a people seems to them worth a great deal of
effort.

In conjunction with other events on the world calendar, these conditions help produce predictable historical consequences. The rulers of the expanding Egyptian empire, represented for us in the figure of "Pharaoh," both value and fear this tough, prolific crowd of aliens. Pharaoh needs the strength and industry of the Hebrews for his building program, but he is reasonably apprehensive about maintaining a growing population of potential enemies within his own borders. In chapter 1 we see Pharaoh attempting a familiar solution to this political problem: oppression and limited genocide. He proposes to make life so difficult for the Israelites that they will be too tired or too busy to make trouble. He tries to limit the number of male Jewish babies by having them murdered by midwives. In response, the Hebrews can only devise temporary expedients to save their infants. They cannot leave Egypt because Pharaoh requires their labor, and perhaps they can imagine no place to go which might not be worse. At this point, the children of Israel appear to have no historical future worth living for.

Of course, a man named Moses refutes this dismal prognosis. In doing so, he becomes a historical figure, an important cause for a significant change in human events. He is not the only cause for the escape of the Jews from Egypt and the foundation of the nation of Israel. He could not, for example, have made the Hebrews accede to his plans if they had not already a general commitment to the God of Abraham, Isaac, and Jacob. Yet the Exodus writer is obviously not one of those writers of historical literature who think that the heroic personality either does not exist or is irrelevant to the course of history. Along with the other Biblical authors, the Exodus writer depicts a world in which the decisions of particular men and women, as well as their abilities to carry out such decisions, are, for good and ill, terribly important.

Moses is one of the great heroes of the Bible. He is the dominant character in the books called Exodus, Leviticus, Numbers, and Deuteronomy. As his continuing appearance in modern novels and films suggests, he can be viewed as a hero in the romantic sense: the brave, resourceful man who overcomes perilous hardships and formidable problems. He is superior to the people around him in character and intellect. As a national leader he becomes a heroic legend during his lifetime and remains one for succeeding generations. Perhaps most interesting of all, he has a special personal relationship with a reality beyond the ordinary material reality known to the mass of mankind. In literature that does not assume divine involvement in the affairs of men, such a special relationship may be considered as an inspiration or intuition from sources unknown. In the Bible the relationship is mystical in the religious sense, and the reality is God.

That the character of Moses must be deemed heroic is something we must agree to if we are to understand Exodus. Yet we should also note that this hero is neither Superman nor a demigod. Moses has human fears, weaknesses, and limitations of vision. He must contend with the ills of his own mortality as well as with external problems. Much of his story's interest is a result of the author's decision to include evidence of his hero's human frailty.

In the readings from Exodus which follow this introduction, and which bring Moses and his people out of Egypt to wander for decades as a landless nation, we see a great deal not only of the heroism but also of the common mortality of Moses. We see a man make notable decisions and demonstrate remarkable powers of leadership, but we also see a man "grow up"—as ordinary men do. Note, for example, the false start of Moses in the hero business. His first actions on his people's behalf are to assassinate an Egyptian who was smiting one of his kinsmen and to attempt a lecture on the need for solidarity among the oppressed to a couple of casually quarreling Hebrews. This kind of violent personal militance is about as productive for the youthful Moses as it has been for most of its practitioners in our own time. His futile efforts lead him to disillusionment with his vaguely defined cause and a sense of hopelessness about any sort of social change. He must leave the country to escape punishment as a revolutionary terrorist, and like some other aging radicals he settles down as a respectable family man somewhere else. At the age of forty he seems to have concluded that being a hero is not for him.

As I have tried to imply, these episodes from the life of Moses are familiar or even "realistic" to most modern readers. We see destructive, useless acts prompted by immature passions all around us. And we often see the people who indulge in such acts slump later into apathy. If the story of Moses were to end with his marriage we might conclude that he was just another over-privileged young person who took on the romantic role of scourge-of-the-establishment in behalf of an oppressed "people" that neither wanted nor understood his efforts.

Even before we come to this realistic account of the career of Moses as a radical terrorist, however, the Exodus story has strongly implied that this man is a great deal more than a garden-variety revolutionary. His birth and infancy include circumstances which myth and legend teach us to associate not with ordinary people but with heroes. One of the most widespread ideas humanity has attached to heroes of the first magnitude is that they do not enter the world in the ordinary way. Somehow, the general human consciousness feels, heroes are marked out from the beginning by incidents outside ordinary human reality. Remarkable, sometimes miraculous, births and childhoods make concrete what we sense about people of extraordinary destiny.

Compared to the nativities of mythic Hercules or legendary King Arthur, the circumstances of the birth of Moses are not particularly magic or miraculous. They may, in fact, be taken as a series of happy coincidences. Yet readers are likely to agree that these coincidences and their fortuitous connections are unusual and exciting and do in some measure distinguish Moses as one marked by destiny for important things from the beginning. These early chapters of Exodus, by the way, do not explicitly state that the strange rescue of the infant Moses is by the personal intervention of the God of Abraham, Isaac, and Jacob. Until he is a mature man in Midian, he is in no way connected with the religious traditions of his people. Up to that point when he experiences the first of his theophanies (direct encounters with the divine), Exodus presents his life without mystical implications.

Both the life of Moses and the emphasis of the narrative change radically after the incident of the burning bush. No one, of course, can look at life as he once did after he becomes certain that he has literally talked with God. And the story of any person who talks with God must be told very differently from the story of one who does not. Yet even here the Exodus narrative includes details to remind us of the human weaknesses of the developing hero. As I have suggested, Moses has become disillusioned with heroic resistance. He has married the daughter of a successful man and is apparently doing well enough as a settled stock-raiser. He has passed the age of romantic political idealism. He does not see in himself the leader required by the voice from the burning bush. Even as they are swept away by the imperious will of the Lord, his presumptuous arguments provide a convincing transition for the reader who must accept the transformation of a middle-aged shepherd, who has once been an Egyptian prince and young revolutionary, to a divinely inspired leader and founder of a nation.

Do not let a certain primitive quality in the scene of the burning bush cause you to miss what Exodus offers as a historical event of extraordinary and complex importance. This is the coming to conviction by Moses that the godhead is not only the local embodiment of an idea (although in the burning bush He is that), not only the legendary identity of one's group (although as the God of Abraham He is that also), but also the supreme ruler of all events and conditions for Whom nothing can be impossible—the Lord of history. With this realization, Moses starts off to accomplish the impossible. Now *that* is a historic event.

Exodus

1:6,7 And Joseph died, and all his brethren, and all that generation. And the children of Israel were fruitful, and increased abundantly, and multiplied, and waxed exceeding mighty; and the land was filled with them.

8 Now there arose up a new king over Egypt, which knew not Joseph.
9 And he said unto his people, Behold, the people of the children of Israel are
10 more and mightier than we: Come on, let us deal wisely with them; lest they multiply, and it come to pass, that, when there falleth out any war, they join also unto our enemies, and fight against us, and so get them up
11 out of the land. Therefore they did set over them taskmasters to afflict them with their burdens. And they built for Pharaoh treasure cities, Pithom and
12 Raamses. But the more they afflicted them, the more they multiplied and
13 grew. And they were grieved because of the children of Israel. And the
14 Egyptians made the children of Israel to serve with rigor: And they made their lives bitter with hard bondage, in mortar, and in brick, and in all manner of service in the field: all their service, wherein they made them serve, was with rigor.

15 And the king of Egypt spake to the Hebrew midwives, of which the name
16 of the one was Shiphrah, and the name of the other Puah; And he said, When ye do the office of a midwife to the Hebrew women, and see them upon the stools, if it be a son, then ye shall kill him; but if it be a daughter, then she
17 shall live. But the midwives feared God, and did not as the king of Egypt
18 commanded them, but saved the men children alive. And the king of Egypt called for the midwives, and said unto them, Why have ye done this thing,
19 and have saved the men children alive? And the midwives said unto Pharaoh, Because the Hebrew women are not as the Egyptian women; for they are
20 lively, and are delivered ere the midwives come in unto them. Therefore God dealt well with the midwives: and the people multiplied, and waxed very mighty.
22 And Pharaoh charged all his people, saying, Every son that is born ye shall cast into the river, and every daughter ye shall save alive.

2 And there went a man of the house of Levi, and took to wife a daughter
2 of Levi. And the woman conceived, and bare a son: and when she saw him
3 that he was a goodly child, she hid him three months. And when she could not longer hide him, she took for him an ark of bulrushes, and daubed it with slime and with pitch, and put the child therein; and she laid it in the
4 flags by the river's brink. And his sister stood afar off, to wit what would be done to him.

5 And the daughter of Pharaoh came down to wash herself at the river; and her maidens walked along by the river's side: and when she saw the ark
6 among the flags, she sent her maid to fetch it. And when she had opened it, she saw the child: and, behold, the babe wept. And she had compassion on
7 him, and said, This is one of the Hebrews' children. Then said his sister to Pharaoh's daughter, Shall I go and call to thee a nurse of the Hebrew women,
8 that she may nurse the child for thee? And Pharaoh's daughter said to her, Go. And the maid went and called the child's mother.

9 And Pharaoh's daughter said unto her, Take this child away, and nurse it

for me, and I will give thee thy wages. And the woman took the child, and
10 nursed it. And the child grew, and she brought him unto Pharaoh's daughter, and he became her son. And she called his name Moses: and she said,
Because I drew him out of the water.

11 And it came to pass in those days, when Moses was grown, that he went
out unto his brethren, and looked on their burdens: and he spied an Egyptian
12 smiting a Hebrew, one of his brethren. And he looked this way and that
way, and when he saw that there was no man, he slew the Egyptian, and hid
13 him in the sand. And when he went out the second day, behold, two men
of the Hebrews strove together: and he said to him that did the wrong,
14 Wherefore smitest thou thy fellow? And he said, Who made thee a prince
and a judge over us? intendest thou to kill me, as thou killedst the Egyptian?
And Moses feared, and said, Surely this thing is known.
15 Now when Pharaoh heard this thing, he sought to slay Moses. But
Moses fled from the face of Pharaoh, and dwelt in the land of Midian:
16 and he sat down by a well. Now the priest of Midian had seven daughters:
and they came and drew water, and filled the troughs to water their father's
17 flock. And the shepherds came and drove them away: but Moses stood up
18 and helped them, and watered their flock. And when they came to Reuel
19 their father, he said, How is it that ye are come so soon to-day? And they
said, An Egyptian delivered us out of the hand of the shepherds, and also
20 drew water enough for us, and watered the flock. And he said unto his
daughters, And where is he? why is it that ye have left the man? call him,
that he may eat bread.
21 And Moses was content to dwell with the man: and he gave Moses Zip-
22 porah his daughter. And she bare him a son, and he called his name Gershom:
for he said, I have been a stranger in a strange land.
23 And it came to pass in process of time, that the king of Egypt died: and
the children of Israel sighed by reason of the bondage, and they cried, and
24 their cry came up unto God by reason of the bondage. And God heard their
groaning, and God remembered his covenant with Abraham, with Isaac,
25 and with Jacob. And God looked upon the children of Israel, and God had
respect unto them.
3 Now Moses kept the flock of Jethro his father-in-law, the priest of
Midian: and he led the flock to the back side of the desert, and came to the
2 mountain of God, even to Horeb. And the Angel of the Lord appeared
unto him in a flame of fire out of the midst of a bush: and he looked, and,
3 behold, the bush burned with fire, and the bush was not consumed. And
Moses said, I will now turn aside, and see this great sight, why the bush is
not burnt.
4 And when the Lord saw that he turned aside to see, God called unto him
out of the midst of the bush, and said, Moses, Moses. And he said, Here
5 am I. And he said, Draw not nigh hither: put off thy shoes from off thy feet;
6 for the place whereon thou standest is holy ground. Moreover he said, I am
the God of thy father, the God of Abraham, the God of Isaac, and the God
of Jacob. And Moses hid his face; for he was afraid to look upon God.
7 And the Lord said, I have surely seen the affliction of my people which
are in Egypt, and have heard their cry by reason of their taskmasters; for I
8 know their sorrows; And I am come down to deliver them out of the hand
of the Egyptians, and to bring them up out of that land unto a good land and

a large, unto a land flowing with milk and honey; unto the place of the Canaanites, and the Hittites, and the Amorites, and the Perizzites, and the

9 Hivites, and the Jebusites. Now therefore, behold, the cry of the children of Israel is come unto me: and I have also seen the oppression wherewith the

10 Egyptians oppress them. Come now therefore, and I will send thee unto Pharaoh, that thou mayest bring forth my people the children of Israel out of Egypt.

11, 12 And Moses said unto God, Who am I, that I should go unto Pharaoh, and that I should bring forth the children of Israel out of Egypt? And he said, Certainly I will be with thee; and this shall be a token unto thee, that I have sent thee: When thou hast brought forth the people out of Egypt, ye shall serve God upon this mountain.

13 And Moses said unto God, Behold, when I come unto the children of Israel, and shall say unto them, The God of your fathers hath sent me unto you; and they shall say to me, What is his name? what shall I say unto them?

14 And God said unto Moses, I AM THAT I AM: and he said, Thus shalt

15 thou say unto the children of Israel, I AM hath sent me unto you. And God said moreover unto Moses, Thus shalt thou say unto the children of Israel, The Lord God of your fathers, the God of Abraham, the God of Isaac, and the God of Jacob, hath sent me unto you: this is my name for ever, and this is my memorial unto all generations.

19 And I am sure that the king of Egypt will not let you go, no, not by a

20 mighty hand. And I will stretch out my hand, and smite Egypt with all my wonders which I will do in the midst thereof: and after that he will let you go

21 And I will give this people favor in the sight of the Egyptians: and it shall

22 come to pass, that, when ye go, ye shall not go empty: But every woman shall borrow of her neighbor, and of her that sojourneth in her house, jewels of silver, and jewels of gold, and raiment: and ye shall put them upon your sons, and upon your daughters; and ye shall spoil the Egyptians.

4 And Moses answered and said, But, behold, they will not believe me, nor hearken unto my voice: for they will say, The Lord hath not appeared unto

2 thee. And the Lord said unto him, What is that in thine hand? And he said,

3 A rod. And he said, Cast it on the ground. And he cast it on the ground, and

4 it became a serpent; and Moses fled from before it. And the Lord said unto Moses, Put forth thine hand, and take it by the tail. And he put forth his

5 hand, and caught it, and it became a rod in his hand: That they may believe that the Lord God of their fathers, the God of Abraham, the God of Isaac, and the God of Jacob, hath appeared unto thee.

6 And the Lord said furthermore unto him, Put now thine hand into thy bosom. And he put his hand into his bosom: and when he took it out, behold,

7 his hand was leprous as snow. And he said, Put thine hand into thy bosom again. And he put his hand into his bosom again; and plucked it out of his

8 bosom, and, behold, it was turned again as his other flesh. And it shall come to pass, if they will not believe thee, neither hearken to the voice of the first

9 sign, that they will believe the voice of the latter sign. And it shall come to pass, if they will not believe also these two signs, neither hearken unto thy voice, that thou shalt take of the water of the river, and pour it upon the dry land: and the water which thou takest out of the river shall become blood upon the dry land.

10 And Moses said unto the Lord, O my Lord, I am not eloquent, neither heretofore, nor since thou hast spoken unto thy servant; but I am slow of
11 speech, and of a slow tongue. And the Lord said unto him, Who hath made man's mouth? or who maketh the dumb, or deaf, or the seeing, or the blind?
12 have not I the Lord? Now therefore go, and I will be with thy mouth, and
13 teach thee what thou shalt say. And he said, O my Lord, send, I pray thee, by the hand of him whom thou wilt send.

14 And the anger of the Lord was kindled against Moses, and he said, Is not Aaron the Levite thy brother? I know that he can speak well. And also, behold, he cometh forth to meet thee: and when he seeth thee, he will be glad
15 in his heart. And thou shalt speak unto him, and put words in his mouth: and I will be with thy mouth, and with his mouth, and will teach you what ye
16 shall do. And he shall be thy spokesman unto the people: and he shall be, even he shall be to thee instead of a mouth, and thou shalt be to him instead
17 of God. And thou shalt take this rod in thine hand, wherewith thou shalt do signs.

18 And Moses went and returned to Jethro his father-in-law, and said unto him, Let me go, I pray thee, and return unto my brethren which are in Egypt, and see whether they be yet alive. And Jethro said to Moses, Go in peace.

19 And the Lord said unto Moses in Midian, Go, return into Egypt: for all
20 the men are dead which sought thy life. And Moses took his wife and his sons, and set them upon an ass, and he returned to the land of Egypt: and
21 Moses took the rod of God in his hand. And the Lord said unto Moses, When thou goest to return into Egypt, see that thou do all those wonders before Pharaoh, which I have put in thine hand: but I will harden his heart, that he shall not let the people go.

27 And the Lord said to Aaron, Go into the wilderness to meet Moses. And
28 he went, and met him in the mount of God, and kissed him. And Moses told Aaron all the words of the Lord who had sent him, and all the signs which
29 he had commanded him. And Moses and Aaron went and gathered together
30 all the elders of the children of Israel: And Aaron spake all the words which the Lord had spoken unto Moses, and did the signs in the sight of the people.
31 And the people believed: and when they heard that the Lord had visited the children of Israel, and that he had looked upon their affliction, then they bowed their heads and worshipped.

5 And afterward Moses and Aaron went in, and told Pharaoh, Thus saith the Lord God of Israel, Let my people go, that they may hold a feast unto
2 me in the wilderness. And Pharaoh said, Who is the Lord, that I should obey his voice to let Israel go? I know not the Lord, neither will I let Israel go.
3 And they said, The God of the Hebrews hath met with us: let us go, we pray thee, three days' journey into the desert, and sacrifice unto the Lord our God; lest he fall upon us with pestilence, or with the sword.
4 And the king of Egypt said unto them, Wherefore do ye, Moses and
5 Aaron, let the people from their works? get you unto your burdens. And Pharaoh said, Behold, the people of the land now are many, and ye make
6 them rest from their burdens. And Pharaoh commanded the same day the
7 taskmasters of the people, and their officers, saying, Ye shall no more give the people straw to make brick, as heretofore: let them go and gather straw

8 for themselves. And the tale of the bricks, which they did make heretofore, ye shall lay upon them; ye shall not diminish aught thereof: for they be idle;

9 therefore they cry, saying, Let us go and sacrifice to our God. Let there more work be laid upon the men, that they may labor therein; and let them not regard vain words.

10 And the taskmasters of the people went out, and their officers, and they spake to the people, saying, Thus saith Pharaoh, I will not give you straw.

11 Go ye, get you straw where ye can find it: yet not aught of your work shall

12 be diminished. So the people were scattered abroad throughout all the land

13 of Egypt to gather stubble instead of straw. And the taskmasters hasted them, saying, Fulfill your works, your daily tasks, as when there was straw.

14 And the officers of the children of Israel, which Pharaoh's taskmasters had set over them, were beaten, and demanded, Wherefore have ye not fulfilled your task in making brick both yesterday and to-day, as heretofore?

15 Then the officers of the children of Israel came and cried unto Pharaoh,

16 saying, Wherefore dealest thou thus with thy servants? There is no straw given unto thy servants, and they say to us, Make brick: and, behold, thy

17 servants are beaten; but the fault is in thine own people. But he said, Ye are

18 idle, ye are idle: therefore ye say, Let us go and do sacrifice to the Lord. Go therefore now, and work; for there shall no straw be given you, yet shall ye

19 deliver the tale of bricks. And the officers of the children of Israel did see that they were in evil case, after it was said, Ye shall not minish aught from your bricks of your daily task.

20 And they met Moses and Aaron, who stood in the way, as they came

21 forth from Pharaoh: And they said unto them, The Lord look upon you, and judge; because ye have made our savor to be abhorred in the eyes of Pharaoh, and in the eyes of his servants, to put a sword in their hand to

22 slay us. And Moses returned unto the Lord, and said, Lord, wherefore hast

23 thou so evil entreated this people? why is it that thou hast sent me? For since I came to Pharaoh to speak in thy name, he hath done evil to this people; neither hast thou delivered thy people at all.

6 Then the Lord said unto Moses, Now shalt thou see what I will do to Pharaoh: for with a strong hand shall he let them go, and with a strong hand

2 shall he drive them out of his land. And God spake unto Moses, and said

3 unto him, I am the Lord: And I appeared unto Abraham, unto Isaac, and unto Jacob, by the name of God Almighty; but by my name JEHOVAH was

4 I not known to them. And I have also established my covenant with them, to give them the land of Canaan, the land of their pilgrimage, wherein they

5 were strangers. And I have also heard the groaning of the children of Israel, whom the Egyptians keep in bondage; and I have remembered my covenant.

6 Wherefore say unto the children of Israel, I am the Lord, and I will bring you out from under the burdens of the Egyptians, and I will rid you out of their bondage, and I will redeem you with a stretched out arm, and with great judgments:

9 And Moses spake so unto the children of Israel: but they hearkened not

10 unto Moses for anguish of spirit, and for cruel bondage. And the Lord spake

11 unto Moses, saying, Go in, speak unto Pharaoh king of Egypt, that he let

12 the children of Israel go out of his land. And Moses spake before the Lord, saying, Behold, the children of Israel have not hearkened unto me; how then shall Pharaoh hear me, who am of uncircumcised lips?

13   And the Lord spake unto Moses and unto Aaron, and gave them a charge unto the children of Israel, and unto Pharaoh king of Egypt, to bring the children of Israel out of the land of Egypt.

7   And the Lord said unto Moses, See, I have made thee a god to Pharaoh;

2 and Aaron thy brother shall be thy prophet. Thou shalt speak all that I command thee; and Aaron thy brother shall speak unto Pharaoh, that he

3 send the children of Israel out of his land. And I will harden Pharaoh's heart,

4 and multiply my signs and my wonders in the land of Egypt. But Pharaoh shall not hearken unto you, that I may lay my hand upon Egypt, and bring forth mine armies, and my people the children of Israel, out of the land of

5 Egypt by great judgments. And the Egyptians shall know that I am the Lord, when I stretch forth mine hand upon Egypt, and bring out the children

6 of Israel from among them. And Moses and Aaron did as the Lord com-

7 manded them, so did they. And Moses was fourscore years old, and Aaron fourscore and three years old, when they spake unto Pharaoh.

8,9   And the Lord spake unto Moses and unto Aaron, saying, When Pharaoh shall speak unto you, saying, Show a miracle for you: then thou shalt say unto Aaron, Take thy rod, and cast it before Pharaoh, and it shall become a

10 serpent. And Moses and Aaron went in unto Pharaoh, and they did so as the Lord had commanded: and Aaron cast down his rod before Pharaoh, and be-

11 fore his servants, and it became a serpent. Then Pharaoh also called the wise men and the sorcerers: now the magicians of Egypt, they also did in like

12 manner with their enchantments. For they cast down every man his rod, and they became serpents: but Aaron's rod swallowed up their rods.

14   And the Lord said unto Moses, Pharaoh's heart is hardened, he refuseth

15 to let the people go. Get thee unto Pharaoh in the morning; lo, he goeth out unto the water; and thou shalt stand by the river's brink against he come;

16 and the rod which was turned to a serpent shalt thou take in thine hand. And thou shalt say unto him, The Lord God of the Hebrews hath sent me unto thee, saying, Let my people go, that they may serve me in the wilderness:

17 and, behold, hitherto thou wouldest not hear. Thus saith the Lord, In this thou shalt know that I am the Lord: behold, I will smite with the rod that is in mine hand upon the waters which are in the river, and they shall be

18 turned to blood. And the fish that is in the river shall die, and the river shall stink; and the Egyptians shall loathe to drink of the water of the river.

19   And the Lord spake unto Moses, Say unto Aaron, Take thy rod, and

20 stretch out thine hand upon the waters of Egypt, . . . And Moses and Aaron did so, as the Lord commanded; and he lifted up the rod, and smote the waters that were in the river, in the sight of Pharaoh, and in the sight of his

21 servants; and all the waters that were in the river were turned to blood. And the fish that was in the river died; and the river stank, and the Egyptians could not drink of the water of the river; and there was blood throughout

22 all the land of Egypt. And the magicians of Egypt did so with their en-chantments: and Pharaoh's heart was hardened, neither did he hearken unto them; as the Lord had said.

8   And the Lord spake unto Moses, Go unto Pharaoh, and say unto him,

2 Thus saith the Lord, Let my people go, that they may serve me. And if thou refuse to let them go, behold, I will smite all thy borders with frogs:

3 And the river shall bring forth frogs abundantly, which shall go up and come into thine house, and into thy bedchamber, and upon thy bed, and into the

house of thy servants, and upon thy people, and into thine ovens, and into thy kneadingtroughs:

5 And the Lord spake unto Moses, Say unto Aaron, Stretch forth thine hand with thy rod over the streams, over the rivers, and over the ponds, and cause
6 frogs to come up upon the land of Egypt. And Aaron stretched out his hand over the waters of Egypt; and the frogs came up, and covered the land of
7 Egypt. And the magicians did so with their enchantments, and brought up frogs upon the land of Egypt.

8 Then Pharaoh called for Moses and Aaron, and said, Entreat the Lord, that he may take away the frogs from me, and from my people; and I will
9 let the people go, that they may do sacrifice unto the Lord. And Moses said unto Pharaoh, Glory over me: when shall I entreat for thee, and for thy servants, and for thy people, to destroy the frogs from thee and thy houses,
10 that they may remain in the river only? And he said, To-morrow. And he said, Be it according to thy word; that thou mayest know that there is none
11 like unto the Lord our God. And the frogs shall depart from thee, and from thy houses, and from thy servants, and from thy people; they shall remain in the river only.

12 And Moses and Aaron went out from Pharaoh: and Moses cried unto the
13 Lord because of the frogs which he had brought against Pharaoh. And the Lord did according to the word of Moses; and the frogs died out of the
14 houses, out of the villages, and out of the fields. And they gathered them to-
15 gether upon heaps; and the land stank. But when Pharaoh saw that there was respite, he hardened his heart, and hearkened not unto them; as the Lord had said.

9 Then the Lord said unto Moses, Go in unto Pharaoh, and tell him, Thus saith the Lord God of the Hebrews, Let my people go, that they may serve
2,3 me. For if thou refuse to let them go, and wilt hold them still, Behold, the hand of the Lord is upon thy cattle which is in the field, upon the horses, upon the asses, upon the camels, upon the oxen, and upon the sheep: there
5 shall be a very grievous murrain. And the Lord did that thing on the mor-row, and all the cattle of Egypt died: but of the cattle of the children of
7 Israel died not one. And Pharaoh sent, and, behold, there was not one of the cattle of the Israelites dead. And the heart of Pharaoh was hardened, and he did not let the people go.

13 And the Lord said unto Moses, Rise up early in the morning, and stand before Pharaoh, and say unto him, Thus saith the Lord God of the Hebrews,
15 Let my people go, that they may serve me. For now I will stretch out my hand, that I may smite thee and thy people with pestilence; and thou shalt
17 be cut off from the earth. As yet exaltest thou thyself against my people,
18 that thou wilt not let them go? Behold, to-morrow about this time I will cause it to rain a very grievous hail, such as hath not been in Egypt since
19 the foundation thereof even until now. Send therefore now, and gather thy cattle, and all that thou hast in the field; for upon every man and beast which shall be found in the field, and shall not be brought home, the hail shall come down upon them, and they shall die.

23 And Moses stretched forth his rod toward heaven: and the Lord sent thunder and hail, and the fire ran along upon the ground; and the Lord rained
24 hail upon the land of Egypt. So there was hail, and fire mingled with the

hail, very grievous, such as there was none like it in all the land of Egypt
25 since it became a nation. And the hail smote throughout all the land of Egypt all that was in the field, both man and beast; and the hail smote every herb
26 of the field, and brake every tree of the field. Only in the land of Goshen, where the children of Israel were, was there no hail.

27 And Pharaoh sent, and called for Moses and Aaron, and said unto them, I have sinned this time: the Lord is righteous, and I and my people are
28 wicked. Entreat the Lord (for it is enough) that there be no more mighty thunderings and hail; and I will let you go, and ye shall stay no longer.

31 And the flax and the barley was smitten: for the barley was in the ear, and
32 the flax was bolled. But the wheat and the rye were not smitten: for they
33 were not grown up. And Moses went out of the city from Pharaoh, and spread abroad his hands unto the Lord: and the thunders and hail ceased, and
34 the rain was not poured upon the earth. And when Pharaoh saw that the rain and the hail and the thunders were ceased, he sinned yet more, and
35 hardened his heart, he and his servants. And the heart of Pharaoh was hardened, neither would he let the children of Israel go; as the Lord had spoken by Moses.

10: 3 And Moses and Aaron came in unto Pharaoh, and said unto him, Thus saith the Lord God of the Hebrews, How long wilt thou refuse to humble
4 thyself before me? let my people go, that they may serve me. Else, if thou refuse to let my people go, behold, to-morrow will I bring the locusts into
5 thy coast: And they shall cover the face of the earth, that one cannot be
6 able to see the earth: . . . And he turned himself, and went out from Pharaoh.

7 And Pharaoh's servants said unto him, How long shall this man be a snare unto us? let the men go, that they may serve the Lord their God: knowest
8 thou not yet that Egypt is destroyed? And Moses and Aaron were brought again unto Pharaoh: and he said unto them, Go, serve the Lord your God:
9 but who are they that shall go? And Moses said, We will go with our young and with our old, with our sons and with our daughters, with our flocks and
10 with our herds will we go; for we must hold a feast unto the Lord. And he said unto them, Let the Lord be so with you, as I will let you go, and your
11 little ones: look to it; for evil is before you. Not so: go now ye that are men, and serve the Lord; for that ye did desire. And they were driven out from Pharaoh's presence.

12 And the Lord said unto Moses, Stretch out thine hand over the land of Egypt for the locusts, that they may come up upon the land of Egypt, and
13 eat every herb of the land, even all that the hail hath left. And Moses stretched forth his rod over the land of Egypt, and the Lord brought an east wind upon the land all that day, and all that night; and when it was morning,
14 the east wind brought the locusts. And the locusts went up over all the land of Egypt, and rested in all the coasts of Egypt: very grievous were they; before them there were no such locusts as they, neither after them shall
15 be such. For they covered the face of the whole earth, so that the land was darkened; and they did eat every herb of the land, and all the fruit of the trees which the hail had left: and there remained not any green thing in the trees, or in the herbs of the field, through all the land of Egypt.

16 Then Pharaoh called for Moses and Aaron in haste; and he said, I have

17 sinned against the Lord your God, and against you. Now therefore forgive, I pray thee, my sin only this once, and entreat the Lord your God, that he 18 may take away from me this death only. And he went out from Pharaoh, and 19 entreated the Lord. And the Lord turned a mighty strong west wind, which took away the locusts, and cast them into the Red sea; there remained not 20 one locust in all the coasts of Egypt. But the Lord hardened Pharaoh's heart, so that he would not let the children of Israel go.

21 And the Lord said unto Moses, Stretch out thine hand toward heaven, that there may be darkness over the land of Egypt, even darkness which 22 may be felt. And Moses stretched forth his hand toward heaven; and there 23 was a thick darkness in all the land of Egypt three days: They saw not one another, neither rose any from his place for three days: but all the children of Israel had light in their dwellings.

24 And Pharaoh called unto Moses, and said, Go ye, serve the Lord; only let your flocks and your herds be stayed: let your little ones also go with you. 25 And Moses said, Thou must give us also sacrifices and burnt offerings, that 26 we may sacrifice unto the Lord our God. Our cattle also shall go with us; there shall not a hoof be left behind; for thereof must we take to serve the Lord our God; and we know not with what we must serve the Lord, until we come thither.

27 But the Lord hardened Pharaoh's heart, and he would not let them go. 28 And Pharaoh said unto him, Get thee from me, take heed to thyself, see 29 my face no more; for in that day thou seest my face thou shalt die. And Moses said, Thou hast spoken well, I will see thy face again no more.

11 And the Lord said unto Moses, Yet will I bring one plague more upon Pharaoh, and upon Egypt; afterward he will let you go hence: when he shall 2 let you go, he shall surely thrust you out hence altogether. Speak now in the ears of the people, and let every man borrow of his neighbor, and every 3 woman of her neighbor, jewels of silver, and jewels of gold. And the Lord gave the people favor in the sight of the Egyptians. Moreover, the man Moses was very great in the land of Egypt, in the sight of Pharaoh's servants, and in the sight of the people.

4 And Moses said, Thus saith the Lord, About midnight will I go out into 5 the midst of Egypt: And all the firstborn in the land of Egypt shall die, from the firstborn of Pharaoh that sitteth upon his throne, even unto the firstborn of the maidservant that is behind the mill; and all the firstborn of beasts. 6 And there shall be a great cry throughout all the land of Egypt, such as 7 there was none like it, nor shall be like it any more. But against any of the children of Israel shall not a dog move his tongue, against man or beast: that ye may know how that the Lord doth put a difference between the 8 Egyptians and Israel. And all these thy servants shall come down unto me, and bow down themselves unto me, saying, Get thee out, and all the people that follow thee: and after that I will go out. And he went out from Pharaoh in a great anger.

9 And the Lord said unto Moses, Pharaoh shall not hearken unto you; that 10 my wonders may be multiplied in the land of Egypt. And Moses and Aaron did all these wonders before Pharaoh: and the Lord hardened Pharaoh's heart, so that he would not let the children of Israel go out of his land.

12   And the Lord spake unto Moses and Aaron in the land of Egypt, saying,

3 Speak ye unto all the congregation of Israel, saying, In the tenth day of this month they shall take to them every man a lamb, according to the house of

4 their fathers, a lamb for a house: And if the household be too little for the lamb, let him and his neighbor next unto his house take it according to the number of the souls; every man according to his eating shall make your

5 count for the lamb. Your lamb shall be without blemish, a male of the first

6 year: ye shall take it out from the sheep, or from the goats: And ye shall keep it up until the fourteenth day of the same month: and the whole as-

7 sembly of the congregation of Israel shall kill it in the evening. And they shall take of the blood, and strike it on the two side posts and on the upper

8 doorpost of the houses, wherein they shall eat it. And they shall eat the flesh in that night, roast with fire, and unleavened bread; and with bitter herbs they shall eat it.

11   And thus shall ye eat it; with your loins girded, your shoes on your feet, and your staff in your hand; and ye shall eat it in haste: it is the Lord's

12 passover. For I will pass through the land of Egypt this night, and will smite all the firstborn in the land of Egypt, both man and beast; and against all the

13 gods of Egypt I will execute judgment: I am the Lord. And the blood shall be to you for a token upon the houses where ye are: and when I see the blood, I will pass over you, and the plague shall not be upon you to destroy

14 you, when I smite the land of Egypt. And this day shall be unto you for a memorial; and ye shall keep it a feast to the Lord throughout your genera-

15 tions: ye shall keep it a feast by an ordinance for ever. Seven days shall ye eat unleavened bread; even the first day ye shall put away leaven out of your houses: for whosoever eateth leavened bread from the first day until

16 the seventh day, that soul shall be cut off from Israel. And in the first day there shall be a holy convocation, and in the seventh day there shall be a holy convocation to you; no manner of work shall be done in them, save that which every man must eat, that only may be done of you.

21   Then Moses called for all the elders of Israel, and said unto them, Draw out and take you a lamb according to your families, and kill the passover.

24 And ye shall observe this thing for an ordinance to thee and to thy sons for

25 ever. And it shall come to pass, when ye be come to the land which the Lord will give you, according as he hath promised, that ye shall keep this service.

26 And it shall come to pass, when your children shall say unto you, What

27 mean ye by this service? That ye shall say, It is the sacrifice of the Lord's passover, who passed over the houses of the children of Israel in Egypt, when he smote the Egyptians, and delivered our houses. And the people

28 bowed the head and worshipped. And the children of Israel went away, and did as the Lord had commanded Moses and Aaron, so did they.

29   And it came to pass, that at midnight the Lord smote all the firstborn in the land of Egypt, from the firstborn of Pharaoh that sat on his throne unto the firstborn of the captive that was in the dungeon; and all the firstborn of

30 cattle. And Pharaoh rose up in the night, he, and all his servants, and all the Egyptians; and there was a great cry in Egypt: for there was not a house

31 where there was not one dead. And he called for Moses and Aaron by night, and said, Rise up, and get you forth from among my people, both ye and the

32 children of Israel; and go, serve the Lord, as ye have said. Also take your
33 flocks and your herds, as ye have said, and be gone; and bless me also. And
the Egyptians were urgent upon the people, that they might send them out of
the land in haste; for they said, We be all dead men.

34 And the people took their dough before it was leavened, their kneading-
35 troughs being bound up in their clothes upon their shoulders. And the children of Israel did according to the word of Moses; and they borrowed of the
36 Egyptians jewels of silver, and jewels of gold, and raiment: And the Lord
gave the people favor in the sight of the Egyptians, so that they lent unto
37 them such things as they required: and they spoiled the Egyptians. And the
children of Israel journeyed from Rameses to Succoth, about six hundred
38 thousand on foot that were men, beside children. And a mixed multitude
39 went up also with them; and flocks, and herds, even very much cattle. And
they baked unleavened cakes of the dough which they brought forth out of
Egypt, for it was not leavened; because they were thrust out of Egypt, and
could not tarry, neither had they prepared for themselves any victuals.

40 Now the sojourning of the children of Israel, who dwelt in Egypt, was
41 four hundred and thirty years. And it came to pass at the end of the four
hundred and thirty years, even the selfsame day it came to pass, that all the
42 hosts of the Lord went out from the land of Egypt. It is a night to be much
observed unto the Lord for bringing them out from the land of Egypt: this
is that night of the Lord to be observed of all the children of Israel in their
generations.

17 And it came to pass, when Pharaoh had let the people go, that God led
them not through the way of the land of the Philistines, although that was
near; for God said, Lest peradventure the people repent when they see war,
18 and they return to Egypt: But God led the people about, through the way
of the wilderness of the Red sea: and the children of Israel went up harnessed
19 out of the land of Egypt. And Moses took the bones of Joseph with him: for
he had straitly sworn the children of Israel, saying, God will surely visit
20 you; and ye shall carry up my bones away hence with you. And they took
their journey from Succoth, and encamped in Etham, in the edge of the wil-
21 derness. And the Lord went before them by day in a pillar of a cloud, to lead
them the way; and by night in a pillar of fire, to give them light; to go by
22 day and night. He took not away the pillar of the cloud by day, nor the pillar
of fire by night, from before the people.

14: 5 And it was told the king of Egypt that the people fled: and the heart of
Pharaoh and of his servants was turned against the people, and they said,
6 Why have we done this, that we have let Israel go from serving us? And he
7 made ready his chariot, and took his people with him: And he took six hundred chosen chariots, and all the chariots of Egypt, and captains over every
8 one of them. And the Lord hardened the heart of Pharaoh king of Egypt,
and he pursued after the children of Israel: and the children of Israel went
9 out with a high hand. But the Egyptians pursued after them, all the horses
and chariots of Pharaoh, and his horsemen, and his army, and overtook them
encamping by the sea, . . .
10 And when Pharaoh drew nigh, the children of Israel lifted up their eyes,
and, behold, the Egyptians marched after them; and they were sore afraid:
11 and the children of Israel cried out unto the Lord. And they said unto Moses,
Because there were no graves in Egypt, hast thou taken us away to die in

the wilderness? wherefore hast thou dealt thus with us, to carry us forth out
12 of Egypt? Is not this the word that we did tell thee in Egypt, saying, Let us
alone, that we may serve the Egyptians? For it had been better for us to
serve the Egyptians, than that we should die in the wilderness.

13 And Moses said unto the people, Fear ye not, stand still, and see the salvation of the Lord, which he will show to you to-day: for the Egyptians
14 whom ye have seen to-day, ye shall see them again no more for ever. The
Lord shall fight for you, and ye shall hold your peace.

19 And the Angel of God, which went before the camp of Israel, removed
and went behind them; and the pillar of the cloud went from before their
20 face, and stood behind them: And it came between the camp of the Egyptians and the camp of Israel; and it was a cloud and darkness to them, but it
gave light by night to these: so that the one came not near the other all the
21 night. And Moses stretched out his hand over the sea; and the Lord caused
the sea to go back by a strong east wind all that night, and made the sea dry
22 land, and the waters were divided. And the children of Israel went into the
midst of the sea upon the dry ground: and the waters were a wall unto them
23 on their right hand, and on their left. And the Egyptians pursued, and went
in after them to the midst of the sea, even all Pharaoh's horses, his chariots,
24 and his horsemen. And it came to pass, that in the morning watch the Lord
looked unto the host of the Egyptians through the pillar of fire and of the
25 cloud, and troubled the host of the Egyptians, And took off their chariot
wheels, that they drave them heavily: so that the Egyptians said, Let us flee
from the face of Israel; for the Lord fighteth for them against the Egyptians.

26 And the Lord said unto Moses, Stretch out thine hand over the sea, that
the waters may come again upon the Egyptians, upon their chariots, and
27 upon their horsemen. And Moses stretched forth his hand over the sea, and
the sea returned to his strength when the morning appeared; and the Egyptians fled against it; and the Lord overthrew the Egyptians in the midst of
28 the sea. And the waters returned, and covered the chariots, and the horsemen, and all the host of Pharaoh that came into the sea after them; there re-
29 mained not so much as one of them. But the children of Israel walked upon
dry land in the midst of the sea;   and the waters were a wall unto them on
their right hand, and on their left.

30 Thus the Lord saved Israel that day out of the hand of the Egyptians; and
31 Israel saw the Egyptians dead upon the seashore. And Israel saw that great
work which the Lord did upon the Egyptians: and the people feared the
Lord, and believed the Lord, and his servant Moses.

15 Then sang Moses and the children of Israel this song unto the Lord, and
spake, saying,

> I will sing unto the Lord, for he hath triumphed gloriously:
>   the horse and his rider hath he thrown into the sea.

2   The Lord is my strength and song,
>   and he is become my salvation:
> he is my God, and I will prepare him a habitation;
>   my father's God, and I will exalt him.

3   The Lord is a man of war:
>   the Lord is his name.

4   Pharaoh's chariots and his host hath he cast into the sea:

From the History of Ancient Israel

his chosen captains also are drowned in the Red sea.
5   The depths have covered them:
      they sank into the bottom as a stone.

6   Thy right hand, O Lord, is become glorious in power:
      thy right hand, O Lord, hath dashed in pieces the enemy.
7   And in the greatness of thine excellency thou hast overthrown them
      that rose up against thee:
    thou sentest forth thy wrath,
      which consumed them as stubble.
8   And with the blast of thy nostrils the waters were gathered together,
      the floods stood upright as a heap,
      and the depths were congealed in the heart of the sea.

9   The enemy said,
    I will pursue, I will overtake,
      I will divide the spoil;
      my lust shall be satisfied upon them;
    I will draw my sword,
      my hand shall destroy them.
10   Thou didst blow with thy wind, the sea covered them:
      they sank as lead in the mighty waters.

11   Who is like unto thee, O Lord, among the gods?
     who is like thee, glorious in holiness,
      fearful in praises, doing wonders?
17   Thou shalt bring them in, and plant them
     in the mountain of thine inheritance,
     in the place, O Lord, which thou hast made for thee to dwell in;
     in the sanctuary, O Lord, which thy hands have established.
18   The Lord shall reign for ever and ever.

20   And Miriam the prophetess, the sister of Aaron, took a timbrel in her
hand; and all the women went out after her with timbrels and with dances.
21 And Miriam answered them,

    Sing ye to the Lord, for he hath triumphed gloriously:
      the horse and his rider hath he thrown into the sea.

Considerations and Questions

1. "Bricks without straw," "which knew not Joseph," "the flesh pots," "a land of milk and honey"—along with countless other Biblical phrases, each of these expressions is a standard figure of speech in modern English. To what does each specifically refer in Exodus? To what sort of circumstances might one apply them in ordinary life today?

2. The second chapter of Exodus as we give it here is only twenty-five verses long. What block of time does it cover? What social circumstances does it reveal? What are its geographical settings? What details are provided to lend credibility to the various episodes of Moses' life?

3. Here are two sentences in which Exodus compresses two violent events: "And he looked this way and that, and when he saw that there was no man, he slew the Egyptian, and hid him in the sand" (2:12). "And the shepherds came and drove them away: but Moses stood up and helped them, and watered their flock" (2:17). What do both events reveal about Moses? How, on the other hand, are the actions and attitudes of Moses different? What details of style make the first sentence more intense or exciting than the second? Why is this appropriate to the situation?

4. Although Exodus does not indicate that Moses has any particular religious orientation until his encounter with the burning bush, we must assume that he knows something about the religious traditions of Israel. Why?

5. The Egyptians, particularly "Pharaoh," are the conventional bad guys of the Exodus story, and perhaps especially to those who have, as they say, "seen the movie but not read the book." From your study of the text what case can you make for the Egyptians (including "Pharaoh") as fairly ordinary people who react in a fairly ordinary sort of way, morally speaking, to their historical situation?

6. Does Exodus characterize the Israelites (including Moses) as a uniformly blameless band of saints? Explain.

7. How does the upbringing of Moses as an Egyptian prince relate to his subsequent accomplishments?

8. It was generally believed at the time that the events of Exodus take place that gods are local; the gods of Egypt would provide good fortune and bad to the people of Egypt, for example, but would not trouble themselves with other lands and populations. When Pharaoh answers Moses in the second verse of chapter 5 with, "Who is the Lord that I should obey his voice to let Israel go? I know not the Lord, neither will I let Israel go," he reflects something of this attitude. That the tribal god stubbornly imported by his Hebrews (whoever *he* is) might exert control over Egyptians is not a notion that occurs to Pharaoh. The events which follow in Egypt, notably the plagues and the destruction of Pharaoh's army at the Red Sea, are the immediate evidence that Pharaoh is wrong.

9. When Moses demands of Pharaoh that the Hebrews be allowed to depart from Egypt, he has himself already come to the conviction that God's power is universal. But this conviction represents an expansion of the older concept about gods rather than a simple rejection of it. The all-powerful God encountered by Moses in the burning bush is still local in that He favors the children of Israel over all other peoples. He is a God who can and will do things *for* his particular people, and at the same time He is a God who can and will do things *to* their competition. (In Exodus their competition includes just about everyone and everything with whom this landless horde comes in contact.) As an idea, this combination of absolute power and local favor is a potentially mighty propellent for historical action, but in Exodus Moses is the only character who is absolutely convinced that it is true. How does the inability of other Israelites to accept the Mosaic doctrine heart and soul damage them and their enterprise? How does the great leader, Moses, recoup the damages?

10. The magic tricks with Aaron's rod, the plagues of Egypt, and the parting of the Red Sea, as well as its cataclysmic closing, have for centuries been the favorite targets of skeptics. Their concern, however, has primarily been to establish the invalidity of certain religious beliefs; ours is with the understanding of literature. Where the religious skeptic may find in a Biblical "scientific impossibility" the grounds for refuting a belief in God, the student of Biblical literature may see no more than a matter of style—an imaginative means of expressing something.

So we will put religious or antireligious sentiments about these miracles aside and concentrate on what the writer of Exodus really means his readers to grasp. As I see them, the gist of his story is as follows:

(a) First Moses tries to persuade the Egyptians on their own local terms—magic demonstrations. This is unsuccessful; Pharaoh does not agree to let the Israelites go.

(b) But the Egyptian government is forced to temporary concessions by the effects on the Egyptian population of an unusual series of national disasters. (Note that none of the disasters is itself without precedent; what is unusual in Exodus is that they apparently follow one another so closely.)

(c) The escape of the Israelites from Pharaoh's army is not because this nonmilitary caravan of men, women, children, and livestock can win a battle against professional soldiers but because of conditions beyond their expectation or control. I suggest that the vast body of literature which most religious believers and skeptics alike accept as "history" is littered with events like these. You should not have to know much history to find analogies to them.

11. Ritual is a necessary part of every social unit which hopes to survive. All human groups, large and small, have either practiced some sort of self-identifying ceremonial form or have soon disappeared. As everyone knows, Israel has not disappeared, although Israel has been under considerable practical pressure to do so since the time of Moses. The ritual of the Passover has not disappeared either.

Unlike many ceremonial forms which assert for people in a particular group, "I am a member . . . we are members," the Passover as reported in Exodus begins as an act of special creation rather than as a practice on loan from another group or as a gradually developed evolution. What are the most important details of the Passover ritual in Exodus? Consider their appropriateness for the group that adopts them.

12. One of my favorite lines in Exodus is in the eleventh verse of chapter 14: "And they said unto Moses, Because there were no graves in Egypt, hast thou taken us away to die in the wilderness?" Now the complaint of the Israelites is serious; but their style is sardonically humorous. In books, what people say *and* how they say it is one way in which readers can know what those people are like. (This is also true in "real" or ordinary life, but we react so automatically that we hardly notice.) What does the writer of Exodus suggest about the Israelites in this sentence? What implications about their chances for survival occur to you from the suggestion?

3. Religion, Law, and Politics: Moses

She stood holding the glass and I saw Robert Cohn look at her. He looked a great deal as his compatriot must have looked when he saw the promised land. Cohn, of course, was younger.
ERNEST HEMINGWAY, *The Sun Also Rises*

Although the legendary destination of Israel since Abraham has been "Canaan," and although God promised that land "flowing with milk and honey" to Moses from the burning bush in Midian, the Israelites, when they left Egypt, did not take a direct route to the promised land. As a matter of fact, they did not move into Canaan until about forty years after the first Passover. Moses himself never set foot there. Most of the book of Exodus and the books of Leviticus, Numbers, and Deuteronomy °are historical reports about those forty years. They contain narrative episodes, the great "adventures" of Israel on the journey, but the reader will find increasingly that they are not in the simple chronological sequence of earlier parts of the Bible and that they are overwhelmed in bulk by vast stretches of nonnarrative historical materials. These are for the most part descriptive documents dealing in detail with the religious doctrines, the legal codes, and the governmental policies of the new nation.

In this introduction to the study of Old Testament literature, we will concern ourselves principally with *events* when we consider these historical books. But we should note that the common theme of the narrative fragments is also that of the mass of instruction we will only touch on. That theme is the molding of an itinerant horde of ignorant nomads into a civilized, settled nation. The forty years of gypsy wandering is for the tribes of Israel a period of educational discipline. Beset on the way by other peoples who fear or dislike them, by thirst and by famine, by all the internal weaknesses that human beings suffer from as individuals and in groups, the Israelites finally do reach Canaan with a body of laws to govern them. This is, in effect, a constitution, a blueprint of common beliefs, shared ritual, and codified ethical practices and techniques. It is a hard come-by code, but it is indispensable for their destiny.

Unfortunately, as we know, the existence of a national constitution is no guarantee of a universal adherence to it. During the forty years of wandering and even after they have entered Canaan, various in-

---

° By legend, these four books, along with Genesis, have been ascribed to the authorship of Moses himself and grouped under the title of The Pentateuch (five books).

dividuals and groups of Israelites fall away from their national principles and policies. The consequences of such defections are always bad. The Biblical writers look upon these consequences, which take such forms as military defeats, plagues, and captivities, as the justice of the Lord.

In our times we should be conscious of the special vulnerabilities of constitutional government as well as appreciative of its special advantages. As in the times of ancient Israel, there is always the temptation to sacrifice the advantages of it in order to avoid the perils. The great advantage is, of course, individual liberty and the consequence that every human being may function as a fully responsible person. Laws exist; I can choose to obey them or take the consequences. If enough people choose *not* to obey them, however, or if those in charge of enforcing them do not enforce them, chaos appears to be the inevitable social consequence. As the Eden myth of Genesis proclaims, and most readers of today's newspapers would agree, men seem to be afflicted with a strong tendency to disobey laws on the one hand and not to enforce them on the other. The perverse inclination of a "free" society to be indifferent to its codes is the main vulnerability of constitutional government or government by law.

Now most of the countries with which ancient Israel came in contact in the Bible knew no such vulnerability. They never conceived of a body of laws or principles beyond the manipulation of men. They did not burden their peoples with the choice of obeying such laws or taking certain consequences. The decisions, whims, and inclinations of kings directed what their subjects should do or think. Instead of a body of ordinances established by an invisible moral power beyond man, like the God of Moses, subjects of such kingdoms enjoyed the services of a visible god who commanded them minute by minute. Their choice was limited to mindless obedience or rebellion. For obvious reasons they seldom chose the latter. With something very like this sort of political organization in the twentieth century, Mussolini made the trains run on time and Hitler overran most of Europe. This nonconstitutional sort of society appeals to a human yen for functional efficiency as well as for avoiding responsibility. Of course, to enjoy these apparent advantages of ease and efficiency mankind must regard other men—kings, pharaohs, dictators—as though they were gods.

It would appear that this nonconstitutional sort of society, ruled by the "king-as-god," is the earliest of human political structures. Whether or not such a constitutional government as Israel's came later than such nonconstitutional governments as, say, Egypt's, it is certain that in the Bible, as in recent history, the old cry, "Give us a king," goes up when a government of laws is corrupted by its people.

In Biblical literature, the difference between the constitutional structure of ancient Israel and the totalitarian organizations of the nations around it is essentially religious. The constitution of Israel, we must remember, did not emerge from a convention of rational gentlemen trying to be detached from merely personal concerns in an attempt to find workable socio-political compromises. The constitution of ancient Israel is an article of religious conviction; Israel believes that it comes from God Himself.

The totalitarian nations of the ancient world had, of course, other gods than their kings, but the gods of the ancient nations ruled by kings without law embody very different conceptions of divinity from the God of Moses. For one thing, they are not jealously exclusive. They don't seem to take it personally if people switch their interests and worship from one to another. They don't appear much interested in politics and are available for ceremonial use by anyone who happens to be in charge. They like sacrifices to themselves and payments to their priests, but they are not concerned with standards of good or bad behavior or with justice. They represent mysterious forces in life like fertility, the fortunes of war, death, and the weather, and are thus worth trying to propitiate to the peoples who acknowledge them. If a man is lucky, such gods may be said to be on his side, but this in no way means that they approve of his obedience to any standard of law or morality. They are the ideal sorts of divinity for a society organized with the "king as god." They are absolutely intolerable sorts for a society organized with *God as king*.

Exodus

15:22 So Moses brought Israel from the Red sea, and they went out into the wilderness of Shur; and they went three days in the wilderness, and found no
23 water. And when they came to Marah, they could not drink of the waters of Marah, for they were bitter: therefore the name of it was called Marah.
24 And the people murmured against Moses, saying, What shall we drink?
25 And he cried unto the Lord; and the Lord showed him a tree, which when he had cast into the waters, the waters were made sweet: . . .
27 And they came to Elim, where were twelve wells of water, and three-score and ten palm trees: and they encamped there by the waters.

16 And they took their journey from Elim, and all the congregation of the children of Israel came unto the wilderness of Sin, which is between Elim and Sinai, on the fifteenth day of the second month after their departing out
2 of the land of Egypt. And the whole congregation of the children of Israel
3 murmured against Moses and Aaron in the wilderness: And the children of Israel said unto them, Would to God we had died by the hand of the Lord in the land of Egypt, when we sat by the fleshpots, and when we did eat bread to the full; for ye have brought us forth into this wilderness, to kill this whole assembly with hunger.
4 Then said the Lord unto Moses, Behold, I will rain bread from heaven for you; and the people shall go out and gather a certain rate every day, that I
5 may prove them, whether they will walk in my law, or no. And it shall come to pass, that on the sixth day they shall prepare that which they bring
11 in; and it shall be twice as much as they gather daily. And the Lord spake
12 unto Moses, saying, I have heard the murmurings of the children of Israel: speak unto them, saying, At even ye shall eat flesh, and in the morning ye shall be filled with bread; and ye shall know that I am the Lord your God.
13 And it came to pass, that at even the quails came up, and covered the
14 camp: and in the morning the dew lay round about the host. And when the dew that lay was gone up, behold, upon the face of the wilderness there lay
15 a small round thing, as small as the hoar frost on the ground. And when the children of Israel saw it, they said one to another, It is manna: for they wist not what it was. And Moses said unto them, This is the bread which the Lord hath given you to eat.
19,20 And Moses said, Let no man leave of it till the morning. Notwithstanding they hearkened not unto Moses; but some of them left of it until the morning,
21 and it bred worms, and stank: and Moses was wroth with them. And they gathered it every morning, every man according to his eating: and when the sun waxed hot, it melted.
27 And it came to pass, that there went out some of the people on the seventh
28 day for to gather, and they found none. And the Lord said unto Moses, How
29 long refuse ye to keep my commandments and my laws? See, for that the Lord hath given you the sabbath, therefore he giveth you on the sixth day the bread of two days: abide ye every man in his place, let no man go out of
30 his place on the seventh day. So the people rested on the seventh day.
31 And the house of Israel called the name thereof Manna: and it was like

coriander seed, white; and the taste of it was like wafers made with honey.

35 And the children of Israel did eat manna forty years, until they came to a land inhabited: they did eat manna, until they came unto the borders of the land of Canaan.

17   And all the congregation of the children of Israel journeyed from the
3 wilderness of Sin, after their journeys, . . . And the people thirsted there for water; and the people murmured against Moses, and said, Wherefore is this that thou hast brought us up out of Egypt, to kill us and our children and
4 our cattle with thirst? And Moses cried unto the Lord, saying, What shall I do unto this people? they be almost ready to stone me.
5   And the Lord said unto Moses, Go on before the people, and take with thee of the elders of Israel; and thy rod, wherewith thou smotest the river,
6 take in thine hand, and go. Behold, I will stand before thee there upon the rock in Horeb; and thou shalt smite the rock, and there shall come water out of it, that the people may drink. And Moses did so in the sight of the elders of Israel.

18   When Jethro, the priest of Midian, Moses' father-in-law, heard of all that God had done for Moses, and for Israel his people, and that the Lord
5 had brought Israel out of Egypt; And Jethro, Moses' father-in-law, came with his sons and his wife unto Moses into the wilderness, where he
6 encamped at the mount of God: And he said unto Moses, I thy father-in-law
7 Jethro am come unto thee, and thy wife, and her two sons with her. And Moses went out to meet his father-in-law, and did obeisance, and kissed him;
8 and they asked each other of their welfare; and they came into the tent. And Moses told his father-in-law all that the Lord had done unto Pharaoh and to the Egyptians for Israel's sake, and all the travail that had come upon them by the way, and how the Lord delivered them.
9   And Jethro rejoiced for all the goodness which the Lord had done to
10 Israel, whom he had delivered out of the hand of the Egyptians. And Jethro said, Blessed be the Lord, who hath delivered you out of the hand of the Egyptians, and out of the hand of Pharaoh, who hath delivered the people
11 from under the hand of the Egyptians. Now I know that the Lord is greater than all gods: for in the thing wherein they dealt proudly he was above them.
12 And Jethro, Moses' father-in-law, took a burnt offering and sacrifices for God: and Aaron came, and all the elders of Israel, to eat bread with Moses' father-in-law before God.
13   And it came to pass on the morrow, that Moses sat to judge the people:
14 and the people stood by Moses from the morning unto the evening. And when Moses' father-in-law saw all that he did to the people, he said, What is this thing that thou doest to the people? Why sittest thou thyself alone,
15 and all the people stand by thee from morning unto even? And Moses said unto his father-in-law, Because the people come unto me to inquire of God:
16 When they have a matter, they come unto me; and I judge between one and another, and I do make them know the statutes of God, and his laws.
17   And Moses' father-in-law said unto him, The thing that thou doest is not
18 good. Thou wilt surely wear away, both thou, and this people that is with thee: for this thing is too heavy for thee; thou art not able to perform it
19 thyself alone. Hearken now unto my voice, I will give thee counsel, and God
21 shall be with thee: . . . Moreover thou shalt provide out of all the people

Introduction to Biblical Literature

able men, such as fear God, men of truth, hating covetousness; and place such over them, to be rulers of thousands, and rulers of hundreds, rulers of

22 fifties, and rulers of tens: And let them judge the people at all seasons: and it shall be, that every great matter they shall bring unto thee, but every small matter they shall judge: so shall it be easier for thyself, and they shall bear

23 the burden with thee. If thou shalt do this thing, and God command thee so, then thou shalt be able to endure, and all this people shall also go to their place in peace.

24 So Moses hearkened to the voice of his father-in-law, and did all that he

25 had said. And Moses chose able men out of all Israel, and made them heads over the people, rulers of thousands, rulers of hundreds, rulers of fifties, and

26 rulers of tens. And they judged the people at all seasons: the hard causes they

27 brought unto Moses, but every small matter they judged themselves. And Moses let his father-in-law depart; and he went his way into his own land.

19 In the third month, when the children of Israel were gone forth out of the

2 land of Egypt, the same day came they into the wilderness of Sinai. . . . and

3 there Israel camped before the mount. And Moses went up unto God, and the Lord called unto him out of the mountain, saying, Thus shalt thou say

4 to the house of Jacob, and tell the children of Israel; Ye have seen what I did unto the Egyptians, and how I bare you on eagles' wings, and brought

5 you unto myself. Now therefore, if ye will obey my voice indeed, and keep my covenant, then ye shall be a peculiar treasure unto me above all people:

6 for all the earth is mine: And ye shall be unto me a kingdom of priests, and a holy nation. These are the words which thou shalt speak unto the children of Israel.

7 And Moses came and called for the elders of the people, and laid before

8 their faces all these words which the Lord commanded him. And all the people answered together, and said, All that the Lord hath spoken we will

9 do. And Moses returned the words of the people unto the Lord. And the Lord said unto Moses, Lo, I come unto thee in a thick cloud, that the people may hear when I speak with thee, and believe thee for ever. And Moses told the words of the people unto the Lord.

10 And the Lord said unto Moses, Go unto the people, and sanctify them

11 to-day and to-morrow, and let them wash their clothes, And be ready against the third day: for the third day the Lord will come down in the sight of all

12 the people upon mount Sinai. And thou shalt set bounds unto the people round about, saying, Take heed to yourselves, that ye go not up into the mount, or touch the border of it: whosoever toucheth the mount shall be

13 surely put to death: There shall not a hand touch it, but he shall surely be stoned, or shot through; whether it be beast or man, it shall not live: when the trumpet soundeth long, they shall come up to the mount.

14 And Moses went down from the mount unto the people, and sanctified

15 the people; and they washed their clothes. And he said unto the people, Be

16 ready against the third day: come not at your wives. And it came to pass on the third day in the morning, that there were thunders and lightnings, and a thick cloud upon the mount, and the voice of the trumpet exceeding loud;

17 so that all the people that was in the camp trembled. And Moses brought forth the people out of the camp to meet with God; and they stood at the

18 nether part of the mount. And mount Sinai was altogether on a smoke, be-

From the History of Ancient Israel

cause the Lord descended upon it in fire: and the smoke thereof ascended as

19 the smoke of a furnace, and the whole mount quaked greatly. And when the voice of the trumpet sounded long, and waxed louder and louder, Moses spake, and God answered him by a voice.

20 And the Lord came down upon mount Sinai, on the top of the mount: and

24 the Lord called Moses up to the top of the mount; and Moses went up. And the Lord said unto him, Away, get thee down, and thou shalt come up, thou, and Aaron with thee: but let not the priests and the people break through

25 to come up unto the Lord, lest he break forth upon them. So Moses went down unto the people, and spake unto them.

20:1,2 And God spake all these words, saying, I am the Lord thy God, which have brought thee out of the land of Egypt, out of the house of bondage.

3 Thou shalt have no other gods before me.

4 Thou shalt not make unto thee any graven image, or any likeness of any thing that is in heaven above, or that is in the earth beneath, or that is in the

5 water under the earth: Thou shalt not bow down thyself to them, nor serve them: for I the Lord thy God am a jealous God, visiting the iniquity of the fathers upon the children unto the third and fourth generation of them that

6 hate me; And showing mercy unto thousands of them that love me, and keep my commandments.

7 Thou shalt not take the name of the Lord thy God in vain: for the Lord will not hold him guiltless that taketh his name in vain.

8,9 Remember the sabbath day, to keep it holy. Six days shalt thou labor,

10 and do all thy work: But the seventh day is the sabbath of the Lord thy God: in it thou shalt not do any work, thou, nor thy son, nor thy daughter, thy manservant, nor thy maidservant, nor thy cattle, nor thy stranger that is

11 within thy gates: For in six days the Lord made heaven and earth, the sea, and all that in them is, and rested the seventh day: wherefore the Lord blessed the sabbath day, and hallowed it.

12 Honor thy father and thy mother: that thy days may be long upon the land which the Lord thy God giveth thee.

13 Thou shalt not kill.

14 Thou shalt not commit adultery.

15 Thou shalt not steal.

16 Thou shalt not bear false witness against thy neighbor.

17 Thou shalt not covet thy neighbor's house, thou shalt not covet thy neighbor's wife, nor his manservant, nor his maidservant, nor his ox, nor his ass, nor any thing that is thy neighbor's.

18 And all the people saw the thunderings, and the lightnings, and the noise of the trumpet, and the mountain smoking: and when the people saw it, they

19 removed, and stood afar off. And they said unto Moses, Speak thou with us, and we will hear: but let not God speak with us, lest we die.

20 And Moses said unto the people, Fear not: for God is come to prove you,

21 and that his fear may be before your faces, that ye sin not. And the people stood afar off, and Moses drew near unto the thick darkness where God was.

22 And the Lord said unto Moses, Thus thou shalt say unto the children of

23 Israel, Ye have seen that I have talked with you from heaven. Ye shall not make with me gods of silver, neither shall ye make unto you gods of gold.

24 An altar of earth thou shalt make unto me, and shalt sacrifice thereon thy burnt offerings, and thy peace offerings, thy sheep, and thine oxen: in all

places where I record my name I will come unto thee, and I will bless thee.
25 And if thou wilt make me an altar of stone, thou shalt not build it of hewn stone: for if thou lift up thy tool upon it, thou hast polluted it.

32   And when the people saw that Moses delayed to come down out of the mount, the people gathered themselves together unto Aaron, and said unto him, Up, make us gods, which shall go before us; for as for this Moses, the man that brought us up out of the land of Egypt, we wot not what is become
2 of him. And Aaron said unto them, Break off the golden earrings, which are in the ears of your wives, of your sons, and of your daughters, and bring
3 them unto me. And all the people brake off the golden earrings which were
4 in their ears, and brought them unto Aaron. And he received them at their hand, and fashioned it with a graving tool, after he had made it a molten calf: and they said, These be thy gods, O Israel, which brought thee up out of the
5 land of Egypt. And when Aaron saw it, he built an altar before it; and Aaron
6 made proclamation, and said, To-morrow is a feast to the Lord. And they rose up early on the morrow, and offered burnt offerings, and brought peace offerings; and the people sat down to eat and to drink, and rose up to play.
7   And the Lord said unto Moses, Go, get thee down; for thy people, which
8 thou broughtest out of the land of Egypt, have corrupted themselves: They have turned aside quickly out of the way which I commanded them: they have made them a molten calf, and have worshipped it, and have sacrificed thereunto, and said, These be thy gods, O Israel, which have brought thee
9 up out of the land of Egypt. And the Lord said unto Moses, I have seen this
10 people, and, behold, it is a stiffnecked people: Now therefore let me alone, that my wrath may wax hot against them, and that I may consume them: and I will make of thee a great nation.
11   And Moses besought the Lord his God, and said, Lord, why doth thy wrath wax hot against thy people, which thou hast brought forth out of the
12 land of Egypt with great power, and with a mighty hand? Wherefore should the Egyptians speak, and say, For mischief did he bring them out, to slay them in the mountains, and to consume them from the face of the earth?
13 Turn from thy fierce wrath, and repent of this evil against thy people. Remember Abraham, Isaac, and Israel, thy servants, to whom thou swarest by thine own self, and saidst unto them, I will multiply your seed as the stars of heaven, and all this land that I have spoken of will I give unto your seed,
14 and they shall inherit it for ever. And the Lord repented of the evil which he thought to do unto his people.
15   And Moses turned, and went down from the mount, and the two tables of the testimony were in his hand: the tables were written on both their
16 sides; on the one side and on the other were they written. And the tables were the work of God, and the writing was the writing of God, graven upon
17 the tables. And when Joshua heard the noise of the people as they shouted,
18 he said unto Moses, There is a noise of war in the camp. And he said, It is not the voice of them that shout for mastery, neither is it the voice of them that cry for being overcome; but the noise of them that sing do I hear.
19   And it came to pass, as soon as he came nigh unto the camp, that he saw the calf, and the dancing: and Moses' anger waxed hot, and he cast the
20 tables out of his hands, and brake them beneath the mount. And he took the calf which they had made, and burnt it in the fire, and ground it to powder, and strewed it upon the water, and made the children of Israel drink of it.

From the History of Ancient Israel

21 And Moses said unto Aaron, What did this people unto thee, that thou
22 hast brought so great a sin upon them? And Aaron said, Let not the anger
of my lord wax hot: thou knowest the people, that they are set on mischief.
23 For they said unto me, Make us gods, which shall go before us: for as for
this Moses, the man that brought us up out of the land of Egypt, we wot not
24 what is become of him. And I said unto them, Whosoever hath any gold, let
them break it off. So they gave it me: then I cast it into the fire, and there
came out this calf.
30 And it came to pass on the morrow, that Moses said unto the people, Ye
have sinned a great sin: and now I will go up unto the Lord; peradventure
31 I shall make an atonement for your sin. And Moses returned unto the Lord,
and said, Oh, this people have sinned a great sin, and have made them gods
32 of gold. Yet now, if thou wilt forgive their sin —; and if not, blot me, I pray
thee, out of thy book which thou hast written.
33 And the Lord said unto Moses, Whosoever hath sinned against me, him
34 will I blot out of my book. Therefore now go, lead the people unto the place
of which I have spoken unto thee: behold, mine Angel shall go before thee:
35 nevertheless, in the day when I visit, I will visit their sin upon them. And
the Lord plagued the people, because they made the calf, which Aaron made.

Deuteronomy

34 And Moses went up from the plains of Moab unto the mountain of Nebo,
to the top of Pisgah, that is over against Jericho: and the Lord showed him
2 all the land of Gilead, unto Dan, And all Naphtali, and the land of Ephraim,
3 and Manasseh, and all the land of Judah, unto the utmost sea, And the south,
4 and the plain of the valley of Jericho, the city of palm trees, unto Zoar. And
the Lord said unto him, This is the land which I sware unto Abraham, unto
Isaac, and unto Jacob, saying, I will give it unto thy seed: I have caused
thee to see it with thine eyes, but thou shalt not go over thither.
5 So Moses the servant of the Lord died there in the land of Moab, according
6 to the word of the Lord. And he buried him in a valley in the land of Moab,
over against Beth-peor: but no man knoweth of his sepulchre unto this day.
7 And Moses was a hundred and twenty years old when he died: his eye was
8 not dim, nor his natural force abated. And the children of Israel wept for
Moses in the plains of Moab thirty days: so the days of weeping and mourning for Moses were ended.
10 And there arose not a prophet since in Israel like unto Moses, whom the
11 Lord knew face to face, In all the signs and the wonders which the Lord
sent him to do in the land of Egypt, to Pharaoh, and to all his servants, and
12 to all his land, And in all that mighty hand, and in all the great terror which
Moses showed in the sight of all Israel.

Considerations and Questions

1. "Manna" is another Biblical term that has become a figure of standard English speech generally understood by many who have never read Exodus 16. Not "generally," but *exactly,* what would you mean if you said, "That twenty dollars was like manna from heaven"?
2. In the course of Exodus 16 we find indications that, understandably, the Israelites still have the idea that the whim and power of Moses himself are the ultimate authorities controlling their existence. What are these indications? What events in this episode demonstrate that Moses does not in fact control the manna?
3. What, according to Moses in chapter 18, are the terms in which he administers justice to the people "from the morning unto the evening"? What is his father-in-law's recommendation and what is his immediate reason for making it? Why is Jethro's recommendation applicable to Moses as it would not be to a king who acknowledged no other principle than his own will?
4. On the other hand, what aspect of the judicial system suggested by Jethro does maintain the authority of Moses over the people? How do events in chapter 19 serve to reinforce and increase that authority?
5. Moses tells the assembled people that the Lord has given them evidence of His reality and of His concern for them. What is that evidence? What else does the Lord propose to do for them? Under what conditions? What is their response?
6. As students of Biblical literature we should commit to memory the Ten Commandments as they appear in Exodus 20. Having done so, we are in some position to see how this basic summary of law fits into what we are reading. If this seems too obvious for mention, let me challenge you to ask at random a few non-Bible readers what the Ten Commandments are. I think you will find that otherwise well-informed persons will give you such mistaken notions as these:

    (a) One of the Ten Commandments is that you should do unto others as you would have them do unto you.
    (b) Another is "Thou shalt not lie."
    (c) The Ten Commandments provide *complete* answers for every moral question which may confront all good Jews and Christians in every time and place.
    (d) The Ten Commandments are a "mystical" ideal rather than a practical legal code for a human society in this world.

7. With particular reference to notion (c) in question 6, scan the books of Leviticus, Numbers, and Deuteronomy in an unabridged Bible. What can you find that indicates the general or summary quality of the Ten Commandments—even for the Israel of Moses?

8. In our reading, Moses receives the Decalogue (the Ten Commandments) shortly after he has taken Jethro's advice about organizing a system of higher and lower courts in Israel. What reasonable connection can you determine between these two events?

9. Consider Exodus 32. What have the Israelites been up to while Moses is on Sinai receiving the Decalogue? Why? What is the ironic and dramatic relationship between what they are doing and what he is doing?

10. From the beginning of his biography we have seen two sides of Moses. He is a devoted, self-sacrificing man, and he is a harsh, unforgiving, violent man. How do these apparent contradictions in character manifest themselves when he comes down from Mt. Sinai to find the Israelites exalting a golden calf? One of the Commandments he brings with him is "Thou shalt not kill." How do you square that with his behavior on this occasion?

11. The episode of the golden calf is only one example of the problems Moses has in keeping the tribes of Israel faithfully united. All through the forty years between Egypt and Canaan they "murmur," complain, and rebel in various ways. It is their flaw and their strength that they are, as Moses characterizes them, "a stiff-necked people." Convinced of his own divine justification, Moses deals with all these defections successfully, sometimes with concessions but often with savage sternness. The theme of his life and a central attribute of his God is *justice*. For Moses, God owes the terms of His promise to His people: to preserve and cherish them. But the God of Moses owes these terms only to the extent that the people, on their side, fulfill their promise to obey Him and His commandments. Through Moses, these commandments have been thoroughly expounded; the Israelites cannot plead ignorance. Through Moses, the children have been divinely rescued, "as on eagles' wings," from Egypt; they cannot plead ignorance of the reality of their God. Under the guidance of Moses, they do, of course, keep the faith sufficiently to reach the borders of their promised Canaan. However, God has exacted just payment for their failures to meet their obligations. Moses himself is not exempt from the operations of divine justice. When the time comes for him to die, as we learn in Deuteronomy 34, Moses is permitted to see the promised land from the top of Mt. Pisgah, but because of a single failure in humility to the Lord, he is not permitted to go there.

Put in simple and nonreligious terms, the life of Moses as leader of Israel is dominated by the conviction that, for good and ill, all actions have their appropriate consequences. His parallel religious conviction is that this pattern of act and consequence reflects the will of a Supreme Goodness and that he must dedicate himself utterly to the service of that goodness. In what respects do you think that these convictions account for the greatness of Moses as (1) a prophet, (2) a religious teacher, and (3) a national leader?

12. Although the narrative makes clear that the death of Moses before the children of Israel actually reach Canaan is his just punishment, we should note that Deuteronomy also implies just rewards for the great prophet, priest, and leader. What are these?

4. The Holy Land: Joshua

But now it shall be seen that the Lord hath sanctified this wilderness for his peculiar people. Woe unto them that would defile it!

NATHANIEL HAWTHORNE, *The Maypole of Merry Mount*

The death of Moses within sight of Canaan but not within its borders is not only appropriate to the Mosaic conception of divine justice but dramatically appropriate as the culmination of the historical narrative of the Pentateuch. With Israel on the banks of Jordan, the work of the holy and terrible man "whom the Lord knew face to face" is done. Israel has its law and its identity, its faith and its discipline. To be a nation in the world all Israel now needs is land. Across the river the tough and hungry tribes can see the land which by legend, prophecy, and the divinely inspired words of Moses belongs to them. But that land is presently occupied by various petty city-kingdoms whose rulers are unconvinced of Israel's property rights. So the dirty work of conquest begins, and the day of the prophet, priest, and law-giver is superseded by the day of the soldier. Pre-eminent among these is Joshua, whose name is linked forever with the siege and fall of Jericho.

Joshua

1   Now after the death of Moses the servant of the Lord, it came to pass, that the Lord spake unto Joshua the son of Nun, Moses' minister, saying,

2 Moses my servant is dead; now therefore arise, go over this Jordan, thou, and all this people, unto the land which I do give to them, even to the children

3 of Israel. Every place that the sole of your foot shall tread upon, that have

4 I given unto you, as I said unto Moses. From the wilderness and this Lebanon even unto the great river, the river Euphrates, all the land of the Hittites, and unto the great sea toward the going down of the sun, shall be your

5 coast. There shall not any man be able to stand before thee all the days of thy life: as I was with Moses, so I will be with thee: I will not fail thee, nor

9 forsake thee. Have not I commanded thee? Be strong and of a good courage; be not afraid, neither be thou dismayed: for the Lord thy God is with thee whithersoever thou goest.

10,11   Then Joshua commanded the officers of the people, saying, Pass through the host, and command the people, saying, Prepare you victuals; for within three days ye shall pass over this Jordan, to go in to possess the land, which the Lord your God giveth you to possess it.

2   And Joshua the son of Nun sent out of Shittim two men to spy secretly, saying, Go view the land, even Jericho. And they went, and came into a

2 harlot's house, named Rahab, and lodged there. And it was told the king of Jericho, saying, Behold, there came men in hither to-night of the children of

3 Israel to search out the country. And the king of Jericho sent unto Rahab, saying, Bring forth the men that are come to thee, which are entered into

4 thine house: for they be come to search out all the country. And the woman took the two men, and hid them, and said thus, There came men unto me,

5 but I wist not whence they were: And it came to pass about the time of shutting of the gate, when it was dark, that the men went out; whither the men went, I wot not: pursue after them quickly; for ye shall overtake them.

6 But she had brought them up to the roof of the house, and hid them with the

7 stalks of flax, which she had laid in order upon the roof. And the men pursued after them the way to Jordan unto the fords: and as soon as they which pursued after them were gone out, they shut the gate.

8   And before they were laid down, she came up unto them upon the roof;

9 And she said unto the men, I know that the Lord hath given you the land, and that your terror is fallen upon us, and that all the inhabitants of the land

12 faint because of you. Now therefore, I pray you, swear unto me by the Lord, since I have showed you kindness, that ye will also show kindness unto my

13 father's house, and give me a true token: And that ye will save alive my father, and my mother, and my brethren, and my sisters, and all that they have, and deliver our lives from death.

14   And the men answered her, Our life for yours, if ye utter not this our business. And it shall be, when the Lord hath given us the land, that we will

15 deal kindly and truly with thee. Then she let them down by a cord through the window: for her house was upon the town wall, and she dwelt upon the

16 wall. And she said unto them, Get you to the mountain, lest the pursuers

meet you; and hide yourselves there three days, until the pursuers be re-
17 turned: and afterward may ye go your way. And the men said unto her,
18 We will be blameless of this thine oath which thou hast made us swear. Behold, when we come into the land, thou shalt bind this line of scarlet thread
in the window which thou didst let us down by: and thou shalt bring thy
father, and thy mother, and thy brethren, and all thy father's household,
21 home unto thee. And she said, According unto your words, so be it. And she
sent them away, and they departed: and she bound the scarlet line in the
22 window. And they went, and came unto the mountain, and abode there three
days, until the pursuers were returned: and the pursuers sought them
throughout all the way, but found them not.

23 So the two men returned, and descended from the mountain, and passed
over, and came to Joshua the son of Nun, and told him all things that befell
24 them: And they said unto Joshua, Truly the Lord hath delivered into our
hands all the land; for even all the inhabitants of the country do faint because
of us.

3 And Joshua rose early in the morning; and they removed from Shittim,
and came to Jordan, he and all the children of Israel, and lodged there before
they passed over.

7 And the Lord said unto Joshua, This day will I begin to magnify thee in
the sight of all Israel, that they may know that, as I was with Moses, so I
8 will be with thee. And thou shalt command the priests that bear the ark of
the covenant, saying, When ye are come to the brink of the water of
Jordan, ye shall stand still in Jordan.

9 And Joshua said unto the children of Israel, Come hither, and hear the
10 words of the Lord your God. And Joshua said, Hereby ye shall know that
the living God is among you, and that he will without fail drive out from
before you the Canaanites, and the Hittites, and the Hivites, and the Periz-
11 zites, and the Girgashites, and the Amorites, and the Jebusites. Behold, the
ark of the covenant of the Lord of all the earth passeth over before you into
12 Jordan. Now therefore take you twelve men out of the tribes of Israel, out
13 of every tribe a man. And it shall come to pass, as soon as the soles of the
feet of the priests that bear the ark of the Lord, the Lord of all the earth,
shall rest in the waters of Jordan, that the waters of Jordan shall be cut off
from the waters that come down from above;   and they shall stand upon a
heap.

14 And it came to pass, when the people removed from their tents, to pass
over Jordan, and the priests bearing the ark of the covenant before the people;
15 And as they that bare the ark were come unto Jordan, and the feet of the
priests that bare the ark were dipped in the brim of the water, (for Jordan
16 overfloweth all his banks all the time of harvest,) That the waters which
came down from above stood and rose up upon a heap very far from the city
17 Adam. . . . And the priests that bare the ark of the covenant of the Lord
stood firm on dry ground in the midst of Jordan, and all the Israelites passed
over on dry ground, until all the people were passed clean over Jordan.
4:13 About forty thousand prepared for war passed over before the Lord unto
19 battle, to the plains of Jericho. . . . And the people came up out of Jordan on

the tenth day of the first month, and encamped in Gilgal, in the east border of Jericho.

5:13   And it came to pass, when Joshua was by Jericho, that he lifted up his eyes and looked, and, behold, there stood a man over against him with his sword drawn in his hand: and Joshua went unto him, and said unto him, Art thou

14   for us, or for our adversaries? And he said, Nay; but as captain of the host of the Lord am I now come. And Joshua fell on his face to the earth, and did

15   worship, and said unto him, What saith my lord unto his servant? And the captain of the Lord's host said unto Joshua, Loose thy shoe from off thy foot; for the place whereon thou standest is holy. And Joshua did so.

6   Now Jericho was straitly shut up because of the children of Israel: none

2   went out, and none came in. And the Lord said unto Joshua, See, I have given into thine hand Jericho, and the king thereof, and the mighty men of valor.

3   And ye shall compass the city, all ye men of war, and go round about the

4   city once. Thus shalt thou do six days. And seven priests shall bear before the ark seven trumpets of rams' horns: and the seventh day ye shall compass

5   the city seven times, and the priests shall blow with the trumpets. And it shall come to pass, that when they make a long blast with the ram's horn, and when ye hear the sound of the trumpet, all the people shall shout with a great shout; and the wall of the city shall fall down flat, and the people shall ascend up every man straight before him.

12   And Joshua rose early in the morning, and the priests took up the ark of

13   the Lord. And seven priests bearing seven trumpets of rams' horns before the ark of the Lord went on continually, and blew with the trumpets: and the armed men went before them; but the rearward came after the ark of the

14   Lord, the priests going on, and blowing with the trumpets. And the second day they compassed the city once, and returned into the camp. So they did

15   six days. And it came to pass on the seventh day, that they rose early about the dawning of the day, and compassed the city after the same manner seven times: only on that day they compassed the city seven times.

16   And it came to pass at the seventh time, when the priests blew with the trumpets, Joshua said unto the people, Shout; for the Lord hath given you

17   the city. And the city shall be accursed, even it, and all that are therein, to the Lord: only Rahab the harlot shall live, she and all that are with her in the

18   house, because she hid the messengers that we sent. And ye, in any wise keep yourselves from the accursed thing, lest ye make yourselves accursed, when ye take of the accursed thing, and make the camp of Israel a curse, and

19   trouble it. But all the silver, and gold, and vessels of brass and iron, are consecrated unto the Lord: they shall come into the treasury of the Lord.

20   So the people shouted when the priests blew with the trumpets: and it came to pass, when the people heard the sound of the trumpet, and the people shouted with a great shout, that the wall fell down   flat, so that the people went up into the city, every man straight before him, and they took the city.

21   And they utterly destroyed   all that was in the city, both man and woman,

24   young and old, and ox, and sheep, and ass, with the edge of the sword. And they burnt the city with fire, and all that was therein: only the silver, and the gold, and the vessels of brass and of iron, they put into the treasury of

From the History of Ancient Israel

25 the house of the Lord. And Joshua saved Rahab the harlot alive, and her father's household, and all that she had; and she dwelleth in Israel even unto this day; because she hid the messengers, which Joshua sent to spy out
27 Jericho. So the Lord was with Joshua; and his fame was noised throughout all the country.

7: 2 And Joshua sent men from Jericho to Ai, which is beside Beth-aven, on the east side of Beth-el, and spake unto them, saying, Go up and view the
3 country. And the men went up and viewed Ai. And they returned to Joshua, and said unto him, Let not all the people go up; but let about two or three thousand men go up and smite Ai; and make not all the people to labor
4 thither; for they are but few. So there went up thither of the people about
5 three thousand men; and they fled before the men of Ai. And the men of Ai smote of them about thirty and six men: for they chased them from before the gate even unto Shebarim, and smote them in the going down: wherefore the hearts of the people melted, and became as water.

6 And Joshua rent his clothes, and fell to the earth upon his face before the ark of the Lord until the eventide, he and the elders of Israel, and put dust
7 upon their heads. And Joshua said, Alas, O Lord God, wherefore hast thou at all brought this people over Jordan, to deliver us into the hand of the Amorites, to destroy us? would to God we had been content, and dwelt on
8 the other side Jordan! O Lord, what shall I say, when Israel turneth their
9 backs before their enemies! For the Canaanites and all the inhabitants of the land shall hear of it, and shall environ us round, and cut off our name from the earth: and what wilt thou do unto thy great name?

10 And the Lord said unto Joshua, Get thee up; wherefore liest thou thus
11 upon thy face? Israel hath sinned, and they have also transgressed my covenant which I commanded them: for they have even taken of the accursed thing, and have also stolen, and dissembled also, and they have put it even
13 among their own stuff. Up, sanctify the people, and say, Sanctify yourselves against to-morrow: for thus saith the Lord God of Israel, There is an accursed thing in the midst of thee, O Israel: thou canst not stand before thine enemies, until ye take away the accursed thing from among you.
14 In the morning therefore ye shall be brought according to your tribes: and it shall be, that the tribe which the Lord taketh shall come according to the families thereof; and the family which the Lord shall take shall come by households; and the household which the Lord shall take shall come man by
15 man. And it shall be, that he that is taken with the accursed thing shall be burnt with fire, he and all that he hath: because he hath transgressed the covenant of the Lord, and because he hath wrought folly in Israel.

16 So Joshua rose up early in the morning, and brought Israel by their tribes;
17 and the tribe of Judah was taken: And he brought the family of Judah; and he took the family of the Zarhites: and he brought the family of the Zarhites
18 man by man; and Zabdi was taken: And he brought his household man by man; and Achan, the son of Carmi, the son of Zabdi, the son of Zerah, of the tribe of Judah, was taken.

19 And Joshua said unto Achan, My son, give, I pray thee, glory to the Lord God of Israel, and make confession unto him; and tell me now what thou
20 hast done; hide it not from me. And Achan answered Joshua, and said, Indeed I have sinned against the Lord God of Israel, and thus and thus have I done:

21 When I saw among the spoils a goodly Babylonish garment, and two hundred shekels of silver, and a wedge of gold of fifty shekels weight, then I coveted them, and took them; and, behold, they are hid in the earth in the midst of my tent, and the silver under it. So Joshua sent messengers, and they ran

22
23 unto the tent; and, behold, it was hid in his tent, and the silver under it. And they took them out of the midst of the tent, and brought them unto Joshua, and unto all the children of Israel, and laid them out before the Lord.

24 And Joshua, and all Israel with him, took Achan the son of Zerah, and the silver, and the garment, and the wedge of gold, and his sons, and his daughters, and his oxen, and his asses, and his sheep, and his tent, and all that he

25 had: and they brought them unto the valley of Achor. And Joshua said, Why hast thou troubled us? the Lord shall trouble thee this day. And all Israel stoned him with stones, and burned them with fire, after they had stoned them with stones.

23 And it came to pass, a long time after that the Lord had given rest unto Israel from all their enemies round about, that Joshua waxed old and stricken

2 in age. And Joshua called for all Israel, and for their elders, and for their heads, and for their judges, and for their officers, and said unto them, I am

3 old and stricken in age: And ye have seen all that the Lord your God hath done unto all these nations because of you; for the Lord your God is he

4 that hath fought for you. Behold, I have divided unto you by lot these nations that remain, to be an inheritance for your tribes, from Jordan, with all

5 the nations that I have cut off, even unto the great sea westward. And the Lord your God, he shall expel them from before you, and drive them from out of your sight; and ye shall possess their land, as the Lord your God hath promised unto you.

6 Be ye therefore very courageous to keep and to do all that is written in the book of the law of Moses, that ye turn not aside therefrom to the right hand

7 or to the left; That ye come not among these nations, these that remain among you; neither make mention of the name of their gods, nor cause to

11 swear by them, neither serve them, nor bow yourselves unto them: Take

12 good heed therefore unto yourselves, that ye love the Lord your God. Else, if ye do in any wise go back, and cleave unto the remnant of these nations, even these that remain among you, and shall make marriages with them,

13 and go in unto them, and they to you: Know for a certainty that the Lord your God will no more drive out any of these nations from before you; but they shall be snares and traps unto you, and scourges in your sides, and thorns in your eyes, until ye perish from off this good land which the Lord your God hath given you.

14 And, behold, this day I am going the way of all the earth: and ye know in all your hearts and in all your souls, that not one thing hath failed of all the good things which the Lord your God spake concerning you; all are come to pass unto you, and not one thing hath failed thereof.

Considerations and Questions

1. The successor of Moses is also a religious leader to whom the Lord speaks. But there are significant differences between the religious attitudes of Joshua and of Moses. What do they appear to be? How might it be demonstrated that Joshua's rather simple ideas about his God are, in a practical sense, appropriate to the fighting soldier? °

2. Consider our selections about the battle of Jericho to be representative of the Book of Joshua's account of the conquest of Canaan in general. What appear to be the general conditions of this war? Who are "the enemy"? How are they organized? Where and how do armies seem to do their fighting?

3. How does Joshua's military professionalism appear in his preparations for the capture of Jericho? How does he get his troops ready to fight? How does he discover certain exploitable weaknesses in the enemy? How does he exploit these weaknesses?

4. The story of Rahab and the spies provides a realistic touch to what sometimes seems a rather idealized version of the battle of Jericho. The details of a prostitute's place in society and conditions of work are commonplace in world history. Why is the harlot Rahab a practical person for the espionage agents to deal with?

° A number of successful generals in history have had religious attitudes very like Joshua's. Stonewall Jackson and George S. Patton come to mind; both were, incidentally, staunch defenders of the Book of Joshua.

5. One of the Judges: Samson

Ask for this great deliverer now, and find him
Eyeless in Gaza, at the mill with slaves.
JOHN MILTON, *Samson Agonistes*

Theoretically, the "Judges" of the Book of Judges are successors to Moses and Joshua as the chief magistrates or chief justices of Israel. By Mosaic tradition, the judicial system suggested by Jethro administers Israel without the help of such executive and legislative authorities as we associate with democratic political structures. There is no congress of law-makers in Israel because the God of Moses has provided the completed Law. There is no executive head of state in Israel because the God of Moses Himself provides the enforcement of His Law. There is a nonpolitical priesthood, whose official function is to keep the lines open between the Israelites and the God who fulfills their legislative and executive functions. Positions of social and military leadership are filled as needs arise by those whose eminence, seniority, or abilities seem immediately appropriate for them. As a political ideal, the children of Israel bring with them to the bloody conquest of Canaan a remarkably pure and optimistic form of democracy. Note some of the principles on which it is based:

1. All members of all the tribes are equal before the law.
2. The only official government consists of servants to the law.
3. Society agrees that its laws have been demonstrated to be beyond moral or practical challenge.

Here is theory to solve the political problems of any nation, ancient or modern—if only theoretical principles were able to command compliance.

As we know too well, the ideal does not inevitably ensure the reality. It seems that in practice men do not always want to be equal before the law, to be without the convenience of kings, or to adhere to their own moral and rational standards. And as the Eden myth insists, men are inclined to do what they want to do.

What is remarkable is not that Israel, like every other society, falls short of its principles, but that Israel, unlike most other societies, does not quickly lose those principles entirely. Even in the times of Moses and Joshua we see "judges" exceeding judicial powers and practicing certain inequalities before the law. In the period of the Book of Judges such failures to live up to the ideal increase in number and importance. But somehow the strength and profundity of Israel's faith in its God and its unity are enough to ensure the continuing life of the nation.

The historical message of the Book of Judges is how challenges to the ideal of Israel multiplied after the tribes, under Joshua, established their precarious residence in Canaan. Although the Book of Joshua, and notably the battle of Jericho, would seem to suggest that the Israelites made a clean military sweep of the Canaan conquest, we see in Judges that this is clearly not the case. After significant victories and some defeats, what the Israelites actually managed to do was to establish themselves as one of the various peoples living in the promised land. Although it starts with Joshua's military operations, the domination of Canaan by the Israelites is not simply the result of armed conflict but of a long process. This process consists not only of battles but of accommodations, treaties, and bargains. At bottom, however, it is mainly a victory in a cultural endurance contest between Israel's codes and those of such other peoples in Canaan as the Moabites and Philistines.

Israel's pattern of belief and behavior is, of course, based on adherence to the God of Moses and the Law. In the contest for Canaan, Israel has the advantages and the disadvantages of being culturally unique. The other peoples of the region sacrifice for luck to various local gods whose interests are anything but universal and live in societies administered for the convenience and comfort of their kings. Israel, on the one hand, must stand out as particularly special and desirable by contrast. On the other hand, local "luck" (with fertility, for example) can seem very important to people living on the land, and absolute rulers do save people the pain and effort of making political and military decisions. Once Joshua has apportioned lands to the various tribes and once the former wandering shepherds are settled among other peoples, in cities and on farmlands, their religious and political unity comes seriously under pressure. Indeed, it is threatened with extinction.

The "judges" of the Book of Judges do little literal "judging." The author (or authors) of that book presents them as rallying points for Israel's survival—as battle leaders, priests, prophets, and individual heroes. The "plot" of Judges is a series of tidal actions. Israel in some sense falls away from the Lord and His Law. Israel is then punished by defeat, domination, or an "oppression" at the hands of another nation. Then the Lord raises up a "judge" who temporarily cleanses and strengthens Israel. As a historical development, the story of Judges is not uniformly hopeful. After the last "judge," Samuel, Israel demands and gets a king. Although this is surely a serious compromising of the Mosaic tradition, we will see that the monarchy of Israel is designed in theory to retain the essence of that tradition and to be significantly different from the monarchies of the surrounding despotisms.

The one episode from the Book of Judges that I have chosen

to include in this book is probably the most famous. It is also, I think, one of the least optimistic about the future of Israel's continuing identity as a free and vigorous society. It is the story of that particularly injudicious athlete, Samson. Selfish, bad-tempered, undisciplined, lustful, and rather stupid, nonetheless Samson "judged Israel in the days of the Philistines twenty years."

Judges

13   And the children of Israel did evil again in the sight of the Lord; and the
2 Lord delivered them into the hand of the Philistines forty years. And there
was a certain man of Zorah, of the family of the Danites, whose name was
3 Manoah; and his wife was barren, and bare not. And the angel of the Lord
appeared unto the woman, and said unto her, Behold now, thou art barren,
4 and bearest not: but thou shalt conceive, and bear a son. Now therefore beware, I pray thee, and drink not wine nor strong drink, and eat not any un-
5 clean thing: For, lo, thou shalt conceive, and bear a son; and no razor shall
come on his head: for the child shall be a Nazarite unto God from the womb:
24 and he shall begin to deliver Israel out of the hand of the Philistines. And the
woman bare a son, and called his name Samson: and the child grew, and the
25 Lord blessed him. And the Spirit of the Lord began to move him at times in
the camp of Dan between Zorah and Eshtaol.

14   And Samson went down to Timnath, and saw a woman in Timnath of the
2 daughters of the Philistines. And he came up, and told his father and his
mother, and said, I have seen a woman in Timnath of the daughters of the
3 Philistines: now therefore get her for me to wife. Then his father and his
mother said unto him, Is there never a woman among the daughters of thy
brethren, or among all my people, that thou goest to take a wife of the uncircumcised Philistines? And Samson said unto his father, Get her for me; for
4 she pleaseth me well. But his father and his mother knew not that it was of
the Lord, that he sought an occasion against the Philistines: for at that time
the Philistines had dominion over Israel.
5   Then went Samson down, and his father and his mother, to Timnath, and
came to the vineyards of Timnath: and, behold, a young lion roared against
6 him. And the Spirit of the Lord came mightily upon him, and he rent him as
he would have rent a kid, and he had nothing in his hand: but he told not his
7 father or his mother what he had done. And he went down, and talked with
the woman; and she pleased Samson well.
8   And after a time he returned to take her, and he turned aside to see the
carcass of the lion: and, behold, there was a swarm of bees and honey in the
9 carcass of the lion. And he took thereof in his hands, and went on eating, and
came to his father and mother, and he gave them, and they did eat: but he
10 told not them that he had taken the honey out of the carcass of the lion. So
his father went down unto the woman: and Samson made there a feast; for
so used the young men to do.
11   And it came to pass, when they saw him, that they brought thirty com-
12 panions to be with him. And Samson said unto them, I will now put forth a
riddle unto you: if ye can certainly declare it me within the seven days of the
feast, and find it out, then I will give you thirty sheets and thirty change of
13 garments: But if ye cannot declare it me, then shall ye give me thirty sheets
and thirty change of garments. And they said unto him, Put forth thy riddle,
14 that we may hear it. And he said unto them,

> Out of the eater came forth meat,
>   and out of the strong came forth sweetness.

And they could not in three days expound the riddle.

15 And it came to pass on the seventh day, that they said unto Samson's wife, Entice thy husband, that he may declare unto us the riddle, lest we burn thee and thy father's house with fire: have ye called us to take that we have? is it
16 not so? And Samson's wife wept before him, and said, Thou dost but hate me, and lovest me not: thou hast put forth a riddle unto the children of my people, and hast not told it me. And he said unto her, Behold, I have not told
17 it my father nor my mother, and shall I tell it thee? And she wept before him the seven days, while their feast lasted: and it came to pass on the seventh day, that he told her, because she lay sore upon him: and she told the riddle
18 to the children of her people. And the men of the city said unto him on the seventh day before the sun went down,

What is sweeter than honey?
and what is stronger than a lion?

And he said unto them,

If ye had not plowed with my heifer,
ye had not found out my riddle.

19 And the Spirit of the Lord came upon him, and he went down to Ashkelon, and slew thirty men of them, and took their spoil, and gave change of garments unto them which expounded the riddle. And his anger was kindled,
20 and he went up to his father's house. But Samson's wife was given to his companion, whom he had used as his friend.

15 But it came to pass within a while after, in the time of wheat harvest, that Samson visited his wife with a kid; and he said, I will go in to my wife into
2 the chamber. But her father would not suffer him to go in. And her father said, I verily thought that thou hadst utterly hated her; therefore I gave her to thy companion: is not her younger sister fairer than she? take her, I pray
3 thee, instead of her. And Samson said concerning them, Now shall I be more
4 blameless than the Philistines, though I do them a displeasure. And Samson went and caught three hundred foxes, and took firebrands, and turned tail to
5 tail, and put a firebrand in the midst between two tails. And when he had set the brands on fire, he let them go into the standing corn of the Philistines, and burnt up both the shocks, and also the standing corn, with the vineyards and olives.
6 Then the Philistines said, Who hath done this? And they answered, Samson, the son-in-law of the Timnite, because he had taken his wife, and given her to his companion. And the Philistines came up, and burnt her and her
7 father with fire. And Samson said unto them, Though ye have done this, yet
8 will I be avenged of you, and after that I will cease. And he smote them hip and thigh with a great slaughter: and he went down and dwelt in the top of the rock Etam.
9 Then the Philistines went up, and pitched in Judah, and spread themselves
10 in Lehi. And the men of Judah said, Why are ye come up against us? And they answered, To bind Samson are we come up, to do to him as he hath
11 done to us. Then three thousand men of Judah went to the top of the rock Etam, and said to Samson, Knowest thou not that the Philistines are rulers over us? what is this that thou hast done unto us? And he said unto them,
12 As they did unto me, so have I done unto them. And they said unto him, We

are come down to bind thee, that we may deliver thee into the hand of the Philistines. And Samson said unto them, Swear unto me, that ye will not fall
13 upon me yourselves. And they spake unto him, saying, No; but we will bind thee fast, and deliver thee into their hand: but surely we will not kill thee. And they bound him with two new cords, and brought him up from the rock.
14 And when he came unto Lehi, the Philistines shouted against him: and the Spirit of the Lord came mightily upon him, and the cords that were upon his arms became as flax that was burnt with fire, and his bands loosed from off
15 his hands. And he found a new jawbone of an ass, and put forth his hand,
16 and took it, and slew a thousand men therewith. And Samson said,

> With the jawbone of an ass, heaps upon heaps,
> with the jaw of an ass have I slain a thousand men.

17 And it came to pass, when he had made an end of speaking, that he cast away the jawbone out of his hand, and called that place Ramath-lehi.

16 Then went Samson to Gaza, and saw there a harlot, and went in unto her.
2 And it was told the Gazites, saying, Samson is come hither. And they compassed him in, and laid wait for him all night in the gate of the city, and were quiet all the night, saying, In the morning, when it is day, we shall kill him.
3 And Samson lay till midnight, and arose at midnight, and took the doors of the gate of the city, and the two posts, and went away with them, bar and all, and put them upon his shoulders, and carried them up to the top of a hill that is before Hebron.
4 And it came to pass afterward, that he loved a woman in the valley of
5 Sorek, whose name was Delilah. And the lords of the Philistines came up unto her, and said unto her, Entice him, and see wherein his great strength lieth, and by what means we may prevail against him, that we may bind him to afflict him: and we will give thee every one of us eleven hundred pieces of silver.
6 And Delilah said to Samson, Tell me, I pray thee, wherein thy great
7 strength lieth, and wherewith thou mightest be bound to afflict thee. And Samson said unto her, If they bind me with seven green withes that were
8 never dried, then shall I be weak, and be as another man. Then the lords of the Philistines brought up to her seven green withes which had not been
9 dried, and she bound him with them. Now there were men lying in wait, abiding with her in the chamber. And she said unto him, The Philistines be upon thee, Samson. And he brake the withes, as a thread of tow is broken when it toucheth the fire. So his strength was not known.
10 And Delilah said unto Samson, Behold, thou hast mocked me, and told me
11 lies: now tell me, I pray thee, wherewith thou mightest be bound. And he said unto her, If they bind me fast with new ropes that never were occupied,
12 then shall I be weak, and be as another man. Delilah therefore took new ropes, and bound him therewith, and said unto him, The Philistines be upon thee, Samson. And there were liers in wait abiding in the chamber. And he
13 brake them from off his arms like a thread. And Delilah said unto Samson, Hitherto thou hast mocked me, and told me lies: tell me wherewith thou mightest be bound. And he said unto her, If thou weavest the seven locks of
14 my head with the web. And she fastened it with the pin, and said unto him,

The Philistines be upon thee, Samson. And he awaked out of his sleep, and went away with the pin of the beam, and with the web.

15 And she said unto him, How canst thou say, I love thee, when thine heart is not with me? Thou hast mocked me these three times, and hast not told
16 me wherein thy great strength lieth. And it came to pass, when she pressed him daily with her words, and urged him, so that his soul was vexed unto
17 death; That he told her all his heart, and said unto her, There hath not come a razor upon mine head; for I have been a Nazarite unto God from my mother's womb: if I be shaven, then my strength will go from me, and I shall become weak, and be like any other man.

18 And when Delilah saw that he had told her all his heart, she sent and called for the lords of the Philistines, saying, Come up this once, for he hath showed me all his heart. Then the lords of the Philistines came up unto her, and
19 brought money in their hand. And she made him sleep upon her knees; and she called for a man, and she caused him to shave off the seven locks of his
20 head; and she began to afflict him, and his strength went from him. And she said, The Philistines be upon thee, Samson. And he awoke out of his sleep, and said, I will go out as at other times before, and shake myself. And he
21 wist not that the Lord was departed from him. But the Philistines took him, and put out his eyes, and brought him down to Gaza, and bound him with
22 fetters of brass; and he did grind in the prison house. Howbeit the hair of his head began to grow again after he was shaven.

23 Then the lords of the Philistines gathered them together for to offer a great sacrifice unto Dagon their god, and to rejoice: for they said, Our god hath
24 delivered Samson our enemy into our hand. And when the people saw him, they praised their god: for they said, Our god hath delivered into our hands
25 our enemy, and the destroyer of our country, which slew many of us. And it came to pass, when their hearts were merry, that they said, Call for Samson, that he may make us sport. And they called for Samson out of the prison
26 house; and he made them sport: and they set him between the pillars. And Samson said unto the lad that held him by the hand, Suffer me that I may feel
27 the pillars whereupon the house standeth, that I may lean upon them. Now the house was full of men and women; and all the lords of the Philistines were there; and there were upon the roof about three thousand men and women, that beheld while Samson made sport.

28 And Samson called unto the Lord, and said, O Lord God, remember me, I pray thee, and strengthen me, I pray thee, only this once, O God, that I may
29 be at once avenged of the Philistines for my two eyes. And Samson took hold of the two middle pillars upon which the house stood, and on which it was
30 borne up, of the one with his right hand, and of the other with his left. And Samson said, Let me die with the Philistines. And he bowed himself with all his might; and the house fell upon the lords, and upon all the people that were therein. So the dead which he slew at his death were more than they which
31 he slew in his life. Then his brethren and all the house of his father came down, and took him, and brought him up, and buried him between Zorah and Eshtaol in the buryingplace of Manoah his father. And he judged Israel twenty years.

From the History of Ancient Israel

Considerations and Questions

1. What is a Nazarite? ° How does Samson happen to be one?
2. Exactly what acts of violence does Samson perform against the Philistines? What are his motives?
3. On what occasion does Samson pray? What feeling inspires him to do so?
4. How is the reader of this story informed that Samson is officially a holy man and a Judge of Israel?
5. How is the reader informed of his *personal* characteristics?
6. Why do the men of Judah (a strong tribe of Israel) bind Samson and turn him over to the Philistines? On what terms does Samson allow them to do so?
7. What are the likenesses and differences among Samson's three involvements with women in this story?
8. In the first sentence of the story we learn that the children of Israel, having *again* done evil in the sight of the Lord, are oppressed for forty years by the Philistines. What, by intent and achievement, does Samson do to remedy this situation?
9. As a hero, Samson is a recognizable type in many folklores. He is one of those figures, neither statesman nor soldier, whose natural superiority allows him to stand up to some kind of oppressive establishment. Some popular heroes of this sort, Hercules, for example, are more like Samson than others. Many, like Robin Hood, are outlaws and admired as such. Others are simply wild men or mavericks whose natural wit and power show up the corruptions of a decadent ruling class. Some are actual historical figures whose biographies objectively considered would not support the roles assigned them by folklore. Others are purely "literary," brought into being by the imagination of storytellers. Whatever his provenance, however, each hero of this sort appeals because he presents the illusion, temporarily at least, that we common people can best the captains and the kings whose taxes impoverish and whose laws afflict us.

    The historical importance of these Samsonian popular heroes is generally not that they directly change the course of social, political, or economic events by their actions. It is rather that by becoming popular heroes and by remaining so in song and story they demonstrate the existence of group attitudes in particular times and places. The continuing "life" of Jesse James in the folklore particularly of Missouri and East Texas is not convincing historical evidence of how much that outlaw robbed the rich to give to the poor, but it is evidence about certain social and political attitudes current among a population.

° See Numbers 6.

The tales of Samson, Jesse James, Hercules, Robin Hood, and others of this ilk do not remain popular simply because each reflects a universal attitude of resistance to established authority. There are also some standard character traits among these heroes which appear to have had mass appeal over the centuries of our recorded civilization. Consider whether the following apply to Samson and to any of his folklore relatives you may be familiar with.

(a) Most such heroes possess one particular ability in which they far surpass anyone around them.

(b) They are frequently "rascals" who entertain us by tricking their enemies—and sometimes their friends.

(c) Very often they are also rascals in their disregard of local proprieties, particularly property rights and sexual ethics. Their stories are generally told, however, in such a style that the audience is not invited to disapprove seriously of these shortcomings, if at all.

(d) They are self-directed, willful individuals who, for good or ill, make their own decisions and follow them through despite advice or warning. Such decisions are generally impulsive since these heroes are not given to extended contemplation of consequences.

(e) Often the stories about their lineage, birth, or infancy contain strange or marvelous details which may suggest that they are destined for the roles they play.

(f) In the end such heroes are betrayed by people they trust.

(g) They are primitives: childlike and childish, trusting and untrustworthy, innocent and homicidal, romantic and unrestrained, attractive and dangerous.

10. What, on the other hand, are Samson's credentials as a hero of Biblical literature? The folklore hero we have considered is simple and universal. He is heroic simply because he acts as most people would like to act at times but cannot because they are unable or afraid. Although the author of the Samson tale clearly exploits the appeal of this sort of hero, it seems equally clear that to do so is not his main intention. That intention, like that of the other Old Testament writers, is to depict the revelation of Israel's God to Israel and the historical consequences of that revelation.

Is there not something seriously comic about the role of Samson as a protagonist for such a theme? In some ways the career of our muscular "judge" seems almost a parody of that of his great predecessor, Moses. Moses speaks with the Lord face to face; Samson's only theophanic contacts are through his mother and father. Moses obeys the word of the Lord against his own fearful inclinations; Samson never obeys anyone and is apparently incapable of reasonable fear or any inclinations but the most immediate physical ones. Moses works unceasingly for the unity of Israel; as a marrying man and a brawler, Samson, without apparently working at all, contributes to just the opposite. Moses makes a solemn historical covenant with the Lord in behalf of his people; Samson asks God for a last surge of strength so that he can be revenged for his lost eyesight. Intensely religious, Moses makes his God the public reference point for all his actions; Samson gives God credit for none of his exploits. The rectitude of Moses staunchly counteracts the pressures of emotion or sentiment; sexual desire and irritation easily and invariably overcome any principles that Samson may have. Moses gives and, in detail, explains the Law; Samson is either unaware of or simply disregards the Law. Moses composes songs in praise of the Lord and His deliverance of Israel; Samson tosses off riddles and barnyard sayings. The life of Moses, in spite of certain incongruous episodes, is serious and lofty; the life of Samson, in spite of its spectacular ending, is really rather funny. Moses is a mighty man of God; Samson is a mighty buffoon.

It has been said that, among other things, comedy is a criticism of life. Certainly the comic literary artist puts his focus on the follies rather than on the greatnesses of man. Can this be part of what the writer of the Samson tale is up to in Judges? Or do you think that the writer takes Samson seriously as a great hero of Israel? What appears to be the state of the nation in the Samson story? From the writer's point of view does the Lord *need* great men (like Moses) in order to preserve His people? What are the implications of *that?*

6. The Last of the Judges: Samuel

Thou setter up and plucker down of kings.
WILLIAM SHAKESPEARE, *Henry VI, Part III*

Significantly, Samuel is a priest and a prophet, a learned man of moral courage and firm character. He is everything, in fact, that Samson is not. The plight of Israel, however, is as bad at the beginning of Samuel's judgeship as it was during Samson's. In some respects the situation is worse. The Philistines have become more persistent and powerful as oppressors; the Israelites less unified and more disillusioned. It appears that the longer the tribes inhabit their promised land of Canaan, the less effective are their unique political and religious practices. Surrounding nations, ruled by autocratic kings and their professional captains, beat Israel's amateur armies. Religious and moral patterns have weakened with the lack of central authority. Israel's judicial system has lost popular confidence; some judges, like Samson, are incompetent, and many others are corrupt.

One encouraging sign for Israel in Samuel's time is, ironically, the dissatisfaction and disillusionment of its people. At least the Israelites at this point do not shrug apathetic shoulders and mutter, "Well, that is the way things are, and that is the way they have to be." They are not cheered up by folk tales of exhibitionist heroes who kill thousands of Philistines on individual occasions. They object to the corrupted clergy and dishonest judges who dissipate their national integrity. They object to having their lands, possessions, liberties, and the sacred Ark of the Covenant itself taken from them by uncircumsized Philistines. This is *not*, they cry, the way things are supposed to be.

No doubt the existence of such dissatisfaction throughout the disorganized nation has a good deal to do with the rise and rule of the honest reformer, Samuel. He must seem to many like a new Moses, sternly dedicated to the Law of the Lord. Like Moses also, he is a mystic who does not hesitate to ·announce the results of his personal confrontations with God. He becomes high judge of Israel, officially or otherwise its high priest, and, most important, the one leader whom the various tribes unite in trusting.

But, of course, Samuel is not Moses and he is dealing with problems more complex than those of a single band of families on the trail from Goshen to Sinai to Canaan. And his time must run out. As we pick up the narrative, Samuel is aging; the worried people are bitterly aware there is no other leader of genius and integrity who can take his place when he dies.

I Samuel

8   And it came to pass, when Samuel was old, that he made his sons judges
2 over Israel. Now the name of his firstborn was Joel; and the name of his
3 second, Abiah: they were judges in Beer-sheba. And his sons walked not in
his ways, but turned aside after lucre, and took bribes, and perverted judg-
4 ment. Then all the elders of Israel gathered themselves together, and came
5 to Samuel unto Ramah, And said unto him, Behold, thou art old, and thy
sons walk not in thy ways: now make us a king to judge us like all the
nations.
6   But the thing displeased Samuel, when they said, Give us a king to judge
7 us. And Samuel prayed unto the Lord. And the Lord said unto Samuel,
Hearken unto the voice of the people in all that they say unto thee: for they
have not rejected thee, but they have rejected me, that I should not reign
8 over them. According to all the works which they have done since the day
that I brought them up out of Egypt even unto this day, wherewith they
9 have forsaken me, and served other gods, so do they also unto thee. Now
therefore hearken unto their voice: howbeit yet protest solemnly unto them,
and show them the manner of the king that shall reign over them.
10   And Samuel told all the words of the Lord unto the people that asked of
11 him a king. And he said, This will be the manner of the king that shall reign
over you: He will take your sons, and appoint them for himself, for his
12 chariots, and to be his horsemen; and some shall run before his chariots. And
he will appoint him captains over thousands, and captains over fifties; and
will set them to ear his ground, and to reap his harvest, and to make his in-
13 struments of war, and instruments of his chariots. And he will take your
14 daughters to be confectionaries, and to be cooks, and to be bakers. And he
will take your fields, and your vineyards, and your oliveyards, even the best
15 of them, and give them to his servants. And he will take the tenth of your
16 seed, and of your vineyards, and give to his officers, and to his servants. And
he will take your menservants, and your maidservants, and your goodliest
17 young men, and your asses, and put them to his work. He will take the tenth
18 of your sheep: and ye shall be his servants. And ye shall cry out in that day
because of your king which ye shall have chosen you; and the Lord will not
hear you in that day.
19   Nevertheless the people refused to obey the voice of Samuel; and they
20 said, Nay; but we will have a king over us; That we also may be like all the
nations; and that our king may judge us, and go out before us, and fight our
21 battles. And Samuel heard all the words of the people, and he rehearsed them
22 in the ears of the Lord. And the Lord said to Samuel, Hearken unto their
voice, and make them a king. And Samuel said unto the men of Israel, Go ye
every man unto his city.
9   Now there was a man of Benjamin, whose name was Kish, the son of Abiel,
the son of Zeror, the son of Bechorath, the son of Aphiah, a Benjamite, a
2 mighty man of power. And he had a son, whose name was Saul, a choice
young man, and a goodly: and there was not among the children of Israel a
goodlier person than he: from his shoulders and upward he was higher than

3 any of the people. And the asses of Kish Saul's father were lost. And Kish
said to Saul his son, Take now one of the servants with thee, and arise, go
4 seek the asses. And he passed through mount Ephraim, and passed through
the land of Shalisha, but they found them not: then they passed through the
land of Shalim, and there they were not: and he passed through the land of
the Benjamites, but they found them not.

5 And when they were come to the land of Zuph, Saul said to his servant
that was with him, Come, and let us return; lest my father leave caring for
6 the asses, and take thought for us. And he said unto him, Behold now, there is
in this city a man of God, and he is an honorable man; all that he saith
cometh surely to pass: now let us go thither; peradventure he can show us
our way that we should go.

7 Then said Saul to his servant, But, behold, if we go, what shall we bring
the man? for the bread is spent in our vessels, and there is not a present to
8 bring to the man of God: what have we? And the servant answered Saul
again, and said, Behold, I have here at hand the fourth part of a shekel of
9 silver: that will I give to the man of God, to tell us our way. (Beforetime in
Israel, when a man went to inquire of God, thus he spake, Come, and let us
go to the seer: for he that is now called a Prophet was beforetime called a
10 Seer.) Then said Saul to his servant, Well said; come, let us go. So they
went unto the city where the man of God was.

15 Now the Lord had told Samuel in his ear a day before Saul came, saying,
16 To-morrow about this time I will send thee a man out of the land of Benjamin, and thou shalt anoint him to be captain over my people Israel, that he
may save my people out of the hand of the Philistines: for I have looked upon
17 my people, because their cry is come unto me. And when Samuel saw Saul,
the Lord said unto him, Behold the man whom I spake to thee of! this same
shall reign over my people.

18 Then Saul drew near to Samuel in the gate, and said, Tell me, I pray thee,
19 where the seer's house is. And Samuel answered Saul, and said, I am the
seer: go up before me unto the high place; for ye shall eat with me to-day,
and to-morrow I will let thee go, and will tell thee all that is in thine heart.
20 And as for thine asses that were lost three days ago, set not thy mind on
them; for they are found. And on whom is all the desire of Israel? Is it not
21 on thee, and on all thy father's house? And Saul answered and said, Am not
I a Benjamite, of the smallest of the tribes of Israel? and my family the least
of all the families of the tribe of Benjamin? wherefore then speakest thou so
22 to me? And Samuel took Saul and his servant, and brought them into the
parlor, and made them sit in the chiefest place among them that were bidden,
which were about thirty persons.

25 And when they were come down from the high place into the city, Samuel
26 communed with Saul upon the top of the house. And they arose early: and it
came to pass about the spring of the day, that Samuel called Saul to the top
of the house, saying, Up, that I may send thee away. And Saul arose, and
27 they went out both of them, he and Samuel, abroad. And as they were going
down to the end of the city, Samuel said to Saul, Bid the servant pass on
before us, (and he passed on,) but stand thou still a while, that I may show
thee the word of God.

10 Then Samuel took a vial of oil, and poured it upon his head, and kissed him,

and said, Is it not because the Lord hath anointed thee to be captain over his
2,3 inheritance? When thou art departed from me to-day, . . . Then shalt thou go
on forward from thence, and thou shalt come to the plain of Tabor, and there
5 shall meet thee three men going up to God to Beth-el, . . . After that thou
shalt come to the hill of God, where is the garrison of the Philistines: and it
shall come to pass, when thou art come thither to the city, that thou shalt
meet a company of prophets coming down from the high place with a psaltery, and a tabret, and a pipe, and a harp, before them; and they shall
6 prophesy: And the Spirit of the Lord will come upon thee, and thou shalt
7 prophesy with them, and shalt be turned into another man. And let it be,
when these signs are come unto thee, that thou do as occasion serve thee;
for God is with thee.

9 And it was so, that, when he had turned his back to go from Samuel, God
10 gave him another heart: and all those signs came to pass that day. And when
they came thither to the hill, behold, a company of prophets met him; and
11 the Spirit of God came upon him, and he prophesied among them. And it
came to pass, when all that knew him beforetime saw that, behold, he prophesied among the prophets, then the people said one to another, What is this
12 that is come unto the son of Kish? Is Saul also among the prophets? And one
of the same place answered and said, But who is their father? Therefore it
13 became a proverb, Is Saul also among the prophets?

12 And Samuel said unto all Israel, Behold, I have hearkened unto your voice
2 in all that ye said unto me, and have made a king over you. And now, behold,
the king walketh before you: and I am old and gray-headed; and, behold,
my sons are with you: and I have walked before you from my childhood
3 unto this day. Behold, here I am: witness against me before the Lord, and
before his anointed: whose ox have I taken? or whose ass have I taken? or
whom have I defrauded? whom have I oppressed? or of whose hand have I
received any bribe to blind mine eyes therewith? and I will restore it you.
4 And they said, Thou hast not defrauded us, nor oppressed us, neither hast
5 thou taken aught of any man's hand. And he said unto them, The Lord is
witness against you, and his anointed is witness this day, that ye have not
found aught in my hand. And they answered, He is witness.

6 And Samuel said unto the people, It is the Lord that advanced Moses and
7 Aaron, and that brought your fathers up out of the land of Egypt. Now
therefore stand still, that I may reason with you before the Lord of all the
12 righteous acts of the Lord, which he did to you and to your fathers. And
when he saw that Nahash the king of the children of Ammon came against
you, ye said unto me, Nay; but a king shall reign over us: when the Lord
13 your God was your king. Now therefore, behold the king whom ye have
chosen, and whom ye have desired! and, behold, the Lord hath set a king
22 over you. For the Lord will not forsake his people for his great name's sake:
23 because it hath pleased the Lord to make you his people. Moreover as for
me, God forbid that I should sin against the Lord in ceasing to pray for you:
24 but I will teach you the good and the right way: Only fear the Lord, and
serve him in truth with all your heart: for consider how great things he hath
25 done for you. But if ye shall still do wickedly, ye shall be consumed, both ye
and your king.

13 Saul reigned one year; and when he had reigned two years over Israel,
2 Saul chose him three thousand men of Israel; whereof two thousand were

with Saul in Michmash and in mount Beth-el, and a thousand were with Jonathan in Gibeah of Benjamin: and the rest of the people he sent every
3 man to his tent. And Jonathan smote the garrison of the Philistines that was in Geba, and the Philistines heard of it. And Saul blew the trumpet through-
4 out all the land, saying, Let the Hebrews hear. And all Israel heard say that Saul had smitten a garrison of the Philistines, and that Israel also was had in abomination with the Philistines. And the people were called together after Saul to Gilgal.
5 And the Philistines gathered themselves together to fight with Israel, thirty thousand chariots, and six thousand horsemen, and people as the sand which is on the seashore in multitude: and they came up, and pitched in
6 Michmash, eastward from Beth-aven. When the men of Israel saw that they were in a strait, (for the people were distressed,) then the people did hide themselves in caves, and in thickets, and in rocks, and in high places, and in
7 pits. And some of the Hebrews went over Jordan to the land of Gad and Gilead. As for Saul, he was yet in Gilgal, and all the people followed him trembling.
8 And he tarried seven days, according to the set time that Samuel had appointed: but Samuel came not to Gilgal; and the people were scattered from
9 him. And Saul said, Bring hither a burnt offering to me, and peace offerings.
10 And he offered the burnt offering. And it came to pass, that as soon as he had made an end of offering the burnt offering, behold, Samuel came; and Saul went out to meet him, that he might salute him.
11 And Samuel said, What hast thou done? And Saul said, Because I saw that the people were scattered from me, and that thou camest not within the days appointed, and that the Philistines gathered themselves together at
12 Michmash; Therefore said I, The Philistines will come down now upon me to Gilgal, and I have not made supplication unto the Lord: I forced myself therefore, and offered a burnt offering.
13 And Samuel said to Saul, Thou hast done foolishly: thou hast not kept the commandment of the Lord thy God, which he commanded thee: for now would the Lord have established thy kingdom upon Israel for ever.

14:   Then Saul went up from
52 following the Philistines: and the Philistines went to their own place. And there was sore war against the Philistines all the days of Saul: and when Saul saw any strong man, or any valiant man, he took him unto him.

15 Samuel also said unto Saul, The Lord sent me to anoint thee to be king over his people, over Israel: now therefore hearken thou unto the voice of the
2 words of the Lord. Thus saith the Lord of hosts, I remember that which Amalek did to Israel, how he laid wait for him in the way, when he came
3 up from Egypt. Now go and smite Amalek, and utterly destroy all that they have, and spare them not; but slay both man and woman, infant and suckling, ox and sheep, camel and ass.
7 And Saul smote the Amalekites from Havilah until thou comest to Shur,
8 that is over against Egypt. And he took Agag the king of the Amalekites
9 alive, and utterly destroyed all the people with the edge of the sword. But Saul and the people spared Agag, and the best of the sheep, and of the oxen, and of the fatlings, and the lambs, and all that was good, and would not utterly destroy them: but every thing that was vile and refuse, that they destroyed utterly.

From the History of Ancient Israel

10,11   Then came the word of the Lord unto Samuel, saying, It repenteth me that I have set up Saul to be king: for he is turned back from following me, and hath not performed my commandments. And it grieved Samuel; and he
12 cried unto the Lord all night. And when Samuel rose early to meet Saul in the morning, it was told Samuel, saying, Saul came . . . down to Gilgal.

13   And Samuel came to Saul: and Saul said unto him, Blessed be thou of the Lord: I have performed the commandment of the Lord.

14   And Samuel said, What meaneth then this bleating of the sheep in mine ears, and the lowing of the oxen which I hear?

15   And Saul said, They have brought them from the Amalekites: for the people spared the best of the sheep and of the oxen, to sacrifice unto the Lord thy God; and the rest we have utterly destroyed.

16   Then Samuel said unto Saul, Stay, and I will tell thee what the Lord hath
17 said to me this night. And he said unto him, Say on. And Samuel said, When thou wast little in thine own sight, wast thou not made the head of the tribes
18 of Israel, and the Lord anointed thee king over Israel? And the Lord sent thee on a journey, and said, Go and utterly destroy the sinners the Amalek-
19 ites, and fight against them until they be consumed. Wherefore then didst thou not obey the voice of the Lord, but didst fly upon the spoil, and didst evil in the sight of the Lord?

20   And Saul said unto Samuel, Yea, I have obeyed the voice of the Lord, and have gone the way which the Lord sent me, and have brought Agag the king
21 of Amalek, and have utterly destroyed the Amalekites. But the people took of the spoil, sheep and oxen, the chief of the things which should have been utterly destroyed, to sacrifice unto the Lord thy God in Gilgal.

22   And Samuel said, Hath the Lord as great delight in burnt offerings and sacrifices, as in obeying the voice of the Lord? Behold, to obey is better than
23 sacrifice, and to hearken than the fat of rams. For rebellion is as the sin of witchcraft, and stubbornness is as iniquity and idolatry. Because thou hast rejected the word of the Lord, he hath also rejected thee from being king.

24   And Saul said unto Samuel, I have sinned: for I have transgressed the commandment of the Lord, and thy words: because I feared the people, and
25 obeyed their voice. Now therefore, I pray thee, pardon my sin, and turn again with me, that I may worship the Lord.

26   And Samuel said unto Saul, I will not return with thee: for thou hast rejected the word of the Lord, and the Lord hath rejected thee from being king
27 over Israel. And as Samuel turned about to go away, he laid hold upon the
28 skirt of his mantle, and it rent. And Samuel said unto him, The Lord hath rent the kingdom of Israel from thee this day, and hath given it to a neighbor
29 of thine, that is better than thou. And also the Strength of Israel will not lie nor repent: for he is not a man, that he should repent.

30   Then he said, I have sinned: yet honor me now, I pray thee, before the elders of my people, and before Israel, and turn again with me, that I may
31 worship the Lord thy God. So Samuel turned again after Saul; and Saul worshipped the Lord.

32   Then said Samuel, Bring ye hither to me Agag the king of the Amalekites. And Agag came unto him delicately. And Agag said, Surely the bitterness of
33 death is past. And Samuel said, As thy sword hath made women childless, so

shall thy mother be childless among women. And Samuel hewed Agag in pieces before the Lord in Gilgal.

34 Then Samuel went to Ramah; and Saul went up to his house to Gibeah of
35 Saul. And Samuel came no more to see Saul until the day of his death: nevertheless Samuel mourned for Saul: and the Lord repented that he had made Saul king over Israel.

16 And the Lord said unto Samuel, How long wilt thou mourn for Saul, seeing I have rejected him from reigning over Israel? fill thine horn with oil, and go, I will send thee to Jesse the Bethlehemite: for I have provided me a king
2 among his sons. And Samuel said, How can I go? if Saul hear it, he will kill me. And the Lord said, Take a heifer with thee, and say, I am come to sacri-
3 fice to the Lord. And call Jesse to the sacrifice, and I will show thee what thou shalt do: and thou shalt anoint unto me him whom I name unto thee.
4 And Samuel did that which the Lord spake, and came to Bethlehem. And the elders of the town trembled at his coming, and said, Comest thou peace-
5 ably? And he said, Peaceably: I am come to sacrifice unto the Lord: sanctify yourselves, and come with me to the sacrifice. And he sanctified Jesse and his sons, and called them to the sacrifice.
6 And it came to pass, when they were come, that he looked on Eliab, and
7 said, Surely the Lord's anointed is before him. But the Lord said unto Samuel, Look not on his countenance, or on the height of his stature; because I have refused him: for the Lord seeth not as man seeth; for man looketh on
8 the outward appearance, but the Lord looketh on the heart. Then Jesse called Abinadab, and made him pass before Samuel. And he said, Neither hath the
9 Lord chosen this. Then Jesse made Shammah to pass by. And he said, Neither
10 hath the Lord chosen this. Again, Jesse made seven of his sons to pass before Samuel. And Samuel said unto Jesse, The Lord hath not chosen these.
11 And Samuel said unto Jesse, Are here all thy children? And he said, There remaineth yet the youngest, and, behold, he keepeth the sheep. And Samuel said unto Jesse, Send and fetch him: for we will not sit down till he come
12 hither. And he sent, and brought him in. Now he was ruddy, and withal of a beautiful countenance, and goodly to look to. And the Lord said, Arise,
13 anoint him: for this is he. Then Samuel took the horn of oil, and anointed him in the midst of his brethren: and the Spirit of the Lord came upon David from that day forward. So Samuel rose up, and went to Ramah.
14 But the Spirit of the Lord departed from Saul, and an evil spirit from the
15 Lord troubled him. And Saul's servants said unto him, Behold now, an evil
16 spirit from God troubleth thee. Let our lord now command thy servants, which are before thee, to seek out a man, who is a cunning player on a harp: and it shall come to pass, when the evil spirit from God is upon thee, that he
17 shall play with his hand, and thou shalt be well. And Saul said unto his serv-
18 ants, Provide me now a man that can play well, and bring him to me. Then answered one of the servants, and said, Behold, I have seen a son of Jesse the Bethlehemite, that is cunning in playing, and a mighty valiant man, and a man of war, and prudent in matters, and a comely person, and the Lord is with him.
19 Wherefore Saul sent messengers unto Jesse, and said, Send me David thy
20 son, which is with the sheep. And Jesse took an ass laden with bread, and a
21 bottle of wine, and a kid, and sent them by David his son unto Saul. And

David came to Saul, and stood before him: and he loved him greatly; and he
22 became his armor-bearer. And Saul sent to Jesse, saying, Let David, I pray
23 thee, stand before me; for he hath found favor in my sight. And it came to
pass, when the evil spirit from God was upon Saul, that David took a harp,
and played with his hand: so Saul was refreshed, and was well, and the evil
spirit departed from him.

17   Now the Philistines gathered together their armies to battle, and were
2 gathered together at Shochoh, which belongeth to Judah, . . . And Saul and
the men of Israel were gathered together, and pitched by the valley of Elah,
3 and set the battle in array against the Philistines. And the Philistines stood
on a mountain on the one side, and Israel stood on a mountain on the other
side: and there was a valley between them.

4   And there went out a champion out of the camp of the Philistines, named
5 Goliath, of Gath, whose height was six cubits and a span. And he had a
helmet of brass upon his head, and he was armed with a coat of mail; and
6 the weight of the coat was five thousand shekels of brass. And he had greaves
7 of brass upon his legs, and a target of brass between his shoulders. And the
staff of his spear was like a weaver's beam; and his spear's head weighed six
8 hundred shekels of iron: and one bearing a shield went before him. And he
stood and cried unto the armies of Israel, and said unto them, Why are ye
come out to set your battle in array? am not I a Philistine, and ye servants
9 to Saul? choose you a man for you, and let him come down to me. If he be
able to fight with me, and to kill me, then will we be your servants: but if
I prevail against him, and kill him, then shall ye be our servants, and serve
10 us. And the Philistine said, I defy the armies of Israel this day; give me a
11 man, that we may fight together. When Saul and all Israel heard those words
of the Philistine, they were dismayed, and greatly afraid.

13   And the three eldest sons of Jesse went and followed Saul to the battle:
14,15 . . . And David was the youngest: and the three eldest followed Saul. But
David went and returned from Saul to feed his father's sheep at Bethlehem.
16   And the Philistine drew near morning and evening, and presented himself
17 forty days. And Jesse said unto David his son, Take now for thy brethren
an ephah of this parched corn, and these ten loaves, and run to the camp to
18 thy brethren; And carry these ten cheeses unto the captain of their thousand,
and look how thy brethren fare, and take their pledge.
20   And David rose up early in the morning, and left the sheep with a keeper,
and took, and went, as Jesse had commanded him; and he came to the trench,
21 as the host was going forth to the fight, and shouted for the battle. For Israel
22 and the Philistines had put the battle in array, army against army. And David
left his carriage in the hand of the keeper of the carriage, and ran into the
23 army, and came and saluted his brethren. And as he talked with them, behold, there came up the champion, the Philistine of Gath, Goliath by name,
out of the armies of the Philistines, and spake according to the same words:
24 and David heard them. And all the men of Israel, when they saw the man,
25 fled from him, and were sore afraid. And the men of Israel said, Have ye
seen this man that is come up? surely to defy Israel is he come up: and it
26 shall be, that the man who killeth him, the king will enrich him . . . And
David spake to the men that stood by him, saying, What shall be done to the
man that killeth this Philistine, and taketh away the reproach from Israel?

for who is this uncircumcised Philistine, that he should defy the armies of
27 the living God? And the people answered him after this manner, saying, So
shall it be done to the man that killeth him.

28 And Eliab his eldest brother heard when he spake unto the men; and
Eliab's anger was kindled against David, and he said, Why camest thou down
hither? and with whom hast thou left those few sheep in the wilderness? I
know thy pride, and the naughtiness of thine heart; for thou art come down
29 that thou mightest see the battle. And David said, What have I now done?
Is there not a cause?

31 And when the words were heard which David spake, they rehearsed them
32 before Saul: and he sent for him. And David said to Saul, Let no man's heart
33 fail because of him; thy servant will go and fight with this Philistine. And
Saul said to David, Thou art not able to go against this Philistine to fight
with him: for thou art but a youth, and he a man of war from his youth.

34 And David said unto Saul, Thy servant kept his father's sheep, and there
35 came a lion, and a bear, and took a lamb out of the flock: And I went out
after him, and smote him, and delivered it out of his mouth: and when he
arose against me, I caught him by his beard, and smote him, and slew him.
36 Thy servant slew both the lion and the bear: and this uncircumcised Philistine shall be as one of them, seeing he hath defied the armies of the living God.
37 David said moreover, The Lord that delivered me out of the paw of the
lion, and out of the paw of the bear, he will deliver me out of the hand of this
Philistine. And Saul said unto David, Go, and the Lord be with thee.

38 And Saul armed David with his armor, and he put a helmet of brass upon
39 his head; also he armed him with a coat of mail. And David girded his sword
upon his armor, and he assayed to go; for he had not proved it. And David
said unto Saul, I cannot go with these; for I have not proved them. And
40 David put them off him. And he took his staff in his hand, and chose him five
smooth stones out of the brook, and put them in a shepherd's bag which he
had, even in a scrip; and his sling was in his hand: and he drew near to the
Philistine.

41 And the Philistine came on and drew near unto David; and the man that
42 bare the shield went before him. And when the Philistine looked about, and
saw David, he disdained him: for he was but a youth, and ruddy, and of a
43 fair countenance. And the Philistine said unto David, Am I a dog, that thou
comest to me with staves? And the Philistine cursed David by his gods.
44 And the Philistine said to David, Come to me, and I will give thy flesh unto
the fowls of the air, and to the beasts of the field.
45 Then said David to the Philistine, Thou comest to me with a sword, and
with a spear, and with a shield: but I come to thee in the name of the Lord of
46 hosts, the God of the armies of Israel, whom thou hast defied. This day will
the Lord deliver thee into mine hand; and I will smite thee, and take thine
head from thee; and I will give the carcasses of the host of the Philistines
this day unto the fowls of the air, and to the wild beasts of the earth; that
47 all the earth may know that there is a God in Israel. And all this assembly
shall know that the Lord saveth not with sword and spear: for the battle is
the Lord's, and he will give you into our hands.
48 And it came to pass, when the Philistine arose, and came and drew nigh
to meet David, that David hasted, and ran toward the army to meet the

49 Philistine. And David put his hand in his bag, and took thence a stone, and slang it, and smote the Philistine in his forehead, that the stone sunk into his

50 forehead; and he fell upon his face to the earth. So David prevailed over the Philistine with a sling and with a stone, and smote the Philistine, and slew

51 him; but there was no sword in the hand of David. Therefore David ran, and stood upon the Philistine, and took his sword, and drew it out of the sheath thereof, and slew him, and cut off his head therewith. And when the Philistines saw their champion was dead, they fled.

52 And the men of Israel and of Judah arose, and shouted, and pursued the Philistines, until thou come to the valley, and to the gates of Ekron. And the wounded of the Philistines fell down by the way to Shaaraim, even unto

53 Gath, and unto Ekron. And the children of Israel returned from chasing after

54 the Philistines, and they spoiled their tents. And David took the head of the Philistine, and brought it to Jerusalem; but he put his armor in his tent.

55 And when Saul saw David go forth against the Philistine, he said unto Abner, the captain of the host, Abner, whose son is this youth? And Abner

56 said, As thy soul liveth, O king, I cannot tell. And the king said, Inquire thou

57 whose son the stripling is. And as David returned from the slaughter of the Philistine, Abner took him, and brought him before Saul with the head of the

58 Philistine in his hand. And Saul said to him, Whose son art thou, thou young man? And David answered, I am the son of thy servant Jesse the Bethlehemite.

18 And it came to pass, when he had made an end of speaking unto Saul, that the soul of Jonathan was knit with the soul of David, and Jonathan loved him

2 as his own soul. And Saul took him that day, and would let him go no more

3 home to his father's house. Then Jonathan and David made a covenant, be-

4 cause he loved him as his own soul. And Jonathan stripped himself of the robe that was upon him, and gave it to David, and his garments, even to his sword, and to his bow, and to his girdle.

5 And David went out whithersoever Saul sent him, and behaved himself wisely: and Saul set him over the men of war, and he was accepted in the

6 sight of all the people, and also in the sight of Saul's servants. And it came to pass as they came, when David was returned from the slaughter of the Philistine, that the women came out of all cities of Israel, singing and dancing, to

7 meet king Saul, with tabrets, with joy, and with instruments of music. And the women answered one another as they played, and said,

Saul hath slain his thousands,
and David his ten thousands.

8 And Saul was very wroth, and the saying displeased him; and he said, They have ascribed unto David ten thousands, and to me they have ascribed but

9 thousands: and what can he have more but the kingdom? And Saul eyed David from that day and forward.

20 And Michal Saul's daughter loved David: and they told Saul, and the thing

21 pleased him. And Saul said, I will give him her, that she may be a snare to

22 him, and that the hand of the Philistines may be against him. . . . And Saul commanded his servants, saying, Commune with David secretly, and say, Behold, the king hath delight in thee, and all his servants love thee: now

23 therefore be the king's son-in-law. And Saul's servants spake those words

in the ears of David. And David said, Seemeth it to you a light thing to be a
24 king's son-in-law, seeing that I am a poor man, and lightly esteemed? And
the servants of Saul told him, saying, On this manner spake David.

25   And Saul said, Thus shall ye say to David, The king desireth not any
dowry, but a hundred foreskins of the Philistines, to be avenged of the king's
enemies. But Saul thought to make David fall by the hand of the Philistines.
26 And when his servants told David these words, it pleased David well to be
27 the king's son-in-law: and the days were not expired. Wherefore David arose
and went, he and his men, and slew of the Philistines two hundred men; and
David brought their foreskins, and they gave them in full tale to the king,
that he might be the king's son-in-law. And Saul gave him Michal his daughter to wife.

28   And Saul saw and knew that the Lord was with David, and that Michal
29 Saul's daughter loved him. And Saul was yet the more afraid of David; and
30 Saul became David's enemy continually. Then the princes of the Philistines
went forth: and it came to pass, after they went forth, that David behaved
himself more wisely than all the servants of Saul; so that his name was much
set by.

Considerations and Questions

1. "And [they] said unto him, Behold, thou art old, and thy sons walk not in thy ways: now make us a king to judge us like all the nations." (I Samuel 8:5) Thus the elders of Israel approach old Samuel. What apparently is the only solution they can think of to their problems? Why?

2. Samuel answers the elders with a practical argument. What, he says, will be the result if he does what they ask? Do they refute the details of his argument? What do they conclude?

3. Samuel has a profounder objection to the political change proposed on this occasion by the elders. It is based on his concern for the very identity of Israel. What is it? What is its relationship to the practical points he has made first to the elders?

4. Like other great architects of social structure, Samuel must compromise. From his compromise emerges a political idea familiar to us but not to the world in which he makes it. He agrees to give Israel a king, but clearly he does not plan to set up or support a monarchy like those of "all the nations." How do the details of his selection and preparation of Saul indicate Samuel's determination to provide a strictly "constitutional" monarchy?

5. At first Samuel thinks that Saul is just the right man for what he has in mind. Why? What leads Samuel to change his mind later?

6. When Samuel does decide that Saul is not the right man for the job, we see that Saul goes right on being King of Israel anyway. How do you explain this? What does it suggest about the vulnerabilities of Samuel's constitutional monarchy? What does Samuel do at this point?

7. Partly because of Samuel's blunt rejection of him, but mainly because of David's status as a popular hero, there has long been a tendency to think of King Saul as a Biblical villain. Certainly Saul fails to live up to Samuel's standards and he does behave badly in various other ways, but some of the things Samuel wants Saul to do must seem as savage or impractical to Saul as they would to us. (What, for example?) We might do well to remember, too, that Saul has not asked to be King; he tries to keep the office once it has been thrust upon him. Furthermore, Saul is afflicted with periodic attacks of melancholia or some related psychosis which the writer significantly calls "an evil spirit from the Lord." Can you make a case for Saul as a pathetic or even a tragic figure who is caught in circumstances that he manfully tries to overcome?

8. Note that there are three accounts in our selections of David's introduction to public life and therefore into the affairs of King Saul. What immediate inconsistencies do you find among them? How can you explain and resolve these inconsistencies?

9. Certainly the best known episode involving David and Saul is the former's conquest of the Philistine giant, Goliath. The defeat of the huge veteran

braggart by the modest and dedicated stripling represents mythically a familiar idea. In wars between large nations and small, in sports events between famous and unknown contestants, even in competitions of commerce, art, and love, mankind has entertained that persistent but not always dependable hope that the small but good will beat the big but evil. But the David and Goliath chapter (I Samuel 17) has more to show than a general version of the notion that big bullies lose. As a matter of fact, studied carefully, it may not support that dubious proposition after all.

What, as you consider each of them in the context of the Biblical history of Israel, do you find significant about these points from the David and Goliath chapter?

(a) David puts aside the weapons of well-equipped contemporary warriors and uses shepherds' tools to defeat Goliath.

(b) David's brother, Eliab, a soldier in Saul's army, is indignant with David for coming to the front lines with questions about Goliath.

(c) The entire army of Israel is held at bay by one big Philistine.

(d) King Saul accepts the services of this unknown and unlikely champion.

(e) When Goliath sees David he thinks that David has only a staff with which to fight. The young hero actually knocks Goliath down with a secret weapon. Missile-warfare is apparently a complete surprise to the Philistine.

(f) David tells Saul that it was the Lord who delivered him from the paws of the marauding beasts when he was a shepherd and that it will be the Lord who is his weapon against Goliath. (He tells Goliath this also.) He claims that his victory over the giant will be in order to show "that there is a God in Israel."

After David's victory over Goliath and the consequent destruction of the Philistine army, Saul's first reaction is to reward the young man generously and appropriately. David is a national hero and a young success. He is an intimate member of the King's household, the best friend of the crown prince, and he continues to perform marvelously as a staff officer and a field commander. What ironic result do such aspects of his success produce? What further results do you think they foreshadow? Why?

7. The Story of a Monarchy: Saul, David, and Solomon

*Consider the lilies of the field, how they grow;
they toil not, neither do they spin: And yet I say
unto you, That even Solomon in all his glory was
not arrayed like one of these.*

The Gospel According to St. Matthew

Biblical literature is full of kings, and a number of them are descendants of Abraham and rulers of various divisions of Israel. Only Saul, David, and Solomon, however, are the anointed kings of all Israel. So in the brief story of three generations we see the political birth, maturity, and decadence of a monarchy that as an inspirational and symbolic institution has outlasted thousands of political empires.

The selections to follow begin with the last desperate days of King Saul. He is without Samuel, without David, without health of mind or body, and without hope that his God is with him. As a king and as a man he has lost most of his capacity to keep control of things. Around his kingdom the enemies, Philistines and others, smell blood and increase their ever more successful attacks on his uneasy people. David, once his best soldier, is now an outlaw who wanders with a guerilla band in and out of the wilderness. Perhaps Saul's misfortunes stem from his own decisions; perhaps they are the inevitable consequences of what is beyond his power. In any case, he keeps trying, and he does maintain to the end, and in the face of every pressure, that there is an anointed King of Israel. This prepares the way for David, the greatest of the three kings, the high point of the monarchy, and one of the two or three mighty heroes of Old Testament literature.

Besides taking over an existing and accepted monarchal establishment, David has various other advantages not enjoyed by his predecessor. Saul comes out of the back country with only his imposing physical appearance and the backing of an elder statesman to start him off on his royal career. David becomes king after many years as a popular national hero who has saved the armies of Israel. Furthermore, David has a more recent reputation as a gallant, romantic figure, reluctantly an outlaw, who has survived unjust oppression from a king to whom he remains nobly loyal. While Saul is always uneasy and unfortunate in his personal and professional relationships, David has the happy gift of making people love and admire him. Compared to Saul, David is intelligent, educated, and morally sophisticated. He thinks clearly, knows what he believes, and understands that the God he serves is not manifested only in the immediacies of good and bad luck. Therefore, in contrast to Saul, David is a man capable of detached observation: he can see things as they are, and in consequence can make military, political, and personal judgments of which Saul appears incapable. The kingdom of Israel, with its capital in Jerusalem, is the construction of the gifted soldier, diplomat, and administrator, David. But the necessary foundation material on which David builds his remarkable career consists in part of the dogged and blundering efforts of King Saul.

As we shall see, in spite of his gifts and greatness, David is by no means perfect. By the standards of his world he is a great gentleman, accomplished and magnanimous beyond other men. He is also, on occasion, treacherous, murderous, lustful, and sometimes emotionally inconsistent. But he is generally true to his basic code of duty and always true to his belief in his God. When he does wrong and gets in trouble he blames himself, not the Lord.

Shortly before his death as an old man, David expresses confidence in his son Solomon's ability to administer the kingdom. As world folklore has it, Solomon is extremely wise. We are also informed early in the chapters about his reign that he "loved the Lord." What he actually *does* in the accounts of his kingship may lead serious readers to some careful skepticism both about Solomon's wisdom and his piety.

But however we may evaluate Solomon's qualities, the deeds of his administration are not sufficient to hold the kingdom together after his death. As the Lord informs him at the end of the following section of readings, because Solomon has not kept the Lord's statutes and Covenant, the kingdom will be divided when he dies. This in fact happens. After a bloody civil war between Solomon's willful and unwise son, Rehoboam (supported by the single powerful tribe of Judah), and the popular leader, Jeroboam (with the other eleven tribes), David's kingdom of Israel is divided into two separate kingdoms: "Israel" in the north and "Judah" in the south.

I Samuel

28: 3   Now Samuel was dead, and all Israel had lamented him, and buried him in Ramah, even in his own city. And Saul had put away those that had familiar
4 spirits, and the wizards, out of the land. And the Philistines gathered themselves together, and came and pitched in Shunem: and Saul gathered all Israel
5 together, and they pitched in Gilboa. And when Saul saw the host of the
6 Philistines, he was afraid, and his heart greatly trembled. And when Saul inquired of the Lord, the Lord answered him not, neither by dreams, nor by Urim, nor by prophets.
7   Then said Saul unto his servants, Seek me a woman that hath a familiar spirit, that I may go to her, and inquire of her. And his servants said to him,
8 Behold, there is a woman that hath a familiar spirit at En-dor. And Saul disguised himself, and put on other raiment, and he went, and two men with him, and they came to the woman by night: and he said, I pray thee, divine unto me by the familiar spirit, and bring me him up, whom I shall name unto
9 thee. And the woman said unto him, Behold, thou knowest what Saul hath done, how he hath cut off those that have familiar spirits, and the wizards, out of the land: wherefore then layest thou a snare for my life, to cause me
10 to die? And Saul sware to her by the Lord, saying, As the Lord liveth, there shall no punishment happen to thee for this thing.
11   Then said the woman, Whom shall I bring up unto thee? And he said,
12 Bring me up Samuel. And when the woman saw Samuel, she cried with a loud voice: and the woman spake to Saul, saying, Why hast thou deceived me? for thou art Saul.
13   And the king said unto her, Be not afraid: for what sawest thou? And the
14 woman said unto Saul, I saw gods ascending out of the earth. And he said unto her, What form is he of? And she said, An old man cometh up; and he is covered with a mantle. And Saul perceived that it was Samuel, and he stooped with his face to the ground, and bowed himself.
15   And Samuel said to Saul, Why hast thou disquieted me, to bring me up? And Saul answered, I am sore distressed; for the Philistines make war against me, and God is departed from me, and answereth me no more, neither by prophets, nor by dreams: therefore I have called thee, that thou mayest make known unto me what I shall do.
16   Then said Samuel, Wherefore then dost thou ask of me, seeing the Lord
17 is departed from thee, and is become thine enemy? And the Lord hath done to him, as he spake by me: for the Lord hath rent the kingdom out of thine
18 hand, and given it to thy neighbor, even to David: Because thou obeyedst not the voice of the Lord, nor executedst his fierce wrath upon Amalek,
19 therefore hath the Lord done this thing unto thee this day. Moreover the Lord will also deliver Israel with thee into the hand of the Philistines: and to-morrow shalt thou and thy sons be with me: the Lord also shall deliver
20 the host of Israel into the hand of the Philistines. Then Saul fell straightway all along on the earth, and was sore afraid, because of the words of Samuel; and there was no strength in him; for he had eaten no bread all the day, nor
21 all the night. And the woman came unto Saul, and saw that he was sore

22 troubled, and said unto him, . . . let me set a morsel of bread before thee; and
23 eat, that thou mayest have strength, when thou goest on thy way. But he refused, and said, I will not eat. But his servants, together with the woman,
compelled him; and he hearkened unto their voice. So he arose from the
24 earth, and sat upon the bed. And the woman had a fat calf in the house; and
she hasted, and killed it, and took flour, and kneaded it, and did bake un-
25 leavened bread thereof: And she brought it before Saul, and before his servants; and they did eat. Then they rose up, and went away that night.

31   Now the Philistines fought against Israel: and the men of Israel fled from
2 before the Philistines, and fell down slain in mount Gilboa. And the Philistines followed hard upon Saul and upon his sons; and the Philistines slew
3 Jonathan, and Abinadab, and Melchi-shua, Saul's sons. And the battle went
sore against Saul, and the archers hit him; and he was sore wounded of the
archers.
4   Then said Saul unto his armor-bearer, Draw thy sword, and thrust me
through therewith; lest these uncircumcised come and thrust me through,
and abuse me. But his armor-bearer would not; for he was sore afraid.
5 Therefore Saul took a sword, and fell upon it. And when his armor-bearer
saw that Saul was dead, he fell likewise upon his sword, and died with him.
6 So Saul died, and his three sons, and his armor-bearer, and all his men, that
same day together.
7   And when the men of Israel that were on the other side of the valley, and
they that were on the other side Jordan, saw that the men of Israel fled, and
that Saul and his sons were dead, they forsook the cities, and fled; and the
Philistines came and dwelt in them.
8   And it came to pass on the morrow, when the Philistines came to strip
9 the slain, that they found Saul and his three sons fallen in mount Gilboa. And
they cut off his head, and stripped off his armor, and sent into the land of the
Philistines round about, to publish it in the house of their idols, and among
10 the people. And they put his armor in the house of Ashtaroth: and they
fastened his body to the wall of Beth-shan.
11   And when the inhabitants of Jabesh-gilead heard of that which the Philis-
12 tines had done to Saul, All the valiant men arose, and went all night, and took
the body of Saul and the bodies of his sons from the wall of Beth-shan, and
13 came to Jabesh, and burnt them there. And they took their bones, and buried
them under a tree at Jabesh, and fasted seven days.

II Samuel

1   Now it came to pass after the death of Saul, when David was returned
from the slaughter of the Amalekites, and David had abode two days in Zik-
2 lag; It came even to pass on the third day, that, behold, a man came out of
the camp from Saul with his clothes rent, and earth upon his head: and so it
was, when he came to David, that he fell to the earth, and did obeisance.
3   And David said unto him, From whence comest thou? And he said unto
4 him, Out of the camp of Israel am I escaped. And David said unto him, How

went the matter? I pray thee, tell me. And he answered, That the people are fled from the battle, and many of the people also are fallen and dead; and Saul and Jonathan his son are dead also.

5 And David said unto the young man that told him, How knowest thou that Saul and Jonathan his son be dead?

6 And the young man that told him said, As I happened by chance upon mount Gilboa, behold, Saul leaned upon his spear; and, lo, the chariots and 7 horsemen followed hard after him. And when he looked behind him, he saw 8 me, and called unto me. And I answered, Here am I. And he said unto me, 9 Who art thou? And I answered him, I am an Amalekite. He said unto me again, Stand, I pray thee, upon me, and slay me: for anguish is come upon 10 me, because my life is yet whole in me. So I stood upon him, and slew him, because I was sure that he could not live after that he was fallen: and I took the crown that was upon his head, and the bracelet that was on his arm, and have brought them hither unto my lord.

11 Then David took hold on his clothes, and rent them; and likewise all the 12 men that were with him: And they mourned, and wept, and fasted until even, for Saul, and for Jonathan his son, and for the people of the Lord, and for the house of Israel; because they were fallen by the sword.

13 And David said unto the young man that told him, Whence art thou? And 14 he answered, I am the son of a stranger, an Amalekite. And David said unto him, How wast thou not afraid to stretch forth thine hand to destroy the 15 Lord's anointed? And David called one of the young men, and said, Go near, 16 and fall upon him. And he smote him that he died. And David said unto him, Thy blood be upon thy head; for thy mouth hath testified against thee, saying, I have slain the Lord's anointed.

17 And David lamented with this lamentation over Saul and over Jonathan 18 his son: (Also he bade them teach the children of Judah the use of the bow: behold, it is written in the book of Jasher:)

19   The beauty of Israel is slain upon thy high places:
        how are the mighty fallen!

20   Tell it not in Gath,
        publish it not in the streets of Askelon;
    lest the daughters of the Philistines rejoice,
        lest the daughters of the uncircumcised triumph.

21   Ye mountains of Gilboa, let there be no dew,
        neither let there be rain, upon you, nor fields of offerings:
    for there the shield of the mighty is vilely cast away,
        the shield of Saul, as though he had not been anointed with oil.

22   From the blood of the slain,
        from the fat of the mighty,
    the bow of Jonathan turned not back,
        and the sword of Saul returned not empty.

23   Saul and Jonathan were lovely and pleasant in their lives,
        and in their death they were not divided:
    they were swifter than eagles,
        they were stronger than lions.

24   Ye daughters of Israel, weep over Saul,
        who clothed you in scarlet, with other delights;
        who put on ornaments of gold upon your apparel.

25   How are the mighty fallen in the midst of the battle!
        O Jonathan, thou wast slain in thine high places.

26   I am distressed for thee, my brother Jonathan:
        very pleasant hast thou been unto me:
    thy love to me was wonderful,
        passing the love of women.

27   How are the mighty fallen,
        and the weapons of war perished!

5   Then came all the tribes of Israel to David unto Hebron, and spake, say-
2 ing, Behold, we are thy bone and thy flesh. Also in time past, when Saul was king over us, thou wast he that leddest out and broughtest in Israel: and the Lord said to thee, Thou shalt feed my people Israel, and thou shalt be a
3 captain over Israel. So all the elders of Israel came to the king to Hebron; and king David made a league with them in Hebron before the Lord: and
4 they anointed David king over Israel. David was thirty years old when he
5 began to reign, and he reigned forty years. In Hebron he reigned over Judah seven years and six months: and in Jerusalem he reigned thirty and three years over all Israel and Judah.
6   And the king and his men went to Jerusalem unto the Jebusites, the in-habitants of the land: which spake unto David, saying, Except thou take away the blind and the lame, thou shalt not come in hither: thinking, David
7 cannot come in hither. Nevertheless, David took the stronghold of Zion: . . .
9 So David dwelt in the fort, and called it the city of David. And David built
10 round about from Millo and inward. And David went on, and grew great, and the Lord God of hosts was with him.
11   And Hiram king of Tyre sent messengers to David, and cedar trees, and
12 carpenters, and masons: and they built David a house. And David perceived that the Lord had established him king over Israel, and that he had exalted
13 his kingdom for his people Israel's sake. And David took him more concu-bines and wives out of Jerusalem, after he was come from Hebron: and there were yet sons and daughters born to David.

11   And it came to pass, . . . that David sent Joab, and his servants with him, and all Israel; and they destroyed the children of Ammon, and besieged Rabbah. But David tarried still at Jerusalem.
2   And it came to pass in an eveningtide, that David arose from off his bed, and walked upon the roof of the king's house: and from the roof he saw a woman washing herself; and the woman was very beautiful to look upon.
3 And David sent and inquired after the woman. And one said, Is not this
4 Bath-sheba, the daughter of Eliam, the wife of Uriah the Hittite? And David sent messengers, and took her; and she came in unto him, and he lay with her; for she was purified from her uncleanness: and she returned unto her
5 house. And the woman conceived, and sent and told David, and said, I am with child.
6   And David sent to Joab, saying, Send me Uriah the Hittite. And Joab sent
7 Uriah to David. And when Uriah was come unto him, David demanded of

From the History of Ancient Israel

him how Joab did, and how the people did, and how the war prospered.
8 And David said to Uriah, Go down to thy house, and wash thy feet. And Uriah departed out of the king's house, and there followed him a mess of
9 meat from the king. But Uriah slept at the door of the king's house with all the servants of his lord, and went not down to his house.

10 And when they had told David, saying, Uriah went not down unto his house, David said unto Uriah, Camest thou not from thy journey? why then didst thou not go down unto thine house?

11 And Uriah said unto David, The ark, and Israel, and Judah, abide in tents; and my lord Joab, and the servants of my lord, are encamped in the open fields; shall I then go into mine house, to eat and to drink, and to lie with my wife? as thou livest, and as thy soul liveth, I will not do this thing.

12 And David said to Uriah, Tarry here to-day also, and to-morrow I will
13 let thee depart. So Uriah abode in Jerusalem that day, and the morrow. And when David had called him, he did eat and drink before him; and he made him drunk: and at even he went out to lie on his bed with the servants of his lord, but went not down to his house.

14 And it came to pass in the morning, that David wrote a letter to Joab,
15 and sent it by the hand of Uriah. And he wrote in the letter, saying, Set ye Uriah in the forefront of the hottest battle, and retire ye from him, that he
16 may be smitten, and die. And it came to pass, when Joab observed the city, that he assigned Uriah unto a place where he knew that valiant men were.
17 And the men of the city went out, and fought with Joab: and there fell some of the people of the servants of David; and Uriah the Hittite died also.

18,19 Then Joab sent and told David all the things concerning the war; And charged the messenger, saying, When thou hast made an end of telling the
20 matters of the war unto the king, And if so be that the king's wrath arise, and he say unto thee, Wherefore approached ye so nigh unto the city when
21 ye did fight? knew ye not that they would shoot from the wall? Who smote Abimelech the son of Jerubbesheth? did not a woman cast a piece of a mill-stone upon him from the wall, that he died in Thebez? why went ye nigh the wall? then say thou, Thy servant Uriah the Hittite is dead also.

22 So the messenger went, and came and showed David all that Joab had sent
23 him for. And the messenger said unto David, Surely the men prevailed against us, and came out unto us into the field, and we were upon them even
24 unto the entering of the gate. And the shooters shot from off the wall upon thy servants; and some of the king's servants be dead, and thy servant Uriah the Hittite is dead also.

25 Then David said unto the messenger, Thus shalt thou say unto Joab, Let not this thing displease thee, for the sword devoureth one as well as another: make thy battle more strong against the city, and overthrow it: and en-courage thou him.

26 And when the wife of Uriah heard that Uriah her husband was dead, she
27 mourned for her husband. And when the mourning was past, David sent and fetched her to his house, and she became his wife, and bare him a son. But the thing that David had done displeased the Lord.

12 And the Lord sent Nathan unto David. And he came unto him, and said unto him,

2 There were two men in one city; the one rich, and the other poor. The

3   rich man had exceeding many flocks and herds: But the poor man had
nothing, save one little ewe lamb, which he had bought and nourished
up: and it grew up together with him, and with his children; it did eat
of his own meat, and drank of his own cup, and lay in his bosom, and was
4   unto him as a daughter. And there came a traveler unto the rich man, and
he spared to take of his own flock and of his own herd, to dress for the
wayfaring man that was come unto him; but took the poor man's lamb,
and dressed it for the man that was come to him.

5   And David's anger was greatly kindled against the man; and he said to
Nathan, As the Lord liveth, the man that hath done this thing shall surely die:
6 And he shall restore the lamb fourfold, because he did this thing, and because
he had no pity.
7   And Nathan said to David, Thou art the man. Thus saith the Lord God of
Israel, I anointed thee king over Israel, and I delivered thee out of the hand
8 of Saul; And I gave thee thy master's house, and thy master's wives into thy
bosom, and gave thee the house of Israel and of Judah; and if that had been
too little, I would moreover have given unto thee such and such things.
9 Wherefore hast thou despised the commandment of the Lord, to do evil in
his sight? thou hast killed Uriah the Hittite with the sword, and hast taken
his wife to be thy wife, and hast slain him with the sword of the children of
10 Ammon. Now therefore the sword shall never depart from thine house; . . .
11   Thus saith the Lord, Behold, I will raise up evil against thee out of thine
own house, and I will take thy wives before thine eyes, and give them unto
12 thy neighbor, and he shall lie with thy wives in the sight of this sun. For thou
didst it secretly: but I will do this thing before all Israel, and before the sun.
13   And David said unto Nathan, I have sinned against the Lord. And Nathan
said unto David, The Lord also hath put away thy sin; thou shalt not die.
14 Howbeit, because by this deed thou hast given great occasion to the enemies
of the Lord to blaspheme, the child also that is born unto thee shall surely die.
15 And Nathan departed unto his house.
    And the Lord struck the child that Uriah's wife bare unto David, and it
16 was very sick. David therefore besought God for the child; and David
17 fasted, and went in, and lay all night upon the earth. And the elders of his
house arose, and went to him, to raise him up from the earth: but he would
not, neither did he eat bread with them.
18   And it came to pass on the seventh day, that the child died. And the servants of David feared to tell him that the child was dead: for they said, Behold,
while the child was yet alive, we spake unto him, and he would not hearken
unto our voice: how will he then vex himself, if we tell him that the child is
19 dead? But when David saw that his servants whispered, David perceived that
the child was dead: therefore David said unto his servants, Is the child dead?
And they said, He is dead.
20   Then David arose from the earth, and washed, and anointed himself, and
changed his apparel, and came into the house of the Lord, and worshipped:
then he came to his own house; and when he required, they set bread before
him, and he did eat.
21   Then said his servants unto him, What thing is this that thou hast done?
thou didst fast and weep for the child, while it was alive; but when the child
22 was dead, thou didst rise and eat bread. And he said, While the child was yet

alive, I fasted and wept: for I said, Who can tell whether God will be gra-
23 cious to me, that the child may live? But now he is dead, wherefore should I fast? can I bring him back again? I shall go to him, but he shall not return to me.

24 And David comforted Bath-sheba his wife, and went in unto her, and lay with her: and she bare a son, and he called his name Solomon: and the Lord loved him.

15 And it came to pass after this, that Absalom prepared him chariots and
2 horses, and fifty men to run before him. And Absalom rose up early, and stood beside the way of the gate: and it was so, that when any man that had a controversy came to the king for judgment, then Absalom called unto him, and said, Of what city art thou? And he said, Thy servant is of one of the
3 tribes of Israel. And Absalom said unto him, See, thy matters are good and
4 right; but there is no man deputed of the king to hear thee. Absalom said moreover, Oh that I were made judge in the land, that every man which hath
5 any suit or cause might come unto me, and I would do him justice! And it was so, that when any man came nigh to him to do him obeisance, he put
6 forth his hand, and took him, and kissed him. And on this manner did Absalom to all Israel that came to the king for judgment: so Absalom stole the hearts of the men of Israel.

7 And it came to pass after forty years, that Absalom said unto the king, I pray thee, let me go and pay my vow, which I have vowed unto the Lord,
8 in Hebron. For thy servant vowed a vow while I abode at Geshur in Syria, saying, If the Lord shall bring me again indeed to Jerusalem, then I will serve
9 the Lord. And the king said unto him, Go in peace. So he arose, and went to Hebron.

10 But Absalom sent spies throughout all the tribes of Israel, saying, As soon as ye hear the sound of the trumpet, then ye shall say, Absalom reigneth in
11 Hebron. And with Absalom went two hundred men out of Jerusalem, that were called; and they went in their simplicity, and they knew not any thing.
12 And Absalom sent for Ahithophel the Gilonite, David's counselor, from his city, even from Giloh, while he offered sacrifices. And the conspiracy was strong; for the people increased continually with Absalom.

13 And there came a messenger to David, saying, The hearts of the men of
14 Israel are after Absalom. And David said unto all his servants that were with him at Jerusalem, Arise, and let us flee; for we shall not else escape from Absalom: make speed to depart, lest he overtake us suddenly, and
15 bring evil upon us, and smite the city with the edge of the sword. And the king's servants said unto the king, Behold, thy servants are ready to do
16 whatsoever my lord the king shall appoint. And the king went forth, and all his household after him. And the king left ten women, which were concu-
18 bines, to keep the house. And all his servants passed on beside him; and all the Cherethites, and all the Pelethites, and all the Gittites, six hundred men
23 which came after him from Gath, passed on before the king. And all the country wept with a loud voice, and all the people passed over: the king also himself passed over the brook Kidron, and all the people passed over, toward the way of the wilderness.

30 And David went up by the ascent of mount Olivet, and wept as he went up, and had his head covered, and he went barefoot: and all the people that was with him covered every man his head, and they went up, weeping as

31 they went up. And one told David, saying, Ahithophel is among the conspirators with Absalom. And David said, O Lord, I pray thee, turn the counsel of Ahithophel into foolishness.

32 And it came to pass, that when David was come to the top of the mount, where he worshipped God, behold, Hushai the Archite came to meet him
33 with his coat rent, and earth upon his head: Unto whom David said, If thou
34 passest on with me, then thou shalt be a burden unto me: But if thou return to the city, and say unto Absalom, I will be thy servant, O king; as I have been thy father's servant hitherto, so will I now also be thy servant: then
35 mayest thou for me defeat the counsel of Ahithophel. And hast thou not there with thee Zadok and Abiathar the priests? therefore it shall be, that what thing soever thou shalt hear out of the king's house, thou shalt tell it to
36 Zadok and Abiathar the priests. Behold, they have there with them their two sons, Ahimaaz Zadok's son, and Jonathan Abiathar's son; and by them ye
37 shall send unto me every thing that ye can hear. So Hushai David's friend came into the city, and Absalom came into Jerusalem.

18 And David numbered the people that were with him, and set captains of
2 thousands and captains of hundreds over them. And David sent forth a third part of the people under the hand of Joab, and a third part under the hand of Abishai the son of Zeruiah, Joab's brother, and a third part under the hand of Ittai the Gittite. And the king said unto the people, I will surely go forth
3 with you myself also. But the people answered, Thou shalt not go forth: for if we flee away, they will not care for us; neither if half of us die, will they care for us: but now thou art worth ten thousand of us: therefore now it is
4 better that thou succor us out of the city. And the king said unto them, What seemeth you best I will do. And the king stood by the gate side, and all the people came out by hundreds and by thousands.

5 And the king commanded Joab and Abishai and Ittai, saying, Deal gently for my sake with the young man, even with Absalom. And all the people heard when the king gave all the captains charge concerning Absalom.

6 So the people went out into the field against Israel: and the battle was in
7 the wood of Ephraim; Where the people of Israel were slain before the servants of David, and there was there a great slaughter that day of twenty
8 thousand men. For the battle was there scattered over the face of all the country: and the wood devoured more people that day than the sword devoured.

9 And Absalom met the servants of David. And Absalom rode upon a mule, and the mule went under the thick boughs of a great oak, and his head caught hold of the oak, and he was taken up between the heaven and the earth; and
10 the mule that was under him went away. And a certain man saw it, and told Joab, and said, Behold, I saw Absalom hanged in an oak.

11 And Joab said unto the man that told him, And, behold, thou sawest him, and why didst thou not smite him there to the ground? and I would have
12 given thee ten shekels of silver, and a girdle. And the man said unto Joab, Though I should receive a thousand shekels of silver in mine hand, yet would I not put forth mine hand against the king's son: for in our hearing the king charged thee and Abishai and Ittai, saying, Beware that none touch the young
13 man Absalom. Otherwise I should have wrought falsehood against mine own life: for there is no matter hid from the king, and thou thyself wouldest have set thyself against me.

From the History of Ancient Israel

14 Then said Joab, I may not tarry thus with thee. And he took three darts
in his hand, and thrust them through the heart of Absalom, while he was yet
15 alive in the midst of the oak. And ten young men that bare Joab's armor com-
16 passed about and smote Absalom, and slew him. And Joab blew the trumpet,
and the people returned from pursuing after Israel: for Joab held back the
17 people. And they took Absalom, and cast him into a great pit in the wood,
and laid a very great heap of stones upon him: and all Israel fled every one to
his tent.

19 Then said Ahimaaz the son of Zadok, Let me now run, and bear the king
20 tidings, how that the Lord hath avenged him of his enemies. And Joab said
unto him, Thou shalt not bear tidings this day, but thou shalt bear tidings another day: but this day thou shalt bear no tidings, because the king's son is
21 dead. Then said Joab to Cushi, Go tell the king what thou hast seen. And
22 Cushi bowed himself unto Joab, and ran. Then said Ahimaaz the son of Zadok yet again to Joab, But howsoever, let me, I pray thee, also run after
Cushi. And Joab said, Wherefore wilt thou run, my son, seeing that thou
23 hast no tidings ready? But howsoever, said he, let me run. And he said unto
him, Run. Then Ahimaaz ran by the way of the plain, and overran Cushi.
24 And David sat between the two gates: and the watchman went up to the
roof over the gate unto the wall, and lifted up his eyes, and looked, and be-
25 hold a man running alone. And the watchman cried, and told the king. And
the king said, If he be alone, there is tidings in his mouth. And he came
26 apace, and drew near. And the watchman saw another man running: and the
watchman called unto the porter, and said, Behold another man running alone.
27 And the king said, He also bringeth tidings. And the watchman said, Me-
thinketh the running of the foremost is like the running of Ahimaaz the son
of Zadok. And the king said, He is a good man, and cometh with good tid-
28 ings. And Ahimaaz called, and said unto the king, All is well. And he fell
down to the earth upon his face before the king, and said, Blessed be the
Lord thy God, which hath delivered up the men that lifted up their hand
against my lord the king.
29 And the king said, Is the young man Absalom safe? And Ahimaaz answered, When Joab sent the king's servant, and me thy servant, I saw a
30 great tumult, but I knew not what it was. And the king said unto him, Turn
aside, and stand here. And he turned aside, and stood still.
31 And, behold, Cushi came; and Cushi said, Tidings, my lord the king:
for the Lord hath avenged thee this day of all them that rose up against thee.
32 And the king said unto Cushi, Is the young man Absalom safe? And Cushi
answered, The enemies of my lord the king, and all that rise against thee to
33 do thee hurt, be as that young man is. And the king was much moved, and
went up to the chamber over the gate, and wept: and as he went, thus he
said, O my son Absalom! my son, my son Absalom! would God I had died
for thee, O Absalom, my son, my son!

19 And it was told Joab, Behold, the king weepeth and mourneth for Absa-
2 lom. And the victory that day was turned into mourning unto all the people:
for the people heard say that day how the king was grieved for his son.
3 And the people gat them by stealth that day into the city, as people being
4 ashamed steal away when they flee in battle. But the king covered his face,
and the king cried with a loud voice, O my son Absalom! O Absalom, my
son, my son!

Introduction to Biblical Literature

5   And Joab came into the house to the king, and said, Thou hast shamed this
day the faces of all thy servants, which this day have saved thy life, and the
lives of thy sons and of thy daughters, and the lives of thy wives, and the
6 lives of thy concubines; In that thou lovest thine enemies, and hatest thy
friends. For thou hast declared this day, that thou regardest neither princes
nor servants: for this day I perceive, that if Absalom had lived, and all we
7 had died this day, then it had pleased thee well. Now therefore arise, go
forth, and speak comfortably unto thy servants: for I swear by the Lord, if
thou go not forth, there will not tarry one with thee this night: and that will
be worse unto thee than all the evil that befell thee from thy youth until now.
8 Then the king arose, and sat in the gate. And they told unto all the people,
saying, Behold, the king doth sit in the gate. And all the people came before
the king.

I Kings

2   Now the days of David drew nigh that he should die; and he charged Solo-
2 mon his son, saying, I go the way of all the earth: be thou strong therefore,
3 and show thyself a man; And keep the charge of the Lord thy God, to walk
in his ways, to keep his statutes, and his commandments, and his judgments,
and his testimonies, as it is written in the law of Moses, that thou mayest
5 prosper in all that thou doest, and whithersoever thou turnest thyself: Moreover thou knowest also what Joab the son of Zeruiah did to me, and what he
did to the two captains of the hosts of Israel, unto Abner the son of Ner, and
unto Amasa the son of Jether, whom he slew, and shed the blood of war in
peace, and put the blood of war upon his girdle that was about his loins, and
6 in his shoes that were on his feet. Do therefore according to thy wisdom, and
let not his hoar head go down to the grave in peace.
7   But show kindness unto the sons of Barzillai the Gileadite, and let them
be of those that eat at thy table: for so they came to me when I fled because
8 of Absalom thy brother. And, behold, thou hast with thee Shimei the son of
Gera, a Benjamite of Bahurim, which cursed me with a grievous curse in the
day when I went to Mahanaim: but he came down to meet me at Jordan,
and I sware to him by the Lord, saying, I will not put thee to death with the
9 sword. Now therefore hold him not guiltless: for thou art a wise man, and
knowest what thou oughtest to do unto him; but his hoar head bring thou
down to the grave with blood.
10   So David slept with his fathers, and was buried in the city of David.
11 And the days that David reigned over Israel were forty years: seven years
reigned he in Hebron, and thirty and three years reigned he in Jerusalem.
12   Then sat Solomon upon the throne of David his father; and his kingdom
was established greatly.
3   And Solomon made affinity with Pharaoh king of Egypt, and took Pha-
2 raoh's daughter, and brought her into the city of David, . . . Only the people
sacrificed in high places, because there was no house built unto the name of
3 the Lord, until those days. And Solomon loved the Lord, walking in the
statutes of David his father: only he sacrificed and burnt incense in high

From the History of Ancient Israel

4 places. And the king went to Gibeon to sacrifice there; for that was the great high place: a thousand burnt offerings did Solomon offer upon that altar.

5 In Gibeon the Lord appeared to Solomon in a dream by night: and God
6 said, Ask what I shall give thee. And Solomon said, Thou hast showed unto
7 thy servant David my father great mercy, . . . And now, O Lord my God, thou hast made thy servant king instead of David my father: and I am but a little
8 child: I know not how to go out or come in. And thy servant is in the midst of thy people which thou hast chosen, a great people, that cannot be num-
9 bered nor counted for multitude. Give therefore thy servant an understand-ing heart to judge thy people, that I may discern between good and bad: for who is able to judge this thy so great a people?

10,11 And the speech pleased the Lord, that Solomon had asked this thing. And God said unto him, Because thou hast asked this thing, and hast not asked for thyself long life; neither hast asked riches for thyself, nor hast asked the life of thine enemies; but hast asked for thyself understanding to discern
12 judgment; Behold, I have done according to thy word: lo, I have given thee a wise and an understanding heart; so that there was none like thee before
13 thee, neither after thee shall any arise like unto thee. And I have also given thee that which thou hast not asked, both riches, and honor: so that there
14 shall not be any among the kings like unto thee all thy days. And if thou wilt walk in my ways, to keep my statutes and my commandments, as thy father David did walk, then I will lengthen thy days.

15 And Solomon awoke; and, behold, it was a dream. And he came to Jerusa-lem, and stood before the ark of the covenant of the Lord, and offered up burnt offerings, and offered peace offerings, and made a feast to all his servants.

16 Then came there two women, that were harlots, unto the king, and stood
17 before him. And the one woman said, O my lord, I and this woman dwell in
18 one house; and I was delivered of a child with her in the house. And it came to pass the third day after that I was delivered, that this woman was deliv-ered also: and we were together; there was no stranger with us in the house,
19 save we two in the house. And this woman's child died in the night; because
20 she overlaid it. And she arose at midnight, and took my son from beside me, while thine handmaid slept, and laid it in her bosom, and laid her dead child
21 in my bosom. And when I rose in the morning to give my child suck, behold, it was dead: but when I had considered it in the morning, behold, it was not
22 my son, which I did bear. And the other woman said, Nay; but the living is my son, and the dead is thy son. And this said, No; but the dead is thy son, and the living is my son. Thus they spake before the king.

23 Then said the king, The one saith, This is my son that liveth, and thy son is the dead: and the other saith, Nay; but thy son is the dead, and my son is
24 the living. And the king said, Bring me a sword. And they brought a sword
25 before the king. And the king said, Divide the living child in two, and give half to the one, and half to the other.

26 Then spake the woman whose the living child was unto the king, for her bowels yearned upon her son, and she said, O my lord, give her the living child, and in no wise slay it. But the other said, Let it be neither mine nor
27 thine, but divide it. Then the king answered and said, Give her the living
28 child, and in no wise slay it: she is the mother thereof. And all Israel heard

of the judgment which the king had judged; and they feared the king: for they saw that the wisdom of God was in him to do judgment.

10 And all king Solomon's drinking vessels were of gold, and all the vessels of the house of the forest of Lebanon were of pure gold; none were of silver: it was nothing accounted of in the days of Solo-
22 mon. For the king had at sea a navy of Tharshish with the navy of Hiram: once in three years came the navy of Tharshish, bringing gold, and silver,
23 ivory, and apes, and peacocks. So king Solomon exceeded all the kings of the earth for riches and for wisdom.
24 And all the earth sought to Solomon, to hear his wisdom, which God had
25 put in his heart. And they brought every man his present, vessels of silver, and vessels of gold, and garments, and armor, and spices, horses, and mules,
26 a rate year by year. And Solomon gathered together chariots and horsemen: and he had a thousand and four hundred chariots, and twelve thousand horsemen, whom he bestowed in the cities for chariots, and with the king at
27 Jerusalem. And the king made silver to be in Jerusalem as stones, and cedars
28 made he to be as the sycamore trees that are in the vale, for abundance. And Solomon had horses brought out of Egypt, and linen yarn: the king's mer-
29 chants received the linen yarn at a price. And a chariot came up and went out of Egypt for six hundred shekels of silver, and a horse for a hundred and fifty: and so for all the kings of the Hittites, and for the kings of Syria, did they bring them out by their means.

11 But king Solomon loved many strange women, together with the daughter of Pharaoh, women of the Moabites, Ammonites, Edomites, Zidonians, and
2 Hittites; Of the nations concerning which the Lord said unto the children of Israel, Ye shall not go in to them, neither shall they come in unto you: for surely they will turn away your heart after their gods: Solomon clave unto
3 these in love. And he had seven hundred wives, princesses, and three hun-
4 dred concubines: and his wives turned away his heart. For it came to pass, when Solomon was old, that his wives turned away his heart after other gods: and his heart was not perfect with the Lord his God, as was the heart of
5 David his father. For Solomon went after Ashtoreth the goddess of the Zi-
7 donians, and after Milcom the abomination of the Ammonites. Then did Solomon build a high place for Chemosh, the abomination of Moab, in the hill that is before Jerusalem, and for Molech, the abomination of the children
8 of Ammon. And likewise did he for all his strange wives, which burnt incense and sacrificed unto their gods.
9 And the Lord was angry with Solomon, because his heart was turned from
10 the Lord God of Israel, which had appeared unto him twice, And had commanded him concerning this thing, that he should not go after other gods:
11 but he kept not that which the Lord commanded. Wherefore the Lord said unto Solomon, Forasmuch as this is done of thee, and thou hast not kept my covenant and my statutes, which I have commanded thee, I will surely
12 rend the kingdom from thee, and will give it to thy servant. Notwithstanding, in thy days I will not do it for David thy father's sake: but I will rend it
13 out of the hand of thy son. Howbeit I will not rend away all the kingdom; but will give one tribe to thy son for David my servant's sake, and for Jerusalem's sake which I have chosen.

From the History of Ancient Israel

Considerations and Questions

1. The woman whom Saul goes to see in order to consult with the late Samuel is generally referred to as "the witch of Endor," even though the word "witch" does not appear in the actual text. How is she like or not like what you mean by witch? What exactly is her line of work? Does she appear to have a supernatural connection with evil or "the Evil One"? Why do you suppose that King Saul has passed an ordinance against such activities as hers? What implicit admission about his condition as a king and as a man does Saul make by undertaking this visit?

2. What have we encountered thus far in our study that suggests the idea of personal survival after death as part of the religion of the Israelites? What appear to be the terms of Samuel's survival? To what extent does he bring Saul special news from "beyond the grave"?

3. We have here two accounts of the death of Saul. The first is directly set forth by the writer of I Samuel 31. The second is in the words of a disheveled Amalekite (II Samuel 1), whom David hacks to pieces. If the Amalekite is lying, what might be his reasons for doing so? How do David's reactions to the Amalekite's story serve to display David as a character and, perhaps, as a skilled politician?

4. One of the most significant and interesting episodes in the biography of King David is that of his affair with Bath-sheba, the wife of Uriah the Hittite. Now adultery is common enough in most ages, and the murder of the "third man" (or third woman) is committed in books, cinema, and TV programs too many times to count corpses. The fact is that sexual passion is and has been one of the great motives for criminal homicide.

   An account of adultery and murder, then, does not make this story so special. But what about the inclusion of these bleak facts in an official biography of the greatest king of Israel? Are we to assume that the author is one of the "debunking" school of historical biographers? Is he trying to excite an audience with the announcement that the great and religious king is just as bad as, or sensationally worse than, most ordinary people? You should find, I think, a good deal in the text to make you reject such a notion.

   On the other hand, should the modern reader assume that in the primitive setting of the story what King David does is not really so terrible? In that world of polygamous marriages, concubinage, and bloody violence, does the writer suggest that David's elimination of a subordinate in order to supplement the royal harem should not be judged by the standards of more fastidious times? I think that you should find ample reason to reject this idea also.

5. The story of David and Bath-sheba begins in the season when kings go forth to battle. But this great soldier-king sends out his army under a

trusted general and remains himself in Jerusalem. Does he stay home in order to court Bath-sheba? No, he does not notice her until Joab is actually in the field against the Ammonites. David's remaining in the capital would appear to be evidence of the success and stability of his administration. At this point the nation of Israel has power and unity; their king need no longer rule from a tent; he is the head of state, not merely a war-chief.

But this head of state is also by temperament a warrior, that most physical and elemental sort of "human" creature. It is as a man of appetite and action that he sees and takes what he wants. As we know, heads of state are not gods nor are they often saints. As flesh and blood they differ from the rest of us not so much in what they want but in what they can take. How many ordinary people remain uncorrupted, free from crimes like David's, only because they lack opportunity, power, and daring? No doubt we are right to hope for and expect great moral self-control from our leaders, but unless we choose to be governed by the despotism of "the king as god," we had better not assume perfection.° Lest in our less ethical moments we entertain a naive envy for the freedom provided King David and other heads of state by their opportunities and powers, we might recall a price paid for it. The opportunities and powers of public rulers are public matters. Although rulers frequently try to cover up their missteps, as do the rest of us, their chances of doing so are much slimmer than those of private persons.

What attempts does David make to keep his affair with Bath-sheba secret? What likelihood of success in such an endeavor is ever evident in the story? How do David's dealings with Bath-sheba herself, with his servants, and with Joab indicate the extent of his authority and command of allegiance? What about Nathan?

6. How and why does the teller of this tale take particular pains to show us that Uriah the Hittite is a fine man? Ironically, Uriah's virtues help to destroy him. Is David aware of Uriah's noble qualities? Years before, Saul had sent his young officer David into the most dangerous parts of a battle in order to get rid of him. Compare the motives and actions of the two kings.

7. Ordinary humanity at its worst, extraordinary power at its most unjust are what we see in King David during much of the Bath-sheba story. But we should see other things as well. What is the unusual, not ordinary, reaction of the great king to the words of the lone prophet, Nathan? What is David's reaction to what he believes to be God's judgment on what he has done? What is the composite picture of David as a man which this

---

° The Law of Moses, the ideal of Israel's monarchy, and the thematic insistence of the whole Bible assert that a king is *not* a god and that one of the great evils which afflict mankind occurs when a ruler presumes, or his people assume, otherwise.

story presents? What speculative relationship can you make between that personality and the historical triumph of the kingdom of Israel?

8. Another important incident from this account of David's reign involves his son Absalom. Here is a summary-outline of the episode's main events:

    (a) Absalom foments a rebellion against his father.
    (b) A significant number of Israelites join Absalom's cause.
    (c) David's throne seems in jeopardy.
    (d) David's aggressive and efficient general, Joab, defeats and kills Absalom.
    (e) David mourns Absalom.
    (f) Joab gives the King some straight talk and David makes an effort to restore national peace and unity.

Let me suggest, but only as a starting point, that you ask yourself two basic questions about each of these: "how?" and "why?"

9. By what means does David characteristically receive the directions of his God? How does Solomon receive divine assurance that he will have wisdom and riches and honor and a long life? What implications do you find in a comparison of David's religious experiences with Solomon's? What does David actually *do* about God? How about Solomon?

10. Consider in detail the story of the baby, the two mothers, and King Solomon. It appears to be offered as evidence for his celebrated wisdom.

11. Both David and Solomon maintain large collections of beautiful women. Although Solomon's seven hundred wives and three hundred concubines have received more public attention through the ages than has David's "family," can you see reasons to infer that David is in fact the more virile and sexually emotional of the two? Can you support (or attack) the suggestion that Solomon's huge battalion of famous beauties may have something to do with public relations? Or that it is part of a larger and ominous display of despotic splendor? What does Solomon do for his women that David never does for his?

12. At the end of this account of Solomon's life, the Lord foretells the division of the kingdom in judgment upon the King's sacrilegious acts. How do such acts and other of Solomon's royal policies suggest on a historical level the likelihood of national disaster for Israel?

8. The Prophets of Israel

He has heard the prayer of His servant your shepherd and will grant it if such shall be your desire after I, His messenger, shall have explained to you its import . . . that is to say, its full import. For it is like unto many of the prayers of men, in that it asks for more than he who utters it is aware of . . . except he pause and think.

MARK TWAIN, *The War Prayer*

Do not assume that the space I give to the Biblical Prophets in this book is a reflection of how important I think they are. The Old Testament Prophets are indeed so profoundly important that a serious study of them is out of the question in a mere "Introduction" to Biblical literature. Their various personalities, beliefs, and actions permeate in complex ways almost everything else in the Bible. With the help of a few illustrative selections, here we will only attempt some basic points about how this line of remarkable people fits into the history of ancient Israel.

We are used to "prophets" simply as people who foretell the future. When we call predictors "prophets" perhaps we are inclined to give the term a skeptical or derisive tone. Who, after all, can really tell us what tomorrow will bring? Twentieth-century society is, however, cluttered with such prophets, and twentieth-century society, whether skeptical about them or not, supports them well. We attend to weather prophets, political prophets, economic prophets, sports prophets, and even a few prophets who claim some mystical wire service from Beyond. We generally go confidently to bed with a prophecy about election results long before the votes are all counted. Increasingly, our most revered prophet is not a person but a computer.

Every society about which we know anything has maintained in some form such agencies for prediction. The yen to hear about the future is apparently part of the human condition. That false predictions do mingle with true ones in every place and time does not seem to make much difference.

Ancient Israel's history includes prophets of this sort, seers or mediums like the witch of Endor. Even Samuel has an apparent reputation as a "seer," for Saul first seeks him out to predict where the lost donkeys will be found. But the Prophets of Israel who populate the continuing narrative of the Old Testament are not in the business of fortunetelling. Their vocation is to be the moral critics of society.

173

That is the function of Nathan when he proclaims to King David, "Thou art the man." Nathan does tell David of disasters to come but not as a display of clairvoyance nor as the main point of the interview. His prophetic message is that the great King has sinned and must, in the nature of things, pay for it. Like later and more sophisticated Prophets, Nathan is a teacher rather than a wizard or wonder-worker. His concern with the future is that it is the result of the present.

In that relatively primitive but certainly vivid episode about David and Nathan we have in outline the work of Israel's Prophets. As Biblical history continues there are narratives about Prophets that are much more complex. Many of the Biblical documents about the Prophets of Israel are not narratives but writings of the Prophets themselves, persuasive and critical sermons to their own contemporaries. But common to Nathan and the gifted literary or "writing" Prophets of later days are such essential matters as:

1. The Prophet is a man of words. He is not a captain, king, or a Samson.
2. The Prophet speaks or writes from the spiritual conviction that God has commanded him to do so. Therefore, he has no doubt about the truth of what he says and he dares to speak out at the risk of offending the most powerful of the earth.
3. The prophetic demand is that men turn from evil and do right because it is God's explicit will. Crimes like David's or Ahab's, or the occasional idolatries of the people of Israel, are not mere offenses against other people or institutions. For the Prophet they are intolerable insults to God Almighty.
4. The Prophet emphasizes Divine (or "natural") *justice.* The consequences, whether good or bad, of human behavior are public demonstrations of the truth he preaches. He needs no crystal ball to foretell the evil that will result from evil acts. That such evil will surely come is for him a principle of existence.

I Kings

18:17   And it came to pass, when Ahab saw Elijah, that Ahab said unto him, Art
18 thou he that troubleth Israel? And he answered, I have not troubled Israel;
but thou, and thy father's house, in that ye have forsaken the commandments
19 of the Lord, and thou hast followed Baalim. Now therefore send, and gather
to me all Israel unto mount Carmel, and the prophets of Baal four hundred
and fifty, and the prophets of the groves four hundred, which eat at Jezebel's
20 table. So Ahab sent unto all the children of Israel, and gathered the prophets
together unto mount Carmel.
21   And Elijah came unto all the people, and said, How long halt ye between
two opinions? if the Lord be God, follow him: but if Baal, then follow him.
22 And the people answered him not a word. Then said Elijah unto the people,
I, even I only, remain a prophet of the Lord; but Baal's prophets are four
23 hundred and fifty men. Let them therefore give us two bullocks; and let them
choose one bullock for themselves, and cut it in pieces, and lay it on wood,
and put no fire under: and I will dress the other bullock, and lay it on wood,
24 and put no fire under: And call ye on the name of your gods, and I will call
on the name of the Lord: and the God that answereth by fire, let him be God.
And all the people answered and said, It is well spoken.
25   And Elijah said unto the prophets of Baal, Choose you one bullock for
yourselves, and dress it first; for ye are many; and call on the name of your
26 gods, but put no fire under. And they took the bullock which was given them,
and they dressed it, and called on the name of Baal from morning even until
noon, saying, O Baal, hear us. But there was no voice, nor any that answered.
27 And they leaped upon the altar which was made. And it came to pass at noon,
that Elijah mocked them, and said, Cry aloud: for he is a god; either he is
talking, or he is pursuing, or he is in a journey, or peradventure he sleepeth,
28 and must be awaked. And they cried aloud, and cut themselves after their
29 manner with knives and lancets, till the blood gushed out upon them. And it
came to pass, when midday was past, and they prophesied until the time of
the offering of the evening sacrifice, that there was neither voice, nor any to
answer, nor any that regarded.
30   And Elijah said unto all the people, Come near unto me. And all the people
came near unto him. And he repaired the altar of the Lord that was broken
31 down. And Elijah took twelve stones, according to the number of the tribes
of the sons of Jacob, unto whom the word of the Lord came, saying, Israel
32 shall be thy name: And with the stones he built an altar in the name of the
Lord: and he made a trench about the altar, as great as would contain two
33 measures of seed. And he put the wood in order, and cut the bullock in pieces,
and laid him on the wood, and said, Fill four barrels with water, and pour it
34 on the burnt sacrifice, and on the wood. And he said, Do it the second time.
And they did it the second time. And he said, Do it the third time. And they
35 did it the third time. And the water ran round about the altar; and he filled
the trench also with water.
36   And it came to pass at the time of the offering of the evening sacrifice,
that Elijah the prophet came near, and said, Lord God of Abraham, Isaac,
and of Israel, let it be known this day that thou art God in Israel, and that I

37 am thy servant, and that I have done all these things at thy word. Hear me,
O Lord, hear me, that this people may know that thou art the Lord God, and
38 that thou hast turned their heart back again. Then the fire of the Lord fell,
and consumed the burnt sacrifice, and the wood, and the stones, and the dust,
39 and licked up the water that was in the trench. And when all the people saw
it, they fell on their faces: and they said, The Lord, he is the God; the Lord,
40 he is the God. And Elijah said unto them, Take the prophets of Baal; let not
one of them escape. And they took them: and Elijah brought them down to
the brook Kishon, and slew them there.
41 And Elijah said unto Ahab, Get thee up, eat and drink; for there is a sound
42 of abundance of rain. So Ahab went up to eat and to drink. And Elijah went
up to the top of Carmel; and he cast himself down upon the earth, and put his
43 face between his knees, And said to his servant, Go up now, look toward the
sea. And he went up, and looked, and said, There is nothing. And he said,
44 Go again seven times. And it came to pass at the seventh time, that he said,
Behold, there ariseth a little cloud out of the sea, like a man's hand. And he
said, Go up, say unto Ahab, Prepare thy chariot, and get thee down, that the
45 rain stop thee not. And it came to pass in the mean while, that the heaven was
black with clouds and wind, and there was a great rain. And Ahab rode, and
46 went to Jezreel. And the hand of the Lord was on Elijah; and he girded up
his loins, and ran before Ahab to the entrance of Jezreel.

21 And it came to pass after these things, that Naboth the Jezreelite had a
vineyard, which was in Jezreel, hard by the palace of Ahab king of Samaria.
2 And Ahab spake unto Naboth, saying, Give me thy vineyard, that I may
have it for a garden of herbs, because it is near unto my house: and I will give
thee for it a better vineyard than it; or, if it seem good to thee, I will give
3 thee the worth of it in money. And Naboth said to Ahab, The Lord forbid
4 it me, that I should give the inheritance of my fathers unto thee. And Ahab
came into his house heavy and displeased because of the word which Naboth
the Jezreelite had spoken to him: for he had said, I will not give thee the inheritance of my fathers. And he laid him down upon his bed, and turned
away his face, and would eat no bread.
5 But Jezebel his wife came to him, and said unto him, Why is thy spirit so
6 sad, that thou eatest no bread? And he said unto her, Because I spake unto
Naboth the Jezreelite, and said unto him, Give me thy vineyard for money;
or else, if it please thee, I will give thee another vineyard for it: and he an-
7 swered, I will not give thee my vineyard. And Jezebel his wife said unto him,
Dost thou now govern the kingdom of Israel? arise, and eat bread, and let
thine heart be merry: I will give thee the vineyard of Naboth the Jezreelite.
8 So she wrote letters in Ahab's name, and sealed them with his seal, and
sent the letters unto the elders and to the nobles that were in his city, dwell-
9 ing with Naboth. And she wrote in the letters, saying, Proclaim a fast, and
10 set Naboth on high among the people: And set two men, sons of Belial, before him, to bear witness against him, saying, Thou didst blaspheme God
11 and the king. And then carry him out, and stone him, that he may die. And
the men of his city, even the elders and the nobles who were the inhabitants
in his city, did as Jezebel had sent unto them, and as it was written in the
12 letters which she had sent unto them. They proclaimed a fast, and set Naboth
13 on high among the people. And there came in two men, children of Belial,
and sat before him: and the men of Belial witnessed against him, even

against Naboth, in the presence of the people, saying, Naboth did blaspheme God and the king. Then they carried him forth out of the city, and stoned
14 him with stones, that he died. Then they sent to Jezebel, saying, Naboth is stoned, and is dead.
15 And it came to pass, when Jezebel heard that Naboth was stoned, and was dead, that Jezebel said to Ahab, Arise, take possession of the vineyard of Naboth the Jezreelite, which he refused to give thee for money: for Naboth
16 is not alive, but dead. And it came to pass, when Ahab heard that Naboth was dead, that Ahab rose up to go down to the vineyard of Naboth the Jezreelite, to take possession of it.
17,18 And the word of the Lord came to Elijah the Tishbite, saying, Arise, go down to meet Ahab king of Israel, which is in Samaria: behold, he is in the
19 vineyard of Naboth, whither he is gone down to possess it. And thou shalt speak unto him, saying, Thus saith the Lord, Hast thou killed, and also taken possession? And thou shalt speak unto him, saying, Thus saith the Lord, In the place where dogs licked the blood of Naboth shall dogs lick thy blood,
20 even thine. And Ahab said to Elijah, Hast thou found me, O mine enemy? And he answered, I have found thee: because thou hast sold thyself to work
21 evil in the sight of the Lord. Behold, I will bring evil upon thee, and will take
23 away thy posterity, . . . And of Jezebel also spake the Lord, saying, The
24 dogs shall eat Jezebel by the wall of Jezreel. Him that dieth of Ahab in the city the dogs shall eat; and him that dieth in the field shall the fowls of the air eat.
27 And it came to pass, when Ahab heard those words, that he rent his clothes, and put sackcloth upon his flesh, and fasted, and lay in sackcloth,
28 and went softly. And the word of the Lord came to Elijah the Tishbite, say-
29 ing, Seest thou how Ahab humbleth himself before me? because he humbleth himself before me, I will not bring the evil in his days: but in his son's days will I bring the evil upon his house.

II Isaiah

40: 1   Comfort ye, comfort ye my people, saith your God.
2   Speak ye comfortably to Jerusalem, and cry unto her,
           that her warfare is accomplished,
           that her iniquity is pardoned:
    for she hath received of the Lord's hand double for all her sins.

3   The voice of him that crieth in the wilderness,
    Prepare ye the way of the Lord,
           make straight in the desert a highway for our God.
4   Every valley shall be exalted,
           and every mountain and hill shall be made low:
           and the crooked shall be made straight,
           and the rough places plain:
5   And the glory of the Lord shall be revealed,
           and all flesh shall see it together:
           for the mouth of the Lord hath spoken it.

From the History of Ancient Israel

6 The voice said, Cry.
    And he said, What shall I cry?
All flesh is grass,
    and all the goodliness thereof is as the flower of the field:
7 The grass withereth, the flower fadeth;
    because the spirit of the Lord bloweth upon it:
    surely the people is grass.
8 The grass withereth, the flower fadeth:
    but the word of our God shall stand for ever.

9 O Zion, that bringest good tidings,
    get thee up into the high mountain;
O Jerusalem, that bringest good tidings,
    lift up thy voice with strength;
    lift it up, be not afraid;
say unto the cities of Judah, Behold your God!
10   Behold, the Lord God will come with strong hand,
    and his arm shall rule for him:
behold, his reward is with him,
    and his work before him.
11 He shall feed his flock like a shepherd:
    he shall gather the lambs with his arm,
    and carry them in his bosom,
    and shall gently lead those that are with young.

12 Who hath measured the waters in the hollow of his hand,
    and meted out heaven with the span,
    and comprehended the dust of the earth in a measure,
    and weighed the mountains in scales,
    and the hills in a balance?
13 Who hath directed the Spirit of the Lord,
    or being his counselor hath taught him?
14 With whom took he counsel, and who instructed him,
    and taught him in the path of judgment,
    and taught him knowledge,
    and showed to him the way of understanding?
15 Behold, the nations are as a drop of a bucket,
    and are counted as the small dust of the balance:
    behold, he taketh up the isles as a very little thing.
17 All nations before him are as nothing;
    and they are counted to him less than nothing, and vanity.

18 To whom then will ye liken God?
    or what likeness will ye compare unto him?
21 Have ye not known? have ye not heard?
    hath it not been told you from the beginning?
    have ye not understood from the foundations of the earth?
22 It is he that sitteth upon the circle of the earth,
    and the inhabitants thereof are as grasshoppers;
that stretcheth out the heavens as a curtain,
    and spreadeth them out as a tent to dwell in:

23   That bringeth the princes to nothing;
            he maketh the judges of the earth as vanity.

25   To whom then will ye liken me, or shall I be equal?
            saith the Holy One.

26   Lift up your eyes on high,
            and behold who hath created these things,
            that bringeth out their host by number:
        he calleth them all by names
            by the greatness of his might,
            for that he is strong in power;
            not one faileth.

27   Why sayest thou, O Jacob, and speakest, O Israel,
            My way is hid from the Lord,
            and my judgment is passed over from my God?

28   Hast thou not known?
            hast thou not heard,
        that the everlasting God, the Lord,
            the Creator of the ends of the earth,
        fainteth not, neither is weary?
            there is no searching of his understanding.

29   He giveth power to the faint;
            and to them that have no might he increaseth strength.

30   Even the youths shall faint and be weary,
            and the young men shall utterly fall:

31   But they that wait upon the Lord shall renew their strength;
            they shall mount up with wings as eagles;
        they shall run, and not be weary;
            and they shall walk, and not faint.

Jeremiah

7:1,2 The word that came to Jeremiah from the Lord, saying, Stand in the gate of the Lord's house, and proclaim there this word, and say, Hear the word of the Lord, all ye of Judah, that enter in at these gates to worship the Lord.
3 Thus saith the Lord of hosts, the God of Israel, Amend your ways and your
4 doings, and I will cause you to dwell in this place. Trust ye not in lying words, saying, The temple of the Lord, The temple of the Lord, The temple
5 of the Lord, are these. For if ye thoroughly amend your ways and your doings; if ye thoroughly execute judgment between a man and his neighbor;
6 If ye oppress not the stranger, the fatherless, and the widow, and shed not
7 innocent blood in this place, neither walk after other gods to your hurt; Then will I cause you to dwell in this place, in the land that I gave to your fathers, for ever and ever.
8,9 Behold, ye trust in lying words, that cannot profit. Will ye steal, murder, and commit adultery, and swear falsely, and burn incense unto Baal, and

10 walk after other gods whom ye know not; And come and stand before me in this house, which is called by my name, and say, We are delivered to do
11 all these abominations? Is this house, which is called by my name, become a den of robbers in your eyes? Behold, even I have seen it, saith the Lord.
12 But go ye now unto my place which was in Shiloh, where I set my name at
13 the first, and see what I did to it for the wickedness of my people Israel. And now, because ye have done all these works, saith the Lord, and I spake unto you, rising up early and speaking, but ye heard not; and I called you, but ye
14 answered not; Therefore will I do unto this house, which is called by my name, wherein ye trust, and unto the place which I gave to you and to your fathers, as I have done to Shiloh.

21 Thus saith the Lord of hosts, the God of Israel; Put your burnt offerings
22 unto your sacrifices, and eat flesh. For I spake not unto your fathers, nor commanded them in the day that I brought them out of the land of Egypt,
23 concerning burnt offerings or sacrifices: But this thing commanded I them, saying, Obey my voice, and I will be your God, and ye shall be my people: and walk ye in all the ways that I have commanded you, that it may be well
24 unto you. But they hearkened not, nor inclined their ear, but walked in the counsels and in the imagination of their evil heart, and went backward, and not forward.

28 But thou shalt say unto them, This is a nation that obeyeth not the voice of the Lord their God, nor receiveth correction: truth is perished, and is cut
29 off from their mouth. Cut off thine hair, O Jerusalem, and cast it away, and take up a lamentation on high places; for the Lord hath rejected and forsaken
30 the generation of his wrath. For the children of Judah have done evil in my sight, saith the Lord: they have set their abominations in the house which
31 is called by my name, to pollute it. And they have built the high places of Tophet, which is in the valley of the son of Hinnom, to burn their sons and their daughters in the fire; which I commanded them not, neither came it into my heart.

Considerations and Questions

1. The story of Elijah and the prophets of Baal takes place in the northern kingdom, still called Israel. There has been pressure on this kingdom to adopt or at least accept the worship of the fertility god Baal. The children of Israel living there face, on the one hand, what appear to be the advantages of a local diety who is said to provide good luck with agriculture, and, on the other, the exclusive claims of the God of their ancient Covenant. The King, Ahab, is married to a Baalite and has given official tolerance to that cult, although he is still officially committed to the God of Israel. Why, in the opening lines of this selection, does Ahab accuse Elijah of troubling Israel? What sort of trouble from the King's point of view has the Prophet evidently been making? How does Elijah answer the King? How does the writer of this story show (rather than tell) the state of affairs?

2. How does the second story about Elijah remind us more than the first of the David and Nathan episode? What are the significant differences between Elijah's situation and Nathan's?

3. Jezebel has come to be a symbolic name for a wicked woman. What are the details of her wickedness in our selections?

4. One of the most quoted lines from the chapter about Elijah, Ahab, Jezebel, and the vineyard of Naboth is "Hast thou found me, O mine enemy?" What is the significance of the Prophet's reply? (In what sense is he Ahab's "enemy"?)

5. In Isaiah 40, Isaiah is not denouncing specific wicked behavior and announcing the certainty of divine punishment for it. Still, he is engaged in the prophetic work of teaching what he is convinced is true about God and the state of man. Sophisticated theologian and poet as he is, Isaiah's lecture still reflects the essential "prophetic" attitudes and techniques which I listed in the beginning of the section on the Prophets of Israel. Explain.

6. "Amend your ways and your doings and I will cause you to dwell in this place." (Jeremiah 7:3) Thus begins the message which Jeremiah is commanded by his God to deliver at the gates of the temple in Jerusalem to the people of the southern kingdom of Judah. What does the rest of his message supply in explanation and detail for this general introduction? (What are the alternatives to dwelling in this place? What place? In what sense? What have the people apparently to amend? Why is it just for their God to expect them to do so?)

V

Some Formal Biblical Literature

"Take the whole range of imaginative literature, and we are all wholesale borrowers. In every matter that relates to invention, to use, or beauty or form, we are borrowers."

Wendell Phillips, "The Lost Arts"

1. A Note on Literary Forms

Form is the Cage and Sense the Bird.
HENRY AUSTIN DOBSON, *The Toyman*

I do not call the selections in this part formal literature because they are more important or less sincere or "natural" than any of the rest of the Bible. With the use of the word "formal" I am simply indicating that these selections appear in certain familiar forms or shapes—shapes in which the makers of world literature have consciously organized their creative imaginings.

In this section we will consider, for example, short stories written to be short stories and lyric poems written to be lyric poems. Of course, from the beginning of Genesis we have encountered short narratives; and Biblical literature, as we have it here, is in large part "poetic." The convenient distinction covering the selections here is that each seems to be the self-contained product of a conscious artist. They appear as personal literary creations, constructed by individual writers with literary plans and purposes. We are not likely to think of the writer of the Joseph story saying to himself, "Now I will get to work and imagine a character and some events and determine the ways in which I can make it seem real and interesting." Nor do we imagine the brilliant composer of the first chapter of Genesis thinking, "I will compose this poem to convince an audience of my feelings about how the world began." Yet this is approximately how the writers of formal literature, good and bad, do start out.

2. Short Stories: Ruth, Jonah, Daniel

Ah, my gallant captain, why did ye not give us
Jonah looking out of that eye!
HERMAN MELVILLE, *Moby Dick*

Although poetry is the oldest literary form, we are probably more familiar with short stories, so we will start this little anthology of formal literature with some of them.

What exactly is a short story? Most will agree that it is a prose tale that can be read at a single sitting and that it is fiction. After that agreement, disagreements begin. That is because there are a number of different kinds of short story, short fictions which differ in shape. This has resulted recently in various exclusive definitions of *the* short story, but I think that people who contend that only one kind of short story is *the* short story are really only saying "This is the kind I like." Our narratives about Jonah, Ruth, and Daniel are of different kinds, and we may prefer one to another, but they are all short stories.

They can each be read at a single sitting; short they obviously are. But after all, they are "Bible stories"; by what presumption do I call them fiction? Certainly not to quarrel with the religious conviction that everything in the Bible must be literally historical. If I must quarrel, it will be with those who claim that fiction is by definition false. For fiction, like other art, is an imitation of life. Fiction, like other art, may mislead us about life, as may tape machines, automatic cameras, and other copying agencies, but misleading us about life is not what fiction is for. We recognize great fiction because it does just the opposite.

Ruth

1   Now it came to pass in the days when the judges ruled, that there was a
famine in the land. And a certain man of Bethlehem-judah went to sojourn in
2 the country of Moab, he, and his wife, and his two sons. And the name of the
man was Elimelech, and the name of his wife Naomi, and the name of his
two sons Mahlon and Chilion, . . . And they came into the country of Moab,
3 and continued there. And Elimelech Naomi's husband died; and she was left,
4 and her two sons. And they took them wives of the women of Moab; the
name of the one was Orpah, and the name of the other Ruth: and they dwelt
5 there about ten years. And Mahlon and Chilion died also both of them; and
the woman was left of her two sons and her husband.

6   Then she arose with her daughters-in-law, that she might return from the
country of Moab: for she had heard in the country of Moab how that the
7 Lord had visited his people in giving them bread. Wherefore she went forth
out of the place where she was, and her two daughters-in-law with her; and
8 they went on the way to return unto the land of Judah. And Naomi said unto
her two daughters-in-law, Go, return each to her mother's house: the Lord
9 deal kindly with you, as ye have dealt with the dead, and with me. The Lord
grant you that ye may find rest, each of you in the house of her husband.
Then she kissed them; and they lifted up their voice, and wept.

10   And they said unto her, Surely we will return with thee unto thy people.
11 And Naomi said, Turn again, my daughters: why will ye go with me? are
there yet any more sons in my womb, that they may be your husbands?
12 Turn again, my daughters, go your way; for I am too old to have a husband.
If I should say, I have hope, if I should have a husband also to-night, and
13 should also bear sons; Would ye tarry for them till they were grown? would
ye stay for them from having husbands? nay, my daughters; for it grieveth
me much for your sakes that the hand of the Lord is gone out against me.
14   And they lifted up their voice, and wept again: and Orpah kissed her
15 mother-in-law; but Ruth clave unto her. And she said, Behold, thy sister-in-
law is gone back unto her people, and unto her gods: return thou after thy
16 sister-in-law. And Ruth said,

> Entreat me not to leave thee,
>   or to return from following after thee:
> for whither thou goest, I will go;
>   and where thou lodgest, I will lodge:
> thy people shall be my people,
>   and thy God my God:
17 Where thou diest, will I die,
>   and there will I be buried:
> the Lord do so to me, and more also,
>   if aught but death part thee and me.

18 When she saw that she was steadfastly minded to go with her, then she left
speaking unto her.
19   So they two went until they came to Bethlehem. And it came to pass, when
they were come to Bethlehem, that all the city was moved about them, and

20 they said, Is this Naomi? And she said unto them, Call me not Naomi, call
21 me Mara: for the Almighty hath dealt very bitterly with me. I went out
full, and the Lord hath brought me home again empty: why then call ye me
Naomi, seeing the Lord hath testified against me, and the Almighty hath
22 afflicted me? So Naomi returned, and Ruth the Moabitess, her daughter-in-
law, with her, which returned out of the country of Moab: and they came
to Bethlehem in the beginning of barley harvest.

2   And Naomi had a kinsman of her husband's, a mighty man of wealth, of
the family of Elimelech; and his name was Boaz.

2   And Ruth the Moabitess said unto Naomi, Let me now go to the field, and
glean ears of corn after him in whose sight I shall find grace. And she said
3 unto her, Go, my daughter. And she went, and came, and gleaned in the field
after the reapers: and her hap was to light on a part of the field belonging
unto Boaz, who was of the kindred of Elimelech.

4   And, behold, Boaz came from Bethlehem, and said unto the reapers, The
5 Lord be with you. And they answered him, The Lord bless thee. Then said
Boaz unto his servant that was set over the reapers, Whose damsel is this?
6 And the servant that was set over the reapers answered and said, It is the
Moabitish damsel that came back with Naomi out of the country of Moab:
7 And she said, I pray you, let me glean and gather after the reapers among
the sheaves: so she came, and hath continued even from the morning until
8 now, that she tarried a little in the house. Then said Boaz unto Ruth, Hearest thou not, my daughter? Go not to glean in another field, neither go from
9 hence, but abide here fast by my maidens: Let thine eyes be on the field that
they do reap, and go thou after them: have I not charged the young men that
they shall not touch thee? and when thou art athirst, go unto the vessels, and
10 drink of that which the young men have drawn. Then she fell on her face,
and bowed herself to the ground, and said unto him, Why have I found grace
in thine eyes, that thou shouldest take knowledge of me, seeing I am a
stranger?
11   And Boaz answered and said unto her, It hath fully been showed me, all
that thou hast done unto thy mother-in-law since the death of thine husband;
and how thou hast left thy father and thy mother, and the land of thy nativ-
12 ity, and art come unto a people which thou knewest not heretofore. The
Lord recompense thy work, and a full reward be given thee of the Lord God
13 of Israel, under whose wings thou art come to trust. Then she said, Let me
find favor in thy sight, my lord; for that thou hast comforted me, and for
that thou hast spoken friendly unto thine handmaid, though I be not like
14 unto one of thine handmaidens. And Boaz said unto her, At mealtime come
thou hither, and eat of the bread, and dip thy morsel in the vinegar. And she
sat beside the reapers: and he reached her parched corn, and she did eat, and
15 was sufficed, and left. And when she was risen up to glean, Boaz commanded
his young men, saying, Let her glean even among the sheaves, and reproach
16 her not: And let fall also some of the handfuls of purpose for her, and leave
them, that she may glean them, and rebuke her not.
17   So she gleaned in the field until even, and beat out that she had gleaned:
18 and it was about an ephah of barley. And she took it up, and went into the
city; and her mother-in-law saw what she had gleaned: and she brought
19 forth, and gave to her that she had reserved after she was sufficed. And her

mother-in-law said unto her, Where hast thou gleaned to-day? and where wroughtest thou? blessed be he that did take knowledge of thee. And she showed her mother-in-law with whom she had wrought, and said, The man's

20 name with whom I wrought to-day is Boaz. And Naomi said unto her daughter-in-law, Blessed be he of the Lord, who hath not left off his kindness to the living and to the dead. And Naomi said unto her, The man is near of kin

21 unto us, one of our next kinsmen. And Ruth the Moabitess said, He said unto me also, Thou shalt keep fast by my young men, until they have ended all

22 my harvest. And Naomi said unto Ruth her daughter-in-law, It is good, my daughter, that thou go out with his maidens, that they meet thee not in any

23 other field. So she kept fast by the maidens of Boaz to glean unto the end of barley harvest and of wheat harvest; and dwelt with her mother-in-law.

3 Then Naomi her mother-in-law said unto her, My daughter, shall I not

2 seek rest for thee, that it may be well with thee? And now is not Boaz of our kindred, with whose maidens thou wast? Behold, he winnoweth barley to-

3 night in the threshingfloor. Wash thyself therefore, and anoint thee, and put thy raiment upon thee, and get thee down to the floor: but make not thyself

4 known unto the man, until he shall have done eating and drinking. And it shall be, when he lieth down, that thou shalt mark the place where he shall lie, and thou shalt go in, and uncover his feet, and lay thee down; and he will

5 tell thee what thou shalt do. And she said unto her, All that thou sayest unto me I will do.

6 And she went down unto the floor, and did according to all that her

7 mother-in-law bade her. And when Boaz had eaten and drunk, and his heart was merry, he went to lie down at the end of the heap of corn: and she came

8 softly, and uncovered his feet, and laid her down. And it came to pass at midnight, that the man was afraid, and turned himself: and, behold, a woman lay

9 at his feet. And he said, Who art thou? And she answered, I am Ruth thine handmaid: spread therefore thy skirt over thine handmaid; for thou art a near kinsman.

10 And he said, Blessed be thou of the Lord, my daughter: for thou hast showed more kindness in the latter end than at the beginning, inasmuch as thou fol-

11 lowedst not young men, whether poor or rich. And now, my daughter, fear not; I will do to thee all that thou requirest: for all the city of my people

12 doth know that thou art a virtuous woman. And now it is true that I am thy

13 near kinsman: howbeit there is a kinsman nearer than I. Tarry this night, and it shall be in the morning, that if he will perform unto thee the part of a kinsman, well; let him do the kinsman's part: but if he will not do the part of a kinsman to thee, then will I do the part of a kinsman to thee, as the Lord liveth: lie down until the morning.

14 And she lay at his feet until the morning: and she rose up before one could know another. And he said, Let it not be known that a woman came into

15 the floor. Also he said, Bring the veil that thou hast upon thee, and hold it. And when she held it, he measured six measures of barley, and laid it on her:

16 and she went into the city. And when she came to her mother-in-law, she said, Who art thou, my daughter? And she told her all that the man had done

17 to her. And she said, These six measures of barley gave he me; for he said

18 to me, Go not empty unto thy mother-in-law. Then said she, Sit still, my daughter, until thou know how the matter will fall: for the man will not be in rest, until he have finished the thing this day.

4   Then went Boaz up to the gate, and sat him down there: and, behold, the kinsman of whom Boaz spake came by; unto whom he said, Ho, such a one!
2   turn aside, sit down here. And he turned aside, and sat down. And he took ten men of the elders of the city, and said, Sit ye down here. And they sat
3   down. And he said unto the kinsman, Naomi, that is come again out of the country of Moab, selleth a parcel of land, which was our brother Elime-
4   lech's: And I thought to advertise thee, saying, Buy it before the inhabitants, and before the elders of my people. If thou wilt redeem it, redeem it: but if thou wilt not redeem it, then tell me, that I may know: for there is none to redeem it besides thee; and I am after thee. And he said, I will redeem it.
5   Then said Boaz, What day thou buyest the field of the hand of Naomi, thou must buy it also of Ruth the Moabitess, the wife of the dead, to raise
6   up the name of the dead upon his inheritance. And the kinsman said, I cannot redeem it for myself, lest I mar mine own inheritance: redeem thou my right
7   to thyself; for I cannot redeem it. Now this was the manner in former time in Israel concerning redeeming and concerning changing, for to confirm all things; a man plucked off his shoe, and gave it to his neighbor: and this was
8   a testimony in Israel. Therefore the kinsman said unto Boaz, Buy it for thee. So he drew off his shoe.
9   And Boaz said unto the elders, and unto all the people, Ye are witnesses this day, that I have bought all that was Elimelech's, and all that was Chili-
10   on's and Mahlon's, of the hand of Naomi. Moreover Ruth the Moabitess, the wife of Mahlon, have I purchased to be my wife, to raise up the name of the dead upon his inheritance, that the name of the dead be not cut off from among his brethren, and from the gate of his place: ye are witnesses this day.
11   And all the people that were in the gate, and the elders, said, We are witnesses. The Lord make the woman that is come into thine house like Rachel and like Leah, which two did build the house of Israel: and do thou worthily
12   in Ephratah, and be famous in Bethlehem: And let thy house be like the house of Pharez, whom Tamar bare unto Judah, of the seed which the Lord shall give thee of this young woman.
13   So Boaz took Ruth, and she was his wife: and when he went in unto her,
14   the Lord gave her conception, and she bare a son. And the women said unto Naomi, Blessed be the Lord, which hath not left thee this day without a kins-
15   man, that his name may be famous in Israel. And he shall be unto thee a restorer of thy life, and a nourisher of thine old age: for thy daughter-in-law, which loveth thee, which is better to thee than seven sons, hath borne him.
16   And Naomi took the child, and laid it in her bosom, and became nurse unto it.
17   And the women her neighbors gave it a name, saying, There is a son born to Naomi; and they called his name Obed: he is the father of Jesse, the father of David.

Jonah

1   Now the word of the Lord came unto Jonah the son of Amittai, saying,
2 Arise, go to Nineveh, that great city, and cry against it; for their wicked-
3 ness is come up before me. But Jonah rose up to flee unto Tarshish from the
presence of the Lord, and went down to Joppa; and he found a ship going to
Tarshish: so he paid the fare thereof, and went down into it, to go with them
unto Tarshish from the presence of the Lord.
4   But the Lord sent out a great wind into the sea, and there was a mighty
5 tempest in the sea, so that the ship was like to be broken. Then the mariners
were afraid, and cried every man unto his god, and cast forth the wares that
were in the ship into the sea, to lighten it of them. But Jonah was gone down
6 into the sides of the ship; and he lay, and was fast asleep. So the shipmaster
came to him, and said unto him, What meanest thou, O sleeper? arise, call
upon thy God, if so be that God will think upon us, that we perish not.
7   And they said every one to his fellow, Come, and let us cast lots, that we
may know for whose cause this evil is upon us. So they cast lots, and the
8 lot fell upon Jonah. Then said they unto him, Tell us, we pray thee, for
whose cause this evil is upon us; What is thine occupation? and whence
9 comest thou? what is thy country? and of what people art thou? And he said
unto them, I am a Hebrew; and I fear the Lord, the God of heaven, which
10 hath made the sea and the dry land. Then were the men exceedingly afraid,
and said unto him, Why hast thou done this? For the men knew that he fled
from the presence of the Lord, because he had told them.
11   Then said they unto him, What shall we do unto thee, that the sea may
12 be calm unto us? for the sea wrought, and was tempestuous. And he said
unto them, Take me up, and cast me forth into the sea; so shall the sea be
calm unto you: for I know that for my sake this great tempest is upon you.
13 Nevertheless the men rowed hard to bring it to the land; but they could not:
14 for the sea wrought, and was tempestuous against them. Wherefore they
cried unto the Lord, and said, We beseech thee, O Lord, we beseech thee,
let us not perish for this man's life, and lay not upon us innocent blood: for
15 thou, O Lord, hast done as it pleased thee. So they took up Jonah, and cast
16 him forth into the sea: and the sea ceased from her raging. Then the men
feared the Lord exceedingly, and offered a sacrifice unto the Lord, and made
vows.
17   Now the Lord had prepared a great fish to swallow up Jonah. And Jonah
2   was in the belly of the fish three days and three nights. Then Jonah prayed
2 unto the Lord his God out of the fish's belly, And said,

> 3   I cried by reason of mine affliction unto the Lord,
>   and he heard me;
>   out of the belly of hell cried I,
>   and thou heardest my voice.
>
> 3   For thou hadst cast me into the deep, in the midst of the seas;
>   and the floods compassed me about:
>   all thy billows and thy waves passed over me.
>
> 5   The waters compassed me about, even to the soul:
>   the depth closed me round about,
>   the weeds were wrapped about my head.
>
> 7   When my soul fainted within me I remembered the Lord:

and my prayer came in unto thee, into thine holy temple.

8 They that observe lying vanities forsake their own mercy.

9 But I will sacrifice unto thee with the voice of thanksgiving;
I will pay that that I have vowed.
Salvation is of the Lord.

10 And the Lord spake unto the fish, and it vomited out Jonah upon the dry land.

3:1,2 And the word of the Lord came unto Jonah the second time, saying, Arise, go unto Nineveh, that great city, and preach unto it the preaching that I bid 3 thee. So Jonah arose, and went unto Nineveh, according to the word of the Lord. Now Nineveh was an exceeding great city of three days' journey. 4 And Jonah began to enter into the city a day's journey, and he cried, and said, Yet forty days, and Nineveh shall be overthrown.

5 So the people of Nineveh believed God, and proclaimed a fast, and put on 6 sackcloth, from the greatest of them even to the least of them. For word came unto the king of Nineveh, and he arose from his throne, and he laid 7 his robe from him, and covered him with sackcloth, and sat in ashes. And he caused it to be proclaimed and published through Nineveh by the decree of the king and his nobles, saying, Let neither man nor beast, herd nor flock, 8 taste any thing: let them not feed, nor drink water: But let man and beast be covered with sackcloth, and cry mightily unto God: yea, let them turn every one from his evil way, and from the violence that is in their hands. 9 Who can tell if God will turn and repent, and turn away from his fierce anger, that we perish not?

10 And God saw their works, that they turned from their evil way; and God repented of the evil, that he had said that he would do unto them; and he did it not.

4:1,2 But it displeased Jonah exceedingly, and he was very angry. And he prayed unto the Lord, and said, I pray thee, O Lord, was not this my saying, when I was yet in my country? Therefore I fled before unto Tarshish: for I knew that thou art a gracious God, and merciful, slow to anger, and of great kind- 3 ness, and repentest thee of the evil. Therefore now, O Lord, take, I beseech thee, my life from me; for it is better for me to die than to live.

4,5 Then said the Lord, Doest thou well to be angry? So Jonah went out of the city, and sat on the east side of the city, and there made him a booth, and sat under it in the shadow, till he might see what would become of the city.

6 And the Lord God prepared a gourd, and made it to come up over Jonah, that it might be a shadow over his head, to deliver him from his grief. So 7 Jonah was exceeding glad of the gourd. But God prepared a worm when the 8 morning rose the next day, and it smote the gourd that it withered. And it came to pass, when the sun did arise, that God prepared a vehement east wind; and the sun beat upon the head of Jonah, that he fainted, and wished in himself to die, and said, It is better for me to die than to live.

9 And God said to Jonah, Doest thou well to be angry for the gourd? And he said, I do well to be angry, even unto death.

10 Then said the Lord, Thou hast had pity on the gourd, for the which thou hast not labored, neither madest it grow; which came up in a night, and per- 11 ished in a night: And should not I spare Nineveh, that great city, wherein are more than sixscore thousand persons that cannot discern between their right hand and their left hand; and also much cattle?

Some Formal Biblical Literature

Daniel

3   Nebuchadnezzar the king made an image of gold, whose height was three-score cubits, and the breadth thereof six cubits: he set it up in the plain of
2 Dura, in the province of Babylon. Then Nebuchadnezzar the king sent to gather together the princes, the governors, and the captains, the judges, the treasurers, the counselors, the sheriffs, and all the rulers of the provinces, to come to the dedication of the image which Nebuchadnezzar the king had
3 set up. Then the princes, the governors, and captains, the judges, the treasurers, the counselors, the sheriffs, and all the rulers of the provinces, were gathered together unto the dedication of the image that Nebuchadnezzar the king had set up; and they stood before the image that Nebuchadnezzar had set up.
4   Then a herald cried aloud, To you it is commanded, O people, nations,
5 and languages, That at what time ye hear the sound of the cornet, flute, harp, sackbut, psaltery, dulcimer, and all kinds of music, ye fall down and worship
6 the golden image that Nebuchadnezzar the king hath set up: And whoso falleth not down and worshippeth shall the same hour be cast into the midst
7 of a burning fiery furnace. Therefore at that time, when all the people heard the sound of the cornet, flute, harp, sackbut, psaltery, and all kinds of music, all the people, the nations, and the languages, fell down and worshipped the golden image that Nebuchadnezzar the king had set up.
8   Wherefore at that time certain Chaldeans came near, and accused the
9 Jews. They spake and said to the king Nebuchadnezzar, O king, live for
12 ever. There are certain Jews whom thou hast set over the affairs of the province of Babylon, Shadrach, Meshach, and Abed-nego; these men, O king, have not regarded thee: they serve not thy gods, nor worship the golden image which thou hast set up.
13   Then Nebuchadnezzar in his rage and fury commanded to bring Shadrach, Meshach, and Abed-nego. Then they brought these men before the king.
14 Nebuchadnezzar spake and said unto them, Is it true, O Shadrach, Meshach, and Abed-nego? do not ye serve my gods, nor worship the golden image
15 which I have set up? Now if ye be ready that at what time ye hear the sound of the cornet, flute, harp, sackbut, psaltery, and dulcimer, and all kinds of music, ye fall down and worship the image which I have made; well: but if ye worship not, ye shall be cast the same hour into the midst of a burning fiery furnace; and who is that God that shall deliver you out of my hands?
16   Shadrach, Meshach, and Abed-nego, answered and said to the king, O
17 Nebuchadnezzar, we are not careful to answer thee in this matter. If it be so, our God whom we serve is able to deliver us from the burning fiery fur-
18 nace, and he will deliver us out of thine hand, O king. But if not, be it known unto thee, O king, that we will not serve thy gods, nor worship the golden image which thou hast set up.
19   Then was Nebuchadnezzar full of fury, and the form of his visage was changed against Shadrach, Meshach, and Abed-nego: therefore he spake, and commanded that they should heat the furnace one seven times more than
21 it was wont to be heated. Then these men were bound in their coats, their hose, and their hats, and their other garments, and were cast into the midst

22 of the burning fiery furnace. Therefore because the king's commandment was urgent, and the furnace exceeding hot, the flame of the fire slew those men that took up Shadrach, Meshach, and Abed-nego.

24 Then Nebuchadnezzar the king was astonished, and rose up in haste, and spake, and said unto his counselors, Did not we cast three men bound into the midst of the fire? They answered and said unto the king, True, O king.

25 He answered and said, Lo, I see four men loose, walking in the midst of the fire, and they have no hurt; and the form of the fourth is like the Son of God.

26 Then Nebuchadnezzar came near to the mouth of the burning fiery furnace, and spake, and said, Shadrach, Meshach, and Abed-nego, ye servants of the most high God, come forth, and come hither. Then Shadrach, Me-

27 shach, and Abed-nego, came forth of the midst of the fire. And the princes, governors, and captains, and the king's counselors, being gathered together, saw these men, upon whose bodies the fire had no power, nor was a hair of their head singed, neither were their coats changed, nor the smell of fire had passed on them.

28 Then Nebuchadnezzar spake, and said, Blessed be the God of Shadrach, Meshach, and Abed-nego, who hath sent his angel, and delivered his servants that trusted in him, and have changed the king's word, and yielded their bodies, that they might not serve nor worship any god, except their own

29 God. Therefore I make a decree, That every people, nation, and language, which speak any thing amiss against the God of Shadrach, Meshach, and Abed-nego, shall be cut in pieces, and their houses shall be made a dunghill;

30 because there is no other God that can deliver after this sort. Then the king promoted Shadrach, Meshach, and Abed-nego, in the province of Babylon.

5 Belshazzar the king made a great feast to a thousand of his lords, and

2 drank wine before the thousand. Belshazzar, while he tasted the wine, commanded to bring the golden and silver vessels which his father Nebuchadnezzar had taken out of the temple which was in Jerusalem; that the king

5 and his princes, his wives and his concubines, might drink therein. In the same hour came forth fingers of a man's hand, and wrote over against the candlestick upon the plaster of the wall of the king's palace: and the king

6 saw the part of the hand that wrote. Then the king's countenance was changed, and his thoughts troubled him, so that the joints of his loins were loosed, and his knees smote one against another.

7 The king cried aloud to bring in the astrologers, the Chaldeans, and the soothsayers. And the king spake, and said to the wise men of Babylon, Whosoever shall read this writing, and show me the interpretation thereof, shall be clothed with scarlet, and have a chain of gold about his neck, and shall be

8 the third ruler in the kingdom. Then came in all the king's wise men: but they could not read the writing, nor make known to the king the interpreta-

9 tion thereof. Then was king Belshazzar greatly troubled, and his countenance was changed in him, and his lords were astonished.

10 Now the queen, by reason of the words of the king and his lords, came into the banquet house: and the queen spake and said, O king, live for ever:

11 let not thy thoughts trouble thee, nor let thy countenance be changed: There is a man in thy kingdom, in whom is the spirit of the holy gods; and in the days of thy father light and understanding and wisdom, like the wisdom of the gods, was found in him; whom the king Nebuchadnezzar thy father, the

king, I say, thy father, made master of the magicians, astrologers, Chaldeans,
12 and soothsayers; Forasmuch as an excellent spirit, and knowledge, and understanding, interpreting of dreams, and showing of hard sentences, and dissolving of doubts, were found in the same Daniel, whom the king named Belteshazzar: now let Daniel be called, and he will show the interpretation.

15 Then was Daniel brought in before the king. And the king spake and said unto Daniel, Art thou that Daniel, which art of the children of the captivity
16 of Judah, whom the king my father brought out of Jewry? And I have heard of thee, that thou canst make interpretations, and dissolve doubts: now if thou canst read the writing, and make known to me the interpretation thereof, thou shalt be clothed with scarlet, and have a chain of gold about thy neck, and shalt be the third ruler in the kingdom.

17 Then Daniel answered and said before the king, Let thy gifts be to thyself, and give thy rewards to another; yet I will read the writing unto the king
18 and make known to him the interpretation. O thou king, the most high God gave Nebuchadnezzar thy father a kingdom, and majesty, and glory, and
19 honor: And for the majesty that he gave him, all people, nations, and languages, trembled and feared before him: whom he would he slew; and whom he would he kept alive; and whom he would he set up; and whom he would
20 he put down. But when his heart was lifted up, and his mind hardened in pride, he was deposed from his kingly throne, and they took his glory from him:

22 And thou his son, O Belshazzar, hast not humbled thine heart, though thou
23 knewest all this; But hast lifted up thyself against the Lord of heaven; and they have brought the vessels of his house before thee, and thou and thy lords, thy wives and thy concubines, have drunk wine in them; and thou hast praised the gods of silver, and gold, of brass, iron, wood, and stone, which see not, nor hear, nor know: and the God in whose hand thy breath
24 is, and whose are all thy ways, hast thou not glorified: Then was the part of the hand sent from him; and this writing was written.

25 And this is the writing that was written, MENE, MENE, TEKEL, UPHAR-
26 SIN. This is the interpretation of the thing: MENE; God hath numbered thy
27 kingdom, and finished it. TEKEL; Thou art weighed in the balances, and art
28 found wanting. PERES; Thy kingdom is divided, and given to the Medes and Persians.

29 Then commanded Belshazzar, and they clothed Daniel with scarlet, and put a chain of gold about his neck, and made a proclamation concerning him, that he should be the third ruler in the kingdom.

30,31 In that night was Belshazzar the king of the Chaldeans slain. And Darius the Median took the kingdom, being about threescore and two years old.

6 It pleased Darius to set over the kingdom a hundred and twenty princes,
2 which should be over the whole kingdom; And over these three presidents; of whom Daniel was first: that the princes might give accounts unto them,
3 and the king should have no damage. Then this Daniel was preferred above the presidents and princes, because an excellent spirit was in him; and the
4 king thought to set him over the whole realm. Then the presidents and princes sought to find occasion against Daniel concerning the kingdom; but they could find none occasion nor fault; forasmuch as he was faithful, neither
5 was there any error or fault found in him. Then said these men, We shall

not find any occasion against this Daniel, except we find it against him concerning the law of his God.

6 Then these presidents and princes assembled together to the king, and
7 said thus unto him, King Darius, live for ever. All the presidents of the kingdom, the governors, and the princes, the counselors, and the captains, have consulted together to establish a royal statute, and to make a firm decree, that whosoever shall ask a petition of any God or man for thirty
8 days, save of thee, O king, he shall be cast into the den of lions. Now, O king, establish the decree, and sign the writing, that it be not changed,
9 according to the law of the Medes and Persians, which altereth not. Wherefore king Darius signed the writing and the decree.

10 Now when Daniel knew that the writing was signed, he went into his house; and, his windows being open in his chamber toward Jerusalem, he kneeled upon his knees three times a day, and prayed, and gave thanks be-
11 fore his God, as he did aforetime. Then these men assembled, and found Daniel praying and making supplication before his God.

12 Then they came near, and spake before the king concerning the king's decree; Hast thou not signed a decree, that every man that shall ask a petition of any God or man within thirty days, save of thee, O king, shall be cast into the den of lions?

The king answered and said, The thing is true, according to the law of the Medes and Persians, which altereth not.

13 Then answered they and said before the king, That Daniel, which is of the children of the captivity of Judah, regardeth not thee, O king, nor the
14 decree that thou hast signed, but maketh his petition three times a day. Then the king, when he heard these words, was sore displeased with himself, and set his heart on Daniel to deliver him: and he labored till the going down of the sun to deliver him.

15 Then these men assembled unto the king, and said unto the king, Know, O king, that the law of the Medes and Persians is, That no decree nor
16 statute which the king establisheth may be changed. Then the king commanded, and they brought Daniel, and cast him into the den of lions. Now the king spake and said unto Daniel, Thy God whom thou servest contin-
17 ually, he will deliver thee. And a stone was brought, and laid upon the mouth of the den; and the king sealed it with his own signet, and with the signet of his lords; that the purpose might not be changed concerning Daniel.
18 Then the king went to his palace, and passed the night fasting: neither were instruments of music brought before him: and his sleep went from him.
19 Then the king arose very early in the morning, and went in haste unto the
20 den of lions. And when he came to the den, he cried with a lamentable voice unto Daniel: and the king spake and said to Daniel, O Daniel, servant of the living God, is thy God, whom thou servest continually, able to deliver thee from the lions?
21,22 Then said Daniel unto the king, O king, live for ever. My God hath sent his angel, and hath shut the lions' mouths, that they have not hurt me: forasmuch as before him innocency was found in me; and also before thee, O
23 king, have I done no hurt. Then was the king exceeding glad for him, and commanded that they should take Daniel up out of the den.

So Daniel was taken up out of the den, and no manner of hurt was found

24 upon him, because he believed in his God. And the king commanded, and they brought those men which had accused Daniel, and they cast them into the den of lions, them, their children, and their wives; and the lions had the mastery of them, and brake all their bones in pieces or ever they came at the bottom of the den.

25 Then king Darius wrote unto all people, nations, and languages, that dwell
26 in all the earth; Peace be multiplied unto you. I make a decree, That in every dominion of my kingdom men tremble and fear before the God of Daniel: for he is the living God, and steadfast for ever, and his kingdom that which shall not be destroyed, and his dominion shall be even unto the
27 end. He delivereth and rescueth, and he worketh signs and wonders in heaven and in earth, who hath delivered Daniel from the power of the lions.
28 So this Daniel prospered in the reign of Darius, and in the reign of Cyrus the Persian.

Considerations and Questions

1. A young woman whose husband has died lives with her widowed mother-in-law. The two move back to the older woman's country where the young widow meets a rich and kind man whom she marries. This makes her mother-in-law very happy. Ruth is a simple story, but not quite so simple as this plot summary may suggest. Consider the following:

   (a) Why does Ruth stay with Naomi? What are her alternatives?
   (b) Why do the two women move to Bethlehem?
   (c) What particular problems does this move present for Ruth?
   (d) How does a poor girl like Ruth meet a rich man like Boaz?
   (e) What does Naomi have to do with that?
   (f) What is so appealing about Boaz besides his wealth?
   (g) How do the marriage proposal and acceptance take place?
   (h) What are the specific reasons for Naomi's happiness in the end? What does the story tell or indicate about Ruth's happiness?

2. Plots depend on decisions, the choosing of alternative courses of action. What are the significant decisions in the plot of Ruth?

3. Setting in fiction is a matter of time and place and also a matter of local patterns of behavior and belief. Sometimes a writer explains directly the details of setting necessary to understand his story. Sometimes he simply shows them in action and trusts to the perception of his audience. What does the author of Ruth tell us directly about his setting? What does he leave to our inference? What, for example, are we to assume about cultural differences between Israelites and Moabites? What about family relationships? Marriage laws and customs? Charitable practices? The rights of women and various economic classes?

4. Ruth is that kind of fiction sometimes called historical romance. The author invites his audience back to a time "when the judges ruled" which is about seven hundred years before his own period. Now we have seen something of the historical era he chooses for his story in the Samson folktale and in accounts about Samuel and Saul. In what respect does the Ruth writer idealize the "long-ago" for his readers? What other romantic qualities do you find in his work?

5. Among other things, Ruth is about mixed marriages. Long before this story was written and to this day there has been a strong current of objection in orthodox Jewry to marriages between Israelites and other people. The unfortunate records of Solomon and Ahab, among others, may help make this objection understandable. What, however, appears to be the Ruth author's position on the subject?

6. How does the writer of Ruth go about depicting character? How much of "personality" does he show us in each of his three main characters?

How much does he show us in such minor characters as Ruth's sister-in-law, Orpah, and the "kinsman" of Boaz? What, by the way, are the functions of these minor characters?

7. On what occasions in Ruth does the writer, or do the characters, refer to Israel's God? In what connection? Are there other indications that this is a story concerned with the particular faith of Israel?

8. Some short stories start with an exposition of the background from which the action will emerge; others leap right into the action. Compare Ruth and Jonah in this respect.

9. The command of the Lord with which Jonah begins is of a familiar general sort to anyone acquainted with the Prophets of Israel. But much of what makes this story interesting is that this particular Prophet does not behave as do the characteristic members of his historic line of inspired teachers.

    (a) What is Jonah's immediate reaction to the order of his God? Why? (See chapter 4.)

    (b) Jonah may see himself as the punitive hand of God, but how does it appear that he receives rather than administers most of the divine discipline in the story?

    (c) Jonah's prophetic announcement about future events in Nineveh does not come to pass. Why, however, is this clearly his error and not a matter of his having received the wrong message from God? What is the exact wording of his instruction from the Lord? What does he assume it to mean?

    (d) The historic Prophets of Israel are notable as men absolutely convinced of the truth and justice of their God. What is Jonah's attitude towards the Lord's moral perception and moral character? To what extent has he changed this attitude by the end of the story?

10. For centuries, some fundamentalists and some skeptics have quibbled over Jonah's "great fish." They have solemnly pondered whether the monster is supposed to be a whale or something else and debated the possibility of a man's survival for three days in such a creature's belly. Just now, as readers of a short story, let us accept the event as presented and ask ourselves other questions.

    (a) In world relationships between men and fishes, who do we hope normally eats whom?

    (b) To what extent is being gobbled whole and vomited out in keeping with prophetic dignity?

    (c) In spite of the noble language of Jonah's prayer from the fish's belly, what religious perception has Jonah actually reached at that point? Does he now see that God is right about the Nineveh plan? Is Jonah aware that he is in trouble? Has he learned limits to what he can get away with?

(d) "So Jonah swam for three days and nights until he came to the dry land near Nineveh." What differences in the story would this alternative to the "great fish" make?

11. The Book of Job, as we shall see, begins with this sentence: "There was a man in the land of Uz, whose name was Job; and that man was perfect and upright, and one that feared God, and eschewed evil."

That is one way in which a storyteller can present character; he simply summarizes or tells about it in his own voice. An alternative technique is for the storyteller to "show" us what his characters are like by recounting what they do and say. Obviously, the writer of "Jonah" relies entirely on this second method. This surly and reluctant Prophet is characterized by his own major decisions, courses of action, and words. As well as these principal exhibitions of character, however, the Jonah writer also provides smaller details, sometimes of manner or style, which give the flesh of reality to the fictional man. What do the following points show you about Jonah?

(a) At the time of the storm he has already told the heathen sailors why he is traveling to Tarshish on their ship.

(b) He identifies himself to the sailors: "I am a Hebrew; and I fear the Lord, the God of heaven, which hath made the sea and dry land." (And yet he is enroute to Tarshish).

(c) He immediately assumes that the storm will stop only if they throw *him* overboard.

(d) Although certainly not an untalkative man on certain occasions, his only "preaching" to the people of Nineveh is, "Yet forty days, and Nineveh shall be overthrown."

(e) After he sees that Nineveh will not be destroyed at the time he has predicted, he settles down on an over-looking hill to await developments.

(f) His last comment on the whole business is that he is right to be angry.

12. God is no less a character in this story than Jonah. How does the writer present His personality by what He does and says?

13. Jonah is a more religious story than Ruth. (In what sense?) Can you argue that it is also less romantic, more profound, and considerably more comic?

14. In his essay, "Why I Write," George Orwell sets out four basic impulses as those which move all writers to their work. He calls them (1) "sheer egoism," (2) "esthetic enthusiasm," (3) "historical impulse," and (4) "political purpose." Granting that all four of these are present in every

writer's approach to a particular work, he contends that one of them is likely to take precedence in the author's approach and consequently in the work itself. Orwell claims the fourth, "political purpose," as his own major artistic motivation. He explains that he means by it the purpose to change the world for the better. In short, Orwell's "political purpose" is the moral motive. We should see, I think, that the writers of both Ruth and Jonah express the idea that God is not exclusively concerned with Israel, and that Israelites ought to realize that the Lord is the just and merciful ruler of all mankind (including Moabites and Ninevites). That, if you like, is a general moral with a political purpose evident in both stories. Yet Ruth and Jonah are not dominated by this motif. In this respect, compare them with the three Daniel stories. Can you argue that the sensational events of the latter are meant to serve the writer's main impulse—teaching his readers how good Jews ought to behave?

15. The stories about Daniel and his friends appeared at a time when a Syrian army had occupied Jerusalem and when Jews who refused to give up their own religion and laws to the will of the conquerors were fiercely persecuted. That was in the second century B.C., more than four hundred years after the events of the Daniel stories themselves. In the person of Daniel, the writer creates a kind of religious superman who successfully resists a heathen invader. The truest contribution of Daniel and his associates to their victory is their utter fidelity to God; they receive in return His protection, power, and knowledge. How do each of the following famous occasions illustrate that this is so?

      (a) The Writing on the Wall.
      (b) The Fiery Furnace.
      (c) The Lion's Den.

3. Lyric Poems:
from the Book of Psalms

What should we do but sing His praise ...
ANDREW MARVELL, *Bermudas*

The Book of Psalms as it appears in the King James Version
of the Bible consists of one hundred and fifty poems. They are of various
lengths and on widely differing topics. As Mary Ellen Chase writes in *The
Bible and the Common Reader,* they are "one of the richest collections
of poetry in any language because literally every emotion is within them."
The few we can sample here give only a faint idea of their range and
quality.

Conventionally ascribed to King David, the psalms, scholars
now agree, are almost certainly by a number of later poets. Some refer to
events and circumstances long after David's death. Our selections include
hymns, laments, and meditations. In each case, as in all great poetry, the
expression is from the deepest personal feelings of the poet. And in each
case, as in all great poetry, the poet endeavors with the devices of language
to transfer a sense of those feelings to us.

Two suggestions for your study of these psalms:

1. Most, though not all, poetry is best understood if read aloud.
   Certainly you will grasp the psalms best if you do so.
2. You will encounter, I hope, a number of phrases familiar to
   you. Make a particular note of their context.

The Psalms

Psalm 95

O COME, let us sing unto the Lord:
Let us make a joyful noise to the rock of our salvation.
Let us come before his presence with thanksgiving,
And make a joyful noise unto him with psalms.
For the Lord is a great God,
And a great King above all gods.
In his hand are the deep places of the earth:
The strength of the hills is his also.
The sea is his, and he made it:
And his hands formed the dry land.
O come, let us worship and bow down:
Let us kneel before the Lord our maker.
For he is our God;
And we are the people of his pasture, and the sheep
of his hand.
Today if ye will hear his voice,
Harden not your heart, as in the provocation,
And as in the day of temptation in the wilderness:
When your fathers tempted me,
Proved me, and saw my work.
Forty years long was I grieved with this generation,
And said, It is a people that do err in their heart,
And they have not known my ways:
Unto whom I swore in my wrath
That they should not enter into my rest.

Psalm 96

O SING unto the Lord a new song:
Sing unto the Lord, all the earth.
Sing unto the Lord, bless his name;
Show forth his salvation from day to day.
Declare his glory among the heathen,
His wonders among all people.
For the Lord is great, and greatly to be praised:
He is to be feared above all gods.
For all the gods of the nations are idols:
But the Lord made the heavens.

Honor and majesty are before him:
Strength and beauty are in his sanctuary.
Give unto the Lord, O ye kindreds of the people,
Give unto the Lord glory and strength.
Give unto the Lord the glory due unto his name:
Bring an offering, and come into his courts.
O worship the Lord in the beauty of holiness:
Fear before him, all the earth.
Say among the heathen that the Lord reigneth:
The world also shall be established that it shall not
    be moved:
He shall judge the people righteously.
Let the heavens rejoice, and let the earth be glad;
Let the sea roar, and the fulness thereof.
Let the field be joyful, and all that is therein:
Then shall all the trees of the wood rejoice
Before the Lord: for he cometh,
For he cometh to judge the earth:
He shall judge the world with righteousness,
And the people with his truth.

Considerations and Questions

1. These two poems answer profound questions about the human condition which habit and neglect have made seem superficial or obscure to many of us. If a God exists, what should mankind do about Him? Why?

   Both Psalms 95 and 96 begin with the premise that God *does* exist, and both begin with the urgent invocation to "sing unto the Lord." Both poems quickly develop into hymns, demonstrations of singing unto the Lord, even as they raise the hypothetical question, why worship?

   Since a good many people who generally or vaguely think that God probably exists do *not* "sing unto the Lord" or pay any other ritual attention to Whomever or Whatever, it should not be hard to find popular reasons for not doing so. We are likely to appreciate the affirmation of these poems better if we are clear about what they affirm against. For a start, I suggest this proposition: Total Power and Eternal Creativity is not likely to be interested in the joyful noises of mortal creatures.

   How do these poems respond to that idea? What other arguments do they make in behalf of active worship? How do these psalms themselves exemplify certain acts of worship?

2. Poets, among other things, are makers of metaphors. We read poetry badly when we pass over metaphors as indicating general qualities like good, bad, beautiful, ugly, big, or little. In great poetry, metaphors carry layers of exact meanings, for it is the successful poet's skill to make an idea of similarity exact in detail.

   Here are some metaphorical constructions from Psalms 95 and 96. Explain their meanings in the context of the poems:

   (a) "the rock of our salvation"
   (b) "a great King above all gods"
   (c) "In his hand are the deep places of the earth"
   (d) "The strength of the hills is his"
   (e) "Let the field be joyful"
   (f) "shall all the trees of the wood rejoice"

   Do you agree that these *are* metaphors and not intended to be literal statements? Explain.

3. One of the notable differences between these two similar poems is that in one of them God is directly quoted. What have His words to do with the main idea common to both poems? What is the effect of this device on the unity of the poem that includes it?

The Psalms

Psalm 137

BY the rivers of Babylon,
There we sat down, yea, we wept,
When we remembered Zion.
We hanged our harps
Upon the willows in the midst thereof.
For there they that carried us away captive required
  of us a song;
And they that wasted us required of us mirth, saying,
Sing us one of the songs of Zion.
How shall we sing the Lord's song
In a strange land?
If I forget thee, O Jerusalem,
Let my right hand forget her cunning.
If I do not remember thee,
Let my tongue cleave to the roof of my mouth;
If I prefer not Jerusalem
Above my chief joy.
Remember, O Lord, the children of Edom
In the day of Jerusalem;
Who said, Rase it, rase it,
Even to the foundation thereof.
O daughter of Babylon, who art to be destroyed;
Happy shall he be, that rewardeth thee
As thou hast served us.
Happy shall he be, that taketh and dasheth thy little
  ones
Against the stones.

Considerations and Questions

1. The Babylonian Captivity of the sixth century B.C. involved the deportation of many Israelites to the imperial capital of Babylon. The speaker of Psalm 137, apparently one of these, laments his enforced habitation there. Yet there are apparently rivers and willows and a taste for light music there, and the poem does not indicate that the exiles are physically ill-treated or deprived. What does the poem indicate as the reason for its speaker's intense grief?

2. *How* does the poem indicate the intensity of its speaker's grief?

3. This poem begins with three verses of narrative. What specific events does the speaker put on record? What causal relationships connect these event to one another?

4. The poem concludes with a curse on the "daughter of Babylon." What are the details of this malevolent imprecation? Note that it moves from the general to the particular.

5. The speaker also prays that the Lord remember the children of Edom (vassal-allies of Babylon) who have rejoiced in the conquest of Jerusalem and urged the city's destruction. What do you find in this word "remember" as the speaker employs it?

6. As a symbol, Jerusalem is both a material thing and the representation of a concept beyond the physical. How does the speaker express his attitudes towards both of these aspects of "Jerusalem"?

The Psalms

Psalm 22

MY God, my God, why hast thou forsaken me?
Why art thou so far from helping me, and from the
    words of my roaring?
O my God, I cry in the daytime, but thou hearest not;
And in the night season, and am not silent.
But thou art holy,
O thou that inhabitest the praises of Israel.
Our fathers trusted in thee:
They trusted, and thou didst deliver them.
They cried unto thee, and were delivered:
They trusted in thee, and were not confounded.
But I am a worm, and no man;
A reproach of men, and despised of the people.
All they that see me laugh me to scorn:
They shoot out the lip, they shake the head, saying,
He trusted on the Lord that he would deliver him:
Let him deliver him, seeing he delighted in him.
But thou art he that took me out of the womb:
Thou didst make me hope when I was upon my
    mother's breasts.
I was cast upon thee from the womb:
Thou art my God from my mother's belly.
Be not far from me; for trouble is near;
For there is none to help.
Many bulls have compassed me:
Strong bulls of Bashan have beset me round.
They gaped upon me with their mouths,
As a ravening and a roaring lion.
I am poured out like water,
And all my bones are out of joint:
My heart is like wax;
It is melted in the midst of my bowels.
My strength is dried up like a potsherd;
And my tongue cleaveth to my jaws;
And thou hast brought me into the dust of death.
For dogs have compassed me:
The assembly of the wicked have inclosed me:
They pierced my hands and my feet.
I may tell all my bones:

They look and stare upon me.
They part my garments among them,
And cast lots upon my vesture.
But be not thou far from me, O Lord:
O my strength, haste thee to help me.
Deliver my soul from the sword;
My darling from the power of the dog.
Save me from the lion's mouth:
For thou hast heard me from the horns of the unicorns.
I will declare thy name unto my brethren:
In the midst of the congregation will I praise thee.
Ye that fear the Lord, praise him;
All ye the seed of Jacob, glorify him;
And fear him, all ye the seed of Israel.
For he hath not despised nor abhorred the affliction
    of the afflicted;
Neither hath he hid his face from him;
But when he cried unto him, he heard.
My praise shall be of thee in the great congregation:
I will pay my vows before them that fear him.
The meek shall eat and be satisfied:
They shall praise the Lord that seek him:
Your heart shall live for ever.
All the ends of the world shall remember and turn
    unto the Lord:
And all the kindreds of the nations shall worship
    before thee.
For the kingdom is the Lord's:
And he is the governor among the nations.
All they that be fat upon earth shall eat and worship:
All they that go down to the dust shall bow before him:
And none can keep alive his own soul.
A seed shall serve him;
It shall be accounted to the Lord for a generation.
They shall come, and shall declare his righteousness
Unto a people that shall be born, that he hath done this.

Considerations and Questions

1. I can only guess at its effect in Hebrew, but for me Psalm 22 includes some of the most vivid description of human distress in the English language. With what images and metaphors does this poet express the speaker's plight in the following details?

   (a) He has lost touch with his God.
   (b) He thinks that everyone holds him in contempt.
   (c) He is ridiculed for his beliefs and his misfortunes.
   (d) Nobody cares about him.
   (e) He fears for his life.
   (f) He is in very bad physical condition.
   (g) He is close to psychological despair.
   (h) Evil men threaten and torture him.
   (i) The few material possessions he has are being taken away from him.

2. In what sense might the opening question of the poem be taken as an outrageous complaint? In the context of the whole poem should it rather be taken as an honest application for justice, or even a prayer?

3. How and why does the attitude of the speaker take a turn for the better in the second half of the poem? By the end, what does he seem to expect from God? Why? Have there been indications of this more positive position in the first half of the poem?

The Psalms

Psalm 1

BLESSED is the man that walketh not in the counsel
    of the ungodly,
Nor standeth in the way of sinners,
Nor sitteth in the seat of the scornful.
But his delight is in the law of the Lord;
And in his law doth he meditate day and night.
And he shall be like a tree planted by the rivers of water,
That bringeth forth his fruit in his season;
His leaf also shall not wither;
And whatsoever he doeth shall prosper.
The ungodly are not so:
But are like the chaff which the wind driveth away.
Therefore the ungodly shall not stand in the judgment,
Nor sinners in the congregation of the righteous.
For the Lord knoweth the way of the righteous:
But the way of the ungodly shall perish.

Psalm 90

LORD, thou hast been our dwelling-place
In all generations.
Before the mountains were brought forth,
Or ever thou hadst formed the earth and the world,
Even from everlasting to everlasting, thou art God.
Thou turnest man to destruction;
And sayest, Return, ye children of men.
For a thousand years in thy sight
Are but as yesterday when it is past,
And as a watch in the night.
Thou carriest them away as with a flood; they are as
    a sleep:
In the morning they are like grass which groweth up.
In the morning it flourisheth, and groweth up;
In the evening it is cut down, and withereth.
For we are consumed by thine anger,
And by thy wrath are we troubled.
Thou hast set our iniquities before thee,
Our secret sins in the light of thy countenance.
For all our days are passed away in thy wrath:
We spend our years as a tale that is told.
The days of our years are threescore years and ten;

And if by reason of strength they be fourscore years,
Yet is their strength labor and sorrow;
For it is soon cut off, and we fly away.
Who knoweth the power of thine anger?
Even according to thy fear, so is thy wrath.
So teach us to number our days,
That we may apply our hearts unto wisdom.
Return, O Lord, how long?
And let it repent thee concerning thy servants.
O satisfy us early with thy mercy;
That we may rejoice and be glad all our days.
Make us glad according to the days wherein thou hast
    afflicted us,
And the years wherein we have seen evil.
Let thy work appear unto thy servants,
And thy glory unto their children.
And let the beauty of the Lord our God be upon us:
And establish thou the work of our hands upon us;
Yea, the work of our hands establish thou it.

Psalm 91

HE that dwelleth in the secret place of the most High
Shall abide under the shadow of the Almighty.
I will say of the Lord, He is my refuge and my fortress:
My God; in him will I trust.
Surely he shall deliver thee from the snare of the fowler,
And from the noisome pestilence.
He shall cover thee with his feathers,
And under his wings shalt thou trust:
His truth shall be thy shield and buckler.
Thou shalt not be afraid for the terror by night;
Nor for the arrow that flieth by day;
Nor for the pestilence that walketh in darkness;
Nor for the destruction that wasteth at noonday.
A thousand shall fall at thy side,
And ten thousand at thy right hand;
But it shall not come nigh thee.
Only with thine eyes shalt thou behold
And see the reward of the wicked.
Because thou hast made the Lord, which is my refuge,
Even the most High, thy habitation;
There shall no evil befall thee,
Neither shall any plague come nigh thy dwelling. . . .

Considerations and Questions

1. I group these psalms under the heading of "philosophical and theological meditations." They can be classified in other ways as well, but let us consider them here as statements of each speaker's passionate convictions, expressed in poetic language, about what God is like and about what human life is like. What are the attributes of God as these poems insist on them? What is the state of man? How may man hope to prosper? Is there a moral order which connects what man does with what will happen to him?

2. I have called these selections from the Book of Psalms poems, and I mean by the term that they depend for their effects on devices of language not as essential to the effects of prose. Most of us are likely to think of rhyme and meter as the dominant characteristics by which we identify poetry in the English language. There is no rhyme in the psalms we have here, and their metrical patterns are probably obscure or even absent to many of us. Yet in the translation supplied by the King James Version of the Bible they represent some of the greatest poetry in English.

    Reexamine the psalms we have presented here. With what devices other than rhyme and a metrical pattern do these poems achieve their musical (or lyrical) effects? How do repetitions of words and phrases contribute? What about assonance and alliteration? What about the balance of clauses or other syntactical clusters? What other techniques help to establish the majestic cadence of the psalms?

4. Wisdom Literature:
from Proverbs and Ecclesiastes

Crafty men contemn studies, simple men admire them, and wise men use them.

FRANCIS BACON, *Of Studies*

Proverbs

In every literate age there are books and articles which purport to give instruction in how to live the good life, or, at least, how to make the best of life. The Book of Proverbs and Ecclesiastes (or The Preacher), though different in quality and approach, are both Biblical examples of this kind of literature. Let us take such publications on their own claims and call them "Wisdom" literature. If we do not think that all of each of them deserves being called profound wisdom, at least the word may be used to convey a sense of their mutual product: practical knowledge.

Ancient or modern "Wisdom" literature may or may not assume an orthodox religious doctrine. (In the twentieth century, for example, Norman Vincent Peale's *The Power of Positive Thinking* does so, and Philip Wylie's *An Essay on Morals* most specifically does not.) But in neither case is the aim of such writing to transmit "knowledge" about eternity or the infinite, nor is its goal to establish a relationship with God. Such literature may be about ethics, sanitation, economics, domestic science, sexual behavior, peace of mind, or social and professional success (like the famous Dale Carnegie books), but its underlying purpose is always to give advice about how to get along in today's world. And that, I think, is what the authors of Proverbs and Ecclesiastes, in their separate ways, meant to do in their own day.

A formal difference between Proverbs and Ecclesiastes is that the former, as its title suggests, is a collections of "wise sayings," while Ecclesiastes is a more carefully organized lecture on the conditions of human life and how best to deal with them.

The following examples from Proverbs should give you an idea of its style and content.

> Even a fool, when he holdeth his peace, is counted wise: and he that shutteth his lips is esteemed a man of understanding. (17:28)

> As a dog returneth to his vomit, so a fool returneth to his folly. (26:11)

He that passeth by, and meddleth with strife belonging not to him, is like one that taketh a dog by the ears. (26:17)

Confidence in an unfaithful man in time of trouble is like a broken tooth, and a foot out of joint. (25:19)

Pride goeth before destruction, and a haughty spirit before a fall. (16:18)

Bread of deceit is sweet to a man; but afterwards his mouth shall be filled with gravel. (20:17)

The wicked flee when no man pursueth: but the righteous are bold as a lion. (28:1)

Try turning the "wisdom" of these sayings into your own terms and figurative language. You may see for yourself what "Wisdom" literature is about, and also something about the superiority of Biblical style.

In the thirty-one chapters of Proverbs there is a good deal of repetition among such fragments as these, but there are some more extended and connected passages as well. One such is in chapter 7 which follows here.

Proverbs

My son, keep my words,
And lay up my commandments with thee.
Keep my commandments, and live;
And my law as the apple of thine eye.
Bind them upon thy fingers,
Write them upon the table of thine heart.
Say unto wisdom, Thou art my sister;
And call understanding thy kinswoman:
That they may keep thee from the strange woman,
From the stranger which flattereth with her words.
For at the window of my house
I looked through my casement,
And beheld among the simple ones,
I discerned among the youths,
A young man void of understanding,
Passing through the street near her corner;
And he went the way to her house,
In the twilight, in the evening,
In the black and dark night:
And, behold, there met him a woman
With the attire of an harlot, and subtile of heart.
(She is loud and stubborn;
Her feet abide not in her house:
Now is she without, now in the streets,
And lieth in wait at every corner.)
So she caught him, and kissed him,
And with an impudent face said unto him,
I have peace offerings with me;
This day have I payed my vows.
Therefore came I forth to meet thee,
Diligently to seek thy face, and I have found thee.
I have decked my bed with coverings of tapestry,
With carved works, with fine linen of Egypt.
I have perfumed my bed
With myrrh, aloes, and cinnamon.
Come, let us take our fill of love until the morning:
Let us solace ourselves with loves.
For the goodman is not at home,
He is gone a long journey:
He hath taken a bag of money with him,
And will come home at the day appointed.

With her much fair speech she caused him to yield,
With the flattering of her lips she forced him.
He goeth after her straightway,
As an ox goeth to the slaughter,
Or as a fool to the correction of the stocks;
Till a dart strike through his liver;
As a bird hasteth to the snare,
And knoweth not that it is for his life.
Hearken unto me now therefore, O ye children,
And attend to the words of my mouth.
Let not thine heart decline to her ways,
Go not astray in her paths.
For she hath cast down many wounded:
Yea, many strong men have been slain by her.
Her house is the way to hell,
Going down to the chambers of death.

Considerations and Questions

1. The bulk of this selection is a narrative, but not a story told to entertain, or even, in a more sophisticated sense, to change the world. What is the framework of the story? Who tells it to whom? Why?

2. What are the details of "the strange woman's" part in the incident? She is "with the attire of an harlot." Is she in fact a prostitute? Is she a girl the young man has been planning to seduce? What is the storyteller's apparent point in having her play the role she does? Which of her personal qualities does the storyteller choose to specify?

3. How does the storyteller characterize the young man? Is he an innocent, a Don Juan, or a "swinger"?

4. This passage is concerned with sexual behavior, and it is obviously an admonition against a certain kind of sexual behavior. To what extent does the storyteller indicate that this behavior is *morally* wrong, a sin against God and man? Why shouldn't one indulge in it—according to the storyteller? Why *do* people indulge in it?

5. How does an ox go to the slaughter? Why does a bird haste to the snare?

Ecclesiastes

Ecclesiastes begins: "The words of the Preacher, the son of David, king in Jerusalem," and later, in 1:12 appears: "I the Preacher was king over Israel in Jerusalem." The obvious inference to which the reader is invited is that the author of this book is Solomon, and so many readers have believed. But here, as in the Psalms, we seem to be in the presence of a literary convention rather than literary history. The lyric Psalms are put in the mouth of the musical King David, and the "Wisdom" literature (Proverbs as well as Ecclesiastes) in that of the "wise" King Solomon. The kings are, if you like, the "speakers" of the books assigned to them but not the actual authors of them.°

The language and indeed the "wisdom" of Ecclesiastes is, I think, of a higher order than that of most of Proverbs, but neither the writer of Ecclesiastes nor what he writes about seems directed towards any reality beyond how to survive in the material world. God is mentioned, but there is little indication that the divine has any meaning for the real life of man. Such statements as "Remember now thy Creator in the days of thy youth" (12:1) and "the spirit shall return unto God who gave it" (12:7) are considered by most scholars to be pious additions to the original work. Whether that be the case or not, such hopeful theological suggestions are not consistent with the main current of the work. The Preacher, in truth, is not a very religious man.

° The famous Song of Songs, which I am not including in this Introduction, is fictitiously ascribed to Solomon also, but in his role as a great lover rather than as a great sage. Like Ecclesiastes, the Song of Songs is "religious" literature only with the help of considerable editorial stress and strain.

Ecclesiastes

1 The words of the Preacher, the son of David, king in Jerusalem.

2 Vanity of vanities, saith the Preacher,
   vanity of vanities;
   all is vanity.

3 What profit hath a man of all his labor
   which he taketh under the sun?

4 One generation passeth away, and another generation cometh:
   but the earth abideth for ever.

5 The sun also ariseth, and the sun goeth down,
   and hasteth to his place where he arose.

6 The wind goeth toward the south,
   and turneth about unto the north;
   it whirleth about continually,
   and the wind returneth again according to his circuits.

7 All the rivers run into the sea; yet the sea is not full:
   unto the place from whence the rivers come, thither they
      return again.

8 All things are full of labor;
   man cannot utter it:
   the eye is not satisfied with seeing,
   nor the ear filled with hearing.

9 The thing that hath been, it is that which shall be;
   and that which is done is that which shall be done:
   and there is no new thing under the sun.

12,13 I the Preacher was king over Israel in Jerusalem. And I gave my heart
   to seek and search out by wisdom concerning all things that are done under
   heaven: this sore travail hath God given to the sons of man to be exercised
14 therewith. I have seen all the works that are done under the sun; and, behold, all is vanity and vexation of spirit.

15 That which is crooked cannot be made straight:
   and that which is wanting cannot be numbered.

17 And I gave my heart to know wisdom, and to know madness
      and folly:
   I perceived that this also is vexation of spirit.

18 For in much wisdom is much grief:
   and he that increaseth knowledge increaseth sorrow.

3 To every thing there is a season, and a time to every purpose under the
   heaven:

2   A time to be born,
            and a time to die;
         a time to plant,
            and a time to pluck up that which is planted;

<pre>
3   A time to kill,
               and a time to heal;
           a time to break down,
               and a time to build up;

4   A time to weep,
               and a time to laugh;
           a time to mourn,
               and a time to dance;

5   A time to cast away stones,
               and a time to gather stones together;
           a time to embrace,
               and a time to refrain from embracing;

6   A time to get,
               and a time to lose;
           a time to keep,
               and a time to cast away;

7   A time to rend,
               and a time to sew;
           a time to keep silence,
               and a time to speak;

8   A time to love,
               and a time to hate;
           a time of war,
               and a time of peace.
</pre>

9,10 What profit hath he that worketh in that wherein he laboreth? I have seen the travail, which God hath given to the sons of men to be exercised 19 in it. For that which befalleth the sons of men befalleth beasts; even one thing befalleth them: as the one dieth, so dieth the other; yea, they have all one breath; so that a man hath no preeminence above a beast: for all is 20 vanity. All go unto one place; all are of the dust, and all turn to dust again. 21 Who knoweth the spirit of man that goeth upward, and the spirit of the 22 beast that goeth downward to the earth? Wherefore I perceive that there is nothing better, than that a man should rejoice in his own works; for that is his portion: for who shall bring him to see what shall be after him?

9: 2 All things come alike to all: there is one event to the righteous, and to the wicked; to the good and to the clean, and to the unclean; to him that sacrificeth, and to him that sacrificeth not: as is the good, so is the sinner; and he 3 that sweareth, as he that feareth an oath. This is an evil among all things that are done under the sun, that there is one event unto all: yea, also the heart of the sons of men is full of evil, and madness is in their heart while they live, and after that they go to the dead.

<pre>
4   For to him that is joined to all the living there is hope:
               for a living dog is better than a dead lion.
5   For the living know that they shall die:
               but the dead know not any thing,
               neither have they any more a reward;
               for the memory of them is forgotten.
</pre>

7   Go thy way, eat thy bread with joy, and drink thy wine with a merry

8 heart; for God now accepteth thy works. Let thy garments be always white;

9 and let thy head lack no ointment. Live joyfully with the wife whom thou lovest all the days of the life of thy vanity, which he hath given thee under the sun, all the days of thy vanity: for that is thy portion in this life, and in

10 thy labor which thou takest under the sun. Whatsoever thy hand findeth to do, do it with thy might; for there is no work, nor device, nor knowledge, nor wisdom, in the grave, whither thou goest.

11   I returned, and saw under the sun, that the race is not to the swift, nor the battle to the strong, neither yet bread to the wise, nor yet riches to men of understanding, nor yet favor to men of skill; but time and chance happeneth

12 to them all. For man also knoweth not his time: as the fishes that are taken in an evil net, and as the birds that are caught in the snare; so are the sons of men snared in an evil time, when it falleth suddenly upon them.

12: 1   Remember now thy Creator in the days of thy youth,
        while the evil days come not,
        nor the years draw nigh,
        when thou shalt say, I have no pleasure in them;

2   While the sun, or the light, or the moon, or the stars, be not dark-
        ened,
        nor the clouds return after the rain:

3   In the days when the keepers of the house shall tremble,
        and the strong men shall bow themselves,
    and the grinders cease because they are few,
        and those that look out of the windows be darkened,

4   And the doors shall be shut in the streets,
        when the sound of the grinding is low,
    and he shall rise up at the voice of the bird,
        and all the daughters of music shall be brought low;

5   Also when they shall be afraid of that which is high,
        and fears shall be in the way,
    and the almond tree shall flourish,
        and the grasshopper shall be a burden,
    and desire shall fail:
        because man goeth to his long home,
        and the mourners go about the streets:

6   Or ever the silver cord be loosed,
        or the golden bowl be broken,
    or the pitcher be broken at the fountain,
        or the wheel broken at the cistern.

7   Then shall the dust return to the earth as it was:
        and the spirit shall return unto God who gave it.

8   Vanity of vanities, saith the Preacher; all is vanity.

Considerations and Questions

1. "All is vanity" is the announced theme of the first part of our passages from Ecclesiastes. In the language of the English Bible (and of Shakespeare) the main meaning of "vanity" is worthlessness, lack of reality, emptiness. To what extent does this differ from our contemporary use of the word? What connections remain between the "vanity" of the Preacher and modern "vanity" as applied to, say, beauty, ability, or possessions?

2. In Proverbs we are told that it is disastrous to be a fool and profitable to be wise. What has the Preacher of Ecclesiastes to say on the subject?

3. If we ask the Preacher, "Does history repeat itself?" his answer is that there is "no new thing under the sun" (1:9). What has this to do with his "vanity" theme?

4. Throughout our selections does the Preacher remain consistent to his claim that *all* is vanity, that everything mortal is worthless? Or does it appear that he refers only to a special category of mortal experience? What does he have to say about time, the earth, and history in this regard?

5. Explain the metaphor, "for a living dog is better than a dead lion " (9:4).

6. Ecclesiastes 9:11 is one of the most frequently quoted passages from the Bible. I repeat it here not only because of its great language but as a basic attitude about human life worth memorizing.

> I returned, and saw under the sun, that the race is not to the swift, nor the battle to the strong, neither yet bread to the wise, nor yet riches to men of understanding, nor yet favor to men of skill; but time and chance happeneth to them all.

As literary rhetoric, if not as philosophical or religious thought, this sentence deserves the attention of analysis and the compliment of imitation. Note what a poor thing is my own attempt to reproduce its idea:

> I looked about me and observed that human abilities make no difference in deciding the successes or failures of their possessors, but that all human beings are subject to the deterioration of years and the results of events beyond their control.

Can you do better? Note that the Preacher here is writing about abilities, not moral qualities. What, in our selections from Ecclesiastes, does he have to say about the consequences of being good or evil? What does he say about the prevalence and distribution of moral qualities in mankind?

7. If you have an idea that the Preacher depicts a world in which one can take little if any positive action to ensure a happy and successful life, I do not think that you are being unreasonable. Yet is the tone of his work actually one of despair, as this idea might suggest? To what extent does the vigor and diversity of the imagery in Ecclesiastes dispel such an effect? Does the

Preacher preach *any* courses of action, or even attitudes, by which the futilities and vicissitudes of life as he sees them may be best endured?

8. What appear to be the Preacher's theological views? Compare his ideas about God with those implicit in the early Old Testament myths and legends, in the history of ancient Israel, in the stories, poems, and even in the Proverbs we have read.

9. The last of our selections from Ecclesiastes (its final chapter, 12) is about old age. How does this passage express the following characteristics of the end of natural life?

(a) The quavering weakness of the body.
(b) Failure of teeth, sight, and hearing.
(c) With loss of balance, an increasing fear of heights.
(d) A tendency to break household valuables.

5. A Philosophical Novel: Job

And worse I may be yet. The worst is not,
So long as we can say, 'This is the worst.'
WILLIAM SHAKESPEARE, *King Lear*

Everyone agrees that the Book of Job is a masterpiece. It is, however, quite long, and a good deal of it involves a complicated interplay of concepts and philosophical positions beyond the scope of this Introduction. Consequently, it is represented here in a severely abridged form, but a form which I think will make clear to you what happens to Job and also how it happens.

The Book of Job has been classified variously for various occasions. It has been justly represented as a great poem, a great drama, a great extended essay, or sermon. I choose to treat it here as a novel and have arranged our shortened version accordingly. It is above all the narrative of a man whom circumstances drive to seek answers to the ultimate questions about the nature of existence and who therefore undergoes great changes in fortune and attitude. Short stories, like Jonah, Ruth, and the Daniel tales, generally *reveal* their characters to the characters themselves, to the reader, or to both. Novels ordinarily go further; they deal with *change*. Job starts his story as one kind of man, and emerges at the end of it as another.

Although in this text I am introducing Job after Ecclesiastes, this story was actually written at least a century, probably more, before the Preacher preached. I mention it because this novel is significantly the earliest direct Biblical assertion of the idea that the righteous do not inevitably flourish and the wicked inevitably fall. Now, in fact, this idea must plague all perceptive people who accept the concept of a superhuman moral order in the universe, but the mainstream of orthodoxy in Israel before Job generally ignores the persistent suspicion that the godly do sometimes seem to suffer unjustly while the ungodly prosper. When the facts of particular cases have been too plain to ignore, Biblical orthodoxy has either tended to assume that the godly are not as godly as advertised or that things will soon get better. But that God materially rewards His good and faithful adherents and punishes the wicked and disloyal is, up to this point, the prevailing doctrine of Israel.

In this sense, then, the writer of Job, as a Jew, is a religious radical. In his narrative he presents the disquieting case of a very good man who gets a very raw deal—and from God Himself. Unlike the Preacher of Ecclesiastes, however, the Job writer is profoundly religious. He is not merely concerned with how to endure the injustices of daily life and the frustrations of inevitable decay and death. He is intensely interested in how the observed and apparently unreasonable distribution of rewards and penalties in this life can be reconciled with the idea of Divine Justice.

The situation of the story is established in a prose prologue which is simple and deceptively fanciful. Who on earth dreamed up that council meeting in Heaven? Whoever it was apparently conceived, for the moment, of a remarkably pagan sort of deity, one that would appeal to Homeric Greeks, who did not expect ultimate moral dimensions in divinity. But this fantasy does explain in a primitive way how awful things may occur to people who deserve much better. The God of the prologue simply happens to be in a betting mood, and he is easily talked into destroying Job's life in order to wager with a subordinate god. If the Powers above are really like this one, no wonder life is without justice. Perhaps the worldly Preacher of Ecclesiastes would consider such a version of the Deity casually acceptable, but of course Biblical orthodoxy would not, and neither, as we shall see, does the writer of the Book of Job.

Job

1   There was a man in the land of Uz, whose name was Job; and that man
2 was perfect and upright, and one that feared God, and eschewed evil. And
3 there were born unto him seven sons and three daughters. His substance also
was seven thousand sheep, and three thousand camels, and five hundred yoke
of oxen, and five hundred she asses, and a very great household; so that this
4 man was the greatest of all the men of the east. And his sons went and
feasted in their houses, every one his day; and sent and called for their three
5 sisters to eat and to drink with them. And it was so, when the days of their
feasting were gone about, that Job sent and sanctified them, and rose up
early in the morning, and offered burnt offerings according to the number of
them all: for Job said, It may be that my sons have sinned, and cursed God
in their hearts. Thus did Job continually.
6   Now there was a day when the sons of God came to present themselves
7 before the Lord, and Satan came also among them. And the Lord said unto
Satan, Whence comest thou? Then Satan answered the Lord, and said, From
going to and fro in the earth, and from walking up and down in it.
8   And the Lord said unto Satan, Hast thou considered my servant Job, that
there is none like him in the earth, a perfect and an upright man, one that
feareth God, and escheweth evil?
9   Then Satan answered the Lord, and said, Doth Job fear God for nought?
10 Hast not thou made a hedge about him, and about his house, and about all
that he hath on every side? thou hast blessed the work of his hands, and his
11 substance is increased in the land. But put forth thine hand now, and touch
all that he hath, and he will curse thee to thy face.
12   And the Lord said unto Satan, Behold, all that he hath is in thy power;
only upon himself put not forth thine hand. So Satan went forth from the
presence of the Lord.
13   And there was a day when his sons and his daughters were eating and
14 drinking wine in their eldest brother's house: And there came a messenger
unto Job, and said, The oxen were plowing, and the asses feeding beside
15 them: And the Sabeans fell upon them, and took them away; yea, they have
slain the servants with the edge of the sword; and I only am escaped alone
to tell thee.
16   While he was yet speaking, there came also another, and said, The fire of
God is fallen from heaven, and hath burned up the sheep, and the servants,
and consumed them; and I only am escaped alone to tell thee.
17   While he was yet speaking, there came also another, and said, The Chaldeans made out three bands, and fell upon the camels, and have carried them
away, yea, and slain the servants with the edge of the sword; and I only am
escaped alone to tell thee.
18   While he was yet speaking, there came also another, and said, Thy sons
and thy daughters were eating and drinking wine in their eldest brother's
19 house: And, behold, there came a great wind from the wilderness, and
smote the four corners of the house, and it fell upon the young men, and they
are dead; and I only am escaped alone to tell thee.
20   Then Job arose, and rent his mantle, and shaved his head, and fell down
21 upon the ground, and worshipped, And said,

Naked came I out of my mother's womb,
and naked shall I return thither:
the Lord gave, and the Lord hath taken away;
blessed be the name of the Lord.

22 In all this Job sinned not, nor charged God foolishly.

2 Again there was a day when the sons of God came to present themselves before the Lord, and Satan came also among them to present himself before the Lord.

2 And the Lord said unto Satan, From whence comest thou? And Satan answered the Lord, and said, From going to and fro in the earth, and from walking up and down in it.

3 And the Lord said unto Satan, Hast thou considered my servant Job, that there is none like him in the earth, a perfect and an upright man, one that feareth God, and escheweth evil? and still he holdeth fast his integrity,

4 although thou movedst me against him, to destroy him without cause. And Satan answered the Lord, and said, Skin for skin, yea, all that a man hath

5 will he give for his life. But put forth thine hand now, and touch his bone and

6 his flesh, and he will curse thee to thy face. And the Lord said unto Satan, Behold, he is in thine hand; but save his life.

7 So went Satan forth from the presence of the Lord, and smote Job with

8 sore boils from the sole of his foot unto his crown. And he took him a pot-

9 sherd to scrape himself withal; and he sat down among the ashes. Then said his wife unto him, Dost thou still retain thine integrity? curse God, and die.

10 But he said unto her, Thou speakest as one of the foolish women speaketh. What? shall we receive good at the hand of God, and shall we not receive evil? In all this did not Job sin with his lips.

11 Now when Job's three friends heard of all this evil that was come upon him, they came every one from his own place; Eliphaz the Temanite, and Bildad the Shuhite, and Zophar the Naamathite: for they had made an ap-

12 pointment together to come to mourn with him, and to comfort him. And when they lifted up their eyes afar off, and knew him not, they lifted up their voice, and wept; and they rent every one his mantle, and sprinkled dust

13 upon their heads toward heaven. So they sat down with him upon the ground seven days and seven nights, and none spake a word unto him: for they saw that his grief was very great.

3:1,2 After this opened Job his mouth, and cursed his day. And Job spake, and said,

3
Let the day perish wherein I was born,
and the night in which it was said, There is a man child
conceived.

4
Let that day be darkness;
let not God regard it from above,
neither let the light shine upon it.

5
Let darkness and the shadow of death stain it;
let a cloud dwell upon it;
let the blackness of the day terrify it.

10
Because it shut not up the doors of my mother's womb,
nor hid sorrow from mine eyes.

Some Formal Biblical Literature

227

11	Why died I not from the womb?
	why did I not give up the ghost when I came out of the belly?
13	For now should I have lain still and been quiet,
	I should have slept; then had I been at rest,
17	There the wicked cease from troubling;
	and there the weary be at rest.
18	There the prisoners rest together;
	they hear not the voice of the oppressor.
19	The small and great are there;
	and the servant is free from his master.

20   Wherefore is light given to him that is in misery,
    and life unto the bitter in soul;

21   Which long for death, but it cometh not;
    and dig for it more than for hid treasures;

22   Which rejoice exceedingly, and are glad, when they can find
      the grave?

23   Why is light given to a man whose way is hid,
    and whom God hath hedged in?

24   For my sighing cometh before I eat,
    and my roarings are poured out like the waters.

25   For the thing which I greatly feared is come upon me,
    and that which I was afraid of is come unto me.

26   I was not in safety,
    neither had I rest,
    neither was I quiet;
    yet trouble came.

4   Then Eliphaz the Temanite answered and said,

2   If we assay to commune with thee, wilt thou be grieved?
    but who can withhold himself from speaking?

3   Behold, thou hast instructed many,
    and thou hast strengthened the weak hands.

4   Thy words have upholden him that was falling,
    and thou hast strengthened the feeble knees.

5   But now it is come upon thee, and thou faintest;
    it toucheth thee, and thou are troubled.

6   Is not this thy fear, thy confidence,
    thy hope, and the uprightness of thy ways?

7   Remember, I pray thee, who ever perished, being innocent?
    or where were the righteous cut off?

8   Even as I have seen, they that plow iniquity,
    and sow wickedness, reap the same.

9   By the blast of God they perish,
    and by the breath of his nostrils are they consumed.

17   Shall mortal man be more just than God?
    shall a man be more pure than his Maker?

18   Behold, he put no trust in his servants;
    and his angels he charged with folly:

19   How much less in them that dwell in houses of clay,
        whose foundation is in the dust,
        which are crushed before the moth?

5: 1   Call now, if there be any that will answer thee;
        and to which of the saints wilt thou turn?

2   For wrath killeth the foolish man,
        and envy slayeth the silly one.

6   Although affliction cometh not forth of the dust,
        neither doth trouble spring out of the ground;

7   Yet man is born unto trouble,
        as the sparks fly upward.

8   I would seek unto God,
        and unto God would I commit my cause:

9   Which doeth great things and unsearchable;
        marvelous things without number:

10   Who giveth rain upon the earth,
        and sendeth waters upon the fields:

11   To set up on high those that be low;
        that those which mourn may be exalted to safety.

12   He disappointeth the devices of the crafty,
        so that their hands cannot perform their enterprise.

15   But he saveth the poor from the sword,
        from their mouth, and from the hand of the mighty.

17   Behold, happy is the man whom God correcteth:
        therefore despise not thou the chastening of the Almighty:

18   For he maketh sore, and bindeth up:
        he woundeth, and his hands make whole.

19   He shall deliver thee in six troubles:
        yea, in seven there shall no evil touch thee.

25   Thou shalt know also that thy seed shall be great,
        and thine offspring as the grass of the earth.

26   Thou shalt come to thy grave in a full age,
        like as a shock of corn cometh in in his season.

27   Lo this, we have searched it, so it is;
        hear it, and know thou it for thy good.

6   But Job answered and said,

2   Oh that my grief were thoroughly weighed,
        and my calamity laid in the balances together!

3   For now it would be heavier than the sand of the sea:
        therefore my words are swallowed up.

4   For the arrows of the Almighty are within me,
        the poison whereof drinketh up my spirit:
        the terrors of God do set themselves in array against me.

8   Oh that I might have my request;
        and that God would grant me the thing that I long for!

9   Even that it would please God to destroy me;
        that he would let loose his hand, and cut me off!

11   What is my strength, that I should hope?
        and what is mine end, that I should prolong my life?

12   Is my strength the strength of stones?
        or is my flesh of brass?

14   To him that is afflicted pity should be showed from his friend;
        but he forsaketh the fear of the Almighty.

15   My brethren have dealt deceitfully as a brook,
        and as the stream of brooks they pass away;

16   Which are blackish by reason of the ice,
        and wherein the snow is hid:

17   What time they wax warm they vanish:
        when it is hot, they are consumed out of their place.

24   Teach me, and I will hold my tongue:
        and cause me to understand wherein I have erred.

25   How forcible are right words!
        but what doth your arguing reprove?

27   Yea, ye overwhelm the fatherless,
        and ye dig a pit for your friend.

29   Return, I pray you, let it not be iniquity;
        yea, return again, my righteousness is in it.

30   Is there iniquity in my tongue?
        cannot my taste discern perverse things?

7: 4   When I lie down, I say,
When shall I arise, and the night be gone?
        and I am full of tossings to and fro unto the dawning of the day.

5   My flesh is clothed with worms and clods of dust;
        my skin is broken, and become loathsome.

6   My days are swifter than a weaver's shuttle,
        and are spent without hope.

11   Therefore I will not refrain my mouth;
        I will speak in the anguish of my spirit;
        I will complain in the bitterness of my soul.

13   When I say, My bed shall comfort me,
        my couch shall ease my complaint;

14   Then thou scarest me with dreams,
        and terrifiest me through visions:

15   So that my soul chooseth strangling,
        and death rather than my life.

16   I loathe it; I would not live alway:
        let me alone; for my days are vanity.

20   I have sinned; what shall I do unto thee,
        O thou preserver of men?
why hast thou set me as a mark against thee,
        so that I am a burden to myself?

21 And why dost thou not pardon my transgression,
   and take away mine iniquity?
   for now shall I sleep in the dust;
   and thou shalt seek me in the morning, but I shall not be.

8 Then answered Bildad the Shuhite, and said,

2 How long wilt thou speak these things?
   and how long shall the words of thy mouth be like a strong wind?
3 Doth God pervert judgment?
   or doth the Almighty pervert justice?
6 If thou wert pure and upright;
   surely now he would awake for thee,
   and make the habitation of thy righteousness prosperous.
8 For inquire, I pray thee, of the former age,
   and prepare thyself to the search of their fathers:
10 Shall not they teach thee, and tell thee,
   and utter words out of their heart?

20 Behold, God will not cast away a perfect man,
   neither will he help the evil-doers:
21 Till he fill thy mouth with laughing,
   and thy lips with rejoicing.
22 They that hate thee shall be clothed with shame;
   and the dwelling place of the wicked shall come to nought.

9 Then Job answered and said,

2 I know it is so of a truth:
   but how should man be just with God?
3 If he will contend with him,
   he cannot answer him one of a thousand.
4 He is wise in heart, and mighty in strength:
   who hath hardened himself against him, and hath prospered?
16 If I had called, and he had answered me;
   yet would I not believe that he had hearkened unto my voice.
17 For he breaketh me with a tempest,
   and multiplieth my wounds without cause.
18 He will not suffer me to take my breath,
   but filleth me with bitterness.
20 If I justify myself, mine own mouth shall condemn me:
   if I say, I am perfect, it shall also prove me perverse.
21 Though I were perfect, yet would I not know my soul:
   I would despise my life.
22 This is one thing, therefore I said it,
   He destroyeth the perfect and the wicked.
23 If the scourge slay suddenly,
   he will laugh at the trial of the innocent.
24 The earth is given into the hand of the wicked:
   he covereth the faces of the judges thereof;
   if not, where, and who is he?

Some Formal Biblical Literature

29 If I be wicked,
    why then labor I in vain?
30 If I wash myself with snow water,
    and make my hands never so clean;
34 Let him take his rod away from me,
    and let not his fear terrify me:
35 Then would I speak, and not fear him;
    but it is not so with me.

10: 1 My soul is weary of my life;
    I will leave my complaint upon myself;
    I will speak in the bitterness of my soul.
2 I will say unto God, Do not condemn me;
    show me wherefore thou contendest with me.
3 Is it good unto thee that thou shouldest oppress,
    that thou shouldest despise the work of thine hands,
    and shine upon the counsel of the wicked?
4 Hast thou eyes of flesh?
    or seest thou as man seeth?
5 Are thy days as the days of man?
    are thy years as man's days,
6 That thou inquirest after mine iniquity,
    and searchest after my sin?
7 Thou knowest that I am not wicked;
    and there is none that can deliver out of thine hand.
8 Thine hands have made me and fashioned me together round about;
    yet thou dost destroy me.
9 Remember, I beseech thee, that thou hast made me as the clay;
    and wilt thou bring me into dust again?
11 Thou hast clothed me with skin and flesh,
    and hast fenced me with bones and sinews.
12 Thou hast granted me life and favor,
    and thy visitation hath preserved my spirit.
15 If I be wicked, woe unto me;
    and if I be righteous, yet will I not lift up my head.
I am full of confusion;
    therefore see thou mine affliction;
16   For it increaseth.
Thou huntest me as a fierce lion:
    and again thou showest thyself marvelous upon me.
18 Wherefore then hast thou brought me forth out of the womb?
    Oh that I had given up the ghost, and no eye had seen me!
20 Are not my days few? cease then,
    and let me alone, that I may take comfort a little,
21 Before I go whence I shall not return,
    even to the land of darkness   and the shadow of death;
22 A land of darkness, as darkness itself;
    and of the shadow of death, without any order,
    and where the light is as darkness.

11   Then answered Zophar the Naamathite, and said,

2   Should not the multitude of words be answered?
    and should a man full of talk be justified?

3   Should thy lies make men hold their peace?
    and when thou mockest, shall no man make thee ashamed?

4   For thou hast said, My doctrine is pure,
    and I am clean in thine eyes.

5   But oh that God would speak,
    and open his lips against thee;

6   And that he would show thee the secrets of wisdom,
    that they are double to that which is!
Know therefore that God exacteth of thee less than thine iniquity
    deserveth.

7   Canst thou by searching find out God?
    canst thou find out the Almighty unto perfection?

8   It is as high as heaven; what canst thou do?
    deeper than hell; what canst thou know?

9   The measure thereof is longer than the earth,
    and broader than the sea.

13   If thou prepare thine heart,
    and stretch out thine hands toward him;

14   If iniquity be in thine hand, put it far away,
    and let not wickedness dwell in thy tabernacles.

15   For then shalt thou lift up thy face without spot;
    yea, thou shalt be steadfast, and shalt not fear:

16   Because thou shalt forget thy misery,
    and remember it as waters that pass away:

17   And thine age shall be clearer than the noonday;
thou shalt shine forth, thou shalt be as the morning.

12   And Job answered and said,

2   No doubt but ye are the people,
    and wisdom shall die with you.

3   But I have understanding as well as you;
    I am not inferior to you:
    yea, who knoweth not such things as these?

4   I am as one mocked of his neighbor,
    who calleth upon God, and he answereth him:
    the just upright man is laughed to scorn.

7   But ask now the beasts, and they shall teach thee;
    and the fowls of the air, and they shall tell thee;

8   Or speak to the earth, and it shall teach thee;
    and the fishes of the sea shall declare unto thee.

9   Who knoweth not in all these
    that the hand of the Lord hath wrought this?

15   Behold, he withholdeth the waters, and they dry up:
    also he sendeth them out, and they overturn the earth.

Some Formal Biblical Literature

21	He poureth contempt upon princes,
	and weakeneth the strength of the mighty.
22	He discovereth deep things out of darkness,
	and bringeth out to light the shadow of death.
23	He increaseth the nations, and destroyeth them:
	he enlargeth the nations, and straiteneth them again.

13: 1   Lo, mine eye hath seen all this,
    mine ear hath heard and understood it.

3   Surely I would speak to the Almighty,
    and I desire to reason with God.

4   But ye are forgers of lies,
    Ye are all physicians of no value.

5   Oh that ye would altogether hold your peace!
    and it should be your wisdom.

6   Hear now my reasoning,
    and hearken to the pleadings of my lips.

7   Will ye speak wickedly for God?
    and talk deceitfully for him?

8   Will ye accept his person?
    will ye contend for God?

11   Shall not his excellency make you afraid?
    and his dread fall upon you?

13   Hold your peace, let me alone, that I may speak,
    and let come on me what will.

14   Wherefore do I take my flesh in my teeth,
    and put my life in mine hand?

15   Though he slay me, yet will I trust in him:
    but I will maintain mine own ways before him.

16   He also shall be my salvation:
    for a hypocrite shall not come before him.

23   How many are mine iniquities and sins?
    make me to know my transgression and my sin.

25   Wilt thou break a leaf driven to and fro?
    and wilt thou pursue the dry stubble?

26   For thou writest bitter things against me,
    and makest me to possess the iniquities of my youth.

14: 1   Man that is born of a woman
    is of few days, and full of trouble.

2   He cometh forth like a flower, and is cut down:
    he fleeth also as a shadow, and continueth not.

4   Who can bring a clean thing out of an unclean?
    Not one.

7   For there is hope of a tree, if it be cut down,
    that it will sprout again, and that the tender branch thereof
        will not cease.

8   Though the root thereof wax old in the earth,

and the stock thereof die in the ground;

9 Yet through the scent of water it will bud,
and bring forth boughs like a plant.

10 But man dieth, and wasteth away:
yea, man giveth up the ghost, and where is he?

11 As the waters fail from the sea,
and the flood decayeth and drieth up;

12 So man lieth down, and riseth not:
till the heavens be no more, they shall not awake,
nor be raised out of their sleep.

13 Oh that thou wouldest hide me in the grave,
that thou wouldest keep me secret, until thy wrath be past,
that thou wouldest appoint me a set time, and remember me!

14 If a man die, shall he live again?
all the days of my appointed time will I wait,
till my change come.

19 The waters wear the stones:
thou washest away the things which grow out of the dust of
the earth;
and thou destroyest the hope of man.

38 Then the Lord answered Job out of the whirlwind, and said,

2 Who is this that darkeneth counsel
by words without knowledge?

3 Gird up now thy loins like a man;
for I will demand of thee, and answer thou me.

4 Where wast thou when I laid the foundations of the earth?
declare, if thou hast understanding.

5 Who hath laid the measures thereof, if thou knowest?
or who hath stretched the line upon it?

6 Whereupon are the foundations thereof fastened?
or who laid the corner stone thereof;

7 When the morning stars sang together,
and all the sons of God shouted for joy?

8 Or who shut up the sea with doors,
when it brake forth, as if it had issued out of the womb?

9 When I made the cloud the garment thereof,
and thick darkness a swaddling band for it,

11 And said, Hitherto shalt thou come, but no further:
and here shall thy proud waves be stayed?

16 Hast thou entered into the springs of the sea?
or hast thou walked in the search of the depth?

17 Have the gates of death been opened unto thee?
or hast thou seen the doors of the shadow of death?

18 Hast thou perceived the breadth of the earth?
declare if thou knowest it all.

19 Where is the way where light dwelleth?

and as for darkness, where is the place thereof,

21 Knowest thou it, because thou wast then born?
or because the number of thy days is great?

22 Hast thou entered into the treasures of the snow?
or hast thou seen the treasures of the hail,

24 By what way is the light parted,
which scattereth the east wind upon the earth?

25 Who hath divided a watercourse for the overflowing of waters,
or a way for the lightning of thunder;

26 To cause it to rain on the earth, where no man is;
on the wilderness, wherein there is no man;

27 To satisfy the desolate and waste ground;
and to cause the bud of the tender herb to spring forth?

28 Hath the rain a father?
or who hath begotten the drops of dew?

29 Out of whose womb came the ice?
and the hoary frost of heaven, who hath gendered it?

30 The waters are hid as with a stone,
and the face of the deep is frozen.

31 Canst thou bind the sweet influences of Pleiades,
or loose the bands of Orion?

32 Canst thou bring forth Mazzaroth in his season?
or canst thou guide Arcturus with his sons?

33 Knowest thou the ordinances of heaven?
canst thou set the dominion thereof in the earth?

34 Canst thou lift up thy voice to the clouds,
that abundance of waters may cover thee?

35 Canst thou send lightnings, that they may go,
and say unto thee, Here we are?

36 Who hath put wisdom in the inward parts?
or who hath given understanding to the heart?

37 Who can number the clouds in wisdom?
or who can stay the bottles of heaven, . . .

39: 1 Knowest thou the time when the wild goats of the rock bring forth?
or canst thou mark when the hinds do calve?

9 Will the unicorn be willing to serve thee,
or abide by thy crib?

10 Canst thou bind the unicorn with his band in the furrow?
or will he harrow the valleys after thee?

19 Hast thou given the horse strength?
hast thou clothed his neck with thunder?

20 Canst thou make him afraid as a grasshopper?
the glory of his nostrils is terrible.

21 He paweth in the valley, and rejoiceth in his strength:
he goeth on to meet the armed men.

22	He mocketh at fear, and is not affrighted;
	neither turneth he back from the sword.
23	The quiver rattleth against him,
	the glittering spear and the shield.
24	He swalloweth the ground with fierceness and rage:
	neither believeth he that it is the sound of the trumpet.
25	He saith among the trumpets, Ha, ha!
	and he smelleth the battle afar off,
	the thunder of the captains, and the shouting.

26 Doth the hawk fly by thy wisdom,
    and stretch her wings toward the south?
27 Doth the eagle mount up at thy command,
    and make her nest on high?

40: 2 Shall he that contendeth with the Almighty instruct him?
    he that reproveth God, let him answer it.

3 Then Job answered the Lord, and said,

4 Behold, I am vile; what shall I answer thee?
    I will lay mine hand upon my mouth.
5 Once have I spoken; but I will not answer:
    yea, twice; but I will proceed no further.

6 Then answered the Lord unto Job out of the whirlwind, and said,

7 Gird up thy loins now like a man:
    I will demand of thee, and declare thou unto me.
8 Wilt thou also disannul my judgment?
    wilt thou condemn me, that thou mayest be righteous?
9 Hast thou an arm like God?
    or canst thou thunder with a voice like him?

10 Deck thyself now with majesty and excellency;
    and array thyself with glory and beauty.
12 Look on every one that is proud, and bring him low;
    and tread down the wicked in their place.
14 Then will I also confess unto thee
    that thine own right hand can save thee.

15 Behold now behemoth,
    which I made with thee;
    he eateth grass as an ox.
16 Lo now, his strength is in his loins,
    and his force is in the navel of his belly.
17 He moveth his tail like a cedar:
    the sinews of his stones are wrapped together.
18 His bones are as strong pieces of brass;
    his bones are like bars of iron.

41: 1 Canst thou draw out leviathan with a hook?
    or his tongue with a cord which thou lettest down?

2	Canst thou put a hook into his nose?
	or bore his jaw through with a thorn?
5	Wilt thou play with him as with a bird?
	or wilt thou bind him for thy maidens?
10	None is so fierce that dare stir him up:
	who then is able to stand before me?
14	Who can open the doors of his face?
	his teeth are terrible round about.
15	His scales are his pride,
	shut up together as with a close seal.
19	Out of his mouth go burning lamps,
	and sparks of fire leap out.
20	Out of his nostrils goeth smoke,
	as out of a seething pot or caldron.
21	His breath kindleth coals,
	and a flame goeth out of his mouth.
26	The sword of him that layeth at him cannot hold:
	the spear, the dart, nor the habergeon.
27	He esteemeth iron as straw,
	and brass as rotten wood.
28	The arrow cannot make him flee:
	sling stones are turned with him into stubble.
31	He maketh the deep to boil like a pot:
	he maketh the sea like a pot of ointment.
33	Upon earth there is not his like,
	who is made without fear.

42 Then Job answered the Lord, and said,

2   I know that thou canst do every thing,
       and that no thought can be withholden from thee.

3   . . . therefore have I uttered that I understood not;
       things too wonderful for me, which I knew not.

5   I have heard of thee by the hearing of the ear;
       but now mine eye seeth thee:

6   Wherefore I abhor myself, and repent
       in dust and ashes.

THE EPILOGUE: THE RESTORATION OF JOB

7   And it was so, that after the Lord had spoken these words unto Job, the Lord said to Eliphaz the Temanite, My wrath is kindled against thee, and against thy two friends: for ye have not spoken of me the thing that is right, 8 as my servant Job hath. Therefore take unto you now seven bullocks and seven rams, and go to my servant Job, and offer up for yourselves a burnt offering; and my servant Job shall pray for you: for him will I accept: lest I deal with you after your folly, in that ye have not spoken of me the thing 9 which is right, like my servant Job. So Eliphaz the Temanite and Bildad the Shuhite and Zophar the Naamathite went, and did according as the Lord commanded them: the Lord also accepted Job.

10   And the Lord turned the captivity of Job, when he prayed for his friends:
11 also the Lord gave Job twice as much as he had before. Then came there unto
him all his brethren, and all his sisters, and all they that had been of his ac-
quaintance before, and did eat bread with him in his house: and they be-
moaned him, and comforted him over all the evil that the Lord had brought
upon him: every man also gave him a piece of money, and every one an ear-
12 ring of gold. So the Lord blessed the latter end of Job more than his beginning: for he had fourteen thousand sheep, and six thousand camels, and a
13 thousand yoke of oxen, and a thousand she asses. He had also seven sons and
15 three daughters. And in all the land were no women found so fair as the
daughters of Job: and their father gave them inheritance among their breth-
16 ren. After this lived Job a hundred and forty years, and saw his sons, and his
17 sons' sons, even four generations. So Job died, being old and full of days.

Considerations and Questions

1. Consider the "situation" of the novel as the first two chapters present it. What details depict the virtue of Job? What details give evidence of his prosperity and domestic happiness? To what extent can you agree that the point of view of these chapters is simple, and even, in spite of elements of fantasy, realistic?

2. In these first two chapters the version of how Job's problems begin may offend one's religious sensibilities, but should not strain any reader's comprehension. Does not the scene in Heaven explain what happens to Job in basic primitive terms? If this were the whole story, what would we understand to be its reason why good people are afflicted with apparently undeserved suffering?

3. Unlike the reader, the hero of the novel is not "in on" the conversations between God and Satan. Does Job conceive of his God as a whimsical gambler in the sky?

4. The sequence of Job's catastrophes is significant. The last material thing he loses, for example, is his health. To what extent do his reactions to this disaster differ from his reactions to the others? Can you supply reasonable explanations for this difference?

5. "Such friends my enemies should have" is an old and popular example of Yiddish wit which may well have its origins in Old Testament times. Do you think that it applies in any way to the friends who visit the afflicted Job?

6. After seven days and seven nights Job finally speaks in the presence of his friends. He opens his mouth to curse his day (3:1). What is "his day"? Why does he curse it? His lament is punctuated by a number of significant questions. Generally, what do these questions imply about the justice of God? How?

7. As Job concludes this curse, he makes a revealing statement:

> For the thing which I greatly feared is come upon me, and that which I was afraid of is come unto me. (3:25)

The first two chapters give us no indication that he had any such apprehensions. They merely picture a perfect and upright man who fears God, eschews evil, and is the victim of a cosmic game. How does this admission fill in the silhouette of "the good man" and supply him with a believable inner consciousness?

8. The friends of Job, his "comforters," speak to him at great length, and although their attitude towards him becomes increasingly hostile as the story proceeds, they speak, I think, pretty much to the same effect in each of three separate confrontations. I have decided, therefore, to include only the first. In Bildad the Shuhite's first bit of "comforting," he asserts: "Doth God pervert judgment? or doth the Almighty pervert justice?"

(8:3). And later he insists: "Behold, God will not cast away a perfect man, neither will he help the evil-doers." (8:20)

If Job were to accept this instruction, which Bildad calls the ancient wisdom of Israel, what might he then have to conclude about his present situation? Indeed, Job begins his answer to Bildad with "I know it is so of a truth," but then he adds, "but how should man be just with God?" As he develops this idea it becomes apparent that Job does not really agree with Bildad and the other comforters and that he finds the pious analogy they assume to exist between ideal human justice and God's justice to be insufficient. As he suggests, a plaintiff comes to an ideal human court knowing the laws and principles on which judgment is based, as well as with some human identification with his judge. How does Job describe the relationship between man and the Divine Judge?

9. Many people who suffer terrible things in this world reject a belief in God or any cosmic moral order. Despite his wife's urging, Job does not do so. He does, however, complain.

> I will say unto God, Do not condemn me; show me wherefore thou contendest with me. (10:2)

> Is it good unto thee that thou shouldest oppress, that thou shouldest despise the work of thine hands, and shine upon the counsel of the wicked? (10:3)

How do such complaints go beyond Job's personal circumstances to imply the plight of mankind in general?

10. While Job's complaints and questions are blasphemous in the view of his shocked comforters, they are to a considerable extent approved by God Himself. The Voice from the whirlwind chides Job for "words without knowledge" (38:2), but what knowledge does that Voice then supply for Job? What is Job's reaction to it? And in the conclusion of our selection, the Voice says to the comforters ". . . ye have not spoken of me the thing that is right, as my servant Job hath." (42:7) What exactly do you think the comforters have spoken wrong and Job "right"?

The final verses of the Book of Job (42:7–17) return to the style of the first two chapters and provide Job with new wealth, health, friends, children, and a long life. Would not this seem to validate the orthodox view of divine justice held by Job's friends? If so, why do you suppose the verses are included?

VI

The New Testament

An Introductory Note

There are twenty-seven books in what we call the New Testament, the specifically "Christian" part of the Bible. I am very far from challenging the importance of the New Testament when I suggest that it is less of a *literary* achievement than is the Old Testament. The message of the New Testament has had and continues to have the most profound effects on the lives of people who accept that message and on the lives of people who do not. But the claim of this intensely religious book is somewhat more dependent on non-literary criteria like personal religious conviction than are the claims of the Old Testament. And the Old Testament covers far more time and topics, centuries in the life of an ancient people. It is the work of many authors living in different times under different conditions, inspired by different motives.

The comparatively few authors of the New Testament are products of the same general time and place, and have in common a single purpose. They all write to persuade their audiences that Jesus Christ is the Son of God and the savior of mankind. Without the force of that compelling conviction there would be no New Testament. Remember too that the New Testament writers, as well as the major characters in their narratives, are products of the Old Testament. Everything we have learned from our Old Testament studies they know—and a great deal more. Yet if we agree on the greater literary importance of the Old Testament, the comparison is between giants. No English-speaking adult of any faith or of no faith should claim much literacy without a working knowledge of what goes on in the New Testament and some familiarity with its forms and styles.

The Bible attributes the four Gospels to Matthew, Mark, Luke, and John, sometimes called the four "Evangelists." Each Gospel is about the life of Jesus Christ, but none is really a biography. Unlike most biographers, the Gospel writers are not preoccupied with recording their subject's life for its own sake. Unlike most biographers, the Gospel writers are interested only incidentally in their subject's role in social history. The Gospel writers are instead profoundly and urgently concerned with their subject's *identity*. Each Gospel proclaims that the God revealed in Old Testament scripture became a human being who was executed by society and who rose from the dead. Each "Evangelist" insists that Jesus, an itinerant Jewish preacher and prophet, was the man who was God, and that Jesus' life, death, and resurrection offer deliverance for humanity from sin and from death. Furthermore, each Gospel writer argues that his announcements about Jesus are validated by the Old Testament.

The New Testament books other than the Gospels are in direct response to the Gospel claims about Jesus. The Book of the Acts of the Apostles is an account of what happened to Jesus' followers after his crucifixion. The twenty-one books of Epistles are letters from various "apostles," or leaders among the people, who had accepted the Gospel announcement. The best known of the Epistles are from Paul, and in general they are clarifications of Christian doctrine and practice for the instruction of new "churches." The last book of the Bible is formally called The Revelation of St. John the Divine and by many is believed to be the most difficult and confusing part of the New Testament. Apocalyptic literature—"apocalypse" is the Greek word for "revelation"—ordinarily employs symbols from a dream or vision in order to make its disclosures. For readers accustomed to strictly literal communication or resistant to what the subconscious might have to say, apocalyptic writing like Revelation or certain chapters from the Old Testament Book of Daniel can be rather unyielding.

The nature of what apocalyptic writing is designed to reveal, though, makes the dream approach reasonable and even clear. The writer of Revelation reports his vision of what the Gospel message means, not in the world's mortal terms, but in the terms of eternity. This a mortal writer must do, as the writer John observes, not through the physical senses but "in the spirit." The other New Testament writers make their radical claims about the identity of Jesus in matter of fact terms as direct or indirect witnesses of certain literal events which incredibly have occurred at geographical locations like Jerusalem or Galilee and at calendar dates like the feast of the Passover and the years of administration by secular rulers like Herod or Pontius Pilate. The apocalyptic John feels called upon to reveal events to which there can have been no mortal witness "in the flesh." Since the events of Revelation are in the future, in eternity, and visible only through John's symbolic vision, while they may be hard to understand, they take place in a literary context which makes them easy to accept. There are no "miracles" in Revelation, for there are no natural limitations to be overcome in the "world" of St. John's vision.

Really *knowing* the Bible as a pattern for our literature and language entails, of course, knowing all four of the Gospels as well as the Book of Acts, the Epistles, and Revelation. That sounds like a major educational undertaking, and it is. Here we are getting a start, and as *introduction* to Gospel knowledge will concentrate on only one Gospel: that ascribed to Mark. Mark's is the shortest and in some respects the simplest of the four. Although the central plots of the Gospels are the same, a good deal of incident and detail is omitted or abbreviated in Mark that gets attention in other Gospels. A most obvious example is that the "Christmas" story, the "Nativity," is missing from Mark (and from John) but treated in Matthew and Luke. With or without actually reading about it in the Bible, most of us are amply exposed every December to that episode, but as you will see there are other places in the Mark account where we will want to make a quick leap to another Gospel.

THE GOSPEL ACCORDING TO
Mark

Signs and Portents: Mark 1-6

"Art thou he that troubleth Israel?"
I Kings, 18:17

In James Thurber's story, "The Greatest Man in the World," a dreadful young aviator named Jack ("Pal") Smurch becomes the American public's darling because he flies a homemade plane nonstop around the world. In the context of the story, no one else has done or can do that, so his flight is acclaimed as "miraculous" and Smurch himself as "the greatest man in the world." Unfortunately, this greatest man is a nasty, boorish crook without the slightest regard for the U.S.A., Mom, or God. The nation's leaders soon recognize that "Pal" is a threat to society and that if he is allowed to represent the American Dream, clearly the Dream is a disaster. So the President of the United States orders that by accident Smurch be pushed out a very high window.

We should recognize a familiar pattern in Thurber's funny plot; authorities often have reasons to be uneasy when popular heroes turn up in their bailiwicks. When such a celebrity seems at variance with society's established working values, the unease of authorities is likely to flower into serious hostility.

One of Jesus' roles developing in the first six chapters of Mark is that of public hero. Excited by his force of personality, his miraculous healings, his apparent mastery over natural forces, throngs swarm after him in increasing number. Note the frequency of the word "multitude" in this part of Mark. Like the authorities in Thurber's story, society's leaders in the Gospel are from the beginning uneasy. But how can they not join in public approval of one who heals sick minds and bodies, preaches repentence, feeds the hungry, and is reported to have raised the dead? All the same, may not such wondrous works bode danger to the public welfare? Is there a man here who has more power over the people than have the acknowledged rulers of Israel, the keepers of its Dream?

Those "acknowledged rulers of Israel" are, by the way, in an ambiguous and precarious position even without having to cope with popular heroes. At the time of the Gospel setting, the Promised Land and the Chosen People are ruled not by their own Judges or Kings but ultimately by Italian administrators. The ancient territory of Canaan, the Kingdom of David and Solomon, is now, like the rest of the known world, the property of Roman Caesar. His soldiers occupy it. In Mark we do not encounter the Roman presence as much as in the other Gospels until the closing chapters, but at that point we will realize that the Romans have been available from the beginning of the narrative. The policies of Roman colonial imperialism are not soft, but their practicality dictates that conquered civilizations are best allowed to police their own standards of peace and order. As long as Caesar's tribute is paid fully and on time and as long as there is no serious challenge to Caesar's final authority, his watchful officials and disciplined troops keep what some call a low profile. The Romans are, for example, tolerant of the various religions local to their conquered territories, again just so long as those religions stay out of world politics. Within that important qualification, the Romans support the traditional leaders of Judaism as the "acknowledged rulers of Israel." These established leaders, whose ranks include priests of the Temple at Jerusalem, are mainly Pharisees and Sadducees. These two sects or parties have important theological differences, but are both made up of powerful and well-educated men and are combined in determination to maintain Israel's identity through tradition and scripture.

In the first six chapters of Mark, Jesus not only does things that the Pharisees and Sadducees cannot do, he says things that call their ways into question. Early in the story, the multitudes take note that he teaches and heals "with authority," and it is an authority not possessed and not approved by the Pharisees, the Sadducees, and their scribes. He presumes to forgive sins and to grant occasional waivers from the rules stipulating what good Jews may or may not do on the Sabbath. The Pharisees scent blasphemy; only God can forgive sins; only God can rescind the Laws. The scribes of the Pharisees also accuse Jesus of witchcraft or black magic, implying that his apparent authority over evil spirits show that he is in league with their masters, Satan and Beelzebub.

1: 2 The beginning of the gospel of Jesus Christ, the Son of God; As it is written in the prophets, Behold, I send my messenger before thy face,
3 which shall prepare thy way before thee. The voice of one crying in the wilderness, Prepare ye the way of the Lord, make his paths straight.
4 John did baptize in the wilderness, and preach the baptism of repentance
5 for the remission of sins. And there went out unto him all the land of Judea, and they of Jerusalem, and were all baptized of him in the river of
6 Jordan, confessing their sins. And John was clothed with camel's hair, and with a girdle of a skin about his loins; and he did eat locusts and wild
7 honey; And preached, saying, There cometh one mightier than I after me, the latchet of whose shoes I am not worthy to stoop down and unloose.
8 I indeed have baptized you with water: but he shall baptize you with the Holy Ghost.
9 And it came to pass in those days, that Jesus came from Nazareth of
10 Galilee, and was baptized of John in Jordan. And straightway coming up out of the water, he saw the heavens opened, and the Spirit like a dove
11 descending upon him: And there came a voice from heaven, saying, Thou
12 art my beloved Son in whom I am well pleased. And immediately the
13 spirit driveth him into the wilderness. And he was there in the wilderness forty days, tempted of Satan; and was with the wild beasts; and the angels ministered unto him.
14 Now after that John was put in prison, Jesus came into Galilee, preaching
15 the gospel of the kingdom of God, And saying, The time is fulfilled, and the kingdom of God is at hand: repent ye, and believe the gospel.
16 Now as he walked by the sea of Galilee, he saw Simon and Andrew his
17 brother casting a net into the sea: for they were fishers. And Jesus said unto them, Come ye after me, and I will make you to become fishers of
18 men. And straightway they forsook their nets, and followed him.
19 And when he had gone a little farther thence, he saw James the son of Zebedee, and John his brother, who also were in the ship mending their
20 nets. And straightway he called them: and they left their father Zebedee in the ship with the hired servants, and went after him.
21 And they went into Capernaum; and straightway on the sabbath day he
22 entered into the synagogue, and taught. And they were astonished at his doctrine: for he taught them as one that had authority, and not as the scribes.
23 And there was in their synagogue a man with an unclean spirit; and he
24 cried out, Saying, Let us alone; what have we to do with thee, thou Jesus of Nazareth? art thou come to destroy us? I know thee who thou art, the
25 Holy One of God. And Jesus rebuked him, saying, Hold thy peace, and
26 come out of him. And when the unclean spirit had torn him, and cried with a loud voice, he came out of him.
27 And they were all amazed, insomuch that they questioned among themselves, saying, What thing is this? what new doctrine is this? for with authority commandeth he even the unclean spirits, and they do obey
28 him. And immediately his fame spread abroad throughout all the region round about Galilee.
29 And forthwith, when they were come out of the synagogue, they entered
30 into the house of Simon and Andrew, with James and John. But Simon's
31 wife's mother lay sick of a fever, and anon they tell him of her. And he

came and took her by the hand, and lifted her up; and immediately the fever left her, and she ministered unto them.

32 And at even, when the sun did set, they brought unto him all that were
33 diseased, and them that were possessed with devils. And all the city was
34 gathered together at the door. And he healed many that were sick of divers diseases, and cast out many devils; and suffered not the devils to speak, because they knew him.

35 And in the morning, rising up a great while before day, he went out, and
36 departed into a solitary place, and there prayed. And Simon and they that
37 were with him followed after him. And when they had found him, they
38 said unto him, All men seek for thee. And he said unto them, Let us go into the next towns, that I may preach there also: for therefore came I
39 forth. And he preached in their synagogues throughout all Galilee, and cast out devils.

40 And there came a leper to him, beseeching him, and kneeling down to
41 him, and saying unto him, If thou wilt, thou canst make me clean. And Jesus, moved with compassion, put forth his hand, and touched him, and
42 saith unto him, I will; be thou clean. And as soon as he had spoken,
43 immediately the leprosy departed from him, and he was cleansed. And he
44 straitly charged him, and forthwith sent him away; And saith unto him, See thou say nothing to any man: but go thy way, show thyself to the priest, and offer for thy cleansing those things which Moses commanded,
45 for a testimony unto them. But he went out, and began to publish it much, and to blaze abroad the matter, insomuch that Jesus could no more openly enter into the city, but was without in desert places: and they came to him from every quarter.

2: And again he entered into Capernaum after some days; and it was
2 noised that he was in the house. And straightway many were gathered together, insomuch that there was no room to receive them, no, not so
3 much as about the door: and he preached the word unto them. And they come unto him, bringing one sick of the palsy, which was borne of four.
4 And when they could not come nigh unto him for the press, they uncovered the roof where he was: and when they had broken it up, they
5 let down the bed wherein the sick of the palsy lay. When Jesus saw their faith, he said unto the sick of the palsy, Son, they sins be forgiven thee.
6 But there were certain of the scribes sitting there, and reasoning in their
7 hearts, Why doth this man thus speak blasphemies? who can forgive sins
8 but God only? And immediately when Jesus perceived in his spirit that they so reasoned within themselves, he said unto them, Why reason ye
9 these things in your hearts? Whether is it easier to say to the sick of the palsy, Thy sins be forgiven thee; or to say, Arise, and take up thy bed, and
10 walk? But that ye may know that the Son of man hath power on earth to
11 forgive sins (he saith to the sick of the palsy), I say unto thee, Arise, and
12 take up thy bed, and go thy way into thine house. And immediately he arose, took up the bed, and went forth before them all; insomuch that they were all amazed, and glorified God, saying, We never saw it on this fashion.
13 And he went forth again by the sea side; and all the multitude resorted
14 unto him, and he taught them. And as he passed by, he saw Levi the son of Alpheus sitting at the receipt of custom, and said unto him, Follow me. And he arose and followed him.
15 And it came to pass, that, as Jesus sat at meat in his house, many publicans and sinners sat also together with Jesus and his disciples: for there were

16 many, and they followed him. And when the scribes and Pharisees saw him eat with publicans and sinners, they said unto his disciples, How is it
17 that he eateth and drinketh with publicans and sinners? When Jesus heard it, he saith unto them, They that are whole have no need of the physician, but they that are sick: I came not to call the righteous, but sinners to repentance.
18 And the disciples of John and of the Pharisees used to fast: and they come and say unto him, Why do the disciples of John and of the Pharisees fast,
19 but thy disciples fast not? And Jesus said unto them, Can the children of the bridechamber fast, while the bridegroom is with them? as long as they
20 have the bridegroom with them, they cannot fast. But the days will come, when the bridegroom shall be taken away from them, and then shall they
21 fast in those days. No man also seweth a piece of new cloth on an old garment: else the new piece that filled it up taketh away from the old, and
22 the rent is made worse. And no man putteth new wine into old bottles: else the new wine doth burst the bottles, and the wine is spilled, and the bottles will be marred: but new wine must be put into new bottles.
23 And it came to pass, that he went through the corn fields on the sabbath
24 day; and his disciples began, as they went, to pluck the ears of corn. And the Pharisees said unto him, Behold, why do they on the sabbath day that
25 which is not lawful? And he said unto them, Have ye never read what David did, when he had need, and was an hungred, he, and they that were
26 with him? How he went into the house of God in the days of Abiathar the high priest, and did eat the shewbread, which is not lawful to eat but for
27 the priests, and gave also to them which were with him? And he said unto them, The sabbath was made for man, and not man for the sabbath:
28 Therefore the Son of man is Lord also of the sabbath.
3: And he entered again into the synagogue; and there was a man there
2 which had a withered hand. And they watched him, whether he would
3 heal him on the sabbath day; that they might accuse him. And he saith
4 unto the man which had the withered hand, Stand forth. And he saith unto them, Is it lawful to do good on the sabbath days, or to do evil? to
5 save life, or to kill? But they held their peace. And when he had looked round about on them with anger, being grieved for the hardness of their hearts, he saith unto the man, Stretch forth thine hand. And he stretched it out: and his hand was restored whole as the other.
6 And the Pharisees went forth, and straightway took counsel with the
7 Herodians against him, how they might destroy him. But Jesus withdrew himself with his disciples to the sea: and a great multitude from Galilee
8 followed him, and from Judea, And from Jerusalem, and from Idumea, and from beyond Jordan; and they about Tyre and Sidon, a great multitude, when they had heard what great things he did, came unto him.
9 And he spake to his disciples, that a small ship should wait on him
10 because of the multitude, lest they should throng him. For he had healed many; insomuch that they pressed upon him for to touch him, as many as
11 had plagues. And unclean spirits, when they saw him, fell down before
12 him, and cried, saying, Thou art the Son of God. And he straitly charged them that they should not make him known.
13 And he goeth up into a mountain, and calleth unto him whom he would:
14 and they came unto him. And he ordained twelve, that they should be
15 with him, and that he might send them forth to preach, And to have
16 power to heal sicknesses, and to cast out devils: And Simon he surnamed

17 Peter; And James the son of Zebedee, and John the brother of James; and
18 he surnamed them Boanerges, which is, The sons of thunder: And
Andrew, and Philip, and Bartholomew, and Matthew, and Thomas, and
19 James the son of Alpheus, and Thaddeus, and Simon the Conaanite, And
Judas Iscariot, which also betrayed him: and they went into an house.
20 And the multitude cometh together again, so that they could not so much
21 as eat bread. And when his friends heard of it, they went out to lay hold
on him: for they said, He is beside himself.
22 And the scribes which came down from Jerusalem said, He hath
23 Beelzebub, and by the prince of the devils casteth he out devils. And he
called them unto him, and said unto them in parables, How can Satan cast
24 out Satan? And if a kingdom be divided against itself, that kingdom
25 cannot stand. And if a house be divided against itself, that house cannot
26 stand. And if Satan rise up against himself, and be divided, he cannot
27 stand, but hath an end. No man can enter into a strong man's house, and
spoil his goods, except he will first bind the strong man; and then he will
28 spoil his house. Verily I say unto you, All sins shall be forgiven unto the
sons of men, and blasphemies wherewith soever they shall blaspheme:
29 But he that shall blaspheme against the Holy Ghost hath never forgive-
30 ness, but is in danger of eternal damnation: Because they said, He hath an
unclean spirit.
31 There came then his brethren and his mother, and standing without, sent
32 unto him, calling him. And the multitude sat about him, and they said
unto him, Behold, thy mother and thy brethren without seek for thee.
33 And he answered them, saying, Who is my mother, or my brethren?
34 And he looked round about on them which sat about him, and said,
35 Behold my mother and my brethren! For whosoever shall do the will of
God, the same is my brother, and my sister, and mother.
4 And he began again to teach by the sea side: and there was gathered
unto him a great multitude, so that he entered into a ship, and sat in the
2 sea; and the whole multitude was by the sea on the land. And he taught
them many things by parables, and said unto them in his doctrine,
3 Hearken; Behold, there went out a sower to sow: And it came to pass, as
4 he sowed, some fell by the way side, and the fowls of the air came
5 and devoured it up. And some fell on stony ground, where it
had not much earth; and immediately it sprang up, because it had no
6 depth of earth: But when the sun was up, it was scorched; and because it
7 had no root, it withered away. And some fell among thorns, and the
8 thorns grew up, and choked it, and it yielded no fruit. And other fell on
good ground, and did yield fruit that sprang up and increased; and
9 brought forth, some thirty, and some sixty, and some an hundred. And he
said unto them, He that hath ears to hear, let him hear.
10 And when he was alone, they that were about him with the twelve asked
11 of him the parable. And he said unto them, Unto you it is given to know
the mystery of the kingdom of God: but unto them that are without, all
12 these things are done in parables: That seeing they may see, and not
perceive; and hearing they may hear, and not understand; lest at any time
13 they should be converted, and their sins should be forgiven them. And he
said unto them, Know ye not this parable? and how then will ye know all
parables?

14 The sower soweth the word. And these are they by the way side,
15 where the word is sown; but when they have heard, Satan cometh immediately, and taketh away the word that was sown in their hearts.
16 And these are they likewise which are sown on stony ground; who, when they have heard the word, immediately receive it
17 with gladness; And have no root in themselves, and so endure but for a time: afterward, when affliction or persecution ariseth for the word's
18 sake, immediately they are offended. And these are they which are sown
19 among thorns; such as hear the word, And the cares of this world, and the deceitfulness of riches, and the lusts of other things entering in, choke the
20 word, and it becometh unfruitful. And these are they which are sown on good ground; such as hear the word, and receive it, and bring forth fruit, some thirtyfold, some sixty, and some an hundred.
21 And he said unto them. Is a candle brought to be put under a bushel, or
22 under a bed? and not to be set on a candlestick? For there is nothing hid, which shall not be manifested; neither was any thing kept secret, but that
23 it should come abroad. If any man have ears to hear, let him hear.
24 And he said unto them, Take heed what ye hear: with what measure ye mete, it shall be measured to you: and unto you that hear shall more be
25 given. For he that hath, to him shall be given: and he that hath not, from him shall be taken even that which he hath.
26 And he said, So is the kingdom of God, as if a man should cast seed into
27 the ground; And should sleep, and rise night and day, and the seed should
28 spring and grow up, he knoweth not how. For the earth bringeth forth fruit of herself; first the blade, then the ear, after that the full corn in the
29 ear. But when the fruit is brought forth, immediately he putteth in the sickle, because the harvest is come.
30 And he said, Whereunto shall we liken the kingdom of God? or with what
31 comparison shall we compare it? It is like a grain of mustard seed, which, when it is sown in the earth, is less than all the seeds that be in the earth:
32 But when it is sown, it groweth up, and becometh greater than all herbs, and shooteth out great branches; so that the fowls of the air may lodge
33 under the shadow of it. And with many such parables spake he the word
34 unto them, as they were able to hear it. But without a parable spake he not unto them: and when they were alone, he expounded all things to his disciples.
35 And the same day, when the even was come, he saith unto them, Let us
36 pass over unto the other side. And when they had sent away the multitude, they took him even as he was in the ship. And there were also
37 with him other little ships. And there arose a great storm of wind, and the
38 waves beat into the ship, so that it was now full. And he was in the hinder part of the ship, asleep on a pillow: and they awake him, and say unto
39 him, Master, carest thou not that we perish? And he arose, and rebuked the wind, and said unto the sea, Peace, be still. And the wind ceased, and
40 there was a great calm. And he said unto them, Why are ye so fearful?
41 how is it that ye have no faith? And they feared exceedingly, and said one to another, What manner of man is this, that even the wind and the sea obey him?
5 And they came over unto the other side of the sea, into the country of the
2 Gadarenes. And when he was come out of the ship, immediately there

3 met him out of the tombs a man with an unclean spirit, Who had his dwelling among the tombs; and no man could bind him, no, not with
4 chains: Because that he had been often bound with fetters and chains, and the chains had been plucked asunder by him, and the fetters broken in
5 pieces: neither could any man tame him. And always, night and day, he was in the mountains, and in the tombs, crying, and cutting himself with
6 stones. But when he saw Jesus afar off, he ran and worshipped him,
7 And cried with a loud voice, and said, What have I to do with thee, Jesus, thou Son of the most high God? I adjure thee by God, that thou torment
8 me not. For he said unto him, Come out of the man, thou unclean spirit.
9 And he asked him, What is thy name? And he answered, saying, My name
10 is Legion: for we are many. And he besought him much that he would not send them away out of the country.
11 Now there was there nigh unto the mountains a great herd of swine
12 feeding. And all the devils besought him, saying, Send us into the swine,
13 that we may enter into them. And forthwith Jesus gave them leave. And the unclean spirits went out, and entered into the swine: and the herd ran violently down a steep place into the sea, (they were about two thousand);
14 and were choked in the sea. And they that fed the swine fled, and told it in the city, and in the country. And they went out to see what it was that was
15 done. And they come to Jesus, and see him that was possessed with the devil, and had the legion, sitting, and clothed, and in his right mind: and
16 they were afraid. And they that saw it told them how it befell to him that
17 was possessed with the devil, and also concerning the swine. And they
18 began to pray him to depart out of their coasts. And when he was come into the ship, he that had been possessed with the devil prayed him that
19 he might be with him. Howbeit Jesus suffered him not, but saith unto him, Go home to thy friends, and tell them how great things the Lord
20 hath done for thee, and hath had compassion on thee. And he departed, and began to publish in Decapolis how great things Jesus had done for him: and all men did marvel.
21 And when Jesus was passed over again by ship unto the other side, much
22 people gathered unto him: and he was nigh unto the sea. And, behold, there cometh one of the rulers of the synagogue, Jairus by name; and
23 when he saw him, he fell at his feet, And besought him greatly, saying, My little daughter lieth at the point of death: I pray thee, come and lay thy
24 hands on her, that she may be healed; and she shall live. And Jesus went with him; and much people followed him, and thronged him.
25 And a certain woman, which had an issue of blood twelve years,
26 And had suffered many things of many physicians, and had spent all that
27 she had, and was nothing bettered, but rather grew worse, When she had
28 heard of Jesus, came in the press behind, and touched his garment. For
29 she said, If I may touch but his clothes, I shall be whole. And straightway the fountain of her blood was dried up; and she felt in her body that she
30 was healed of that plague. And Jesus, immediately knowing in himself that virtue had gone out of him. turned him about in the press, and said,
31 Who touched my clothes? And his disciples said unto him, Thou seest the
32 multitude thronging thee, and sayest thou, Who touched me? And he
33 looked round about to see her that had done this thing. But the woman fearing and trembling, knowing what was done in her, came and fell
34 down before him, and told him all the truth. And he said unto her,

Daughter, thy faith hath made thee whole; go in peace, and be whole of thy plague.

35 While he yet spake, there came from the ruler of the synagogue's house certain which said, Thy daughter is dead: why troublest thou the Master
36 any further? As soon as Jesus heard the word that was spoken, he saith
37 unto the ruler of the synagogue, Be not afraid, only believe. And he suffered no man to follow him, save Peter, and James, and John the
38 brother of James. And he cometh to the house of the ruler of the synagogue, and seeth the tumult, and them that wept and wailed greatly.
39 And when he was come in, he saith unto them, Why make ye this ado, and
40 weep? the damsel is not dead, but sleepeth. And they laughed him to scorn. But when he had put them all out, he taketh the father and the mother of the damsel, and them that were with him, and entereth in
41 where the damsel was lying. And he took the damsel by the hand, and said unto her, Talithacumi; which is, being interpreted, Damsel, I say unto
42 thee, arise. And straightway the damsel arose, and walked; for she was of the age of twelve years. And they were astonished with a great
43 astonishment. And he charged them straitly that no man should know it; and commanded that something should be given her to eat.

6 And he went out from thence, and came into his own country; and his
2 disciples follow him. And when the sabbath day was come, he began to teach in the synagogue: and many hearing him were astonished, saying, From whence hath this man these things? and what wisdom is this which is given unto him, that even such mighty works are wrought by his
3 hands? Is not this the carpenter, the son of Mary, the brother of James, and Joses, and of Juda, and Simon? and are not his sisters here with us?
4 And they were offended at him. But Jesus said unto them, A prophet is not without honor, but in his own country. and among his own kin, and in
5 his own house. And he could there do no mighty work, save that he laid
6 his hands upon a few sick folk, and healed them. And he marvelled because of their unbelief. And he went round about the villages, teaching.
7 And he called unto him the twelve, and began to send them forth by two
8 and two; and gave them power over unclean spirits; And commanded them that they should take nothing for their journey, save a staff only; no
9 scrip, no bread, no money in their purse: But be shod with sandals; and
10 not put on two coats. And he said unto them, In what place soever ye
11 enter into an house, there abide till ye depart from that place. And whosoever shall not receive you, nor hear you, when ye depart thence, shake off the dust under your feet for a testimony against them. Verily I say unto you, It shall be more tolerable for Sodom and Gomorrha in the day of judgment, than for that city.
12 And they went out, and preached that men should repent. And
13 they cast out many devils, and anointed with oil many that were sick,
14 and healed them. and king Herod heard of him (for his name was spread abroad): and he said, That John the Baptist was risen from the dead, and
15 therefore mighty works do show forth themselves in him. Others said, That it is Elias. And others said, That it is a prophet, or as one of the
16 prophets. But when Herod heard thereof, he said, It is John, whom I
17 beheaded: he is risen from the dead. For Herod himself had sent forth and laid hold upon John, and bound him in prison for Herodias' sake, his
18 brother Philip's wife: for he had married her. For John had said unto

19 Herod, It is not lawful for thee to have thy brother's wife. Therefore Herodias had a quarrel against him, and would have killed him; but she
20 could not: For Herod feared John, knowing that he was a just man and an holy, and observed him; and when he heard him, he did many things, and heard him gladly.

21 And when a convenient day was come, that Herod on his birthday made a
22 supper to his lords, high captains, and chief estates of Galilee; And when the daughter of the said Herodias came in, and danced, and pleased Herod and them that sat with him, the king said unto the damsel, Ask of me
23 whatsoever thou wilt and I will give it thee. And he sware unto her, Whatsoever thou shalt ask of me, I will give it thee, unto the half of my
24 kingdom. And she went forth, and said unto her mother, What shall I
25 ask? And she said, The head of John the Baptist. And she came in straightway with haste unto the king, and asked, saying, I will that thou give me by and by in a charger the head of John the Baptist.

26 And the king was exceeding sorry; yet for his oath's sake, and for their
27 sakes which sat with him, he would not reject her. And immediately the king sent an executioner, and commanded his head to be brought: and he
28 went and beheaded him in the prison, And brought his head in a charger,
29 and gave it to the damsel: and the damsel gave it to her mother. And when his disciples heard of it, they came and took up his corpse, and laid it in a tomb.

30 And the apostles gathered themselves together unto Jesus, and told him
31 all things, both what they had done, and what they had taught. And he said unto them, Come ye yourselves apart into a desert place, and rest a while: for there were many coming and going, and they had no leisure so
32 much as to eat. And they departed into a desert place by ship privately.
33 And the people saw them departing, and many knew him, and ran afoot thither out of all cities, and outwent them, and came together unto him.
34 And Jesus, when he came out, saw much people, and was moved with compassion toward them, because they were as sheep not having a shepherd: and he began to teach them many things.

35 And when the day was now far spent, his disciples came unto him, and
36 said, This is a desert place, and now the time is far passed: Send them away, that they may go into the country round about, and into the villages,
37 and buy themselves bread: for they have nothing to eat. He answered and said unto them, Give ye them to eat. And they say unto him, Shall we go and buy two hundred pennyworth of bread, and give them to eat? He
38 saith unto them, How many loaves have ye? go and see. And when they knew, they say, Five, and two fishes.

39 And he commanded them to make all sit down by companies upon the
40 green grass. And they sat down in ranks, by hundreds, and by fifties.
41 And when he had taken the five loaves and the two fishes, he looked up to heaven, and blessed, and brake the loaves, and gave them to his disciples
42 to set before them; and the two fishes divided he among them all. And
43 they did all eat, and were filled. And they took up twelve baskets full of
44 the fragments, and of the fishes. And they that did eat of the loaves were about five thousand men.

45 And straightway he constrained his disciples to get into the ship, and to go to the other side before unto Bethsaida, while he sent away the people.

46 And when he had sent them away, he departed into a mountain to pray.
47 And when even was come, the ship was in the midst of the sea, and he
48 alone on the land. And he saw them toiling in rowing; for the wind was
contrary unto them: and about the fourth watch of the night he cometh
49 unto them, walking upon the sea, and would have passed by them. But
when they saw him walking upon the sea, they supposed it had been a
50 spirit, and cried out: For they all saw him, and were troubled. And
immediately he talked with them, and saith unto them, Be of good cheer:
51 it is I; be not afraid. And he went up unto them into the ship; and the
wind ceased: and they were sore amazed in themselves beyond measure,
52 and wondered. For they considered not the miracle of the loaves: for their
heart was hardened.
53   And when they had passed over, they came into the land of Gennesaret,
54 and drew to the shore. And when they were come out of the ship,
55 straightway they knew him, And ran through that whole region round
about, and began to carry about in beds those that were sick, where they
56 heard he was. And whithersoever he entered, into villages, or cities, or
country, they laid the sick in the streets, and besought him that they
might touch if it were but the border of his garment: and as many as
touched him were made whole.

Considerations and Questions

1. Only two of the Gospels, Matthew and Luke, include the "Christmas" story, but all four make a great deal of John the Baptist. Whatever his other importance may be, in all the Gospels this eccentric outdoor preacher serves as a link between Jesus and the Old Testament. In what specific ways does the text of Mark seem to insist that John has, as it were, a foot in each Testament? In this connection, consider the likenesses and differences between John the Baptist and the hero he precedes.

2. For detailed versions of how Jesus is "tempted of Satan" in the wilderness, look at Matthew 4:1-11 and Luke 4:1-13. You will find the order of temptations slightly different in these accounts, but the specific temptations are the same. From the Matthew and Luke "temptation" stories emerge images and ideas whose impact on our thought and literature can hardly be overestimated. In Mark, on the other hand, the single, summary verse (13) is all the attention paid. Mark does not tell us what the temptations precisely are, how they are offered and resisted, nor what they mean. Yet in the apparent vagueness and brevity of the Mark version lurks an emphasis not as strikingly made in the other Gospels. It is in the form of an important implicit question: just what temptations are appropriate for someone who has just been informed that he is the son of God? Matthew and Luke supply answers expressed in the familiar images of this world: stones, bread, cloud-capped towers, gorgeous palaces, solemn temples, and the great globe itself. Mark, in avoiding such material though splendid things, forces us to wonder and to infer. Does "son of God" mean "Superman"? Might not a divinely ordained "Superman" enforce the Kingdom he preaches by changing mankind into a uniformly happy, good, and obedient population, and by rearranging natural laws to that end? Such attempts have been made by *politically* ordained Supermen, but in the Old and New Testaments it is easier to have bricks without straw than deliverance without freedom.

3. Biblical miracles are not simply magical acts which do or should convince people of the divine credentials of whoever seems to perform them. In the first place, Biblical miracles are not magic at all; the Bible takes the view that it is perfectly normal and predictable for God to be omnipotent. Furthermore, in the Bible people take a variety of attitudes towards the various instances of the miraculous they witness. Besides generally noted "healings," the first six chapters of Mark describe eleven specific miracles performed by Jesus. No two are precisely the same, but there are enough likenesses so that all may in some way be classified in a group of two or more.

The headings for such groups may have to do with the nature, effect, or circumstance of the "mighty works," or with how different witnesses react to them.

4. How about that missing twelfth "mighty work," the one Jesus is unable to do in his own country? What explanation does Mark supply for that paradoxical limitation? In the Matthew and Luke "temptation" episodes Satan keeps saying, "If thou be the Son of God...." Is the writer of Mark indicating his own uncertainty about Jesus' true identity?

5. What episodes or statements in these chapters show and explain an increasing attitude of distrust and hostility on the part of the Pharisees, scribes, and Sadducees?

6. Why does Herod's wife trick the tetrarch (an honorary King firmly subservient to Rome) into serving up John the Baptist's head to her? What is the extent and nature of Herod's interest in Jesus? What does the death of the Baptist suggest about future possibilities?

7.   Than telle I hem ensamples many oon
          Of olde stories longe time agoon,
          For lewed peple loven tales olde;
          Swiche thinges can they wel reporte and holde.

   Chaucer's Pardoner is right: most simple folk, and most other folk too, would rather listen to stories they understand than to explanations they don't. So teachers often tell stories, not because telling stories is the most direct way of imparting information, but because telling stories seems a good way to get most people to pay attention and to remember. Stories designed to teach particular lessons are parables. How, in Chapter 4, does Jesus demonstrate both the strengths and the limitations of the parable as a teaching device?

8. Parables are rather more like allegories or even similes than like metaphors. The teacher who uses a parable makes clear that an unknown circumstance is rather like a known one; the metaphorist describes one thing by saying that it *is* another. So when Jesus tells Simon and Andrew that he will make them "fishers of men" (1:17), he is using metaphor rather than parable. He clearly does not mean that the two brothers will be set to casting literal nets or baiting literal hooks in order to catch people for the commericial market. What exactly *does* he mean? What does he mean by calling James and John "the sons of thunder" (3:17)? What apparently does Jesus mean by his repeated references to himself as "the Son of man"? In the context of Mark, is that by intention metaphorical? What about the identification of what we may presume are crazy people as ones possessed of devils or unclean spirits?

The Hero at Noon: Mark 7-13

"How dangerous is it that this man goes loose."
William Shakespeare, *Hamlet*

On the one hand the multitudes acclaim him as having done all things well; they turn out to cheer his entry into the holy city of Jerusalem. On the other, important people increasingly fear and dislike him as a menace to peace, order, and to a tolerable compromise between religion and a wicked world. Make no mistake about it; in this story the enemies of Jesus are not unnatural monsters and idiots. Like most of us and like most people inhabiting Biblical narrative, while responsible for what they do, they identify their choices of action with good intentions or with necessity (what John Milton called "the tyrant's plea"). To get rid of this fascinating healer and preacher who has uncomprehending multitudes trailing after him and who beats highly educated religious authorities in debate seems a public duty to them. He seems to them clearly a danger to what holds Israel together: its religious establishment.

The Pharisees do not believe that Jesus may be the Christ, the Messiah foretold by the prophets as the savior to come. Of course, unlike Peter, they do not *want* to believe it, but no doubt as well, they think the objective evidence is overwhelmingly against such a notion. After all, what oppresses Israel is modern Rome, a gigantic military and economic machine. That, they assume, is what the anointed savior of Israel must deal with. Is there anything in the life and doctrines of this Jesus that remotely suggests the successor to King David the warrior? When his allies suggested enlisting the influence of the Pope during World War II, Joseph Stalin is reported to have asked sarcastically, "And how many infantry divisions has the Pope?" In this wanderer's retinue of fishermen, retired sinners, women, children, demoniacs, the lame, halt, and blind, seasoned with a fair share of that kind of religious faddist the world never runs out of, the Pharisees and Sadducees see no effective answer to the national bondage. They might well have anticipated the Soviet dictator with "And how many legions has this Jesus?"

Now if it is clear to the modern reader that what Jesus means by being the Christ is very different from what his enemies have in mind as the Messiah, it is well for that reader to remember that the Pharisees are not reading the story; they are in it. That "the kingdom of God" must have something to do with the restoration of God's chosen Israel in the material world is a very acceptable idea, not only to the Pharisees but to the multitudes and to the disciples. That is why even the twelve have such a hard time understanding Jesus' parables and paradoxes.

7:     Then came together unto him the Pharisees, and certain of the scribes,
2 which came from Jerusalem. And when they saw some of his disciples eat
bread with defiled, that is to say, with unwashen, hands, they found fault.
3 For the Pharisees, and all the Jews, except they wash their hands oft, eat
4 not, holding the tradition of the elders. And when they come from the
market, except they wash, they eat not. And many other things there be,
which they have received to hold, as the washing of cups, and pots, brasen
vessels, and of tables.
5   Then the Pharisees and scribes asked him, Why walk not thy disciples
according to the tradition of the elders, but eat bread with unwashen
6 hands? He answered and said unto them, Well hath Esaias prophesied of
you hypocrites, as it is written, This people honoreth me with their lips,
7 but their heart is far from me. Howbeit in vain do they worship me,
8 teaching for doctrines the commandments of men. For laying aside the
commandment of God, ye hold the tradition of men, as the washing of
pots and cups: and many other such like things ye do.
9   And he said unto them, Full well ye reject the commandment of God, that
10 ye may keep your own tradition. For Moses said, Honor thy father and thy
mother; and, Whoso curseth father or mother, let him die the death:
11 But ye say, If a man shall say to his father or mother, It is Corban, that is
to say, a gift, by whatsoever thou mightest be profited by me; he shall be
12 free. And ye suffer him no more to do ought for his father or his mother;
13 Making the word of God of none effect through your tradition, which ye
have delivered: and many such like things do ye.
14   And when he had called all the people unto him, he said unto them,
15 Hearken unto me every one of you, and understand: There is nothing
from without a man, that entering into him can defile him: but the things
16 which come out of him, those are they that defile the man. If any man
17 have ears to hear, let him hear. And when he was entered into the house
18 from the people, his disciples asked him concerning the parable. And he
saith unto them, Are ye so without understanding also? Do ye not
perceive, that whatsoever thing from without entereth into the man, it
19 cannot defile him; Because it entereth not into his heart, but into the
20 belly, and goeth out into the draught, purging all meats? And he said,
21 That which cometh out of the man, that defileth the man. For from
within, out of the heart of men, proceed evil thoughts, adulteries,
22 fornications, murders, Thefts, covetousness, wickedness, deceit, lascivi-
23 ousness, an evil eye, blasphemy, pride, foolishness: All these evil things
come from within, and defile the man.
24   And from thence he arose, and went into the borders of Tyre and Sidon,
and entered into an house, and would have no man know it: but he could
25 not be hid. For a certain woman, whose young daughter had an unclean
26 spirit, heard of him, and came and fell at his feet: The woman was a
Greek, a Syrophenician by nation; and she besought him that he would
27 cast forth the devil out of her daughter. But Jesus said unto her, Let the
children first be filled: for it is not meet to take the children's bread, and
28 to cast it unto the dogs. And she answered and said unto him, Yes, Lord:
29 yet the dogs under the table eat of the children's crumbs. And he said unto
30 her, For this saying go thy way; the devil is gone out of thy daughter. And
when she was come to her house, she found the devil gone out, and her
daughter laid upon the bed.

31 And again, departing from the coasts of Tyre and Sidon, he came unto the
32 sea of Galilee, through the midst of the coasts of Decapolis. And they
bring unto him one that was deaf, and had an impediment in his speech;
33 and they beseech him to put his hand upon him. And he took him aside
from the multitude, and put his fingers into his ears, and he spit, and
34 touched his tongue; And looking up to heaven, he sighed, and saith unto
35 him, Ephphatha, that is, Be opened. And straightway his ears were
36 opened, and the string of his tongue was loosed, and he spake plain. And
he charged them that they should tell no man: but the more he charged
37 them, so much the more a great deal they published it; And were beyond
measure astonished, saying, He hath done all things well: he maketh both
the deaf to hear, and the dumb to speak.

8: In those days the multitude being very great, and having nothing to eat,
2 Jesus called his disciples unto him, and saith unto them, I have
compassion on the multitude, because they have now been with me three
3 days, and have nothing to eat: And if I send them away fasting to their
own houses, they will faint by the way: for divers of them came from far.
4 And his disciples answered him, From whence can a man satisfy these
5 men with bread here in the wilderness? And he asked them, How many
6 loaves have ye? And they said, Seven. And he commanded the people to
sit down on the ground: and he took the seven loaves, and gave thanks,
and brake, and gave to his disciples to set before them; and they did set
7 them before the people. And they had a few small fishes: and he blessed,
8 and commanded to set them also before them. So they did eat, and were
filled: and they took up of the broken meat that was left seven baskets.
9 And they that had eaten were about four thousand: and he sent them
away.
10 And straightway he entered into a ship with his disciples, and came into
11 the parts of Dalmanutha. And the Pharisees came forth, and began to
question with him, seeking of him a sign from heaven, tempting him.
12 And he sighed deeply in his spirit, and saith, Why doth this generation
seek after a sign? verily I say unto you, There shall no sign be given unto
13 this generation. And he left them, and entering into the ship again
departed to the other side.
14 Now the disciples had forgotten to take bread, neither had they in the
15 ship with them more than one loaf. And he charged them, saying, Take
heed, beware of the leaven of the Pharisees, and of the leaven of Herod.
16 And they reasoned among themselves, saying, It is because we have no
17 bread. And when Jesus knew it, he saith unto them, Why reason ye,
because ye have no bread? perceive ye not yet, neither understand? have
18 ye your heart yet hardened? Having eyes, see ye not? and having ears,
19 hear ye not? and do ye not remember? When I brake the five loaves
among five thousand, how many baskets full of fragments took ye up?
20 They say unto him, Twelve. And when the seven among four thousand,
how many baskets full of fragments took ye up? And they said, Seven.
21 And he said unto them, How is it that ye do not understand?
22 And he cometh to Bethsaida; and they bring a blind man unto him, and
23 besought him to touch him. And he took the blind man by the hand, and
led him out of the town; and when he had spit on his eyes, and put his
24 hands upon him, he asked him if he saw ought. And he looked up, and

25 said, I see men as trees, walking. After that he put his hands again upon his eyes, and made him look up: and he was restored, and saw every man
26 clearly. And he sent him away to his house, saying, Neither go into the town, or tell it to any in the town.

27 And Jesus went out, and his disciples, into the towns of Caesarea Philippi: and by the way he asked his disciples, saying unto them, Whom do men
28 say that I am? And they answered, John the Baptist: but some say, Elias;
29 and other, One of the prophets. And he saith unto them, But whom say ye that I am? And Peter answereth and saith unto him, Thou art the Christ.
30 And he charged them that they should tell no man of him.

31 And he began to teach them, that the Son of man must suffer many things, and be rejected of the elders, and of the chief priests, and scribes,
32 and be killed, and after three days rise again. And he spake that saying
33 openly. And Peter took him, and began to rebuke him. But when he had turned about and looked on his disciples, he rebuked Peter, saying, Get thee behind me, Satan: for thou savorest not the things that be of God, but the things that be of men.

34 And when he had called the people unto him with his disciples also, he said unto them, Whosoever will come after me, let him deny himself, and
35 take up his cross, and follow me. For whosoever will save his life shall lose it; but whosoever shall lose his life for my sake and the gospel's, the
36 same shall save it. For what shall it profit a man, if he shall gain the
37 whole world, and lose his own soul? Or what shall a man give in exchange
38 for his soul? Whosoever therefore shall be ashamed of me and of my words in this adulterous and sinful generation; of him also shall the Son of man be ashamed, when he cometh in the glory of his Father with the holy angels.

9: And he said unto them, Verily I say unto you, That there be some of them that stand here, which shall not taste of death, till they have seen the kingdom of God come with power.

2 And after six days Jesus taketh with him Peter, and James, and John, and leadeth them up into an high mountain apart by themselves: and he was
3 transfigured before them. And his raiment became shining, exceeding
4 white as snow; so as no fuller on earth can white them. And there appeared unto them Elias with Moses: and they were talking with Jesus.
5 And Peter answered and said to Jesus, Master, it is good for us to be here: and let us make three tabernacles; one for thee, and one for Moses, and
6 one for Elias. For he wist not what to say; for they were sore afraid.
7 And there was a cloud that overshadowed them: and a voice came out of
8 the cloud, saying, This is my beloved Son: hear him. And suddenly, when they had looked round about, they saw no man any more, save Jesus only
9 with themselves. And as they came down from the mountain, he charged them that they should tell no man what things they had seen, till the Son
10 of man were risen from the dead. And they kept that saying with themselves, questioning one with another what the rising from the dead should mean.

11 And they asked him, saying, Why say the scribes that Elias must first
12 come? And he answered and told them, Elias verily cometh first, and restoreth all things; and how it is written of the Son of man, that he must
13 suffer many things, and be set at nought. But I say unto you, That Elias is

indeed come, and they have done unto him whatsoever they listed, as it is written of him.

14 And when he came to his disciples, he saw a great multitude about them,
15 and the scribes questioning with them. And straightway all the people, when they beheld him, were greatly amazed, and running to him saluted
16 him. And he asked the scribes, What question ye with them? And one of
17 the multitude answered and said, Master, I have brought unto thee my
18 son, which hath a dumb spirit; And wheresoever he taketh him, he teareth him: and he foameth, and gnasheth with his teeth, and pineth away: and I spake to thy disciples that they should cast him out; and they could not.

19 He answereth him, and saith, O faithless generation, how long shall I be
20 with you? how long shall I suffer you? bring him unto me. And they brought him unto him: and when he saw him, straightway the spirit tare
21 him; and he fell on the ground, and wallowed foaming. And he asked his father, How long is it ago since this came unto him? And he said, Of a
22 child. And ofttimes it hath cast him into the fire, and into the waters, to destroy him: but if thou canst do any thing, have compassion on us, and
23 help us. Jesus said unto him, If thou canst believe, all things are possible
24 to him that believeth. And straightway the father of the child cried out, and said with tears, Lord, I believe; help thou mine unbelief.

25 When Jesus saw that the people came running together, he rebuked the foul spirit, saying unto him, Thou dumb and deaf spirit, I charge thee,
26 come out of him, and enter no more into him. And the spirit cried, and rent him sore, and came out of him: and he was as one dead; insomuch
27 that many said, He is dead. But Jesus took him by the hand, and lifted him
28 up; and he arose. And when he was come into the house, his disciples
29 asked him privately, Why could not we cast him out? And he said unto them, This kind can come forth by nothing, but by prayer and fasting.

30 And they departed thence, and passed through Galilee; and he would not
31 that any man should know it. For he taught his disciples, and said unto them, The Son of man is delivered into the hands of men, and they shall
32 kill him; and after that he is killed, he shall rise the third day. But they understood not that saying, and were afraid to ask him.

33 And he came to Capernaum: and being in the house he asked them, What
34 was it that ye disputed among yourselves by the way? But they held their peace: for by the way they had disputed among themselves, who should be
35 the greatest. And he sat down, and called the twelve, and saith unto them, If any man desire to be first, the same shall be last of all, and servant of
36 all. And he took a child, and set him in the midst of them: and when he
37 had taken him in his arms, he said unto them, Whosoever shall receive one of such children in my name, receiveth me: and whosoever shall receive me, receiveth not me, but him that sent me.

38 And John answered him, saying, Master, we saw one casting out devils in thy name, and he followeth not us: and we forbad him, because he
39 followeth not us. But Jesus said, Forbid him not: for there is no man which shall do a miracle in my name, that can lightly speak evil of me.
40 For he that is not against us is on our part. For whosoever shall give you a
41 cup of water to drink in my name, because ye belong to Christ, verily I say
42 unto you, he shall not lose his reward. And whosoever shall offend one of these little ones that believe in me, it is better for him that a millstone were hanged about his neck, and he were cast into the sea.

⁴³ And if thy hand offend thee, cut it off: it is better for thee to enter into life maimed, than having two hands to go into hell, into the fire that never ⁴⁴ shall be quenched: Where their worm dieth not, and the fire is not ⁴⁵ quenched. And if thy foot offend thee, cut it off: it is better for thee to enter halt into life, than having two feet to be cast into hell, into the fire ⁴⁶ that never shall be quenched: Where their worm dieth not, and the fire is ⁴⁷ not quenched. And if thine eye offend thee, pluck it out: it is better for thee to enter into the kingdom of God with one eye, than having two eyes ⁴⁸ to be cast into hell fire: Where their worm dieth not, and the fire is not ⁴⁹ quenched. For every one shall be salted with fire, and every sacrifice shall ⁵⁰ be salted with salt. Salt is good: but if the salt have lost his saltness, wherewith will ye season it? Have salt in yourselves, and have peace one with another.

10: And he arose from thence, and cometh into the coasts of Judea by the farther side of Jordan: and the people resort unto him again; and, as he was wont, he taught them again.

² And the Pharisees came to him, and asked him, Is it lawful for a man to ³ put away his wife? tempting him. And he answered and said unto them, ⁴ What did Moses command you? And they said Moses suffered to write a ⁵ bill of divorcement, and to put her away. And Jesus answered and said unto them, For the hardness of your heart he wrote you this precept. ⁶ But from the beginning of the creation God made them male and female. ⁷ For this cause shall a man leave his father and mother, and cleave to his ⁸ wife; And they twain shall be one flesh: so then they are no more twain, ⁹ but one flesh. What therefore God hath joined together, let not man put asunder.

¹⁰ And in the house his disciples asked him again of the same matter. ¹¹ And he saith unto them, Whosoever shall put away his wife, and marry ¹² another, committeth adultery against her. And if a woman shall put away her husband, and be married to another, she committeth adultery.

¹³ And they brought young children to him, that he should touch them: and ¹⁴ his disciples rebuked those that brought them. But when Jesus saw it, he was much displeased, and said unto them, Suffer the little children to come unto me, and forbid them not: for of such is the kingdom of God. ¹⁵ Verily I say unto you, Whosoever shall not receive the kingdom of God as ¹⁶ a little child, he shall not enter therein. And he took them up in his arms, put his hands upon them, and blessed them.

¹⁷ And when he was gone forth into the way, there came one running, and kneeled to him, and asked him, Good Master, what shall I do that I may ¹⁸ inherit eternal life? And Jesus said unto him, Why callest thou me good? ¹⁹ there is none good but one, that is, God. Thou knowest the commandments, Do not commit adultery, Do not kill, Do not steal, Do not bear ²⁰ false witness, Defraud not, Honor thy father and mother. And he answered and said unto him, Master, all these have I observed from my ²¹ youth. Then Jesus beholding him loved him, and said unto him, One thing thou lackest: go thy way, sell whatsoever thou hast, and give to the poor, and thou shalt have treasure in heaven: and come, take up the cross, and ²² follow me. And he was sad at that saying, and went away grieved: for he had great possessions.

²³ And Jesus looked round about, and saith unto his disciples, How hardly ²⁴ shall they that have riches enter into the kingdom of God! And the disciples were astonished at his words. But Jesus answereth again, and

saith unto them, Children, how hard is it for them that trust in riches to
25 enter into the kingdom of God! It is easier for a camel to go through the
eye of a needle, than for a rich man to enter into the kingdom of God.
26 And they were astonished out of measure, saying among themselves,
27 Who then can be saved? And Jesus looking upon them saith. With men it
is impossible, but not with God: for with God all things are possible.
28 Then Peter began to say unto him, Lo, we have left all, and have followed
29 thee. And Jesus answered and said, Verily I say unto you, There is no man
that hath left house, or brethren, or sisters, or father, or mother, or wife,
30 or children, or lands, for my sake, and the gospel's, But he shall receive an
hundredfold now in this time, houses, and brethren, and sisters, and
mothers, and children, and lands, with persecutions; and in the world to
31 come eternal life. But many that are first shall be last; and the last first.
32 And they were in the way going up to Jerusalem; and Jesus went before
them: and they were amazed; and as they followed, they were afraid. And
he took again the twelve, and began to tell them what things should
33 happen unto him, Saying, Behold, we go up to Jerusalem; and the Son of
man shall be delivered unto the chief priests, and unto the scribes; and
they shall condemn him to death, and shall deliver him to the Gentiles:
34 And they shall mock him, and shall scourge him, and shall spit upon him,
and shall kill him: and the third day he shall rise again.
35 And James and John, the sons of Zebedee, come unto him, saying, Master,
36 we would that thou shouldest do for us whatsoever we shall desire. And
37 he said unto them, What would ye that I should do for you? They said
unto him, Grant unto us that we may sit, one on thy right hand, and the
other on thy left hand, in thy glory.
38 But Jesus said unto them, Ye know not what ye ask: can ye drink of the
cup that I drink of? and be baptized with the baptism that I am baptized
39 with? And they said unto him, We can. And Jesus said unto them, Ye shall
indeed drink of the cup that I drink of; and with the baptism that I am
40 baptized withal shall ye be baptized: But to sit on my right hand and on
my left hand is not mine to give; but it shall be given to them for whom it
is prepared.
41 And when the ten heard it, they began to be much displeased with James
42 and John. But Jesus called them to him, and saith unto them, Ye know
that they which are accounted to rule over the Gentiles exercise lordship
43 over them; and their great ones exercise authority upon them. But so shall
it not be among you: but whosoever will be great among you, shall be your
44 minister: And whosoever of you will be the chiefest, shall be servant to
45 all. For even the Son of man came not to be ministered unto, but to
minister, and to give his life a ransom for many.
46 And they came to Jericho: and as he went out of Jericho with his disciples
and a great number of people, blind Bartimeus, the son of Timaeus, sat by
47 the highway side begging. And when he heard that it was Jesus of
Nazareth, he began to cry out, and say, Jesus, thou son of David, have
48 mercy on me. And many charged him that he should hold his peace: but
he cried the more a great deal, Thou son of David, have mercy on me.
49 And Jesus stood still, and commanded him to be called. And they call the
blind man, saying unto him, Be of good comfort, rise; he calleth thee.
50 And he, casting away his garment, rose, and came to Jesus. And Jesus
51 answered and said unto him. What wilt thou that I should do unto thee?
The blind man said unto him, Lord, that I might receive my sight.

52 And Jesus said unto him, Go thy way; thy faith hath made thee whole. And immediately he received his sight, and followed Jesus in the way.

11: And when they came nigh to Jerusalem, unto Bethphage and Bethany,
2 at the mount of Olives, he sendeth forth two of his disciples, And saith unto them, Go your way into the village over against you: and as soon as ye be entered into it, ye shall find a colt tied, whereon never man sat;
3 loose him, and bring him. And if any man say unto you, Why do ye this? say ye that the Lord hath need of him; and straightway he will send him hither.
4 And they went their way, and found the colt tied by the door without in a
5 place where two ways met; and they loose him. And certain of them that
6 stood there said unto them, What do ye, loosing the colt? And they said
7 unto them even as Jesus had commanded: and they let them go. And they brought the colt to Jesus, and cast their garments on him; and he sat upon
8 him. And many spread their garments in the way: and others cut down
9 branches off the trees, and strawed them in the way. And they that went before, and they that followed, cried, saying, Hosanna; Blessed is he that
10 cometh in the name of the Lord: Blessed be the kingdom of our father David that cometh in the name of the Lord: Hosanna in the highest.
11 And Jesus entered into Jerusalem, and into the temple: and when he had looked round about upon all things, and now the eventide was come, he
12 went out unto Bethany with the twelve. And on the morrow, when they
13 were come from Bethany, he was hungry: And seeing a fig tree afar off having leaves, he came, if haply he might find any thing thereon: and when he came to it, he found nothing but leaves; for the time of figs was
14 not yet. And Jesus answered and said unto it, No man eat fruit of thee hereafter for ever. And his disciples heard it.
15 And they come to Jerusalem: and Jesus went into the temple, and began to cast out them that sold and bought in the temple, and overthrew the tables of the moneychangers, and the seats of them that sold doves;
16 And would not suffer that any man should carry any vessel through the
17 temple. And he taught, saying unto them, Is it not written, My house shall be called of all nations the house of prayer? but ye have made it a den of
18 thieves. And the scribes and chief priests heard it, and sought how they might destroy him: for they feared him, because all the people was
19 astonished at his doctrine. And when even was come, he went out of the city.
20 And in the morning, as they passed by, they saw the fig tree dried up from
21 the roots. And Peter calling to remembrance saith unto him, Master,
22 behold, the fig tree which thou cursedst is withered away. And Jesus
23 answering saith unto them, Have faith in God. For verily I say unto you, That whosoever shall say unto this mountain, Be thou removed, and be thou cast into the sea; and shall not doubt in his heart, but shall believe that those things which he saith shall come to pass; he shall have
24 whatsoever he saith. Therefore I say unto you, What things soever ye desire, when ye pray, believe that ye receive them, and ye shall have them.
25 And when ye stand praying, forgive, if ye have ought against any: that
26 your Father also which is in heaven may forgive you your trespasses. But if ye do not forgive, neither will your Father which is in heaven forgive your trespasses.
27 And they come again to Jerusalem: and as he was walking in the temple,
28 there came to him the chief priests, and the scribes, and the elders. And

say unto him, By what authority doest thou these things? and who gave
29 thee this authority to do these things? And Jesus answered and said unto
them, I will also ask of you one question, and answer me, and I will tell
30 you by what authority I do these things. The baptism of John, was it from
31 heaven, or of men? answer me. And they reasoned with themselves,
saying, If we shall say, From heaven; he will say, Why then did ye not
32 believe him? But if we shall say, Of men; they feared the people: for all
33 men counted John, that he was a prophet indeed. And they answered and
said unto Jesus, We cannot tell. And Jesus answering saith unto them,
Neither do I tell you by what authority I do these things.

12:     And he began to speak unto them by parables. A certain man planted a
vineyard, and set an hedge about it, and digged a place for the winefat, and
built a tower, and let it out to husbandmen, and went into a far country.
2 And at the season he sent to the husbandmen a servant, that he might
3 receive from the husbandmen of the fruit of the vineyard. And they
4 caught him, and beat him, and sent him away empty. And again he sent
unto them another servant; and at him they cast stones, and wounded him
5 in the head, and sent him away shamefully handled. And again he sent
another; and him they killed, and many others; beating some, and killing
some.
6   Having yet therefore one son, his well-beloved, he sent him also last unto
7 them, saying, They will reverence my son. But those husbandmen said
among themselves, This is the heir; come, let us kill him, and the
8 inheritance shall be ours. And they took him, and killed him, and cast
9 him out of the vineyard. What shall therefore the lord of the vineyard do?
he will come and destroy the husbandmen, and will give the vineyard unto
10 others. And have ye not read this scripture; The stone which the builders
11 rejected is become the head of the corner: This was the Lord's doing, and
12 it is marvellous in our eyes? And they sought to lay hold on him, but
feared the people: for they knew that he had spoken the parable against
them: and they left him, and went their way.
13   And they send unto him certain of the Pharisees and of the Herodians, to
14 catch him in his words. And when they were come, they say unto him,
Master, we know that thou art true, and carest for no man: for thou
regardest not the person of men, but teachest the way of God in truth: Is
15 it lawful to give tribute to Caesar, or not? Shall we give, or shall we not
give? But he, knowing their hypocrisy, said unto them, Why tempt ye me?
16 bring me a penny, that I may see it. And they brought it. And he saith
unto them, Whose is this image and superscription? And they said unto
17 him, Caesar's. And Jesus answering said unto them, Render to Caesar the
things that are Caesar's, and to God the things that are God's. And they
marvelled at him.
18   Then come unto him the Sadducees, which say there is no resurrection;
19 and they asked him, saying, Master, Moses wrote unto us, If a man's
brother die, and leave his wife behind him, and leave no children, that his
20 brother should take his wife, and raise up seed unto his brother. Now
there were seven brethren: and the first took a wife, and dying left no
21 seed. And the second took her, and died, neither left he any seed: and the
22 third likewise. And the seven had her, and left no seed: last of all the
23 woman died also. In the resurrection therefore, when they shall rise,
whose wife shall she be of them? for the seven had her to wife.
24   And Jesus answering said unto them, Do ye not therefore err, because ye

25 know not the scriptures, neither the power of God? For when they shall rise from the dead, they neither marry, nor are given in marriage; but are
26 as the angels which are in heaven. And as touching the dead, that they rise: have ye not read in the book of Moses, how in the bush God spake unto him, saying, I am the God of Abraham, and the God of Isaac, and the
27 God of Jacob? He is not the God of the dead, but the God of the living: ye therefore do greatly err.
28 And one of the scribes came, and having heard them reasoning together, and perceiving that he had answered them well, asked him, Which is the
29 first commandment of all? And Jesus answered him, The first of all the
30 commandments is, Hear, O Israel; The Lord our God is one Lord: And thou shalt love the Lord thy God with all thy heart, and with all thy soul, and with all they mind, and with all thy strength: this is the first
31 commandment. And the second is like, namely this, Thou shalt love thy neighbor as thyself. There is none other commandment greater than these.
32 And the scribe said unto him, Well, Master, thou hast said the truth: for
33 there is one God; and there is none other but he: And to love him with all the heart, and with all the understanding, and with all the soul, and with all the strength, and to love his neighbor as himself, is more than all
34 whole burnt offerings and sacrifices. And when Jesus saw that he answered discreetly, he said unto him, Thou art not far from the kingdom of God. And no man after that durst ask him any question.
35 And Jesus answered and said, while he taught in the temple, How say the
36 scribes that Christ is the son of David? For David himself said by the Holy Ghost, The Lord said to my Lord, Sit thou on my right hand, till I
37 make thine enemies thy footstool. David therefore himself calleth him Lord; and whence is he then his son? And the common people heard him gladly.
38 And he said unto them in his doctrine, Beware of the scribes, which love
39 to go in long clothing, and love salutations in the marketplaces, And the
40 chief seats in the synagogues, and the uppermost rooms at feasts: Which devour widows' houses, and for a pretence make long prayers: these shall receive greater damnation.
41 And Jesus sat over against the treasury, and beheld how the people cast
42 money into the treasury: and many that were rich cast in much. And there came a certain poor widow, and she threw in two mites, which make a
43 farthing. And he called unto him his disciples, and saith unto them, Verily I say unto you, That this poor widow hath cast more in, than all they
44 which have cast into the treasury: For all they did cast in of their abundance; but she of her want did cast in all that she had, even all her living.
13: And as he went out of the temple, one of his disciples saith unto him,
2 Master, see what manner of stones and what buildings are here? And Jesus answering said unto him. Seest thou these great buildings? there shall not be left one stone upon another, that shall not be thrown down.
3 And as he sat upon the mount of Olives over against the temple, Peter
4 and James and John and Andrew asked him privately, Tell us, when shall these things be? and what shall be the sign when all these things shall be fulfilled?
5 And Jesus answering them began to say, Take heed lest any man deceive
6 you: For many shall come in my name, saying, I am Christ; and shall

7 deceive many. And when ye shall hear of wars and rumors of wars, be ye not troubled: for such things must needs be; but the end shall not be yet.

8 For nation shall rise against nation, and kingdom against kingdom: and there shall be earthquakes in divers places, and there shall be famines and troubles: these are the beginnings of sorrows.

9 But take heed to yourselves: for they shall deliver you up to councils; and in the synagogues ye shall be beaten: and ye shall be brought before rulers 10 and kings for my sake, for a testimony against them. And the gospel must 11 first be published among all nations. But when they shall lead you, and deliver you up, take no thought beforehand what ye shall speak, neither do ye premeditate: but whatsoever shall be given you in that hour, that 12 speak ye: for it is not ye that speak, but the Holy Ghost. Now the brother shall betray the brother to death, and the father the son; and children shall rise up against their parents, and shall cause them to be put to death. 13 And ye shall be hated of all men for my name's sake: but he that shall endure unto the end, the same shall be saved.

14 But when ye shall see the abomination of desolation, spoken of by Daniel the prophet, standing where it ought not (let him that readeth under- 15 stand), then let them that be in Judea flee to the mountains: And let him that is on the housetop not go down into the house, neither enter therein, 16 to take any thing out of his house: And let him that is in the field not turn 17 back again for to take up his garment. But woe to them that are with 18 child, and to them that give suck in those days! And pray ye that your flight be not in the winter.

19 For in those days shall be affliction, such as was not from the beginning of 20 the creation which God created unto this time, neither shall be. And except that the Lord had shortened those days, no flesh should be saved: but for the elect's sake, whom he hath chosen, he hath shortened the days. 21 And then if any man shall say to you, Lo, here is Christ; or, lo, he is there; 22 believe him not: For false Christs and false prophets shall rise, and shall shew signs and wonders, to seduce, if it were possible, even the elect. 23 But take ye heed: behold, I have foretold you all things.

24 But in those days, after that tribulation, the sun shall be darkened, and the 25 moon shall not give her light, And the stars of heaven shall fall, and the 26 powers that are in heaven shall be shaken. And then shall they see the 27 Son of man coming in the clouds with great power and glory. And then shall he send his angels, and shall gather together his elect from the four winds, from the uttermost part of the earth to the uttermost part of 28 heaven. Now learn a parable of the fig tree; When her branch is yet 29 tender, and putteth forth leaves, ye know that summer is near: So ye in like manner, when ye shall see these things come to pass, know that it is 30 nigh, even at the doors. Verily I say unto you, that this generation shall 31 not pass, till all these things be done. Heaven and earth shall pass away: but my words shall not pass away.

32 But of that day and that hour knoweth no man, no, not the angels which 33 are in heaven, neither the Son, but the Father. Take ye heed, watch and 34 pray: for ye know not when the time is. For the Son of man is as a man taking a far journey, who left his house, and gave authority to his servants, and to every man his work, and commanded the porter to watch. 35 Watch ye therefore: for ye know not when the master of the house cometh, at even, or at midnight, or at the cockcrowing, or in the morning: 36 Lest coming suddenly he find you sleeping. And what I say unto you I say 37 unto all, Watch.

Considerations and Questions

1. When in Chapter 7 the Pharisees criticize his disciples' failure to wash before meals, Jesus immediately goes on the offensive. What distinction does he make between such matters as ritual cleansing and the Ten Commandments? How does he make that distinction reflect discredit on the Pharisees?

2. Parents, hygiene classes, and state agencies that license restaurants all approve of and even enforce the practice of washing before handling food. In what we might call Jesus' "digestion" parable, the one about what goes into and out of the system, does he denounce elementary sanitation? Why do you suppose the disciples need an explanation of that parable?

3. A few verses after that explanation in Chapter 7, a Greek woman, "a Syrophenician by nation," begs Jesus to "cast forth the devil out of her daughter." To grasp the situation we must react to the emphasis put on this woman's racial and ethnic identification. She is not of the chosen people of Israel; she is not by religion a Jew; she is an alien and a pagan from the perspective not only of the Pharisees but from that of Jesus and his disciples. His response to her application is the parable about feeding the children before the dogs and appears to be in accord with that perspective. Yet unlike the disciples, this outsider does not need a pretty simple parable explained to her; she even answers Jesus in the terms of his own parable. And he does what she asks: her daughter is cured. What has this incident to do with the tension between the hero and his enemies?

4. In Chapter 8, Jesus repeats the "feeding" miracle of Chapter 6. So similar are the two mass picnics that the easiest distinction between them may be in the numbers of participants. The first feeding is of "the four thousand" and the second of "the five thousand." Mark, as well as Matthew, includes both feedings, and whatever the causes of this seemingly repetitious selection, certain effects on the story are evident. If the disciples have witnessed the feeding of the four thousand, what are we to make of their question in 8:4? If after witnessing *both* feedings they still assume that Jesus is worried about someone's failure to bring enough food in the boat, what are we to assume about their understanding? Note that the very next miracle in the chapter is the healing of a blind man.

5. How does the disciples' apparent obtuseness on certain counts provide a dramatic context for Peter's answer to "But whom say ye that I am?" (8:29). The answer seems plain and positive enough, but as we have already noted, its central term "the Christ" has ample potential to mislead. How do we see something of that in Peter's subsequent reactions to what Jesus says lies ahead and to the "transfiguration" vision of Chapter 9, in which that rather unimaginative disciple sees Jesus in the company of Moses and Elias (Elijah)?

6. The hero's enemies need to make him seem an enemy of the people if they are to justify destroying him. What episodes in the plot emphasize that such is a particularly difficult task? After all, whatever the hero may have *said,* what has he been *doing* throughout the first nine chapters of the story?

How does each of the following incidents represent a particular attempt to discredit Jesus in public estimation?
   a. The questions about divorce. (10:2-12)
   b. The question about his authority. (11:28-33)
   c. The question about paying Roman taxes. (12:13-17)
   d. The question about the afterlife. (12:18-27)

7. Jesus' ride into Jerusalem (11:8-11) and his visit to the temple (11:15-17) make what particular contributions to the plot?

8. At what point in the narrative does Jesus start announcing what lies immediately ahead? In what various forms and on what various occasions does he make these announcements?

Conclusion: Mark 14-16

"And now I live, and now my life is done."
Chidiock Tichborne, "The Night
Before His Execution"

Suffering, death, resurrection: these make up the final sequence common to all four Gospel plots. The Nativity stories of Luke and Matthew translate well into pageant and spectacle, a series of wonderful, almost static scenes whose artistic effects are rather like those of the great paintings that have so frequently depicted them. The other end of the Gospel plots has also been treated by painters and sculptors, but the art form most applicable to it is not painting or sculpture, but drama. This may be better understood if we consider a respect in which "Passion plays" differ in kind from the traditionally popular Christmas pageants based on the beginnings of the Matthew and Luke Gospels. The principal person of the death drama is a hero; the principal person of the birth pageant is a baby. Now babies are fine for pageants; as central figures they may be displayed, adored, or even slaughtered. What they do not do, if they are real babies, is act. What happens to them, for good or ill, is imposed by others and is in no way the consequence of their own decisions. In this sense, if in no other, children are to be seen and not heard.

What serious drama calls for is a hero who decidedly *is* heard. He is seen too, of course, but he is seen in motion, in conflict with the circumstances of outrageous fortune. If outrageous fortune's circumstances, for which the hero of serious drama must be in part responsible, destroy him we are likely to call his drama a tragedy. Thus we might call the Gospel conclusions "tragic" if they ended with the death and burial of Jesus.

14: After two days was the feast of the passover, and of unleavened bread: and the chief priests and the scribes sought how they might take him by

2 craft, and put him to death. But they said, Not on the feast day, lest there be an uproar of the people.

3 And being in Bethany in the house of Simon the leper, as he sat at meat, there came a woman having an alabaster box of ointment of spikenard

4 very precious; and she brake the box, and poured it on his head. And there were some that had indignation within themselves, and said, Why was

5 this waste of the ointment made? For it might have been sold for more than three hundred pence, and have been given to the poor. And they murmured against her.

6 And Jesus said, Let her alone; why trouble ye her? she hath wrought a

7 good work on me. For ye have the poor with you always, and whensoever

8 ye will ye may do them good: but me ye have not always. She hath done what she could: she is come aforehand to anoint my body to the burying.

9 Verily I say unto you, Wheresoever this gospel shall be preached throughout the whole world, this also that she hath done shall be spoken of for a memorial of her.

10 And Judas Iscariot, one of the twelve, went unto the chief priests, to

11 betray him unto them. And when they heard it, they were glad, and promised to give him money. And he sought how he might conveniently betray him.

12 And the first day of unleavened bread, when they killed the passover, his disciples said unto him, Where wilt thou that we go and prepare that thou

13 mayest eat the passover? And he sendeth forth two of his disciples, and saith unto them, Go ye into the city, and there shall meet you a man

14 bearing a pitcher of water: follow him. And wheresoever he shall go in, say ye to the goodman of the house, The Master saith, Where is the

15 guestchamber, where I shall eat the passover with my disciples? And he will show you a large upper room furnished and prepared: there make ready for us.

16 And his disciples went forth, and came into the city, and found as he had

17 said unto them: and they made ready the passover. And in the evening he

18 cometh with the twelve. And as they sat and did eat, Jesus said, Verily I

19 say unto you, One of you which eateth with me shall betray me. And they began to be sorrowful, and to say unto him one by one, Is it I? and another

20 said, Is it I? And he answered and said unto them, It is one of the twelve,

21 that dippeth with me in the dish. The Son of man indeed goeth, as it is written of him: but woe to that man by whom the Son of man is betrayed! good were it for that man if he had never been born.

22 And as they did eat, Jesus took bread, and blessed, and brake it, and gave

23 to them, and said, Take, eat: this is my body. And he took the cup, and when he had given thanks, he gave it to them: and they all drank of it.

24 And he said unto them, This is my blood of the new testament, which is

25 shed for many. Verily I say unto you, I will drink no more of the fruit of the vine, until that day that I drink it new in the kingdom of God.

26 And when they had sung an hymn, they went out into the mount of

27 Olives. And Jesus saith unto them, All ye shall be offended because of me this night: for it is written, I will smite the shepherd, and the sheep shall

28 be scattered. But after that I am risen, I will go before you into Galilee.

29 But Peter said unto him, Although all shall be offended, yet will not I.

30 And Jesus saith unto him, Verily I say unto thee, That this day, even in

31 this night, before the cock crow twice, thou shalt deny me thrice. But he spake the more vehemently, If I should die with thee, I will not deny thee in any wise. Likewise also said they all.

32 And they came to a place which was named Gethsemane: and he saith to 33 his disciples, Sit ye here, while I shall pray. And he taketh with him Peter and James and John, and began to be sore amazed, and to be very heavy; 34 And saith unto them, My soul is exceeding sorrowful unto death: tarry ye 35 here, and watch. And he went forward a little, and fell on the ground, and 36 prayed that, if it were possible, the hour might pass from him. And he said, Abba, Father, all things are possible unto thee; take away this cup from me: nevertheless not what I will, but what thou wilt.

37 And he cometh, and findeth them sleeping, and saith unto Peter, Simon, 38 sleepest thou? couldest not thou watch one hour? Watch ye and pray, lest ye enter into temptation. The spirit truly is ready, but the flesh is weak. 39 And again he went away, and prayed, and spake the same words. 40 And when he returned, he found them asleep again (for their eyes were 41 heavy,) neither wist they what to answer him. And he cometh the third time, and saith unto them, Sleep on now, and take your rest: it is enough, the hour is come; behold, the Son of man is betrayed into the hands of 42 sinners. Rise up, let us go; lo, he that betrayeth me is at hand.

43 And immediately, while he yet spake, cometh Judas, one of the twelve, and with him a great multitude with swords, and staves, from the chief 44 priests and the scribes and the elders. And he that betrayed him had given them a token, saying, Whomsoever I shall kiss, that same is he; take him, 45 and lead him away safely. And as soon as he was come, he goeth 46 straightway to him, and saith, Master, master; and kissed him. And 47 they laid their hands on him, and took him. And one of them that stood by drew a sword, and smote a servant of the high priest, and cut off his 48 ear. And Jesus answered and said unto them, Are ye come out, as against a 49 thief, with swords and with staves to take me? I was daily with you in the 50 temple teaching, and ye took me not: but the scriptures must be fulfilled. And 51 they all forsook him, and fled. And there followed him a certain young man, having a linen cloth cast about his naked body; and the young men 52 laid hold on him: And he left the linen cloth, and fled from them naked.

53 And they led Jesus away to the high priest: and with him were assembled 54 all the chief priests and the elders and the scribes. And Peter followed him afar off, even into the palace of the high priest: and he sat with the 55 servants, and warmed himself at the fire. And the chief priests and all the council sought for witness against Jesus to put him to death; and found 56 none. For many bare false witness against him, but their witness agreed 57 not together. And there arose certain, and bare false witness against him, 58 saying, We heard him say, I will destroy this temple that is made with 59 hands, and within three days I will build another made without hands. But neither so did their witness agree together.

60 And the high priest stood up in the midst, and asked Jesus, saying, 61 Answerest thou nothing? what is it which these witness against thee? But he held his peace, and answered nothing. Again the high priest asked 62 him, and said unto him, Art thou the Christ, the Son of the Blessed? And Jesus said, I am: and ye shall see the Son of man sitting on the right hand 63 of power, and coming in the clouds of heaven. Then the high priest rent 64 his clothes, and saith, What need we any further witnesses? Ye have heard the blasphemy: what think ye? And they all condemned him to be

65 guilty of death. And some began to spit on him, and to cover his face, and to buffet him, and to say unto him, Prophesy: and the servants did strike him with the palms of their hands.

66 And as Peter was beneath in the palace, there cometh one of the maids of
67 the high priest: And when she saw Peter warming himself, she looked
68 upon him, and said, And thou also wast with Jesus of Nazareth. But he denied, saying, I know not, neither understand I what thou sayest. And he
69 went out into the porch; and the cock crew. And a maid saw him again,
70 and began to say to them that stood by, This is one of them. And he denied it again. And a little after, they that stood by said again to Peter, Surely thou are one of them: for thou art a Galilean, and thy speech
71 agreeth thereto. But he began to curse and to swear, saying, I know not
72 this man of whom ye speak. And the second time the cock crew. And Peter called to mind the word that Jesus said unto him, Before the cock crow twice, thou shalt deny me thrice. And when he thought thereon, he wept.

15: And straightway in the morning the chief priests held a consultation with the elders and scribes and the whole council, and bound Jesus, and
2 carried him away, and delivered him to Pilate. And Pilate asked him, Art thou the King of the Jews? And he answering said unto him, Thou sayest
3 it. And the chief priests accused him of many things: but he answered
4 nothing. And Pilate asked him again, saying, Answerest thou nothing?
5 behold how many things they witness against thee. But Jesus yet answered nothing; so that Pilate marvelled.

6 Now at that feast he released unto them one prisoner, whomesoever they
7 desired. And there was one named Barabbas, which lay bound with them that had made insurrection with him, who had committed murder in the
8 insurrection. And the multitude crying aloud began to desire him to do as
9 he had ever done unto them. But Pilate answered them, saying, Will ye
10 that I release unto you the King of the Jews? For he knew that the chief priests had delivered him for envy.

11 But the chief priests moved the people, that he should rather release
12 Barabbas unto them. And Pilate answered and said again unto them, What will ye then that I shall do unto him whom ye call the King of the
13 Jews? And they cried out again, Crucify him. Then Pilate said unto them,
14 Why, what evil hath he done? And they cried out the more exceedingly, Crucify him.

15 And so Pilate, willing to content the people, released Barabbas unto them,
16 and delivered Jesus, when he had scourged him, to be crucified. And the soldiers led him away into the hall, called Pretorium; and they call
17 together the whole band. And they clothed him with purple, and platted a
18 crown of thorns, and put it about his head, And began to salute him, Hail,
19 King of the Jews! And they smote him on the head with a reed, and did spit upon him, and bowing their knees worshipped him.

20 And when they had mocked him, they took off the purple from him, and
21 put his own clothes on him, and led him out to crucify him. And they compel one Simon a Cyrenian, who passed by, coming out of the country,
22 the father of Alexander and Rufus, to bear his cross. And they bring him unto the place Golgotha, which is, being interpreted, The place of a skull.
23 And they gave him to drink wine mingled with myrrh: but he received it
24 not. And when they had crucified him, they parted his garments, casting
25 lots upon them, what every man should take. And it was the third hour,
26 and they crucified him. And the superscription of his accusation was

27 written over, THE KING OF THE JEWS. And with him they crucify two thieves; the one on his right hand, and the other on his left.

28 And the scripture was fulfilled, which saith, And he was numbered with
29 the transgressors. And they that passed by railed on him, wagging their heads, and saying, Ah, thou that destroyest the temple, and buildest it in
30 three days, Save thyself, and come down from the cross. Likewise also
31 the chief priests mocking said among themselves with the scribes, He
32 saved others; himself he cannot save. Let Christ the King of Israel descend now from the cross, that we may see and believe. And they that were crucified with him reviled him.

33 And when the sixth hour was come, there was darkness over the whole
34 land until the ninth hour. And at the ninth hour Jesus cried with a loud voice, saying, Eloi, Eloi, lamasabachthani? which is, being interpreted, My
35 God, my God, why hast thou forsaken me? And some of them that stood
36 by, when they heard it, said, Behold, he calleth Elias. And one ran and filled a spunge full of vinegar, and put it on a reed, and gave him to drink, saying, Let alone; let us see whether Elias will come to take him down.
37 And Jesus cried with a loud voice, and gave up the ghost.
38 And the veil of the temple was rent in twain from the top to the bottom.
39 And when the centurion, which stood over against him, saw that he so cried out, and gave up the ghost, he said, Truly this man was the Son of
40 God. There were also women looking on afar off: among whom was Mary Magdalene, and Mary the mother of James the less and of Joses, and
41 Salome; (Who also, when he was in Galilee, followed him, and ministered unto him); and many other women which came up with him unto Jerusalem.
42 And now when the even was come, because it was the preparation, that is,
43 the day before the sabbath, Joseph of Arimathea, an honorable counsellor, which also waited for the kingdom of God, came, and went in boldly unto
44 Pilate, and craved the body of Jesus. And Pilate marvelled if he were already dead: and calling unto him the centurion, he asked him whether
45 he had been any while dead. And when he knew it of the centurion, he
46 gave the body to Joseph. And he bought fine linen, and took him down, and wrapped him in the linen, and laid him in a sepulchre which was
47 hewn out of a rock, and rolled a stone unto the door of the sepulchre. And Mary Magdalene and Mary the mother of Joses beheld where he was laid.

16: And when the sabbath was past, Mary Magdalene, and Mary the mother of James, and Salome, had bought sweet spices, that they might
2 come and anoint him. And very early in the morning the first day of the
3 week, they came unto the sepulchre at the rising of the sun. And they said among themselves, Who shall roll us away the stone from the door of the
4 sepulchre? And when they looked, they saw that the stone was rolled away: for it was very great.

5 And entering into the sepulchre, they saw a young man sitting on the
6 right side, clothed in a long white garment; and they were affrighted. And he saith unto them, Be not affrighted: Ye seek Jesus of Nazareth, which was crucified: he is risen; he is not here; behold the place where they laid
7 him. But go your way, tell his disciples and Peter that he goeth before you
8 into Galilee: there shall ye see him, as he said unto you. And they went out quickly, and fled from the sepulchre; for they trembled and were amazed: neither said they any thing to any man; for they were afraid.

9 Now when Jesus was risen early the first day of the week, he appeared
10 first to Mary Magdalene, out of whom he had cast seven devils. And she

went and told them that had been with him, as they mourned and wept.

11 And they, when they had heard that he was alive, and had been seen of her, believed not.

12 After that he appeared in another form unto two of them, as they walked,
13 and went into the country. And they went and told it unto the residue: neither believed they them.

14 Afterward he appeared unto the eleven as they sat at meat, and upbraided them with their unbelief and hardness of heart, because they believed not
15 them which had seen him after he was risen. And he said unto them. Go
16 ye into all the world, and preach the gospel to every creature. He that believeth and is baptized shall be saved; but he that believeth not shall be
17 damned. And these signs shall follow them that believe; In my name shall
18 they cast out devils; they shall speak with new tongues; They shall take up serpents; and if they drink any deadly thing, it shall not hurt them; they shall lay hands on the sick, and they shall recover.

19 So then after the Lord had spoken unto them, he was received up into
20 heaven, and sat on the right hand of God. And they went forth, and preached every where, the Lord working with them, and confirming the word with signs following. Amen.

Considerations and Questions

1. In what various direct and indirect ways does Jesus inform his disciples of his approaching death? What are their particular and general reactions to his warnings? How do they react to his arrest when it actually occurs?

2. We may wonder why the chief priests need the services of the betrayer. In the Mark Gospel all Judas Iscariot does for his undisclosed sum of blood money is to identify Jesus for the temple police by kissing him. Surely, if the authorities are so eager to seize Jesus, some of them can recognize him. Mark leaves us to infer a function for the traitor, a function which is suggested in Matthew and more directly indicated in Luke.

   Matthew 26:5. *But they said. Not on the feast day, lest there be an uproar among the people.*
   Luke 22:6. *And he promised, and sought opportunity to betray him unto them in the absence of the multitude.*

   How do events during and after the arrest throw an ironic light on apprehensions about Jesus' public following?

3. At the trial of the Knave of Hearts in *Alice in Wonderland*, the Queen of Hearts, who wants to cut everyone's head off, insists, "Sentence first—verdict afterwards." Something like this rules the trial at the high priest's palace. So eager are Jesus' enemies to put him to death that they have not taken sufficient care to prepare their case, that is, to ensure that their false witnesses agree with one another. When it seems that they are unlikely to get a clear verdict, what does the high priest do to ensure the sentence anyway?

4. We presume that Judas Iscariot betrays Jesus for the money. What accounts for the devoted Peter's denial of his master as it occurs at the end of Chapter 14?

5. Readers of Mark are expected to know that Pilate is the Roman military governor, or *procurator* of Judea. They are also expected to know, or to infer from rather scant textual evidence, that imperial Rome keeps to itself the power to inflict capital punishment in its colonies. If local authorities want someone executed, they must ask their local procurator to do it. He may or he may not, but conquered peoples do learn ways of manipulating their tyrants. Why does Pilate agree, somewhat against his own inclinations, to crucify Jesus?

6. This is a time to take another look at Psalm 22 on page 207. What references to that earlier scripture occur in Mark's account of Jesus' execution in Chapter 15?

7. "Eloi, Eloi, lama sabachthani?" Note that when bystanders hear Jesus' last words from the cross, they misunderstand them. How may this be seen as a final instance of something that has gone on throughout the whole plot of Mark?

8. Most authorities on Biblical text agree that the last twelve verses of Chapter 16 are not by the Mark who wrote the rest of the Gospel. Some contend that the Gospel of Mark properly concludes with the words "they were afraid" in the eighth verse. Not being textual authorities and not being engaged in theological debate, we might only note that whatever it might "properly" do, the English Bible's version of Mark does in fact end with the twentieth not the eighth verse. Still, as students of narrative, we would be less than alert if we did not see significant differences between the chapter's two parts. How does each part offer its own distinct conclusion to the story?